A Keeper Of Royal Secrets: Being The Private And Political Life Of Madame De Genlis

Jean Harmand

Nabu Public Domain Reprints:

You are holding a reproduction of an original work published before 1923 that is in the public domain in the United States of America, and possibly other countries. You may freely copy and distribute this work as no entity (individual or corporate) has a copyright on the body of the work. This book may contain prior copyright references, and library stamps (as most of these works were scanned from library copies). These have been scanned and retained as part of the historical artifact.

This book may have occasional imperfections such as missing or blurred pages, poor pictures, errant marks, etc. that were either part of the original artifact, or were introduced by the scanning process. We believe this work is culturally important, and despite the imperfections, have elected to bring it back into print as part of our continuing commitment to the preservation of printed works worldwide. We appreciate your understanding of the imperfections in the preservation process, and hope you enjoy this valuable book.

A KEEPER OF ROYAL SECRETS

Pamela.   Eugène Adélaide Louise, Princesse d'Orléans.   Mme de Genlis.

Madame de Genlis.
from a painting at Versailles.

A KEEPER OF ROYAL SECRETS

BEING THE PRIVATE AND POLITICAL LIFE
OF MADAME DE GENLIS

BY

JEAN HARMAND

WITH A PREFACE BY ÉMILE FAGUET

NEW YORK
BRENTANOS
1913

A KEEPER OF ROYAL SECRETS

BEING THE PRIVATE AND POLITICAL LIFE
OF MADAME DE GENLIS

BY
JEAN HARMAND

WITH A PREFACE BY ÉMILE FAGUET

NEW YORK
BRENTANO'S
1913

PREFACE

This volume has not had for its aim the rehabilitation of Mme. de Genlis, but it is the truth about her, and a semi-rehabilitation of her has resulted from the truth. The time was ripe for such a book (and it was not an easy book to write), for Mme. de Genlis had come to be only a name remembered only with a smile, inasmuch as it evoked the idea of the most tedious of all the tedious authors of a very tedious epoch; and, for some, the idea of a political *intrigante* of somewhat easy morals, who, in the witty phrase of another woman, "made precepts of the virtues and a practice of the vices."

To many people it would not much matter if these ideas had continued to prevail until the very name of Mme. de Genlis had been forgotten, but it does matter a little to the literary history of France that such an impression should be rectified in so far as it is incorrect.

The reputation of Mme. de Genlis has suffered from two things: from her wit, which was very sardonic and which drew down on her by way of reprisals a certain number of uncomplimentary characterisations that have survived; and her *Memoirs*, which are so manifestly inaccurate and which leave so much untold, that—as often happens in such cases—people have been disposed to believe the worst of her. "I should like to write a book such as nobody has ever written," someone said once to Rivarol. "*Faites votre éloge*," was his reply. In similar fashion, to anyone who should say to me, "I want to write a book that everyone will attack," I would make answer: "Write a panegyric upon yourself." All these autobiographers, in truth, seem bent on making us regard them sceptically. There is no avoiding it.

I may go on to confess that Mme. de Genlis's published works in general still do her a disservice. To begin with, there are too many of them. Secondly, Stendhal was right in his saying: "This woman of infinite wit has not enough in her books, which are glazed with the hypocrisy of the Salons." Yet to my mind it was not so much a case of their being glazed by the hypocrisy of the Salons—it was rather her method of improvisation that prevented them from having the consistency, the substance, the tautness (to use the sailor's term) which they might so well have possessed. Mme. de Genlis treated her books as she treated her royal pupils—she did not allow them to relax. Her guiding hand was tender, even loving—but it never let go. She kept them ceaselessly on the alert, without respite for a moment. She did not realise that a child needs to be left to itself from time to time and to live its own little life; and she did not realise that a book also must be "given rope"—that to some extent it must write itself and be allowed intervals for unconscious meditation and for pulling itself together. She was too impetuous for that, and this is the reason why this astonishing improvisatore has now almost nothing to show for herself. It is only the very carefully prepared improvisations that last!

And this is how it has come about that we can say of Mme. de Genlis, without being unduly epigrammatic, that her life is concealed in her *Memoirs* and her talent in her books. Really to get to know her, therefore—and it was well worth while to get to know a woman who played so considerable a part in history—it was necessary not merely to read her *Memoirs* and more important books attentively, but also to seek out records of her career elsewhere, with diligence and with zest.

But where ? Why, in history—in the whole history of the time—in State archives and in trivial records alike. There was never anyone so equally at home in " la grande histoire " and in " la petite histoire " as Mme. de Genlis !

Now, this is the task to which the author of the present volume set himself with all his heart. He has spent several years over his researches, and if he is the first to acknowledge that many important things may have escaped him, we may at least feel certain that we have the story of Mme. de Genlis set out before us here in its essential outlines for the first time. And she comes out of this ordeal—a very dangerous ordeal for everyone—if not enlarged to heroic size, at least looking all the better for it.

Her political rôle was very much open to criticism, but it was the result of her devotion to the Prince who had welcomed her and to his children, and this is its excuse—perhaps more than an excuse. In the field of education, apart from the shortcoming already indicated, she was nothing less than an inventor. She invented the entire system of modern education, without its defects : a system of education, both literary and scientific, directed towards the true, no less than towards the beautiful, and taking account of history, modern languages, and of *realities*—combining the study of important new discoveries with the study of the great books of ancient and modern times. It was, in the truest and best sense of the word, an encyclopædic system of education ; that is to say, it consisted not in piling up every possible form of knowledge in the children's heads, but, what is really just the opposite method, in opening their minds in all kinds of new directions, and in giving them an appetite for everything : I call this the opposite, because it is opening out instead of filling in.

She was an inventor in this respect also, that she laid herself out to give the same education to her own daughters as to her sons. Like Mme. de Gournay, she believed that women's brains were not less receptive of enlightenment than men's. That is one of the claims of our Feminists, and our anti-Feminists very naturally regard Mme. de Genlis therefore with horror. She was, in truth, a genuine Feminist, and of the best sort, for (and this is the most curious trait in her many-sided character), if she was a *femme savante*, she was so far from neglecting practical, domestic, humdrum matters that she attended more thoroughly to these things than to anything else.

In a word, she is the child of the *Encyclopédie*. She might, rather, have been its mother: according to a contemporary wit, "She proposed to rewrite the *Encyclopédie* in her old age." It is all very well to laugh, but there was something in that idea: Mme. de Genlis could quite well have brought the *Encyclopédie* up to date in 1820; and her learning was a finer thing than the ignorant cleverness of so many of the ladies of that epoch. She was the child of the age—of the serious-minded section of that eighteenth-century world, athirst for knowledge and eager for real progress. She is akin not to the women who read Crébillon *fils* or to the sentimental worshippers of Jean-Jacques, but to the Créquys and the Châtelets. It is a matter of taste, if you will, but without being in love with this type I prefer it.

Napoleon I. was not wrong in his estimate of her—at least he was not far wrong. He granted her quarters in the Arsenal and a pension of 6000 francs a year so that she might write week by week "whatever passed through her head," but more particularly notes and memories in regard to the usages and manners of the *Ancien Régime*. We feel that what he recognised in her above all was the professor of deportment and the authority upon etiquette. Still, he persisted in asking her to record everything that passed through her head. He had satisfied himself that it was a very good head.

It must be admitted that even the books of Mme. de Genlis have been greatly undervalued. In many of them there is a lot of rubbish; in many there is too much acrimony, too much of a carping, querulous spirit. She was essentially a *frondeuse*. But it must not be overlooked that *Mademoiselle de Clermont* remains a very pretty, touching piece of work. M. J. Chénier was not wrong when he said: "The characters of the Princess, of her brother, of her lover, and of the Duc de Melun, are traced with a charming fidelity to truth. Neither the incidents nor the speeches are artificial; the action is simple, the style natural, the narrative animated, the interest grows steadily." He went too far when he added that "one would believe one was reading a posthumous work of Mme. de Lafayette," but as he didn't mean it in the least, that doesn't matter.

I will confess my own liking for certain parts, many parts even, of the *Veillées du Château*. The bloom is on all that no longer, and yet it still seems fresh and pleasing. It may be recalled possibly that I have spoken favourably of one of Mme. de Genlis's dramatic efforts elsewhere, and with sincere respect. George Sand, it is well to remember, did not look down upon Mme. de Genlis. It was from the *Battuecas* (I admit I have not read the *Battuecas*) that George Sand declares she drew "her first socialistic and dramatic instincts."

In conclusion, Mme. de Genlis contended against the philosophy of the eighteenth century throughout forty years. It is not at all because she contended against the philosophy of the eighteenth century that I have a kindness for her; but it is because she did so that she has been depreciated deliberately by a mob of authors, serious, frivolous, violent, satirical; and it is from this depreciation, as unjust as many of her own attacks, that we must lift her up a little.

Sainte-Beuve compares her with Mlle. de Scudéry, and Jean Harmand with Mme. de Maintenon. I should place her lower than these two, but between them; lower, because Mlle. de Scudéry's talent was more real and Mme. de Maintenon was altogether on a higher plane; between them, because she was certainly of their species, and Mme. de Maintenon would have held her in high esteem while Mlle. de Scudéry would have done a very fine portrait of her.

To sum up, this woman had a very fine talent which she squandered a little through her itch to be always displaying it; but, as La Harpe, who was so fond of her but who was so fond also of classifications, might have said, her place is in the front row of women of letters of the second class.

ÉMILE FAGUET.

TABLE OF CONTENTS

	PAGE
Preface by M. Émile Faguet	v
Introduction	xix

PART I

FROM CHILDHOOD TO MARRIAGE

CHAPTER I

Parentage

Champcéry—M. de Mézières, grandfather of Mme. de Genlis—The Romance of Mlle. de Mézières—The Du Crest family—Birth of Félicité—Saint-Aubin—A small Provincial transformed into a Parisienne—Stay at Etiolles—The chapter-house of Saint-Denis d'Alix 1

CHAPTER II

Education

Félicité's first schooling—Mlle. de Mars—In Cupid's guise and in male attire—A first admirer—The salon of Mme. de Bellevaux—An author of twelve—M. de Mondorge, literary tutor—The sale of Saint-Aubin—A loan from the husband of la Pompadour 17

CHAPTER III

Young Womanhood

The Marquise de Saint-Aubin in misfortune—A visit to the Farmer-General La Popelinière—Félicité, a harpist of repute—Her admirers—Dalembert—Suitors—Chevilly—A Professional or a young lady of Society—Mlle. du Crest at fifteen 34

PART II

THE COMTESSE DE GENLIS BEFORE 1789

CHAPTER I

MARRIAGE

Two Prisoners of War—The Romance of the Comte de Genlis and Mlle. du Crest—Genealogy of the Genlis family—Marriage of Félicité—How it was viewed—Whims and Fantasies—Presentation at Court 45

CHAPTER II

THE COMEDY OF SOCIETY

Mme. de Genlis and her Circle—L'Isle Adam—Villers-Cotterets—A Quadrille of Proverbs—Rousseau—Social Successes—Mme. de Montesson and the Duke of Orleans—Lady-in-Waiting to the Duchess of Chartres 63

CHAPTER III

THE PALAIS ROYAL

The Palais Royal in 1772—Mme. de Blot—The Duke of Chartres—Mme. de Genlis wakens up the Ducal Court—Friendship with the Duchess—Marie-Antoinette and Mme. de Genlis . 77

CHAPTER IV

THE VISIT TO FORGES

The Romance of Mme. de Genlis and the Duke of Chartres—An outbreak of Smallpox—Chantilly—The rôle of Egeria—The Chiappini affair—A trip to Spa 88

CHAPTER V

BELLECHASSE

Mme. de Genlis visits Voltaire—The Comte de Genlis and the Gaming-tables—La Harpe—Governess to the Princesses—The Convent at Bellechasse—Marriage of Caroline de Genlis 103

CONTENTS

CHAPTER VI

THE GOVERNOR OF THE PRINCES

A Woman Governor of the Princes—The Appointment ill received—Squibs and Pamphlets—Mme. de Genlis's feelings—The Chevalier de Bonnard—A problem of feminine Antipathy—The Programme of Education—Demonstration at the Théâtre-Français in 1782—Mme. de Genlis hits out at her Enemies 121

CHAPTER VII

A CELEBRATED WOMAN IN 1782

Mme. de Genlis and the French Academy—The Prix Monthyon—Marriage of Pulchérie de Genlis—Mme. de Montesson and the Comte de Valence—The Genlis *ménage* in 1785—Paméla and Hermine—Paméla's Parentage—Mme. de Genlis and her Works—She loses her Daughter—*La Religion Considerée*—"Maman" Genlis 135

PART III

MADAME DE GENLIS AS A REVOLUTIONARY

CHAPTER I

THE PRELIMINARIES

Mme. de Genlis and her disavowals—The Palais Royal in 1787—The Duke of Orleans—His intervention in Parliament—Bernardin de Saint-Pierre—The Bellechasse Saturdays—Mme. de Genlis Goddess of Liberty—Her share of responsibility in the doings of the Orleans Party . . . 159

CHAPTER II

THE *DRAMATIS PERSONÆ*

Exile of the Duke of Orleans—The Marquis du Crest—His Memorial to the King—His disgrace—Return of the Duke—Laclos enters upon the scene—The Bellechasse Salon in 1789—The Palais Royal in 1789—The Fall of the Bastille—The October Days—The Terrace at Passy . . . 169

CHAPTER III

Popularity of the Young Orleans Princes

The Châtelet inquiry—Departure of the Duke of Orleans—The Duke of Chartres—His education and character—The Princes at the Theatre—Mme. de Genlis's "Discourses"—Revolutionary Jewellery—Camille Desmoulins—The Jacobin Club 183

CHAPTER IV

A Family Drama

Troubles of the Duchess of Orleans—Affection of the Duke of Chartres for Mme. de Genlis—The Rupture—The *Journal des Princes*—Mme. de Genlis resigns—Her Departure—Letters to Mademoiselle 200

CHAPTER V

The Journey to England

Return of Mme. de Genlis to Bellechasse—After Varennes—Laclos loses the Game—The *Leçons d'une Gouvernante à ses Elèves*—Bath and London—Walpole—Talleyrand in London—Sheridan and Paméla—Return to Bellechasse—The *Émigrés* 219

PART IV

THE EMIGRATION

CHAPTER I

With Dumouriez

Lord Edward Fitzgerald—He marries Paméla—Tournay—Dumouriez—Mme. de Genlis prepares for flight—Frontier Perils—Quievrain—Mons—The Duke of Chartres rejoins his sister at Basle—Short stay at Zurich—Zug—Bremgarten 241

CONTENTS

CHAPTER II

BREMGARTEN AND ALTONA

The Execution of Philippe-Égalité—Louis-Philippe's change of attitude—Mme. de Elahaut—Mademoiselle leaves Mme. de Genlis—Mme. de Genlis quarrels with the young Duke of Orleans—Her departure—She arrives in Holstein—The Pflock Inn—Life at Altona—Death of Robespierre—The Duke of Orleans leaves Hamburg 258

CHAPTER III

HAMBURG

Hamburg—Among the Émigrés—Paméla and Henriette, Queens of Beauty—Rivarol—How Mme. de Genlis was regarded in Hamburg—Talleyrand—Silk—Mme. de Genlis appeals to the Directorate—*Le Précis de ma Conduite*—Henriette's Marriage—A journey to Berlin—Expulsion . . . 275

CHAPTER IV

THE LIFE OF AN *ÉMIGRÉ* IN GERMANY

The Château of Dollrott—Brevel—An Émigré's misfortunes—A brave pen—Berlin in 1798—Mlle. Itzig—Jewish society—Mme. de Genlis refuses to lecture—Theatricals—A Prussian cicisbeo—Arrival of General Beurnonville—Casimir Boecker—Paméla again 294

PART V

FROM THE CONSULATE TO THE MONARCHY OF JULY

CHAPTER I

THE RETURN TO FRANCE

The Return—Mme. de Montesson—Paris as depicted by Mme. de Genlis—Sillery—Helmina—Mme. de Genlis finds a home at the Arsenal—Her Correspondence with the First Consul 311

CONTENTS

CHAPTER II

AT THE ARSENAL

Letter from La Harpe—Literary vogue of Mme. de Genlis—Her last Salon—The Arsenal—Mme. de Genlis at Sixty—Dr. Gall—Talleyrand—Mme. de Genlis's adopted Children—Her conflicts with Ameilhon—She leaves the Arsenal . . 327

CHAPTER III

1812—THE RESTORATION

Casimir—His Marriage—The Michaud Quarrel—The Hundred Days—Letters from Mme. de Genlis to Talleyrand—She meets her Pupils again—Her Pension—The Carmelite Convent—Her rooms—The Change in Paméla . . 349

CHAPTER IV

THE LAST PHASE OF MME. DE GENLIS

Mme. de Genlis under the Restoration—She converts Valence—*L'Intrépide*—Astolphe de Custine—Religious zeal—*Les Dîners du Baron d'Holbach*—The Memoirs—The Revolution of July—Death of Mme. de Genlis—Her last moments—Her funeral—Her grave 370

PART VI

THE PUBLISHED WORKS OF MME. DE GENLIS

I. MME. DE GENLIS AS MORALIST 403
II. II. MME. DE GENLIS AS DRAMATIST . . . 408
III. MME. DE GENLIS AS EDUCATIONALIST . . . 422

LIST OF HER WORKS 437

LIST OF ILLUSTRATIONS

MME. DE GENLIS WITH HER PUPIL, EUGÈNE ADELAIDE LOUISE, PRINCESS OF ORLEANS, AND PAMELA . . *Frontispiece*
From a painting at Versailles.

                                                          FACING PAGE

CHARLES-ALEXIS, COMTE DE GENLIS 48

THE DUCHESS OF ORLEANS (HENRIETTE DE BOURBON-CONTI, WIFE OF LOUIS-PHILIPPE, DUKE OF ORLEANS) . . 64

LOUIS-PHILIPPE, DUKE OF ORLEANS . . . 70

MME. DE MONTESSON 94

MME. DE GENLIS 122

THE DUKE OF CHARTRES (SON OF PHILIPPE-ÉGALITÉ) . 188

THE DUCHESS OF ORLEANS (LOUISE MARIE ADELAIDE DE BOURBON-PENTHIÈVRE : WIFE OF PHILIPPE-ÉGALITÉ) . 212

PAMELA, LADY FITZGERALD 242

THE DUKE OF ORLEANS (PHILIPPE-ÉGALITÉ) . . 252

M. DE VALENCE 282

MME. DE GENLIS IN LATER LIFE 334
From a painting at Versailles reproduced by permission of Messrs. BRAUN, CLEMENT ET CIE, Paris.

LOUIS-PHILIPPE KING OF FRANCE . . . 390

INTRODUCTION

If it be true that we can appraise our predecessors equitably as soon as the strong feelings they evoked have been quieted by the lapse of time and have sunk into oblivion, it may be said that the hour has come long since for examining into the character and career of Mme. de Genlis.

This all-accomplished woman: educator and politician, author of more than a hundred volumes; leader of society, artist; actress, an adept at everything she undertook, and in spite of certain shortcomings that were then in vogue theologian also and moralist—this famous personage is almost unknown to us.

Posterity remembers nothing of her long career, spanning that troubled epoch in our history which extended from the reign of Louis xv. to the Monarchy of July, except a couple of titles, as it were, summarising a couple of chapters in her life's story: the eminent title of *Gouverneur* to King Philippe, and that of *amie* to Philippe-Égalité.

A veil has continued to hide from us those features, of whose indistinctness Sainte-Beuve complained so many years ago. Mme. de Genlis, in truth, cultivated this atmosphere of mystery; she persisted in concealing her inner self, always wearing a mask alike to her friends and her readers, despite her apparent frankness and naturalness and vivacity; and neither her *Memoirs* nor any of her other works let us into the secret of her real nature.

Those who have been sufficiently interested have had

to look about them for means of elucidating the enigma of this baffling personality.

And it will be admitted that a dozen or so of lines of meagre biographical information in the Dictionaries, two or three estimates based upon contemporary satires and scandalous attacks, with Sainte-Beuve's portrait of her in her rôle as pedagogue and Barbey d'Aurevilly's sketch of her as an old woman in a muffler—a pair of silhouettes: that these things amount to very little when we think of all the thousand facets there were to the character of this Maintenon of the eighteenth century.

Mme. de Maintenon, of course, towers above Mme. de Genlis, but Louis-Philippe's *Gouverneur* does indubitably follow in the footsteps of her great predecessor. Certain points of resemblance stand out conspicuously in the two careers, and when we probe more deeply into the two characters we find that they have this also in common—in the midst of so many human weaknesses: both hungered for renown.

This trait shows itself in Mme. de Genlis in many forms. We see it in the young girl of noble lineage who hopes to shine at Court; in the artist striving for success; in the ardent, insatiable student, exploiting every field of knowledge; in the author eager for admiration; in the instructress jealously moulding her pupils so that they shall outshine all others; in the woman of affairs seeking to exert her sway over men and manners—even over the State; finally in the "*Mère de l'Eglise*" (as she was called satirically) setting herself up as a guardian of virtue, bearing the standard of religion aloft.

A heavy burden for a woman, all these forms of fame! Mme. de Genlis is all the more fascinating a study, however, by reason of them. A difficult study, though, calling for all our patience and attention.

And patience and attention are just what she has been

INTRODUCTION

hitherto denied. Whether it be due to the influence of all the evil rumours which surround her memory, or whether it be that her champions have been impelled by excess of zeal into attempting to rehabilitate her too completely, violence has always characterised the tone of those who have written about her.

The real Mme. de Genlis stands somewhere between the blameless prodigy of virtue and the unscrupulous adventuress that we see depicted by extremists. It is of this real Mme. de Genlis that I have sought to retrace the likeness with the help of such sources of information as have been available, and with the regard for truth and accuracy to which this much-abused woman was entitled, after her death.

In accomplishing this task, I have had the advantage of much invaluable assistance from others, and I am at a loss to express fully my gratitude for the kindness and courtesy of those who have placed at my disposal their documents, their knowledge, and their time.

In the first place, I must record my indebtedness to the descendants in the fraternal line of Mme. de Genlis, and in particular to M. le Colonel du Crest and M. le Comte du Crest, who have given me access to family archives that were of the first importance.

M. Frantz Funck-Brentano, Curator of the Manuscript Department in the Library of the Arsenal, and M. le Dr. Gillard, both of whom undertook delicate researches for me with untiring amiability, and M. Charles Blanchet, of the Bibliothèque Nationale, who placed at my service the very great help of his bibliographical learning, and have all shown me a measure of kindness for which I can never return adequate thanks.

MM. Henry Martin, Curator of the Library of the Arsenal; Cadet de Gassicourt; Louis Laroche, of the Bibliothèque Nationale; Lazard, of the Archives of the Seine; Grave, of Nantes; Sadart, Curator of the Library of Rheims; and

Favier, Curator of the Library of Nancy; Mme. Martin-Cochet, of Saint-Étienne-de-Saint-Geovis, M. le Colonel Piarron de Mondésir; M. le Baron André de Maricourt; M. le Dr. Pol Gosset; Mlles. Mac-Stuartie, Le Maire; M. le Marquis de Bourdeille, and the amiable M. Macon, Curator of the Musée Condé at Chantilly, have all contributed bricks to my building with a good-nature far in excess of the modest recognition which I here make to them.

In addition, I have to thank Mes. Mouchet and Josset, Notaries of Paris, for the very obliging way in which they placed their records at my disposal; and also the very courteous librarians and archivists of Spa, Berlin, and Hamburg, who helped me so much in my researches.

I beg them, each and all, to accept this expression of my deep gratitude.

J. H.

A KEEPER OF ROYAL SECRETS

PART I

FROM CHILDHOOD TO MARRIAGE

CHAPTER I

PARENTAGE

In the early days of December 1745 a man of soldierly bearing and a young, athletic-looking woman, both of them good riders, were making their way light-heartedly on horseback over the upland wastes which stretch across the arid countryside of the Charolais, near Autun.

A cold wind blew, driving the clouds across the wintry sky, heavy with snow; and its icy currents, as they went wailing through the naked branches of the trees, accentuated the harsh severity of this region, in which, failing a highway or even a practicable road, it was necessary to follow a wretched track evolved anyhow from the lie of the ground.

Nothing could be much more uncomfortable than this kind of travelling—nowadays we should have every excuse for grumbling at it. Our ancestors, in their hardier, more intrepid way, relished its picturesque aspects. As, upon the occasion in question, did Messire François du Crest and his bride, Marie-Françoise-Félicité Mauguet de Mézières, now in this fashion nearing the end of their honeymoon journey.

Having driven from Paris in a hired carriage as far as

Issy-l'Évêque, they had secured horses at this stage and were now proceeding to their manor-house at Champcéry, situated on a small property of that name, three miles farther on.

Even in the middle of the eighteenth century there was something strange in the notion of a honeymoon at Champcéry, amid surroundings so gloomy and in a climate so severe.

But solitude is sweet to young married couples, and these could have enjoyed it nowhere else, for they owned no other abode in which they could make their home. Moreover, Champcéry did not belie the meaning of its name, originally Champs de Cérès, for, by contrast with the country all about, it had something of the appearance of an oasis in the wilderness.

The landscape softened as you came to it; the river, which fed a pond of some considerable size, flowed beneath a cluster of lofty trees and turned the wheels of the mill. Beyond lay the fields in cultivation which supplied grain for the mill, and the manor-house stood on the banks of the pond.

It was a large one-storeyed, widespread house, constructed, in accordance with the fashion prevalent in Burgundy among country squires, of the thick and enduring masonry by which our grandfathers flattered themselves they defied the onslaughts of time.

In the courtyard the traditional well displayed the customary curb. It still survives, the sole remaining vestige of what the manor-house once was.

Such was the framework within which the youthful household was to work out its history—a history begun under not unromantic auspices.

Romance is assigned but a small place in most lives, but Marie-Françoise-Félicité was always on the alert for it; her mother had made two love-matches, and it seemed to her only natural that romance should have its part also in her own career.

Claude-Christophe Mauquet de Mézières, *écuyer*, her father, had lost his heart to her mother, Marie-Josèphe Minard, at first sight. He was a man of strong individuality—

a lawyer, a collector, a devotee of manuscripts and antiques, and in particular of Polish genealogies; pluming himself upon his knowledge " of all the things which others never thought of studying," so Moreau records; and standing in no alarm of the learned ladies of the period.

It entered into his head one day to leave Paris, where he lived, and set out on a visit to Rome. On announcing this intention to Mlle. Morisot, a woman belonging to the world of books and learning, who resided, one gathers, at the Louvre, he was persuaded by her to make a journey through Burgundy before taking ship at Marseilles, and to pay a visit to her relative at Avallon, Mme. Minard.

M. de Mézières went no farther. The eldest of Mme. Minard's daughters—there were five or six of them—a beautiful girl, exceptionally well educated, above all as regards history, and something also of a musician, seemed to him a veritable Tenth Muse. The banns were published almost at once, and he and Marie-Josèphe were married on 7th January 1717, the bridegroom relying on his income of seven or eight thousand *livres* a year as means of subsistence, with, in addition, the 900 *livres* a year produced by a small property which constituted the bride's *dot*.

Unfortunately, thrift was always the very last concern of M. de Mézières. To his other expensive habits he now added conjugal affection to such a degree that he could refuse nothing to his wife, and within a very short space of time his munificence in the matter of clothes, carriages, furniture, and social display in general, brought him to financial ruin.

A prey to his creditors, he was living at Avallon as best he could at the Hostel de Chastillon, rue du Petit Bourbon, the house of his friend the Marquis de la Haie, when he died from an attack of ague on 26th August 1734. This " beau la Haye," as he was called, in his youth a page and lover of the Duchesse de Berry, daughter of the Regent (whose princely favours were attended by bountiful generosity), still retained, apparently, and set due store by, the household treasures, plate, and pictures surviving from those days of splendour. Now he took his ease in wealth and comfort, exercising benevolence towards his less fortunate friends, among them this luckless neighbour of his, M. de Mézières, whom he was glad to shelter from duns and bailiffs. It was, of course, whispered by the malicious that Mme. de Mézières recompensed him for his benevolence, though of this no kind of proof was forthcoming.

Barely four months after her husband's death, however, Mme. de Mézières was united in marriage with the Marquis, who had been a widower for several years. And there can be no doubt that she had appealed to M. de la Haie's sense of pity and chivalry to a degree involving some measure of love.

This is a fact that people have been unwilling to admit.

Because her parentage was inferior to that of the family of la Haie, this marriage seemed to minister to her vanity and ambition. It constituted her promotion into the great world (so it has been said) which her people had always regarded as a land inaccessible to them.

With all respect to these carpers, the Minards were far from being so plebeian in their origin. They did not pretend, indeed, to illustrious ancestry, but they were a branch of an honourable Auxon family of lawyers of some antiquity, to whom patents of nobility had been granted, and the new marriage does not seem on examination so very much of a *mésalliance*, apart from its financial side, and in regard to this we find that the Marquis reimbursed himself as fully as possible out of the Mézières estate, putting in a claim for every penny he had lent and drawing a further sum of 250 *livres* from the sale of his old friend's household effects as payment of rent due to him.

La Haie assumed the rank and title of Marquis, but in the official records and in the marriage contract he appears merely as "Chevalier." An arrogant libertine, his whole bearing and character—those of a man who would not suffer anyone to forget the honours that had been accorded to him—bore the stamp of the Regent's Court.

Absorbed in his memories and vanities, he was no fit

guardian for the poor little Mézières children: a daughter of sixteen and a son a year younger. And they needed a guardian to protect them from their mother, who after her second marriage began at once to take a dislike to them. They were too old to be left like Dalembert on the steps of a church, but there were at least convents at hand which offered the inviolable security of perpetual seclusion to those numerous parents who were anxious to get rid of their children. Whether she wished it or not, Mlle. de Mézières was to be made a nun, and to this end was consigned to the convent of the Dames du Bon Secours.

As for her brother, Anatole-Christophe-Fortunat, it appears that the Marquise found a different expedient for ridding herself of him. She took him away from the school at which he was being educated and at which he was achieving a brilliant success, and packed him off to America as a bad lot.

The tranquillity of her new life was now secured. Two children came to fortify it: a daughter, Charlotte, who became—without any element of romance—first, Mme. de Montesson, and then—as the outcome of a romance, both long and made the most of—Duchess of Orleans; and a son, the Marquis de la Haie.

Once in six months, at oftenest, Marie-Françoise-Félicité received a visit from her mother at the convent. This would probably be when payments for her maintenance there became due, and these were as low as possible and included nothing for special lessons. And during these twice-yearly visits, the young girl, who had never received a single caress from her mother, had to sit and listen in silence to her commonplaces upon the dangers of the world and the peace and happiness of the convent.

Now, the convent has hardships only for those who enter it without a vocation. Mlle. de Mézières underwent them, buoyed up with the hope, so enduring in young hearts, of one day escaping. Mme. Rossignol, the Abbess, encouraged her in motherly fashion to confide in her, took the greatest care of her, took her about with her like a favourite daughter, and of her own accord had her taught by a music-master so that she might be able to find consolation playing the organ.

But her terrible mother began to talk of vows, and it was arranged that Marie-Françoise-Félicité should become a nun, despite her tears, prayers, and protestations. The day of the ceremony arrived. The postulant, determined not to allow the irrevocable "Yes" to be drawn from her, declared that she might indeed be taken to the church but that she would say "No." She had her way.

"She resumed that day her ordinary clothes, which she had not worn for two years . . ." says Mme. de Genlis in her *Memoirs*. "As she had grown during the period of her useless novitiate, they were too short for her to an absurd degree, but she resumed them with delight none the less. And she was left at the convent, whence she was never allowed out."

The best years of her girlhood languished thus, seeming to presage an entire life spent in seclusion.

In the spring of her twenty-sixth year, however, an old widowed lady, the Marquise de Fontenille, came to the convent to reside there, withdrawn from the world, as was then a common custom, in a separate suite of rooms in which she could lead her own life, waited on by her own servants, after the fashion of Mme. du Deffand at the Filles-de-Saint-Joseph; and Marie-Françoise-Félicité soon began to lend the charm of her youth to the austere salon in which the Marquise was wont to receive her relatives and friends.

Here it was that her Prince Charming saw and loved her. Living thus sequestered and hidden away, does she not in truth set one thinking of the Sleeping Beauty?

A gentleman of rank this Prince Charming: a man of distinction, educated by the Jesuits of Lyon; tall, well set up; "of perfect beauty," so his daughter will tell us; of winning manners; playing the violin quite tolerably, and not lacking in other charms and accomplishments. He is thirty-five, and his name is Pierre-César du Crest.

He has ample leisure for his visits to Mme. de Fontenille, having no professional ties now that he left the army with the rank of captain, as the result of an escapade of which we know only this: that having come to Paris one night, without leave, and having been attacked by ruffians near the gates of the Louvre, he killed one of them. This mysterious adventure made it necessary for him to reveal his identity and to regain immediately his regiment, then under the command of Duc d'Hostun.

Three months later he resigned. This at least is what happened according to Mme. de Genlis.

Now we are a-sail in the realms of romance! We are in a fairy-tale worthy of Perrault. Nothing is lacking. In the person of the Abbess we have the guileful and beneficent fairy.

Mme. de la Haie, in her rôle of wicked mother, refuses the hand of her daughter to Prince Charming. Her daughter is to have no dowry.

The Abbess, despite all protestations from outside that to unite the two young people is to marry hunger to thirst, exerts herself on their behalf; and her magic ring—or her kind soul—will defray the expenses of the wedding. . . . A delightful tale, for it ends happily with the wedding bells!

But to return to plain facts. The du Crest family was not rich, except in children—a fine tradition in itself and preferable to mere money-bags. Pierre-César, however (according to Mme. de Genlis), would have been in receipt of from 10,000 to 12,000 *livres* a year at the time of his marriage, had not his joyous and careless, not to say spendthrift, temperament already dissipated a large measure of his patrimony.

Descended from a race of soldiers and men of action, warlike and brave, he was the incarnation of the type of those provincial nobles of France who, in the interval between two campaigns in the service of the King, were wont to return to their manors and to spend their time cultivating the soil and clearing the woods of wolves and wild boars. His own titles of nobility were of old origin. The Ducrests, or du Crests, go back, according to a manuscript genealogy, to that Philipes du Crest who, in the fifteenth century (1491), married Charlotte de Gevingi, widow of Guichard, Seigneur de Valette, a native of Savoy; and who came into France in the suite of the French queen, Charlotte de Savoie, second wife of King Louis XI. But traces of a branch of the family may be found earlier than this in Italy.

They have never been *de robe*, according to their family archives. The oldest musters and *revues d'armes* which have been preserved in Burgundy (Courtray, 1842; Chatel-Chignon, 1412; Châtillon, 1414; Beauvais, 1417) mention squires of this name, either as accompanying the Duke in his wars in Flanders in the fourteenth century, or as galloping behind the Bold to the disaster of Nancy. Those who did not carry the sword joined the Church.

The pedigree has no gaps in it dating from 1474, and in the fourteenth century there were sixteen or seventeen branches, all deriving their name from an estate named Le Crest or Ducrest, situated in the parish of Vandenesse-sur-Arroux, in le Charolais, which has never passed out of the family.

Pierre-César belonged to the branch surnamed de Chigy, by no means the least honoured. One of his great-uncles, Claude du Crest, proved his mettle at St. John of Jerusalem, December 1582; another Claude, at Malta, 2nd June 1633. Suffice it to say that the pages of Hozier are full of them, as are the archives of Dijon, Mâcon, Nevers, Moulins; and that they contracted alliances with the families of Semur, Le Bourgoing, Rollin, Vichy, Maurage, Lichy, Murat, Moroges, Rabutin, Villars, Hennezel, Condé, Bonneval, and Leprestre de Vauban.

Fortune, however, was seldom prodigal in their regard. In spite of their military prowess, in spite of their gallant services in the armies and fleets of the King, they came in only for a pension or a cross of St. Louis or of St. Lazare by way of recompense.

It was perhaps a piece of luck, therefore, for the father of Pierre-César that he won for his bride, in August 1706, a rich heiress of his neighbourhood, Catharine Chaussin, daughter of Gilbert Chaussin, described in Hozier as a " rich merchant and dealer in the market-town of Issy-l'Évêque, near Autun."

He cannot be said to have married beneath him in the

literal sense of the words. The Chaussins, without being able to lay claim to such ancient lineage as the du Crests, were awarded titles of nobility in 1667, 1669, and 1698. Gilbert Chaussin himself appears as Seigneur d'Urly previously to 1697. Members of the family are to be found in the King's bodyguard and among the notables of France.

Catharine du Crest was left a widow with three children. François, the eldest, a *mousquetaire* in the army of the Rhine, who died before the marriage of his sister Marie-Madeleine, on the 8th January 1731, to Jean-Jacques de Sercey, Baron du Jeu, Chevalier of St. Louis and captain of dragoons. Catharine died before the marriage of her second son, Pierre-César.

The Seigneur de Champcéry et de Perrigny-la-Plaine, to give him the full title which now belonged to him, inherited half his mother's fortune, which must have amounted to some thousands of *livres* a year. Most of this money he had managed to squander either when with his garrison or in Paris in merry company.

He seems to have behaved chivalrously enough by his penniless *fiancée*, and although she had to forgo wedding presents and trousseau as well as her rightful share of her father's property (in regard to which she was afterwards to bring a legal action against her mother), they were married, it would seem, towards the end of November 1743.

Du Crest imparted some lustre to the ceremony through the names of those who signed the wedding contract. Among the witnesses were Monseigneur de Valette, Bishop of Autun; the Duc de Saint-Aignan, Governor of Burgundy, Member of the French Academy; the Marquis de Bauffremont, Chevalier de la Toison d'Or, Lieutenant-General of the armies of the King; and the Chevalier de Bauffrement de Listenois, Commander of the Order of Malta.

On the bride's side the witnesses are less distinguished: la Haie and his son, and Mme. Minard des Alleurs, an aunt, are there to represent the family. The Abbess also was present. After the wedding was over, the young couple set forth for Champcéry, where we have seen them arrive.

Not quite three years later, 26th January 1746, their first

child was born to them, the daughter, Magdeleine-Félicité, who was to become famous as Mme. de Genlis.[1]

The child is very weak and delicate—so much so that they cannot put her in swaddling-clothes. She has to be wrapped up in a pillow-case, the four corners of which are pinned up. A quaint little parcel of humanity she must have looked, deposited there upon an arm-chair. On one occasion a local official who had come to offer his congratulations to the young couple very nearly sat down upon her by mistake!

She had so little vitality that they had her baptized in the house on the day of her birth. Things looked more serious still when it was found that the nurse could not suckle her and that she had to be fed on crumbs of rye bread passed through a sieve and moistened with wine and water. As soon as she could move about, she fell into a pond. When nearly two, she burnt herself. Another tumble followed soon after, and she nearly split open her head. But she survived all these mishaps miraculously. They were but forewarnings, perhaps, of her stormy career.

Her parents soon began to weary of their small and mournful abode. A son came to them, fifteen months after Félicité — 28th April 1747: Charles-Louis. Impelled by dreams of a fine future for him, they disposed of Champcéry to their brother-in-law, de Sercey, and bought a house with a garden and a terrace overlooking the Loire, at Cosne—a temporary arrangement pending better things.

On 31st July in the following year he acquired by contract the freehold of Saint-Aubin-sur-Loire, marquisate and château together—a step which seems disproportionate to his scanty means. The purchase did in fact bring about pecuniary difficulties, and we shall have to come back to the subject later. The titles of Marquis and of "Seigneur Haut Justicier" of Saint-Aubin and of Sept-Fons (of which the

---

[1] Mme. de Genlis says "fifteen months," but according to the date of the marriage contract, 23rd November 1743, it must have been three years.

Mme. de Genlis is sometimes styled Étiennette-Félicité, sometimes Stéphanie-Félicité—this latter name is the one adopted in her own signatures as a rule. The former name appears in her marriage contract and in the official record of her death.

famous abbey stood opposite the château, on the other bank of the Loire) went with the property. To these du Crest added the titles of Seigneur and Baron of Bourbon-Lancy.

Saint-Aubin was charmingly situated. The château must have been of vast size and magnificent, but at the time when it was purchased by the du Crests its walls, already old, showed many cracks and fissures.

"It resembled the castles which have since been described by Mrs. Radcliffe," says Mme. de Genlis. "It was old and dilapidated, and there were immense courtyards through one of which flowed a canal, bordered by ebony trees which then were very rare. In this canal fine carps were kept." By an extraordinary singularity, impossible to account for, there was no view of the river from the château, none of the windows looking out in that direction.

The château, according to an authentic document, dated September 1752, partook of the nature of a fortress in its construction. It rose in the midst of a vast walled courtyard girt by a moat to the north, west, and south. Two blocks of buildings, enclosing a central courtyard, and flanked by four large round towers which bore the arms of the marquisate and raised aloft their pointed summits surmounted by small spires, constituted the manor-house properly so called. Behind it was a large garden, also walled and defended by two additional round towers. To the left of it were stables, barns, and outhouses.

The principal entrance was from the north. To the west, quite near, but out of sight, ran the Loire. The sun rose upon the pond, and right at the end of the garden might be seen the village church and the cemetery.

Félicité's room was in one of the big towers, that on the right, overlooking the pond: a damp little room on the ground floor. This tower is not one of the portions of the old château which have escaped ruin.

Félicité and her brother would seem to have been free to play about to their hearts' content. Mme. du Crest did not give much time or thought to her daughter's upbringing. The child is said to have been ill dressed and ill cared for. The village schoolmistress, Mlle. Durgon, was, however, called in to initiate her into the mysteries of the alphabet and develop her unformed mind before she was six years old. In the course of six or seven months the little girl learnt how to read. The small brother needed other teachers besides a village schoolmistress. He was sent to Paris to the Pension du Roule or the Pension Bertaud. And when Mme. du Crest de Saint-Aubin had given birth to a second son and recovered her health, she followed to Paris with Félicité.

We find them staying with a relative, Mme. de Bellevaux, *née* du Crest, a resident in Paris since the death of her husband, who had lost his life at the siege of Prague. This lady saw a great many visitors, and poor little seven-year-old Félicité, little Burgundian savage that she was, offered a marked contrast to the elegantly attired Parisians. She had been suffered too long to run wild. She walked ungracefully, her hair was unkempt, her teeth needed looking to, one of her eyes was inclined to squint. These defects needed drastic and painful remedies. She had two teeth extracted; her body was imprisoned in a pitiless contrivance of whalebone; tight shoes tortured her feet; a collar made of iron, hundreds of curl-papers, hoop-petticoats, and a pair of spectacles designed to correct the tendency to squint, combined to complete her transformation.

As soon as she was held to have been sufficiently Parisianised, Félicité was solemnly baptized. (It will be remembered that the earlier baptism was administered in the house.) Mme. de Genlis does not tell us the name of the parish in which the ceremony took place; she confines herself to recording the names of the godfather and godmother, Michel Bouret, the famous financier, and Mme. de Bellevaux. Thanks to the recent discovery, however, of an unpublished document which has been placed at our disposal, we now know that the baptism took place at the church of Saint-Eustache. Great festivities ensued; but for all their brilliancy Félicité preferred the Opera.

Music and dancing and the stage transport her already. Soon people are to say, " This little person was born to be an actress."

Almost before she has reached the age of reason, she

makes her *début* between the folding screens of the château d'Étiolles, the home of Guillaume Le Normand, a friend of Mme. Bellevaux, and very probably a former boon-companion of Pierre-César.

At Étiolles, life was one long endless comedy—the play-acting did not confine itself to the stage. Even during the day the costumes of the guests were redolent of the theatre. Félicité was to find herself transformed into a little Savoyarde, attired, we learn, "in a little monkey's apparel, with a little jacket of brown taffetas, and short petticoat of the same stuff, trimmed with two or three rows of pink ribbons, and for headdress a gauze fichu tied under the chin."

And because she enacted on the stage the allegorical rôle of Friendship and sang a poor couplet or so in her pretty dress, the memory of these doings was never to pass from her mind, "so glorious did this day appear" to her!

It is recorded, too, that she made a conquest—her first! This was in the person of the gouty old Maréchal de Lowendal, a hero, who singled her out from all the others, so pleased he was by her naïve admiration. Little Félicité began to feel she was quite a star.

It was made a matter of reproach to her mother that she paid so long a visit to this château. It was thought imprudent on her part. The supposition was that she was attracted thither, and tempted to remain on, by the continual round of gaiety and frivolity. It was not realised that the poor young woman was chiefly actuated by her hopes of getting financial help from the powerful Farmer-General. Incapable in business matters, like her husband, ignorant and happy-go-lucky, it was her nature to count on strokes of miraculous good luck to extricate her from the morasses in which their improvidence continually landed them.

At the moment in question, Pierre-César has not paid down any of the money due from him for his recently acquired property. Moreover, "failing the payment of the sum of 1200 *livres*," a certain Sieur Dutrou de Villetang has put in a writ of attachment on Saint-Aubin, which is to be put up for auction on the 1st of September 1752 by Edme Vinot, sheriff's officer at Bourbon-Lancy.

In desperation over this, Mme. du Crest had recourse to the rich Le Normand, who being a man of business before anything else, was not inclined to do anything rashly. He took the precaution of informing himself first as to the value of the property. When, in May 1753, he decided not indeed to lend Pierre-César the money needed but to act as his security, thus enabling him to borrow elsewhere, Mme. du Crest and her daughter were able to return home.

They returned in a spirit of gaiety and happiness, accompanied by Mme. de Bellevaux and two little girls who lived with her—children whose origin was a matter of much speculation to contemporaries. They were believed to be the daughters of Le Normand and Mme. de Bellevaux, and unfriendly tongues suggested, of course, that this had something to do with the assistance accorded to Pierre-César.

Mme. de Chastellux told Moreau (and another writer, following in their footsteps, repeats the statement) that a Mademoiselle Chaussin, the twenty-year-old widow of Claude Béraut de Bellevaux, having come to seek her fortunes in Paris, made the acquaintance of Le Normand " and consoled him for his notorious domestic grief. She succeeded so well that two little daughters came into the world, for whom it was necessary to find a father. César du Crest and Mlle. de Mézières would seem to have agreed to recognise them as their children and to legitimise them by their marriage in consideration of the payment of 800,000 crowns, half of which sum is said to have found its way into the hands of intermediaries." And Moreau adds: "One of these children, so the story goes, was the future Mme. de Genlis."

Nobody could be misled for an instant by this last blunder, so serious that it should suffice in itself to discredit the rest of the narrative. A second mistake is obvious in that Mme. de Bellevaux was not a Chaussin but a du Crest. It is clear, none the less, how easily the uncharitable could make capital out of the simple facts.

We shall see presently the outcome of this fable. For the moment it will suffice to explain that the two little girls were in truth the illegitimate children of a cousin of Pierre-César, Lazare du Crest de Chigy, and of a girl of the neighbourhood named Philippe-Julienne de Gayot de Provenchères. Failing the consent of the parents, the lovers had to wait until the young mother attained the age at which she could marry without it, and they had avoided the gossiping of neighbours by confiding their first child to their cousin Mme. de Bellevaux, and by placing their second out at nurse at a village named Ville-Chaux, near Cosne. The children then were du Crests, and, as we shall see, Lazare and Mlle. de Gayot were to legitimise them on the day of their wedding, 19th December 1758. Meanwhile, they are taken with Félicité to the noble chapter-house of Saint-Denis d'Alix, near Lyon, there to be received as " canonesses." [1]

The custom, in great favour with the French nobility, of conferring on their daughters the title of " canoness " involved an excellent method of provision for their future in the event of their not marrying. In this event the chapter-house offered them many advantages, placing at their disposal a highly honoured home, accompanied with titles and prebends and enabling them to continue their lives in an atmosphere of aristocracy, for even the least distinguished of the chapter-houses insisted rigorously upon proofs of noble birth. That of Alix, renowned throughout Lyonnais and Dauphiné, was not as exacting as that of Panthemont and certain of those in Bavaria in respect of their rule that at least sixteen quarterings must be shown; eight quarterings were sufficient, and Félicité and her cousins were able to satisfy the *commissaire*. In three weeks the proofs were verified, and thanks to the influence of a relative on the Minard side, Mme. de Clugny, a canoness resident at the chapter, the ceremony took place without delay. It was very imposing. All the old canonesses, the Abbess at their head, attired in hooped

---

[1] Mme. de Genlis says she travelled with her cousins, but the second child was scarcely out of her cradle, being only eleven months old. It is possible that her memory in regard to this was at fault.

gowns of black silk, with great cloaks faced with ermine, filled the choir. The officiating priest handed to the young aspirants the insignia of the Order—the red ribbon with an enamelled cross, the wide band of watered ribbon, and the tiny headdress of black taffetas which these ladies call " a husband."

It used to be the custom to cut off a lock of hair in every case. The priest, who was short-sighted, cut Félicité's ear slightly, and the blood began to flow a little—" but I bore it heroically," Mme. de Genlis records. The child is in ecstasy over the whole experience. Henceforth she is *Madame!*—Madame la Comtesse de Lancy; this thought, she tells us, gave her more pleasure than anything else. Overwhelmed with bonbons and made much of in every way, it was natural that she should feel strongly drawn to her new condition.

But when Mme. de Clugny offered to bequeath to little Félicité her title and prebend, which would have entailed renouncing marriage and taking the vows, Mme. du Crest refused on her child's behalf. It would not do to commit the future in this way. So they return to Saint-Aubin. Mother and daughter arrive just in time to be present at the death of the youngest born, who had been made a Knight of Malta while still in his cradle.

CHAPTER II

EDUCATION

It is strange to find children so badly neglected in this eighteenth century, so prolific of reform in other directions.

They passed from the arms of their nurses into other mercenary hands, and their parents took no further interest in them. We know that Biron and Talleyrand were the moral offspring of this custom, against which the Genevan Rousseau protested. Mme. du Crest, but lately mixing in the best society, did not dream of acting differently. She saw her daughter for a few moments in the early morning, and for a little while at meal-times, but for the rest of the day Félicité was handed over to the chambermaids.

M. du Crest has taken to the pursuits of a country gentleman. The greater part of his existence is given up to hunting, angling, his pack of hounds, snaring birds and fishing at night. He passes the rest of his days, with the exception of a few visits to the abbey at Sept-Fonts, shut up in his laboratory. But these diversions do not prevent him from becoming a silent and melancholy man.

The Marquise, on the other hand, became a social butterfly. She led the unrestrained life of a châtelaine, and made up for the dull years of her youth, spent in the seclusion of a convent.

The entertainment of her neighbours was to her the most important thing in life.

Félicité remained untaught and neglected to the last degree. The servants, rough peasants for the most part, who were told to teach her a little Catechism, filled her head with ghost-stories.

Occasionally, for want of a better tutor, César du Crest would take his daughter in hand. He wished to make her a hardy woman, and to that end he inured her to touching spiders, mice, and toads without flinching, and took her out with him when he went fishing at night.

When she was seven years old, her parents thought of getting a governess for her, according to the custom in good families. Pierre-César, as we know, was a musician. Félicité had a taste for music and gave promise of a pretty voice. They therefore looked about for a music-mistress.

The one chosen was a poor sixteen-year-old Breton girl. She was the daughter of the organist at Vannes, a gentle, timid girl, grave beyond her years, with a considerable knowledge of the harpsichord. Apart from that, she knew nothing; her piety—the gentle, innocent piety of a St. Francis of Sales—took the place of everything else.

Her name was Mlle. de Mars.

Félicité was "given entirely into her charge." She was to guide and instruct her in everything. The responsibility must have weighed heavily upon one who had never taught anything, yet it was a great improvement when Félicité's days were occupied and turned to account.

Félicité could read, which was considered enough. No one spoke of writing—that would come later.

An oral lesson in the Catechism, another in history, with an abridged edition of P. Buffier, one in music and the harpsichord, formed the daily method of study until the midday dinner. After the meal, student and teacher went to their rooms to recite the office of the Virgin, and the afternoon was devoted to walks.

It was a meagre education. Besides, P. Buffier was abandoned for good at the end of a week. "He bored us dreadfully!" confesses Mme. de Genlis, "and no one ever called us to account."

But gentle Mlle. de Mars felt herself very unprepared in the face of her duty. She had the care of Félicité's mind; she had to teach, and, feeling afraid, she unbosomed herself to the Marquis. They explored the library of the manor together. They chose, perhaps by chance, two books which appeared promising to their inexperienced eyes, the *Célie* and *Le Théâtre* of Mlle. Barbier.

Could the excellent Scudéry ever have foreseen that the adventures of Aronce and Princesse Tullie would one day serve as grammar, history, and text-book of good manners for young girls!

Félicité and her governess delighted in it for many long months, and probably puzzled over the meaning of it all. But P. Buffler's insipid history could hardly be expected to bear comparison with *la carte de Tendre*.

Such was the education of the future Mme. de Genlis. In the beginning she became a very pious little girl.

The saintly Mlle. de Mars never wearied of speaking to her of God, and during the course of their long walks she tried to explain the great mystery of divine love from the eternal book of Nature.

One is really touched by the delightful picture which these two children must have made, conversing of holy things along the paths and forests of this corner of the Bourbon country; the younger vivacious, impulsive, and curious, the elder with the precocious gravity of sixteen summers, "admiring with rapture the sky, the trees, and the flowers as proofs of the existence of God and as His works." When they went to church in the manor chapel, Félicité never tired of contemplating a large statue of coloured plaster, representing an angel holding an enormous bunch of black grapes in his slender hands, who smiled at her and appealed to her young soul.

If one is to believe Mme. de Genlis, her piety had still more fervent aspects to it, since it urged her to get up in the middle of the night to prostrate herself on the floor in prayer; which did not prevent her, it is true, from having recourse to the most barefaced stratagems in the daytime to evade the difficulties in a piece of music.

She acquired, from contact with Scudéry and Barbier, a taste for romance, a love of intrigue and adventure, and a leaning towards sentimentality, which was to be conspicuous in her character later on, and which at this time excited her to the point of inventing stories of romantic events, in which she imagined herself taking part. She became so important in her own eyes that she considered herself able to teach others from her own small store of knowledge. So while her mother and Mlle. de Mars retire for their siesta or are busy attending to their personal affairs, the child goes up to her room and steps over the window-sill on to the terrace, which is raised above the bank of the pond and overlooks a narrow strip of grass, which slopes gently down to the water's edge. Here it is that the urchins of the village, the sons of watermen and ploughmen, come to cut rushes and loiter about. Félicité calls to them, enticing them with promises of cakes, and from the height of her stone balcony, like a magistrate on the bench, suspended between heaven and earth, she recites to them some of Mlle. Barbier's verses or a passage from the Jesuit's history. The boys stand there submissively, with their faces upturned, and go through their spelling exercises, and repeat their lessons to their small mistress, who withholds the manna of cakes until the lesson is over. It appears that Félicité's teaching bore fruit, and was transmitted from father to son in Saint-Aubin.

The child was a born pedagogue, as people came to remark. But this was not her mother's doing, for the latter was more than ever absorbed in her own amusements.

While the lord of Saint-Aubin, who had been called away to Paris, where he remained until 1755, by the differences always pending with the *capitaine du second vol pour corneilles*, Mme. du Crest conceived the idea of passing the time in the preparation of amateur theatricals with which to celebrate his return. She herself composed "a kind of rustic comic opera, with a mythological prologue" in verse, although she knew nothing whatever of the laws of versification. She delighted Félicité by giving her the rôle of Cupid. Racine, it is true, contributed largely to the programme, for besides the comic opera they played *Iphigénie*, and Félicité played the part of Iphigenia.

From that moment life at Saint-Aubin is thrown into confusion. The whole manor, from the Marquise down to the four chambermaids, learn their different parts, prepare the costumes, and rehearse. The neighbours, who were invited to help, ransack their wardrobes, as did Mme. du Crest, and even order a quantity of artificial jewels from Moulins. The dress rehearsals lasted for three months. "A tremendous number of people from Bourbon-Lancy and Moulins came to them," and praised Félicité to the skies.

She was certainly delightfully pretty in her different costumes. In the part of Iphigenia she wore a silver and cherry-coloured silk damask, trimmed with sable; in that of Cupid a "rose-coloured dress, covered with point lace, and decked with artificial flowers," with a quiver and large blue wings on her shoulders. The last dress was so becoming that Félicité never left it off, but would run about in the fields in her little "silver and straw-coloured shoes," and, as Mme. de Genlis says, "with all the paraphernalia of love—a quiver on my shoulder and my bow in my hand." She had duplicates of this costume, one for Sunday and one for "work-days"; but the wings were suppressed on Sundays and her dress was covered with a "kind of mantle of grey taffetas." However, as she used to follow the Corpus Christi processions dressed like an angel, it is to be supposed that the same wings were used for Cupid and the heavenly messenger, which was an odd mixture of sacred and profane ideas, and might almost be taken as "an emblem of a life which, after having known the frailties of love, was to end by aspiring to the purity of an angel's."[1]

Meanwhile, the Marquis de Saint-Aubin did not return, and the Marquise continued to amuse her neighbours for the time being with further sumptuous festivities.

They played *Zaïre*, in which Félicité surpassed Clairon, according to the ladies from Moulins.

She did not yet know how to dance, a defect which they were not long in remedying.

Mme. du Crest secured the services of a Mlle. Mion, a dancing-mistress at Autun, who taught the little star how to dance and enter a room. She was soon replaced, however, on account of her scandalous drinking habits and her mane

[1] Louis Chabaud, *Les Précurseurs du féminisme*, "Mme. de Genlis," p. 201.

of red hair, by a Vestris of the neighbourhood, fifty years of age, who was also a fencing-master.

Fencing! What an opportunity for distinction! Why should not Félicité try it? The professor asked for nothing better, and he taught the child his favourite science.

This was the end of the Cupid's dress.

Félicité, dressed now like a little boy, wore breeches, fenced, jumped ditches, and climbed trees, to the sorrow of Mlle. de Mars. And as the play has become the most important thing with her mother, she gives Félicité the part of Darviane,[1] as it needs someone who can draw a sword and fence. Mme. de Genlis does not tell us that she shocked anyone; on the contrary, everybody was captivated, including Père Antoine, chaplain at Saint-Aubin.

Mlle. de Mars alone appears to have kept a grain of common sense in the general extravagance. She was the only one among so many actresses who dared to criticise and laugh at the costumes, the curious success of which was spoiling her pupil. Her sense of responsibility made her try to bring about a reaction by means of good counsel and exemplary behaviour, and by the continuance of pious practices, so long as they did not take up the time devoted by Mme. de Saint-Aubin to the hobby of play-acting; but she could not do much. The greater part of the morning was taken up with dancing, fencing, and studying the parts, and music and singing took up the rest. Occasionally they read *La Reine de Navarre*, by Mlle. de la Force; and when Mme. de Saint-Aubin is not receiving anyone, the afternoon is passed in making garlands of artificial flowers for decorative purposes—an agreeable pastime in which Père Antoine did not disdain to join.

And so the festivities continue, attracting all the nobility of the neighbourhood, which was very numerous in a district where so many manors adjoined.

Once there was a scare of small-pox, which put a stop to things; but it proved nothing more than a slight attack over which Félicité's fresh complexion triumphed, thanks to good Doctor Pinot, and no one thought any more about it.

[1] Darviane, a character in *Mélanide*, a tragi-comedy by La Chaussée.

But another invalid appeared to be more seriously, if not irremediably, affected. We refer to the manor of Saint-Aubin, which had become even more dilapidated and tumble-down, and was almost uninhabitable. The Marquis seemed to have no remedy for it, since he never returned, and its occupants were forced to leave it without waiting for his problematical return.

Meanwhile, in Paris, Pierre-César was fighting as best he could against reverses. Without money, encumbered with debts, plagued with ruinous lawsuits, the unfortunate man had recourse to every expedient to escape disaster. It does not seem possible that his wife knew the real state of things, in view of her reckless way of living.

We find her settled now at Bourbon-Lancy, with her sister-in-law, Mme. de Sercey, whose husband—after an attack of paralysis—has come there to take the waters.

The establishment, of course, had to have a theatre, which was fitted up specially for Mme. du Crest. It was the autumn of 1755. Comedies and tragedies had been revived since the previous winter, and to the former repertory they now added *George Dandin; Les Plaideurs; Cénie*, a play by Mme. Graffigny; *Attendez-moi sous l'orme*; and *Le Distrait*, in which Félicité aroused general enthusiasm.

Poor little girl! She was exposed to the life behind the scenes, and grew up among the most artificial emotions, the more dangerous by their very exaggeration. At a most impressionable age she was continually rehearsing with pseudo-heroes, giving voice to the most passionate utterances, and playing parts in which love was always, and only, in question. That was her schooling.

It would not have been surprising really if Félicité, who was a precocious child, had fallen in love. But her heart remained untouched, and was not to be the dupe of so many sentimental scenes. Her vanity protected her and screened her from any disturbing thought, beyond the perfection of her acting and the business of the theatre, which absorbed her growing zeal.

But others were not so well balanced. The son of Doctor Pinot of Bourbon-Lancy, probably a weak and simple-minded boy, was a constant partner of Félicité's in tragic parts, and confounded play-acting with reality. He took everything in earnest, and his eighteen-year-old affections were set on fire by the ten-year-old star.

The unfortunate youth was destined to have a fall.

A person of the lower middle-class, "who was not a gentleman," daring to make love to Mlle. du Crest de Saint-Aubin! Actually having the impertinence to hand her a note! She is "exceedingly shocked," and takes the insolent love-letter to her mother and to Mlle. de Mars.

The imprudent lover was sharply rebuked by his father, who had been informed, and had to leave the scene, giving his word to disappear. Young Pinot did not remain a bachelor. He married three years later, and appears to have been very happy.

At length, during the year 1756, Pierre-César returned home. Unfortunately, he brought with him nothing but bad news—unpaid debts, the threats of creditors, a wasted fortune, and the immediate sale of Saint-Aubin and Bourbon-Lancy.

"His wife and he," says Courchamps, "could have devoured two kingdoms. All the available rights to these two manors were mortgaged by them for ninety-nine years."

There is no doubt that the unfortunate du Crests were led astray by their improvidence and prodigality.

They were now forced to give up their salons and the theatre; but rather than undergo the commiseration of the little town, the Marquise preferred to leave everything, allowing it to be believed that a more brilliant future awaited her in Paris.

She therefore embarks upon the passage-boat which goes up the Loire as far as Orleans, together with her daughter, Mlle. de Mars, the servants, and everything that they could take away with them in trunks. It must be explained that this was the cheapest way of travelling. After a rest at Orleans with some friends, who had invited everyone of importance in the town to meet them, our travellers reach Paris and put up at Mme. de Bellevaux's, who, it is probable, was not aware of their pecuniary embarrassments.

And while Pierre-César left as quickly as he could for

Bourbon-Lancy, making money, they say, of the bricks and wood of the manor of Aubin, his wife in Paris set herself to settle the state of affairs as quietly and as advantageously as she could.

Meanwhile, life went on quietly and uneventfully. Mme. de Bellevaux, a witty woman, and an occasional writer,[1] had her box at the Opera and the Française, and was a lady of fashion much sought after. Financiers, men of letters, and musicians frequented her salon and her country-house at Saint-Mandé. Mme. de Saint-Aubin, who had become habituated to a life of ease, witty conversation, and the arts and graces of society, was entirely in her element on her return to the society of Paris. And Félicité, with her prettiness, freshness, and vivacity, and her readiness to recite and allow her beautiful voice to be heard, was a valuable asset to her mother. They praised her to the skies, and she, who was always hungry for success, set herself to provoke it still further. Four hours of music—singing, harpsichord, and guitar, for they were teaching her the guitar now—hardly suffice for the preparation of the " pieces " in which she is to play. She spends a great deal of time, besides, in rehearsing the verses which she recites. Every night she is seen at the play. " In this way," the *Mémoires* tell us, " my days were employed, if not very properly, at least in their entirety, and there was no time left for serious study." And Félicité, who was an intelligent girl, was very conscious of her own inferiority.

How crude and bare is her little provincial mind, compared with the brilliant intellects of these men of letters! How backward and ridiculous she feels! How greedily she listens to the conversations, tormented by the desire for knowledge! How curious, interested, and captivated she is! The intellectual Genlis of the morrow is awakening.

A certain M. de Mondorge, a humorous poet and ballad-writer, and something of a critic, holds a conversation with Marmontel at Mme. de Bellevaux's one day. Helvetius has just published his book *De l'Esprit*, and M. de Mondorge scourges " the infamy of the principles in this book."

[1] She published a novel, *Les Lettres d'une jeune veuve*.

Félicité never tires of listening. She is his frank and gentle admirer, and she conquers him by confiding to him her first and very mediocre quatrain.[1]

M. de Mondorge, says Mme. de Genlis, was inexpressibly delighted and flattered by the artless confidence of this eleven-year-old muse, and willingly became the director of her literary studies.

His principle was to make her read and write a great deal. As she had no books, he gave her the poems of Jean-Baptiste Rousseau, which she conscientiously learned by heart, and La Fontaine's *Fables* and Gresset's *Vert-Vert* on New Year's Day. Nowadays, this choice would appear to us somewhat disquieting, but it was characteristic of the age.

Félicité set to work undaunted. She devoted herself to reading and recitation until bedtime. She was also taught how to hold a pen, and began to practise by writing long letters, some of them sixteen pages in length, in her large, awkward handwriting, to Mlle. Azerote, a cousin of Mlle. Durgon, and niece of the priest at Bourbon-Lancy. When her brother came to spend his summer holidays with Mme. de Bellevaux at her house at Saint-Mandé, he continued to take Latin lessons, in which Félicité joined. At Saint-Mandé, besides, she put together some little plays in dumb show, for which she borrowed from various pieces for the harpsichord and guitar, in combination with some fragments from plays and novels. She always arranged them so that she had the most important part in the play. These *pots-pourris*, it appears, covered their author with glory—which was, after all, what they were meant to do. They are not to be taken too seriously. The little actress, flattered to the top of her bent, was unconscious of the slight value of the praises of society. At her age one may be excused for not seeing beyond so intoxicating a success. However, no one about her ever thought that this delightful time was coming to an end.

[1] This was the work of art, founded on the names of the writer, her governess, and a chambermaid named Victoire:—

"Félicité, Mars, et Victoire
Se trouvent rassemblés chez nous.
Est-il rien de plus grand, est-il rien de plus doux,
Que de fixer chez soi le bonheur et la gloire!"

And when the final crash came, it appears to have been with the suddenness of a catastrophe.

According to Mme. de Genlis, she and her mother lived with Mme. de Bellevaux for two years.

But, from 15th October 1757, one finds them at rue Traversière-Saint-Honoré. They came to Paris during the year 1756, and they left Mme. de Bellevaux before 15th October of the following year, so it appears that Mme. de Genlis's memory has not served her well.

Mme. de Bellevaux, who had received her cousins with open arms, promptly gave them one month in which to find a district and a house to live in, when she learned of their downfall. Mother and daughter therefore went to the Hôtel du Péron, rue Traversière, near the church of Saint-Roch, to a "shabby ground-floor apartment overlooking a damp garden." It is here that Mme. du Crest signed two bills of sale in the presence of Me. Dutartre, a notary, "for which she had obtained a power of attorney from her husband," the first on 15th October 1757, and the second on 28th February 1758. The first was in regard to the lands and manor of Saint-Aubin, and the second related to the barony of Bourbon-Lancy. The purchaser was Le Normand. Around the sale and the purchase of these properties there has since arisen a whole volume of scandal, which it would be as well to clear up.

When, seven years previously, Pierre-César du Crest mortgaged, in consideration of an annuity of twelve hundred odd *livres*, the barony of Bourbon-Lancy, and when, on 31st July 1751, he bought at the price of 76,500 *livres* the marquisate of Saint-Aubin, which had been put up for sale after the death of its owners (Gilbert Le Gendre, Marquis de Saint-Aubin, and his mother, Marguerite Violet de la Forest), he did not possess enough to meet such large sums, it is not surprising that his new status, in view of his prodigality since his marriage and the fact that his wife had no *dot*, proved too much for him. One wonders where the money came from, and since all trace of it has remained hidden in the old minutes of the notaries of the province, it has been believed to have been non-existent. Consequently, it was supposed that du Crest became a marquis at the price of a shameful action; that is to say, on account of the various events which we have already mentioned. People attributed the children of Lazare du Crest and Julienne de Gayot to the relations which existed between the husband of La Pompadour and Mme. de Bellevaux; and Pierre-César and Mlle. de Mézières are supposed—acting as intermediaries between their cousin and Le Normand—to have found a father in their own family for these miraculous children, for which satisfactory brokerage they were to receive the greater part of the promised 800,000 *écus*. The proof, it has been said, lies in the fact that the Crest-Mézières family buys the marquisate of Saint-Aubin in 1752, when " not long before they did not possess anything." Another proof is that the marriage between Lazare du Crest and Julienne de Gayot, which was to legitimise these two children, takes place in 1758 in the home of Pierre-César. Further proofs are found in the following facts: that Félicité's godfather is Bouret, " the tool of Le Normand "; that Pierre-César arranges to pay, by means of a mortgage on his Saint-Aubin property, the annuities for " each of his two nieces " at Alix; and finally, that in spite of the repurchase of Saint-Aubin by Le Normand in 1758, César du Crest continues to bear the titles of Marquis of Saint-Aubin and Baron of Bourbon-Lancy. " What claim," they ask, " had he on such generosity, if it were not on account of verbal promises which Le Normand did not keep, or blackmail, which in the story of an adventurer like du Crest is not incredible?" The words are uncharitable. Without attaching too much importance to them, it is permissible to raise doubts as to their reliability.

A comparison of the exact dates would suffice to destroy these facts. In reality, the Crest-Gayot marriage took place three years after the purchase of Bourbon-Lancy, and more than two years after the acquisition of Saint-Aubin.[1]

---

[1] The purchase of Bourbon-Lancy is dated August 20, 1750, according to a contract of September 23, 1752, entered in the records of the Chambre des Comptes at Dijon on August 8, 1754 (Archives du Crest). See also the marriage contract between Lazare du Crest de Chigy and Philippe-Julienne de Gayot, December 19, 1758 (B.N. catalogue of entries. Original papers, 1036. Du Crest in Burgundy, 23743).

Pierre-César, therefore, did not pay for them with the price of his complaisance towards Le Normand. Moreover, it must be remembered that it was on 1st September 1752 that Dutrou de Villetang issued a writ of attachment against Saint-Aubin in default of the payment to him of 1200 francs due to him. Du Crest was certainly most improvident! Le Normand, they say, was quick to help him. It was he who harboured and protected Mme. du Crest and her daughter at the time of their first journey to Paris; but, given the morals and customs of the age, nothing was more natural. It was he who extricated du Crest from his difficulties. We are going to prove that there was no need to search for a questionable motive to justify the help given to the du Crests by the great financier. He never lent them any money at all. After going into the matter, Le Normand merely becomes surety for his friend, so that he can raise the necessary money elsewhere.

In fact, it is a certain Sieur de Saint-Quentin and his lady who furnish him with 22,000 *livres*; a Sieur de Ligny, trustee of the Colombat children, who were Chaussin's cousins, lends him 18,000 *livres* by deed on 16th May 1753; and nearly a year after the Crest-Gayot marriage, Le Normand again becomes surety for Pierre-César for 40,000 *livres*, which he obtains from a Sieur Baille.[1]

Saint-Aubin was bought for 76,400 *livres*, and 80,000 were borrowed, which covered the purchase.

Thus it is proved that the marriage of his cousin and the legitimation of the children attributed to Le Normand have not brought Pierre-César a farthing of ready money. All he gets out of it is the security already mentioned, and the difference is obvious.

But here, again, the greatest precautions are taken, for Le Normand risked nothing in lending his signature to his friend. The value of the property more than covered his surety.

When du Crest made the purchase, the estate of Saint-Aubin brought him all the creditors of an inheritance

[1] Sale of the land and manor of Saint-Aubin and its appendages by M. and Mme. du Crest to M. Le Normand, October 15, 1767 (Du Crest Archives).

burdened with innumerable debts. Awarded on 24th November 1718 to Messire Charles Le Gendre, a councillor in the Parliament, by right of purchase, as was also the barony of Bourbon-Lancy, it passed on the death of the latter, which occurred some years later, to his son and widow.

Le Gendre was allied to the greatest families in France, to the princes of Lorraine-Armagnac, the Marillac, the La Tremoille, the Rohan-Chabot, and the Chaulnes, but that did not prevent him from leaving debts, which, unfortunately, his widow and son increased instead of paying off.

Five judgments were issued by the Council of State from March 1737 to October 1746, appointing three senior counsel to "judge without appeal all the lawsuits begun or about to begin between the said Messire Gilbert Le Gendre, Marquis of Saint-Aubin, and the Lady Marguerite Violet de la Forest, his mother, and widow on his decease of Messire Charles Le Gendre . . . of the one part, and their creditors and debtors of the other part."[1]

Five injunctions! A great deal of money must have been spent on litigation, and consequently further expenses added to the debts.

The situation is so bad on the death of the unfortunate squire and his mother that no heir dares to accept the inheritance. This is declared vacant, and on 31st May 1748 a Sieur Brisson is appointed trustee. Already, in 1740, the counsel elected by the Council of State replaced a creditor in possession of five pieces of land sold by them to Le Gendre senior, and not yet paid for. And the estate of Saint-Aubin, reduced by these five portions, is put up for sale in 1751 as a vacant inheritance—that is to say, put up for auction by law, under conditions as unfavourable as those consequent on a writ of attachment: a circumstance which was disastrous for the creditors, but extremely advantageous to the purchaser. This was the

---

[1] Auction of the land of Saint-Aubin and appendages, held by M. P. César du Crest, lord of the said place, on July 14, 1753 (Du Crest Archives). This report, which comprises more than fourteen pages of "double-elephant" paper, printed in the most minute characters, is a veritable monument of legal procedure.

way in which Me. Hardy de Huines, procurator to the Paris Parliament, obtained Saint-Aubin for Pierre-César du Crest on 31st July 1751, for the price of 76,500 *livres*, which was barely half the value of the property.

It was just as the sharp Le Normand had foreseen. If the worst came to the worst, and du Crest could pay neither capital nor interest, the property would cover him, and he could take back his surety, certain of selling the land for more than he had risked, and reimbursing the lenders. This was precisely what happened.

On 15th October 1757, Le Normand took over the property of Saint-Aubin by deed at the price of 91,000 *livres*, the amount of capital advanced on his surety, namely, 84,508 *livres* plus 1620 *livres* for expenses. The balance is destined to discharge the costs of the auction of Saint-Aubin, which had been paid for at the end of the five years.

Further, if we wish to know why Pierre-César saddled himself with the board of his nieces, the two young canonesses at Alix, we have only to cast our eyes over another bill of sale, dated 28th February 1758, less than four months after that of Saint-Aubin.

By this deed, and through the medium of Me. Dutartre the notary, Le Normand acquired the barony of Bourbon-Lancy for 80,000 *livres*, on the condition that he paid a life-annuity of 1400 *livres*, assigned by M. and Mme. de Saint-Aubin in behalf of Lazare du Crest and Julienne de Gayot.

It is quite evident that these benevolent cousins helped Pierre-César with their money, and the annuity to their daughters at Alix represented the interest on the loan. Whether from prudence, or from a knowledge of the low price given for this property, César reserves for himself and his family, by the deed of 1757, the right of repurchasing it from Le Normand, by reimbursing the price given for it. It now remains to explain the expedient by means of which Pierre-César continues, until his death, to bear the titles of Marquis of Saint-Aubin and Baron of Bourbon-Lancy, the lands of which no longer belong to him.

The same document will again inform us. It goes to

prove the accuracy of César's estimate of the true value of Bourbon-Lancy.

It is stated that Mme. de Saint-Aubin, in the name of her family, renounces in these words the option of buying back the property which she had reserved in the deed of 1757: "In consideration of the present desistment, the said sieur Le Normand is by these presents bound to pay the sum of 80,000 *livres*. It is agreed that the said sieur and lady of Saint-Aubin may, during their lifetime, bear the name of the said property of Saint-Aubin, and their children that of de Lancy."

Nothing remains, therefore, of this scandalous affair when the dates and figures are known.

What is very clear is that the unfortunate and imprudent du Crest has lost everything—lands and money.

How did the 80,000 *écus* disappear? There is no further trace of them either on the side of the du Crest or on that of de Gayot. Lazare du Crest and Julienne de Gayot married after at least seven years' guilty relations, for want of obtaining earlier the consent of their parents. And they were married under the system of separate estate. It is hardly likely that 800 *livres* worth of "rings and jewellery," and a marriage settlement of 100 *livres*, recoverable by 1000 *livres* in ready money, would be of any importance to people who would have received at least 400,000 francs, half of the promised sum. We may add, to conclude this sad story, that the two lovers had made a written promise of marriage at the beginning of their relations.

This authentic promise, written in the hand of Lazare du Crest and annexed to the minute of the marriage contract, is dated 20th October 1746.[1]

As to the marriage itself, if it were celebrated at Saint-Aubin, it was because Pierre-César was, of all the du Crests,

[1] "We the undersigned Lazare du Crest and Julienne de Gayot promise to take each other for lawful husband and wife at the first request by the one or the other and when I, Julienne de Gayot, shall have reached my majority. The said promise and agreement made upon the forfeiture of a sum of 1500 *livres*, which the first who shall refuse to fulfil the agreement above shall pay. Made under our signatures this 20th day October 1746, at Fléty, Nivernois. . . ." (B.N. catalogue of entries. Original papers, 1036).

the only one who was willing to help his cousin to regularise his false position, and to lend him a home in the circumstances.

Mme. de Genlis, therefore, has no need to blush for her father. Extravagant, adventurous, improvident he undoubtedly was, but the facts prove abundantly that he cannot be accused of a dishonourable complaisance towards Le Normand. Of the two, the financier had the best of it. And Saint-Aubin must have been desirable indeed, if the notification of the right to repurchase, alone, was worth 80,000 francs from the coffers of Le Normand: a notification for which he preferred to waive the title, and by so paying, keep the property.

CHAPTER III

YOUNG WOMANHOOD

"When all our debts were paid," says Mme de Genlis, "there remained only a small life annuity of 1200 francs, on the lives of my father and mother, and not a roof to our heads"; it is poverty with all its humiliations, its anxieties, and its hopeless prospects. They had already had to part with Mlle. de Mars, as they could no longer afford to pay her wages—a terrible separation for both pupil and governess, who had been like sisters.

Their last talk, punctuated by many tears, lasted a whole night, during which they exchange their Books of Hours, like two young monks bound by the vow of poverty, and promise to pray for each other night and morning. When the governess had left, Félicité, prostrated and disfigured by torrents of uninterrupted tears, drew upon herself the severe reprimands of her mother, and, poor child! had to steel herself against the bitterness of destiny.

She recalled her dreams at Saint-Aubin: an inextricable confusion of imaginary adventures and perils, invented at pleasure, which she always overcame by her intelligence and will. "They had," she says, "given to my thoughts I know not what dignity and strength which put them, so to speak, above all the tricks of fate."

Her mother tried to look at things more stoically. Hers was a weak nature, romantic to the last degree, and enervated by six or seven years of excessive pleasures. She, also, had her dreams, but they were idyllic dreams; she felt that women were born to be shepherdesses, and lived only to be adored by shepherds. This idyllic conception of life, which she was to realise later on, made her oddly amusing to the society in which she usually passed for a witty woman. On her face, which is full and rather fat, of a noble air and perfect poise, the world sees only one side of the medal. Félicité saw the reverse: her inefficiency, her horror of domesticity and seclusion, her temper which, apart from society, made her cold, peevish, and unapproachable. When she saw herself doomed to the most prosaic poverty, Mme. du Crest thought only of evading it, of turning her back upon misfortune, and of providing her daughter with social attainments which would—albeit in a servile fashion—eventually give her the entrée to that society where she hoped, in spite of everything, to make her a success. And from the time of their misfortune, she trained Félicité, as Lamartine says, "for the doubtful fate of those women upon whom Nature has lavished wit and beauty, and to whom Society has refused the necessary complement—social adventuresses, sometimes elevated and sometimes debased by it."[1]

In the meantime, until Félicité finds masters who will cultivate her musical gifts, Mme. du Crest—Pierre-César remaining in Burgundy to settle the remaining confusion of debts—set about finding a hospitality similar to that of Le Normand, at the house of one of those rich financiers who filled their homes with parasites in order to keep up a sort of court around them.

I do not know what ill wind took them to La Popelinière, the Farmer-General, where they would have been well advised not to have gone. The consequences cost her and her daughter the ill-will of everyone. Rivers of ink have flowed in connection with this, and many untruths have been circulated. It has been said, not so very long ago either, that Félicité du Crest and her mother were plucked from their wretched Champcéry and afterwards shown the way to brilliant careers in Paris by La Popelinière; Félicité has been compared to Jeanne de la Motte, who was picked up by Mme. de Boulainvilliers.

[1] Lamartine, *Girondins*, I. I. xi.

There is no authority for such statements, which are contradicted by contemporaries. Besides, the two ladies are not literally in the street, like the unfortunate adventuress who imposed upon the Cardinal du Rohan. They at least could hope for help and annuities from the Governor of their province, the Prince de Condé, and they were not backward in asking for them. Finally, had not Mme. du Crest the right to her inheritance, which her mother had retained all this time? Better days may come; but until then they had to live somehow.

It was then that Mme. du Crest approached La Popelinière, whom she had probably met at the house of her cousin de Bellevaux, and obtained an invitation to stay with the financier at Passy.

Apart from his immense fortune, La Popelinière is chiefly noted in history on account of a certain revolving chimney, invented by his unfaithful wife for the benefit of the Duc de Richelieu.[1] After the separation which followed that notorious love-affair, the wealthy Pollio, as he liked to call himself, consoled himself by giving rein to his liking for ostentatious entertainment. His house at Passy was open to everyone, and was, according to Grimm, "the haunt of all grades of society: people of the Court, leaders of fashion, men of letters, artists, foreigners, actors and actresses, *filles-de-joie*—all were assembled there." The master of the house ironically called it his farmyard. Comedies were played there almost every day, very often some of his own rather clever pieces, which were made more enjoyable by suppers and fireworks; and other plays which were full of magnificence, a pleasure to the eye, the senses, and the mind, which had become almost as necessary to Mme. du Crest as her daily bread.

Indeed, she must have considered Passy and Pollio providential blessings.

Now, how did she pay her expenses?

---

[1] Mme. de la Popelinière, or rather the actress Mimi Dancourt. "The financier had, in marrying her, made reparation to her for having wronged her during many years" (Feuillet de Conches, *Salons de conservation au XIIIième siècle*, p. 94).

The financier's gallant disposition is sufficiently notorious, and it has been said again and again that he had a fancy for his original and unhappy guest. Of course, proofs are lacking. Well, we must remember the morals of the period! Moreover, Mme. de Genlis herself allows it to be imagined.

She gives La Popelinière such high praise; she points out "his benevolence, his inexhaustible charity" with such remarkable zeal; she insists so much on "his good heart" and on his "domestic virtues"; she asures us that he had "the highest principles, the most respectable and regular habits"; she gives so much credit to "the protection which he gave to unfortunate artists and authors"; she becomes so indignant that "petty and mean self-conceit could have successfully lampooned a noble self-respect, and often calumniated even the purest and sincerest intentions of Christian charity," that our suspicions are aroused. We must do La Popelinière the justice to say that he really was benevolent. This profligate made his profit out of charity. However, it is quite certain that Félicité saw everything with the eyes of a child, which was fortunate. The proof is that she desired to marry Pollio herself, believing him to be virtuous in all good faith. She would have been delighted—she, who was only thirteen years of age, while La Popelinière was sixty-seven! And he thought of it too.

His constant glances and frequent sighs, and an oft-repeated phrase—"What a pity she is only thirteen!"—speak clearly enough. "I was annoyed," Mme. de Genlis tells us, "that I was not three or four years older, for I admired him so much that I should have been charmed to marry him."

Meanwhile, she acted the parts of Agnès and lady's-maids admirably in the theatre at Passy; she danced constantly and to perfection in La Popelinière's drawing-rooms, and the financier gave her Deshayes, the master of the Italian comedy ballet, and afterwards Gaiffre, an old German harpist of repute, who was nicknamed "King David," to teach her the art of pleasing by the perfection of her dancing and her music.

One can therefore better understand Mme. de Genlis's gratitude towards the generous financier to whom she owed her knowledge of the harp, the gage of her future success in society.

When Mlle. Mondran, a native of Toulouse and the star of the Passy theatre, finally captured La Popelinière and their marriage was announced, the whole fine company fled—Mme. du Crest with the rest.

She returned to Paris, to the rue Neuve-Saint-Paul, and gathered about her many acquaintances whom she had formed at Pollio's house, among whom were the Abbé d'Olivet, Mme. Riccoboni, Bertin, Rameau the musician, Latour the pastellist, and his comrade Van Loo, and Gaiffre. Félicité's heart was heavy with regrets, and she remembered the Farmer-General with disappointment. "I had conceived for him," she says, "a genuine affection."

Pierre-César came to Paris at this time to say good-bye to his wife and daughter before embarking for San Domingo, where he hoped to better his fortunes, and his departure increased the child's unhappiness. She suffered a terrible moral solitude at an age when her heart longed to open itself. Mme. du Crest, who was too little interested in her, and consequently aloof from her, had never been able to gain her daughter's affections. There was no intimacy, no demonstration of affection between mother and daughter. Félicité "did not do justice to her mother and was only affected by the caprices for which she had to suffer,"[1] though she had the greatest affection for her father. To speak the truth, their misfortunes made the two women very bitter, if one can term woman a child who normally would hardly have taken the communicant's white veil. She was far from the pure and innocent state of mind of children of her age! She had passed through the April of her life among the screens and wings of a theatre, and in costumes suitable to romantic comedy; and the atmosphere which she breathed at La Popelinière's house was not precisely edifying. At present, the care for the morrow, or rather, the necessity for self-assertion in order to escape at any price from her

[1] *Souvenirs of the Marquise de Créquy*, ii. 92.

necessitous position, troubled and saddened her. Her chief preoccupation is to become a virtuoso, and all her time is taken up with music. Lessons succeed each other from six in the morning. Pellegrini comes to teach her singing, and Philidor the art of accompaniment, and then it is Gaiffre, whose out-of-date methods she soon outdistanced and reformed. She took up the study of the oboe—in addition to the viola, guitar, and clavecin—so well and so successfully that the fame of Mlle. du Crest was soon noised abroad in Paris.

They came to listen to her as to a prodigy. Everyone became infatuated with the harp, and the rumour reached even to rue Michel-le-Comte, where Dalembert lodged.

The philosopher did not resist "the ardent desire" to make the acquaintance of the youthful artist, and he obtained an introduction to her mother's house. Félicité found "his appearance mean, his falsetto voice harsh and shrill." Briefly, Dalembert displeased her intensely. He began, as he usually did, to tell facetious stories, which is not a method to be recommended when paying court to a young girl. And besides, what was he but a tiresome mathematician, even if he were of the Academy; poor and of doubtful origin, as compared with the high-born people who raved of Félicité's talent?

Mme. de Genlis has complacently enumerated these admirers of her youth, who were aspirants to her hand. They are the Baron de Zurlauben, an octogenarian, and a colonel of the Swiss; and M. de Monville, a magnificent suitor, young, widowed, very rich, handsome, noble, and romantic; besides the mysterious adventurer, the Comte de Saint-Germain, who appears to have entered the lists.

But the first is decidedly too old, the second is not of the Court,—a considerable disadvantage,—and the last waits until she attains the age of eighteen.

Greatly flattered by her success, Félicité du Crest feels that she is destined to a great future.

The prestige of her family is lost—so be it; she feels herself great enough to restore it. All she needs is a husband in a high position in order to get to the top of the tree. La Popelinière, on account of his wealth, would certainly have pleased her more than any other, and she bitterly regrets him. But in default of the Farmer-General, she is determined to accept none other than a gentleman of the Court. The energy of this fifteen-year-old girl, her faith in herself, which would have moved mountains, never allowed her to doubt her future success.

Ambition stimulates her courage. It hardly satisfies her to be considered a child-prodigy. She will do even more if she can. The five hours of harp daily increase to eight and nine, sometimes, Mme. de Genlis confesses, to ten or twelve rounds of the dial. This appalling overwork lasted for more than a year—a year which, spent between her mother, for whom her heart remained cold, and her unremitting work, proved to be of tremendous hardship for her. She was bothered, moreover, with the worries of a regrettable lawsuit, that which had been brought against Mme. de la Haie in order to obtain the restitution of the famous inheritance.

How is one to explain this inheritance, which some people say never existed, seeing that Mézières left nothing but debts behind him? An authentic document tells us, however, that the monetary assets of this inheritance (6605 *livres*) were divided between the creditors, whom it did not suffice to pay in full.

With the exception of some small debts, these creditors were La Haie and his wife. Mme. de la Haie, who demanded her dowry (6000 *livres*) and the settlements agreed to in her marriage contract, swallowed up everything, even to a house situated in Paris, rue Neuve-des-Petits Champs, belonging to Mézières in his own right, with a revenue of 2000 *livres*. She therefore impaired the inheritance of her children. This was undoubtedly the cause of the lawsuit to which Mme. de Genlis refers in her *Mémoires*, where she describes at great length the phases of this regrettable affair. If we are to believe her, Mme. de la Haie acted a revolting farce in a pathetic interview with her unhappy daughter.

Feigning to be ill, she begged her, when they had brought her to her senses again, "to desist, to trust to her, saying that she would lose nothing by giving her this proof of respect."

The child of the second marriage, now Mme. de Montesson, and her brother the Marquis de la Haie joined their entreaties to those of the old Marquise, who was desirous of finishing a scandalous lawsuit.

Mme. du Crest, who was greatly moved, thereupon signed everything they wished. Shortly afterwards, the Marquis de la Haie, who had been the promoter of this negotiation—apparently with the intention of rendering justice to his half-sister—left for the war and was killed at Minden.

It is almost incredible, but Mme. de la Haie appears to have sent word to her daughter "that she had nothing further to claim, having admitted so much herself by signing her non-suit." This is Mme. de Genlis's version. According to Moreau, the lawsuit related to the story of the Bellevaux, and the daughters supposed to be Le Normand's, and continued for many years. The parties came to terms, he says, for fear of annoying Mme. de la Haie by attacking her second marriage, which was entered into with scandalous precipitation barely three months after the death of poor Mézières. However, Moreau so often confounds persons and families that a certain amount of caution is necessary concerning his sayings.

Mme. du Crest, who had anticipated her inheritance to meet inevitable debts, fell again into misfortune. She remembered her former expedient—that of becoming a parasite. We must excuse her for having had recourse to it from the first, and it is a relief to find her quietly installed with M. and Mme. de Jouy, in their fashionable house at Chevilly—a foretaste of Trianon with its farm, its dairy of white marble and pearly shell-work, its terraced gardens, and its orchards dotted about with summer-houses. The two women hid their misfortune here for a while. It was a short-lived protection. M. de Jouy's creditors, and they are numerous, obtain a warrant of imprisonment against him. He is ruined and imprisoned at Pierre-Encise, and Mme de Jouy leaves Chevilly and rejoins her family at Lyons and her husband, whose prison is quite close.

The ladies du Crest return to Paris, to live in gilded misery, and transfer their household gods to rue d'Aguesseau, where one is somewhat astonished to find them apparently living a life of some brilliancy. They have a salon. They gather about them some artists and writers, besides the old fellow-guests at Passy; Saint-Foix, author of *Essais sur Paris*, whom Sevelinges called "Le Ferrailleur," the harpist Honavre, and the famous violinist Gaviniès, etc.

It must be admitted that Félicité met the expenses of this establishment by the exploitation of her talents; not that she went about professionally in the sense that we should understand it nowadays. Several aristocratic families, who were also very fashionable, invited her to supper once a week, and remunerated her for her harp-playing and wit by "certain little presents" according to Garat, and the principal biographers put it at twenty-five *louis* when the performance did not last after midnight.

One among them, however, denies with some spirit both the fact and the indignity. "No decent people," Courchamps declares, "would have been willing to take part in the degradation of a noble family and a girl of rank. . . .

"Besides, Mme. du Crest had two large pensions on the State and Clergy of Burgundy, without counting the money which she was always receiving from M. le Prince de Condé, the Governor of her province. . . . Until the marriage of her daughter, at least, she had never spent less in one year than 15,000 to 18,000 francs honourably received."

With all due deference to this chronicler, who is open to grave doubt although he visited Mme. de Genlis a great deal during the First Empire, the *Mémoires* of the lady herself contradict this. She has never mentioned these important revenues, which might have spared her many humiliations. On the contrary, she does not allow one to overlook the fact that she was received in society on an inferior footing, dressed up in her benefactresses' presents—such as those dresses of Mme. de la Reynière, "at a time when she wanted everything "; she lets one see the revolt of her self-respect, and the bitterness with which she regarded these brilliant gatherings where she and her harp-playing were exhibited, when she has to amuse Society with her singing and dancing. She is flattered and praised " to excess "; and she blushes till the tears come. The favours and promises of indulgent protection are gall to her young pride. She became sullen, ashamed, and unnatural because of it all; at every moment the desire to escape seized her, a passionate longing for solitude so that she might at least hide her mortified vanity. Her secret worries are real and bite into her heart like acid. Yet in all this where is the degradation to be found? Is there anything disgraceful in the fact of a girl of rank accepting tactfully given remuneration from the people of her world for concerts on the harp, which it must be borne in mind were marvellous? The fact that she suffers through her sensitiveness and yet has the courage to sustain her difficult part is all in her favour.

In truth, the imputation against her rests on no other foundation than the hatred and calumny of writers who had no respect for anything, and the enemies of Mme. de Genlis.

Though Talleyrand may say of her shyness that it was assumed, we will none the less keep our sympathy for the Félicité who was at that time so courageous and charming and unspoilt.

We shall never have a better opportunity of looking at her with favourable eyes than at this moment. Let us look at her, therefore. The face is a beautiful oval, very slightly rounded towards the chin, which shows a little dimple in the middle; the cheeks are firm and pink, with the delicate velvety bloom of youth upon them; the nose, with its sensitive nostrils, prettily retroussé; the eyes are rather provoking and are the colour of chestnuts. They sparkle with mischief in a frame of thick, bushy hair, falling on the nape of her plump neck in curls, as black as sloes, innocently seductive. This face, which fifteen summers brighten with an ingenuous smile and a look of roguishness, has about it the look of a wild flower, and you would have to be very keen to detect in it any sign of high ambition.

The shoulders are plump and the bust well curved. Félicité has gained, from her curious early education and her former prowess in boy's costume, a graceful quickness, easy and alert, a buoyancy of movement which her contemporaries, whom it charmed, praised without reticence. Talleyrand, a little later, condemns her elegant figure as "being without nobility." The Abbé of Perigord was doubtless a good judge, but when he was in a position to appreciate her the youthful Genlis was already bordering upon the thirties. According to a woman who did not love her, her figure had, without being tall, "the right proportion which pleases in a woman."[1]

Yes, without a doubt, Mlle. du Crest was attractive. She was so attractive that, after having only seen her portrait, Charles-Alexis Brûlart, Comte de Genlis, fell in love with her at first sight.

And so there was to be another romance in the family.

[1] Duchesse d'Abrantès, *Salons de Paris*, ii. 177.

PART II

THE COMTESSE DE GENLIS BEFORE 1789

CHAPTER I

MARRIAGE

PIERRE-CÉSAR did not foresee, when he returned to his native land in the midst of the Seven Years War, after having unsuccessfully sought his fortune in San Domingo, that he was going to find it coming—not to him, alas!—but to his daughter.

Misfortune would have it—to some misfortune is kind—that the English, meeting the vessel which brought him home, should make him a prisoner of war. Du Crest was sent to Launceston. He became acquainted with a young naval officer, French like himself, covered with glorious wounds gained at the siege of Pondicherry, and taken, like him, by the enemy. Charles-Alexis Brûlart, Comte de Genlis, then twenty-six years old, had a brilliant record in the service; ensign at eighteen, a Chevalier of Saint Louis at twenty-three, and recently promoted captain, he was advancing rapidly towards a high rank.

He formed a friendship for the unfortunate du Crest, who, though having met with great pecuniary losses, transferred his hopes to his children and talked incessantly of his daughter and her loveliness, her wit, and her marvellous talents. One day, the naval officer saw in du Crest's hands a delightful miniature on the lid of a little box—probably a snuff-box—from which he was inseparable. It was the portrait of a little harpist, her delicate hands clasping the royal instrument with a childlike and innocent grace, so touching, that Genlis immediately lost his heart. He enthused. Du Crest allowed him to see certain passages from the letters of this extraordinary child. He marvelled. And from that time there was no subject of conversation except Félicité between the two men.

As soon as he was at liberty — for his uncle, M. de Puysieulx, Minister of Foreign Affairs, had him exchanged for an English prisoner shortly after—Charles-Alexis hastened to the original of the portrait.

We can only imagine that first meeting, which has always remained a mystery, but everything points to the young naval officer not having been disappointed.

As he was actively engaged in obtaining his friend's exchange, Genlis frequently visited the two ladies and kept them informed of his attempts, which were rewarded with prompt success. M. du Crest arrived at the rue d'Aguesseau at the end of three weeks, but his return was the signal for an avalanche of creditors' bills at home.

The unfortunate man brought nothing back from San Domingo except some small dainties for his daughter; however, bailiff's men cannot be appeased with calabash syrup.

A bill of exchange for 600 francs, which he was unable to meet, forced him to join the actors and others arrested for debt at For-l'Évêque, the debtors' prison. Mme. de Genlis speaks of this unhappy event with an unusual show of despair. People have tried to read in her rather dramatic words— which were, however, written some sixty-five years after the event—a " good example of the sort of perversity which her curious education had bred in her." But why should not one take it that this imprisonment came unexpectedly, at a time in her life which was already so unhappy, and grieved her bitterly, so that she looked upon it as a stigma, and was filled with vexation ? Moreover, no help came to alleviate matters for her. Mme. du Crest, deaf to all justifiable spite, applied in vain to her half-sister, Mme. de Montesson : " she received the bluntest and most arbitrary of refusals." The affected, lackadaisical Marquise was hurt to the quick in her delicacy; and besides, M. de Montesson was so parsimonious!

It would appear that if Pierre-César was able to leave For-l'Évêque after a fortnight therein, it was due to M. de Genlis, who "rendered him the great service of paying everything."[1]

However, this last misfortune proved to be the finishing blow to the poor man. He buried himself at home, refused to go out, and grew more feeble and spiritless day by day.

A malignant fever soon carried him off, delivering him from a life full of vicissitudes. His burial took place at the church of Sainte-Marie-Madeleine of the Ville l'Évêque, on 5th July 1763.

Du Crest left nothing but debts behind. Two presses full of linen and clothes which had seen much wear were all that he possessed. It is a curious thing that Le Normand of Étioles is to be found "among the claimants on his meagre estate," and also Me. Hardy de Juines, the attorney, whose fees were still due in part. Mme. du Crest owed 200 francs for rent, and she was not likely to be able to support herself by her literary efforts. She removed again, thankful to be able to go and bury her grief and distress in the convent of the Filles du Précieux Sang,[2] in the rue Cassette, where a compassionate friend offered her a temporary shelter. In this manner she followed the example of many widows of the upper class who, according to an old custom, came to lament—or otherwise—their husbands in the quiet, religious obscurity of a cloister.

Félicité naturally followed her mother. As to her brother, Charles-Louis du Crest, it is not known how he passed his time; at the period when his sister was playing in public it is simply stated that he "had not 100 *pistoles* income."

What happened to the Comte de Genlis?

If he paid the du Crests' creditors, as Michaud has it, the two women at any rate did not count upon him, since Mme.

---

[1] Michaud, Biography.
[2] The Filles du Précieux Sang occupied the site of the house which to-day forms the corner of the rue Cassette and the rue de Vaugirard, opposite the actual church of the Catholic Institute.

du Crest lectured her daughter untiringly and begged her to accept the elderly Baron d'Andlau, who had pestered her with attentions since the death of Pierre-César, whose friend he had been. However, Félicité persisted in refusing her sexagenarian admirer —who was nevertheless younger than La Popelinière—in spite of his having preceded his request by " a large parcel containing his entire genealogy," of very ancient deeds and titles. Agnès would have nothing to do with Arnolphe—this particular one had, besides, a very disagreeable reputation.[1] Had she received a letter ? Had she any means of approaching him ?

Talleyrand's equivocal remark, " being young, pretty and lonely, it was by risking a few visits from gentlemen in the morning that she obtained a husband," would seem to lend colour to this supposition. In any case, it was a fairly long walk from the rue Cassette to the rue de Richelieu, where the young officer lived, and the meetings could not have been frequent.

We know of nothing, however, that goes to support Talleyrand's insinuation, possibly quite baseless.

A deep mystery has always remained round Mme. de Genlis's marriage, and she who " tells us everything " has been careful not to clear it up.

On the other hand, if Genlis has never given up paying court to Mlle. du Crest, we can understand that he hesitates to let himself be drawn into an adventure which can only end in a disadvantageous marriage, and which would annoy his uncle, who is busy arranging a brilliant alliance for him with a young orphan, Mlle. de la Motte, whose 40,000 *livres* income will keep up the family position in proper style.

Charles-Alexis, Comte de Genlis, was descended from the noble lineage of the Bruslart, which dated back to Pierre Bruslart (1487), who in turn traced his origin to Adam Bruslart and his son Geoffroy in the twelfth century—in the year 1150, to be exact. In former times the family comprised three branches, of which the greater number

---

[1] " As for the baron . . . the most foolish and dissolute of men, I would not have allowed him to marry a decent servant-girl to whom I wished well " (J. N. Moreau, *op. cit.* ii. 185).

CHARLES ALEXIS, COMTE DE GENLIS.

of members occupied high offices. The most celebrated of them all is Nicolas Brûlart, Marquis de Sillery, King Henry III.'s ambassador and a Chevalier de France in 1607; there was a Fabio Bruslart, Bishop of Soissons and a member of the French Academy in 1705; there were several presidents of the Burgundian Parlement, bishops, abbés of Saint-Waast, and many chevaliers of various orders, etc. It was a powerful family.

It took the title and the name of Genlis from a large fief situated at Hangest-en-Santerre, near Noyon, which formerly belonged to the Hangest-Genlis, one of the most illustrious families of the province. When it fell to the female line, and the inheritance was sold, the de Genlis manor "fell to Pierre Brûlart, lord of Crosne, Secretary of State, and was made a marquisate for his sons and grandsons in 1645. The descendants in their turn sold it to the Duc d'Aumont, through whom it became the duchy of Villequier, but the Brûlart kept the name of Genlis."

In the eighteenth century there remained only two branches, that of Brûlart-Sillery, represented by the Marquis and Marquise de Puysieulx, and their only daughter, who married the Maréchal d'Estrées—a childless union; and that of Brûlart-Genlis, reduced by the death of Charles de Genlis and his wife, *née* Charlotte-Françoise d'Hallencourt de Droménil, to their two sons, the Marquis de Genlis and Comte Charles-Alexis, who was obviously a great catch.

Three months had passed since the death of Pierre-César. Things dragged on both sides. M. de Puysieulx quietly continued his matrimonial projects, and M. de Genlis decided nothing.

Mme. and Mlle. du Crest then left the Précieux Sang for the convent of Saint-Joseph, rue Saint-Dominique, where Mme. du Deffand lived. They remained too short a time to form a friendship with Walpole's misanthropical friend, and did not even make her acquaintance.[1] At the end

---

[1] The house of the Filles de Saint-Joseph de la Providence occupied the spacious site which is covered to-day by the various buildings for the Administration of War. To the left of the hôtel de Brienne, given up to-day to the dwelling of the Minister, was the body of a separate house, connected

of a month they accept the hospitality of the Comtesse de Sercey, cul-de-sac de Rohan. And then, very suddenly, Félicité du Crest's marriage with the Comte de Genlis took place.

Mme. de Genlis's *Memoirs* affect to mention the event as something very natural, foreseen, and almost unimportant, in two short lines.

Not a word of her betrothal—or of her romance.

However, she cannot persuade us that, even in this "sensible" century, marriages between rich titled gentlemen who are men of mark and impoverished girls of very inferior birth are so common.

It was a love match. For all that, the brave, well-born sailor is by no means a novice to be captivated by the innocent coquetry of a schoolgirl. Biographers have bestowed upon him such flattering and fashionable names as "roué" and "libertin blasé," and attributed to him the "cursed passion for gambling, which outweighed (with him) that for women."[1] His small stature, his handsome lively face with its refined features and delicate lips, his open look, and his long, aristocratic nose revealed his elegance and refinement, while his expression showed daring with that air of premature fatigue of men who have lived hard. Everything about him was eloquent of his breeding and good taste. We know that he bore an extraordinary resemblance to the Abbé de Rancé, or rather to the celebrated portrait by Rigaud of the Trappist reformer. There was a similarity of feature, but not one of character.[2]

Certainly there is no one better able to appreciate the fair musician whose beautiful arms so gracefully clasped the

by a small court, to which access was gained by the rue Saint-Dominique. In this part of the house, independent from that where the nuns shut themselves up, certain apartments of an unobtrusive elegance were let to fashionable ladies, widows, spinsters, or those separated from their husbands (Marquis de Ségur, *Julie de l'Espinasse*, p. 79).

[1] Dufort de Cheverny, *Memoirs*, i. 175.

[2] When Mme. de Genlis and her pupils visited, in 1788, La Trappe, they admired the copy of Rigaud's portrait at the convent, and remarked upon the extraordinary resemblance of the Abbé de Rancé to M. de Genlis. But Mme. de Genlis says that he had not the pallor of the ascetic (Cf. Clarisse Bader, *Les Princes d'Orléans à la Trappe en 1788*, p. 12).

golden harp, who made one think of Saint Cecilia charming the pathetic Valerian. However, she was never Cecilia nor he Valerian, and the Comte de Trémont remarks that "if he married Mlle. du Crest in an entirely romantic manner, M. de Genlis had nothing romantic in his character."[1]

Nevertheless, Félicité was a charming Eve. Could any-one be more naïvely seductive, more innocent, or more youthful and artistic?

Is it the first time that she has played Agnès?

This *roué* was, on the whole, very faithful. He showed it to some extent in politics later on. He did not give way to a moment of feverish emotion, and his very natural hesitation —very natural when one thinks of M. de Puysieulx and his *lettre-de-cachet* with which this terribly vigilant guardian had formerly given his ward three years' imprisonment at Pierre-Encise, for a game of tric-trac which lasted eight days and cost the imprudent young man 100,000 écus—lasted for some time.

Would Félicité have conquered it by herself and the unique charm of her beautiful chestnut eyes, if that clever, worldly match-maker, Mme. de Sercey, besides had not taken a hand?

To her, certainly, is due the success of this uncertain game of love and chance, which is so often unlucky. And if Mme. de Montesson brought to it, as has been supposed—in spite of Mme. de Genlis's contradictions—her already great influence and her support as a great lady in society, so much united feminine skill formed around the undecided and enamoured Genlis a quartette as subtle as it was formidable.

The really mysterious point about the whole affair is the feelings of the young girl. Did Charles-Alexis, who was thoroughly in love with the charming canoness, get back what he gave? Mme. de Genlis affects a reserve to the point of silence on this delicate subject.

When, at seventy-five, she wrote her *Memoirs*, she was absolutely swayed by the doctrines of "good form" and was a qualified professor of deportment, and she does not allow

[1] Comte de Trémont, unpublished document concerning Mme. de Genlis.

anything to appear concerning the state of her heart when she was betrothed (if indeed she still remembered it). She therefore leads us to believe that she accepted her marriage with submission; that she had nothing to do with it, and that it entered into the usual order of things. As Talleyrand remarked maliciously: "Tant bien que mal, elle épousa."

As a matter of fact, the marriage was at least celebrated in the most correct fashion possible.

A formal contract was prepared a fortnight before at Mme. de Sercey's by Me. Lenoir, the notary. Genlis acknowledged having received 40,000 *livres* as Mlle. du Crest's dowry, which dowry was probably never paid over, but served to explain a jointure of 7000 *livres* income allowed to the young wife. Husband and wife bestowed all their worldly goods upon each other in usufruct, which did not bind Félicité in the least. M. de Genlis, it is true, brought no more than 15,000 *livres* to the common estate; the surplus, that is to say, his inheritance, from his father and mother, and that from a brother and a maternal great-uncle, had to revert to his family. Moreover, he admitted having 20,000 francs of debts.

This contract is only signed by near relatives, the Comtesse de Sercey, Félicité's aunt, the Comtesse du Jeu, and Charles-Louis du Crest, the brother. The bridegroom had as witnesses Antoine Hanicque, equerry, a former Governor of the Pages of the King's Stable, the Sieur Bertheaud, a brigadier of Paris, and Démary, the former tutor to the young Marquis de la Haie, and afterwards steward to Mme. de Montesson; these latter were almost unknown people.

In the afternoon of the same day, the 80th October 1763, the Comte de Genlis settled upon his mother-in-law, by special deed, a yearly income of 1200 *livres*, payable every six months, and insured it by means of a mortgage on all her possessions. In consideration of this, he acknowledged having received from Mme. du Crest the sum of 15,000 *livres* "in gold and silver louis and money in currency."

The du Crests, for once, lost nothing in the business.

Their admirable precautions surrounded the chief event with the greatest mystery. Never was a secret so well kept.

Up to the present day it was unknown at which church the marriage took place.

In fact, none of the contemporary memoirists speak of it. Mme. de Genlis simply says: "We left Saint-Joseph and went to live with Madame la Comtesse de Sercey, my aunt, who lived in the cul-de-sac de Rohan. I married there in her parish."

The author of *La Jeunesse d'une femme célèbre* concludes that it was the church of Saint-Roch, relying upon a similarity of names and judging that the cul-de-sac de Rohan must be found in the neighbourhood of the Rue de Rohan itself. Old maps of Paris show a sort of passage named Cours de Rohan, with, in fact, a triple courtyard, connecting the Rue du Jardinet, formerly called Rue de l'Escureul, with the Cour du Commerce. Lefeuve says these courtyards call to mind the fact that in 1584 the Archbishop of Rouen resided in the buildings on this site, which dated back to the Middle Ages. It appears there was still the base of a tower to be seen, which formerly formed part of the body of the place in Philippe-Auguste's time. The de Rohan family had possessed the block until the Revolution. However, these courtyards were nothing but a cul-de-sac in 1714. Almost all this quarter has disappeared since the opening up of the boulevard Saint-Germain, but the rue du Jardinet still exists, and its position leads us to place the Crest-Genlis marriage at the church of Saint-André des Arts.

Nevertheless, this hypothesis—rendered still more probable by the declaration of Félicité's contract of her domicile as "cul-de-sac de Rohan, parish of Saint-André des Arts"—awaits historical confirmation, that undeniable proof without which there can be no certainty; a proof which the destruction of all the old Paris registers makes very unlikely.

We have, however, found a formal document among the old registers: the very declaration of Etiennette-Félicité du Crest's marriage-contract, in the genealogical archives of MM. Pavy and Andriveau. It is certainly at the church of Saint-André des Arts on the 8th November 1768 (not December, nor in 1762, as has been stated), at midnight—according to the custom in great families—and with the greatest secrecy that Charles-Alexis Brûlart joyfully took the final and irretrievable step.[1]

The next day Paris heard the news.

What a scandal it was among the nobility! It raised an outcry on all sides.

People enjoyed themselves to their hearts' content criticising the marriage, and did not hesitate to call the young wife an "intrigante." As always happens, they exceeded the limit: they attacked Félicité's reputation.

M. de Puysieulx's anger was terrible. This alone formed the subject of conversation for many days, and helped not a little (for the Minister was powerful) to rouse public opinion against the young couple, and to make most of their friends and supporters shut their doors in the faces of the unfortunate Brûlarts.

M. de Genlis in vain humbly presented himself and his wife at the hôtel de Puysieulx, and at the house of the Maréchale d'Estrées. They were not received. His grandmother, the Marquise de Droménil, did not even answer Félicité's courteous letter. The only sympathy the Comte and Comtesse de Genlis received the day after their exploit was from the Marquis de Genlis, whom it would have ill become to be shocked by his brother's marriage; and from M. and Mme. de Balincourt, distant relatives, who showed them "tokens of friendship"; and finally from Mme. de Montesson, who paid a polite visit to Mme. du Crest, an act of politeness to which, according to Félicité, she confined herself. "The marriage pleased her vanity."

The young couple did not try the patience of their relatives for more than ten days, and, ceasing to knock at doors which remained stubbornly locked, they left for Genlis, where the Marquis received them with open arms.

The harsh condemnation of a society which showed so much leniency in other respects to many more reprehensible evils than a love-marriage, did not prevent Félicité from enjoying her novel position.

Her new happiness—let us not say unhoped-for—intoxi-

---

[1] We owe this item to M. Andriveau, who has himself had to look up the document in his lists of marriages in Paris from 1740 to 1793.

cates her. She exults in it. She does not know how to show her gratification, and in her joy comes out with a thousand original freaks. She feels she must astonish people in order to justify her fame as an extraordinary girl. Sometimes she lays claim to "the pretensions of a person who was a stranger to no country occupation," and goes off to fish in the ponds in a light dress and little white embroidered shoes; and sometimes, to prove that she is not "a pretty lady from Paris," she devours a live fish without a qualm. "Everyone was amazed," says she. There was some reason for it.

And when the honeymoon was over, M. de Genlis was obliged to rejoin his regiment at Nancy—he had passed from the navy to the army, from the rank of a captain of a ship to that of a colonel of the French Grenadiers, on the 23rd February 1768—and not wishing to expose his young wife to the dangers of Stanislaus's court, he left her for some time at the abbey of Origny, where she amused herself in the most extravagant way at everyone's expense.

Neither the nuns, whom she covered with rouge and patches while they were asleep; nor the abbess, whom she defied by running away, disguised as a peasant, to a village wedding in order to dance all day long; nor her own maid, the unfortunate Mlle. Beaufort, who was nearly fifty years old, whom she dressed up to act sometimes as a Prince Charming and sometimes as an idyllic shepherdess,[1] satisfied her thirst for pleasure. She enjoyed herself so well that, when M. de Genlis came to fetch his wife, she refused to leave, and asked for a month's grace. A " curt and absolute " refusal made her shed many tears, but she obeyed and made up for it at Genlis. It would need a large volume to describe her eccentricities at that time. She takes milk baths. At nightfall she plays ghosts at the doors of inns, crying out: "Good people, do you sell *sacréchien*?"[2] and running away to the back, laughing enough "to fall to the ground."

[1] These were little white dresses edged with ribbons of different colours, a straw hat trimmed with flowers (which was worn over the ear) . . . a shepherd's crook. And Mlle. Beaufort was forty-five years old, her hair was grey, she had a pimply face, and her two front teeth were missing (Genlis, *Memoirs*, i. 184).

[2] A name given to brandy.

She loses herself while hunting, and all the manor turns out to look for her, and her husband feels almost ready to die with fright. She takes a fancy to learn the science of bleeding under the surgeon of la Fère, and afterwards under Chamousset, and you find her running about the countryside with her case of surgical instruments in her hand. As she accompanied each bleeding with a piece of twenty-four or thirty sous, she did not lack customers. Usually the village barber, a M. Racine, the Æsculapius of the place, followed her and managed her consultations, and the patients at any rate gained sometimes by having tisanes and broths, instead of expensive emetics from M. Racine.

She led the dance everywhere with a frenzy of vitality, a fervour of excitement, and an irresistible gaiety and high spirits which made her much talked of.

The Genlis's neighbours—respectable provincial nobility of patriarchal morals—are old and burdened with large families, and are besides very austere and domesticated. That does not stop her. Mme. de Genlis will visit them, shake up their torpor, and make them act in a play.

And in very truth, wherever she shall appear hereafter, a theatre springs up and works as if by magic.

Is the Genlis manor without a stage and wings?

Quick! a builder to construct one, and a painter to paint the scenery!

The painter, a certain Tirmane, brought specially from Saint-Quentin, has a history. He was a curious half-crazy person, in whom Molière would have delighted; a sort of Don Quixote of the brush, who was convinced " that he had the talent of Raphael and Rubens, and could paint the ceiling of a room very well."

Tirmane became—as did the Chevalier de la Mancha formerly—the hero, or scapegoat, of a thousand ludicrous enterprises. Mme. de Genlis, with impish ingenuity, used to hoax him unceasingly. Among other things, she played pranks upon him during his vigils; she had him robbed in the middle of the day by a gardener disguised as a thief, and everyone laughed at the piteous figure of the unfortunate man as he returned to the house in scanty attire. These frivolities went on for eight months. Let us refrain from describing them, as it would take away the freshness of Mme. de Genlis's amusing account, the reading of which can be recommended to people who are bored.

It is a curious thing that these pranks, the outcome merely of heedless youth and a boundless delight in life, have nearly all been brought up against her by her enemies.

The innocent occasion of her first appearance on horseback with old Jean, who placed her astride on the gardener's horse, and in this way initiated her into the mysteries of riding, has seemed an incident of the most vicious intent; and the fact of taking " a course of anatomy, doctoring, bleeding, and purging, etc."—an innovation—has been eagerly turned to ridicule.

However, this foolish yet clever Comtesse could do nothing by halves. The impetus of her desires is such that, at a moment when her life was crammed with agreeable employment, her unusual wish for knowledge and learning—for a time abated and subservient to the material care for her daily bread—awoke stronger, increased tenfold by the compulsory delay during those years of poverty.

Married, and comfortably settled down, living with great freedom the easy and amusing life of a châtelaine, Mme. de Genlis realised as never before the deficiencies in her education. She began to find the country monotonous, and a great desire to read more took possession of her. However, she was so ignorant that she did not know where to begin, and she could make no choice. History attracted her; then a treatise on geometry fell into her hands. "I saw," she says, " by the advertisement that it was so easy that a child of twelve would understand it," and she began on it.

She could not see anything in it, and M. de Genlis laughed " at her silliness," so she fell back on Roman history. She ransacked the splendid library at Genlis, and inaugurated, during the visit of a friend, M. de Sauvigny,[1] whom she had met in other days at the Convent of Saint-Joseph, a series of daily meetings at which they read aloud. In this way she read the *Lettres de Mme. de Sévigné*, the *Provinciales*, and

[1] Edme-Louis Billardon de Sauvigny (1730–1802).

the dramas of Corneille. She also set herself the task of summarising these readings in writing ; and having discovered a large blank book-size folio in the kitchen, intended for the accounts, she took possession of it, and this plebeian portfolio became the "Diary" of the Comtesse, who confided to it every night the account of her occupations and reflections. This curious record has unfortunately been lost. It disappeared after the death of Mme. du Crest.

We may note, finally, the large correspondence which the youthful Genlis kept up. Without counting her daily letter to her mother, she scribbles three a week to Mme. de Montesson ; and the others were to Mme. de Bellevaux, with whom the quarrel was made up : to Mme. de Balincourt, a friend at the convent of Origny, living in Valenciennes : an advocate at Douai ; Feutry, poet and translator of *Robinson Crusoe*, etc. ; which nearly completed a round dozen of weekly epistles.

These pleasant or intellectual pursuits served her only as a palliative. These things could not take the place of Paris. She had been at Genlis for two years, and save for one glorious holiday—three weeks at Arras, where the colonel commanded the garrison, and where, contrary to custom, she followed her husband—an infringement which was heartily welcomed by the Grenadiers—the petulant Comtesse imagined herself exiled in its domains.

How much she must have dreamed and reflected beneath the sad, grey skies of Picardy. What inexhaustible subjects present themselves to her imagination in the Court, the city, and the society which refused her entrance, and into which she longs to gain admittance. Are her youth, her charm, her beauty to fade hidden away from the sun ?

There cannot be many people in that gay and complex Paris to talk about the du Crests after a period of two years.

Her mother has married the rejected suitor, the Baron d'Andlau, eighteen months after the marriage of her daughter. It was an unfortunate choice, for the old man had nothing but his name and a small life annuity.

As to Charles-Louis du Crest, he has taken service and does not live in Paris.

And after all, has not time abated many a resentment?

She was alone one day, and was probably feeling very dull. M. de Genlis has had to go to Paris to his brother, who is ill.

A mad idea crosses the lonely woman's mind—supposing she were to rejoin her husband?

She has no carriage. So much the worse, she will do without one.

Mme. la Comtesse calls her servant, Lemire, and Mlle. Victoire, her maid, and gives them her orders. Lemire lends his top-boots, which are too large, and he remedies this by packing Mme. de Genlis's legs in straw. She dresses herself in her husband's clothes, and Mlle. Victoire puts on Lemire's riding-coat and breeches. Thus equipped, the three are about to ride on horseback along the road to Paris, when the startled and more prudent postmaster brings forward a carriage "without curtain or glass," wherein Mme. de Genlis —cursing and fuming, and regretting "her stout boots and the glory of riding twenty-five leagues at full speed"— starts off in the pouring rain. She sticks to her masculine attire, and is trundled along all night.

M. de Genlis proved "strangely surprised" at the unexpected arrival of his wife. Perhaps he suspected that it was more the attraction of Paris than her love for him which had inspired this foolish escapade.

The young Comtesse, anyhow, gained six weeks of pleasure —in particular, a ball at the Spanish Embassy. Mme. de Montesson opened her salon to her. Mme. de Boulain-Villiers and the Marquise de Saint-Charmant condescended to half-open their own to the young couple, but Mmes. de Puysieulx and d'Estrées rigorously ostracised her.

Shortly afterwards, the Marquis de Genlis married Mlle. de Vilmeur, an orphan, and the young sister-in-law, who acted as mother to the bride, had the humiliation of seeing Mme. de Puysieulx turn aside from her, and all the other ladies present at the wedding imitate the powerful Marquise's frigid silence at her expense.

There was nothing for it but to leave things alone. Mme. de Genlis, who had expectations of becoming a mother, hoped that the de Puysieulx's spiteful indifference would not be able to resist the innocent smile of a baby's lips.

In the meantime, she wrote *Les Réflexions d'une mère de vingt ans.*"[1] "She was a writer above everything," Sainte-Beuve says later, with his usual penetration; as yet he did not know of these early Reflections, which were also lost, together with the kitchen accounts, but their substance seems to have formed in part *Adèle et Théodore.*

Mme. de Genlis, who had been settled for a month in anticipation of the event at the cul-de-sac Saint-Dominique, in the heart of the faubourg Saint-Germain, gave birth on the 4th September 1765 to her first child, a girl, whom they named Caroline.

The birth of the child obliged the relations to make a formal visit. It was Mme. d'Estrées who performed the unpleasant duty, accompanying it with a present of beautiful Indian fabrics. The Marshal's wife added a polite formula: the relations would receive the young mother with much pleasure and would present her at Court.

These words could not be taken as a sign of gracious reconciliation or of forgiveness of old grievances. They were dictated by pride of birth.

Presentation at Court necessitating proofs of nobility, went to prove that the Minister Puysieulx's nephew had not degraded himself, since his wife's claims could bear the closest scrutiny by the royal genealogists without any fear. Mme. de Puysieulx, in chaperoning her new niece at Versailles, vouched merely for the honour of the family, which shone with the same proud integrity, and did not deny her private grudge.

At her first visit, five weeks after her confinement, Mme. de Genlis saw plainly that nothing was changed, by the haughtiness and stiffness of her husband's aunt.

She herself remained "cold and silent." This first interview was void of any sympathy.

The second, a week later, showed more painfully the hostility between the two women. This was for the pre-

---

[1] She was not nineteen years old, and had then only the hope of maternity (Louis Chabaud, *Mme. de Genlis*, p. 203).

sentation, the great day in the lives of well-born ladies. It was a day which needed unending preparation—the rehearsal of curtseys which Gardel had just taught, or the attire, the great Court dress with its long train, or the dressing of the hair, all of which were regulated by an inexorable etiquette.

Mme. de Genlis slept the night before at Versailles, with Mme. d'Estrées, and early the next day, the torture, made even more unbearable by the Puysieulx's ill grace, began.

"Mesdames de Puysieulx and d'Estrées really persecuted me," Mme. de Genlis tells us, ". . . they had my hair dressed three times, and decided upon the style which was most old-fashioned and unbecoming to me. They compelled me to put on a lot of powder and rouge, two things that I hated; they wished me to wear my stiff bodice at dinner, in order, they said, to accustom myself to it. These stiff bodices left the shoulders uncovered, cut the arms, and were horribly uncomfortable; in addition to which, they had me laced to the utmost tightness in order to show my figure off."

"Mother and daughter then had a bitter quarrel on the subject of my collarette, as to the way to fasten it. They were seated and I was standing and tired out during the dispute. That collarette was tried on and taken off me at least four times, and finally Mme. d'Estrées took it away, on the advice of three of her maids, which very much annoyed Mme. de Puysieulx. I was so tired that I could hardly keep up, when we had to go to dinner."

Mme. de Genlis could neither breathe nor eat at dinner, she was so tight-laced. The repast was enhanced by unending discussions on the subject of her toilet. Finally, when her hoop petticoat and skirt were on, and the curtseys rehearsed, Mme. de Genlis thought herself delivered, but Mme. de Puysieulx "forbade her to push her skirt gently back with her foot, as she retired backwards, saying that it was theatrical. I explained to her that I should entangle my feet in it, and should fall. She repeated, with a cold, imperious voice, that it was theatrical. I did not reply."

Happily, the terrible trial passed off well. Beneath the blue eyes of Louis xv., Mme. de Genlis forgets all her tortures. She thinks the King " very handsome," she admires " that royal and majestic something which distinguished him noticeably from all other men."

The Queen appeared to her as " a charming little old lady." Lying upon a couch, " in a lace night-cap with large sprigs of diamonds (ear-rings)," Marie-Leczinska spoke to the young Comtesse with gracious words, said with a charming smile, and in a tone of voice which was faint, but sweet and " went to the heart."

The day ended with Mesdames the daughters of the King, and with the children of France. Mme. de Genlis afterwards lived at Genlis, and continued to revolutionise peasants and neighbours with her theatrical entertainments, her harp, and the doctoring, which she practised with the greatest enthusiasm, her Tissot and lancet in her hand, and always in the company of the barber.

She ended by carrying her zeal to excess; so much so that she felt impelled to abstain from bleeding without the assistance of a surgeon, in order to put a stop to scandal. At this time she wrote a novel of which the title alone has come down to us: *Les dangers de la célébrité.*

CHAPTER II

THE COMEDY OF SOCIETY

THE birth of a second daughter, Pulchérie, interrupts only for a moment the round of gaieties which have come to form the normal existence of Mme. de Genlis. Every kind of entertainment arouses her restless ardour —visits, private theatricals, music, suppers, and the theatre.

Mme. de Montesson, the " tantâtre " so assiduously cultivated, has already introduced her into many of the salons, and she has the *entrée* also to those of former friends : the Marquise de Beuvron, the Comtesse d'Harville, Mmes. de Balincourt and de Custine, and the Duchesse de Liancourt. As yet, Mme. de Genlis is admitted rather than sought after in a society very quick to notice all distinctions, and she anxiously awaits the first steps and expressions of patronage which are undoubtedly doled out according to the attitude of the Puysieulx, whose forgiveness tarries in spite of two or three formal invitations.

She lacks, also, knowledge of Court customs, having had up to the present scant intercourse with the highest society. Her deportment suffers in consequence ; it is not confident, nor has it the supreme ease which is necessary. Her charms continue to be those of a débutante. She has vivacity, piquancy, " few features in her conversation," although her wit was " already very caustic." She has also an intelligent expression, many accomplishments, and good-humour, but she is a little nervous and awkward, because sympathy, which would allow her qualities to appear, is lacking around her. The Duchesse d'Abrantès does not refrain from saying that

"Mme. de Genlis never had the bearing of a great lady in society."[1]

She was not very much of a success at Isle-Adam, where Mme. de Montesson presented her soon after the birth of Pulchérie.

Isle-Adam is the kingdom of the arbiter of fashion. It is even more difficult of access than the Court. The highest nobility and the most aristocratic young people scintillated there in full magnificence under the undisputed direction of Mmes. de Luxembourg and de Boufflers. The old Marquise holds the sceptre here and leads the fashion. Her utterances are oracular. She can launch a young woman into society with a single word. Her support is equivalent to a certificate, and it is advisable to obtain it, for the Prince de Conti has so great an esteem for her that he always ratifies it.

Mme. de Genlis did not omit this social duty, and leads us to believe that she attracted the interest of the Maréchale. Nevertheless, the Prince did not depart from his attitude of rather disdainful haughtiness towards her, which unnerved her to the last degree. She could not overcome her awkwardness and embarrassment, and did not make much impression on him, in spite of her pretty face. The Prince remained cold even after a wonderful sonata on the harp and some verses which she sang in the famous theatre—to say nothing of a certain part in *Le Savetier et le Financier*, in which she almost achieved success, her self-possession having returned. Ordinary fascination was powerless before this great personage.

It was not the same at Villers-Cotterets. The Duke of Orleans[2] is a charming prince, full of good-nature and cordiality. If he receives few ladies, it is because the dowagers and ladies of the Court hesitate to rub elbows in public with Mlle. Le Marquis, a ballet-dancer in the Comédie-Italienne, who has been honoured since the death of the Duchess by an open liaison with the first Prince of the blood. His Highness has therefore restricted his invitations to the

---

[1] Duchesse d'Abrantès, *Paris Salons*, ii. 166.
[2] Louis-Philippe d'Orléans, son-in-law of the Regent, and father of Philippe-Egalité (1725–77), married in 1744 Henriette de Bourbon-Conti; died on 8th February 1759.

THE DUCHESS OF ORLEANS
(HENRIETTE DE BOURBON-CONTI, WIFE OF LOUIS-PHILIPPE, DUKE OF ORLEANS).

ladies of his family; and neither the old Marquise de Ségur, nor the strait-laced Comtesse de Pont, could take umbrage at the youthful appearance of Mmes. de Montesson and de Genlis, who have now an opportunity to make up for the background to which they were relegated at Isle-Adam!

The Duke takes a deep interest in dramatic art and literature, and Mme. de Genlis is very successful in acting proverbs, charades, amateur theatricals, and even operas, elaborately staged by the Prince's builders, Sedaine and Collé, while the stout Prince devours her with his eyes. He himself takes the part of peasants with "great frankness." Mme. de Genlis arouses such enthusiasm that the Prince begs her to act every night, and orders her portrait to be painted by Carmontelle. Her skill on horseback delights him by day.

M. de Puysieulx is moved to indulgence in view of such success. He could scarcely show greater severity than the first prince of the blood. He therefore invites the repentant nephew and niece to Sillery. Mme. de Dromesnil has already forgiven them. As to the Marquise, if at first there was a coolness between her and Mme. de Genlis, it is because our strongest dislikes and feelings of resentment die hard. Mme. de Puysieulx, however, overcame her own in six days. As Talleyrand says, her niece "was well aware that here lay the key to her entry into society, and she therefore brought all her talents into play." A scene of tearful emotion, which she had the wit not to restrain, "disarmed Mme. de Puysieulx's former bitterness."[1] The rubicon was crossed. Finally, the enemy—alternately laughing and kissing her, astonishing her with her witty sallies and her youthful loveliness—became the spoiled darling of the old lady, allowing herself to be corrected, for the Marquise was fond of preaching, "with a perfect equanimity of temper and that natural tractability which never allowed others to suspect that one had the impertinent desire to rule."

M. de Puysieulx, "the most *ennuyé* man of his day," did not resist the charms which his attentive niece displayed in his honour. The clever Countess made little of playing the harp, and composing verses adapted to the

[1] *Memoirs* of the Prince de Talleyrand.

question of the hour, or of getting up proverbs, learning the dulcimer, and dressing herself up—laying herself out in every way on every occasion. One can well imagine her as she accompanied the Minister on his morning rides, when she fascinated him to such an extent that he had a pretty stage and wings erected, in fact a complete theatre, the indispensable accessary to all entertainments. Soon after this he gave further evidence of his affection by a princely gift, the revenue of the governorship of Epernay, which amounted to 7000 *livres* annual income. This, added to the 12,000 *livres* a year and M. de Genlis's pay, allowed of the household being kept up in greater style.

Mme. de Genlis begins to count for something in society from the time she returns to Paris in the winter of 1767. She has been received under the wing of Mme. de Montesson until then—now the foundations are laid.

She throws herself into a whirlpool of pleasures with the incredible eagerness which characterises all her undertakings.

Amateur theatricals form her battlefield—a battlefield upon which her forces are always victorious. She acts at home, at Isle-Adam and elsewhere, with no respite in spite of her condition—a son was born in the spring—and to her alone is due the fashion of social theatricals.

This is Mme. de Genlis's first period of real brilliance. It is all the more intoxicating because it comes to her in the springtime of her youth when she is in the prime of health, and at a time when beauty, youth, and strength develop the body and mind. She is twenty-two years old, and her face has kept the immobility of childhood. There is a bewitching glance in her almond-shaped eyes. The joy of life is always lurking in her marvellous smile, and her mouth, which is perhaps a trifle large, is well cut and shows her pearly and regular teeth. She has a graceful, swanlike neck, and her nose, fairly large and slightly turned up like the famous Roxelana nose, " gave her face a piquant expression which, added to the spirit of observation which dominated everything in this pretty head, made her singularly attractive."[1] As to her figure, which is slighted by Talleyrand, Mme. d'Abrantès

[1] Duchesse d'Abrantès, *Paris Salons*, iii. 177.

will say that "it was charming at this time: it was slender and lissome and prettily rounded, and her every attitude was graceful and unpremeditated."

Everything about her breathed happiness and contentment. At the time of the Proverb quadrilles at the Opera ball, a great deal of jealousy was caused by Gardel writing a ballet specially to Mme. de Genlis's music. According to the description of contemporary writers, the quadrille had hardly begun when an enormous cat with flaming eyes and menacing claws interrupted it with loud caterwauls. It was chased and beaten, and chased again, but it persisted and quite put an end to the figure. The interrupter was merely a little Savoyard disguised, apparently put up to it by the young Duke of Chartres, who revenged himself in this way for not having been invited to help in the organisation of the dancing proverbs.

The general opinion later on was that he fell in love at first sight that evening with Mme. de Genlis, who was dressed as a peasant girl.

However, this ball established the pretty Comtesse, and her salon had a great reputation thenceforth. She gathered about her artists and scholars who made it attractive by their sense of art and poetry and their intellectuality, "which was sufficiently unusual in the highest society."

It is believed that Chamfort and Lemierre took part in the production of charades, ballets, and musical plays in which little social incidents were pictured. The music, thanks to Mme. de Genlis's talent with the harp, guitar, small oboe, and other instruments, held the first place, and the theatricals always ended with a concert conducted by Cramer.

Among the people who frequented her salon were the Comte d'Albaret, a Southerner, the Président de Périgny, the Abbé Arnaud, the Chevaliers de Talleyrand and de Barbentane, the Abbé Delille, M. de Sauvigny, M. de Vérac and his wife, the Vicomte and Vicomtesse de Custine, Mmes. de Brancas, de Rancé, etc. Mme. de Montesson never went; her niece's prestige began to threaten her own. It had received the hall-mark of Jean-Jacques Rousseau, the incomparable.

Mme. de Genlis had, indeed, made the acquaintance of the philosopher shortly before this period. Her husband brought him in one day and introduced him for fun as the actor Préville, who resembled Rousseau slightly.

Mme. de Genlis, quite taken in, had all the difficulty in the world in controlling herself, and replied to him in a very cavalier manner, said many foolish things, and finally appeared to be surprisingly merry—all of which seemed to Jean-Jacques the perfection of artlessness. He went away charmed with such an original young woman, so "free from pretensions." And he returned to dine and play fragments from the *Devin du village*, and to read his *Pygmalion*, for Mme. de Genlis confessed that she did not know his work. He also gave her his novels. It began as it always did— and ended as it always did, so far as he was concerned.

He believed he had found in this young woman a pure heart, an innocent mind, a sweet, uncorrupted nature as free from artificiality as a sunny meadow, such as he was always eagerly seeking. He went towards the meadow and enthusiastically gathered the flowers from it. But at the end of three months he thought such an abundance of charms might be deceptive; he seemed to see a shadow fall across the field, a wicked, deceitful shadow which attracted him only to blind him and strangle his liberty and persecute him. He did not think of the shadow he cast wherever he went.

There came a day when M. de Genlis thought fit to send him a basket of Sillery of a very rare colour, like the skin of an onion. To him—Rousseau! They wanted to bribe him with wine the colour of onion skin? He had the greatest difficulty in calming himself, and it was only after two months of sulks on his part, and of smiles and advances on the part of the Genlis, that he came back. This reconciliation did not last long.

The quarrel reached its height at the Théâtre-Français in a closed box, whither he had accompanied Mme. de Genlis to see the production of *Persifleur*, by M. de Sauvigny. It is not known whether he was annoyed at finding himself the cynosure of the entire house, or at having been less remarked upon than Mme. de Genlis, whom he judged to be "too dressed up for a closed box." He complained that he had been brought to the theatre in order to be made a spectacle of in public, " as they show off the wild beasts at a fair," and a sea of bitterness submerged all that remained of the friendship in his heart. His morbid fancy got the better of him, and he never in his life saw the Genlis again, convinced that they were his bitterest enemies.

But let us return to Mme. de Genlis and her gaieties.

What is the most surprising thing about her is that she is a fashionable doll and yet at the same time a studious woman. She finds time to learn Ancient History and the history of the Lower Empire, Roman history, and mythology, and to practise Pascal's *Pensées*, Bossuet's *Oraisons funèbres*, Massillon's *Petit Carême*, and Buffon's *Natural History*. She writes out long extracts in exercise-books, and recopies the memoirs about the war and the navy which her husband addressed to the Minister, and which she corrected and sometimes entirely rewrote.

She learned from all this how to write correctly, and she thought her own essays only fit for burning, with the exception of two. These she replaced by an historical novel, *Parysatis ou la Nouvelle Médée*, which was a horrible tragedy, and certain *Dialogues des Morts* after the style of Fontenelle, but " more moral."

One wonders by what miracle of intelligence and energy she was able to reconcile so much inclination for study with her frivolities. She mingled one with the other, reading for an hour each day while she dressed and during the rare afternoons when she did not go out until five or six o'clock, studying parts, making up disguises, acting, dancing, singing, writing, visiting the town, the fair, the market, the cabaret, and the country with untiring energy.

In the summer she stayed with various friends for several weeks, visiting Dieppe and Vaudreuil with the Balincours, and Rheims with Mme. de Dromesnil. She enjoys herself there, and amuses everyone with her marvellous energy and aptitude.

It was while she was at Vaudreuil that she rewrote in six or seven days the celebrated comedy of the *Trois Sultanes* with a plot entirely different from that used by Favart. " I gave myself a very brilliant part," she says, " in which I sang, danced and played the clavecin, the harp, the guitar, the small oboe, the dulcimer, and the hurdy-gurdy. . . . I omitted only the viola, but I had not played it for three years, and the mandoline would have had little success beside the guitar, which I played very much better."

It met with triumphant success and was received with deafening applause. On the night of that memorable day, Mme. de Puysieulx, with tears in her eyes, took the hands of her niece in her own, and, gazing at her with tenderness, said to her in an uneasy voice, " Yes, you will have an extraordinary fate ! But what will it be ? "

The good lady probably trembled for her nephew's happiness, but " M. de Genlis, whose intelligence and refinement gave no hint of the feeble apathy of a man who allows himself to be led, accompanied his wife everywhere, was seen at all the entertainments of which she was, so to speak, the moving spirit, and he never left her except to join his regiment." [1]

It was during one of these absences that certain preliminary negotiations were entered into, the result of which —successful on the whole—seems to have been the nomination of Mme. de Genlis to the Palais Royal.

It was during the summer of 1769. M. de Montesson died on 31st July, leaving his wife free to covet the Duke of Orleans. For ten years a romance had been weaving between them, guided by the Marquise with a sure hand, and cleverly kept within the most virtuous, not to say austere, limits. Up to this time they had been obliged to content themselves with pretty sentimentality, a quiet, prudent friendship, founded on affection and kept alive by stolen smiles and glances, and pretty speeches exchanged at the theatre or during private theatricals.

This arsenal of platonic allurement had gradually inflamed the Prince's sentimental heart with a passionate love for Mme. de Montesson, and the time had now come for turning this passion into matrimonial love.

[1] Duchesse d'Abrantès, *Salons de Paris.*

LOUIS-PHILIPPE, DUKE OF ORLEANS
(FATHER OF PHILIPPE-ÉGALITÉ).

This was by no means so simple as it looked, for there had been no culpable love-passages between them. Mme. de Montesson intended to become a princess without in the least appearing to wish for it; on the contrary, she protested that she opposed the idea and that His Highness was the only one to make any advances towards a marriage so unreasonable from the point of view of his children, in particular of his son, the Duke of Chartres. In fact, she came out of the ordeal with skill. In this particular, Mme. de Montesson was equal to any diplomat.

In the first place, she went away. She retired to Barèges for her period of mourning, and left the princely aspirant to reflect upon the situation. However, she left it to Mme. de Genlis, who was, as we know, alone at that time, as the Colonel had returned to his regiment, to receive the Duke of Orleans and to point out quietly for him the way which leads from the heart to the hand.

"Fat Philippe," as he was familiarly called, on account of his stoutness and his joviality, had perhaps measured the distance, for he hesitated and seemed to cool off; and Mme. de Genlis served her aunt's interests in a mischievous manner.

To quote only her own record of the matter, in which, with the most innocent air possible, she lets us into the secret of the lover's state of mind: "The Duke was in love like a good soldier who remains faithfully at his post and does not leave it until he gets permission. But when there was no longer any post, he forgot easily and changed service without regret or disappointment."

The intrigue was really of the slightest description. The Prince called at the hôtel Montesson; he found there a witty young woman, and, falling a victim to her attractions, he set briskly to work from the time of his second visit upon the tale of his love-affairs. The affair had this much humour in it—that the Duke was notorious for his failures. However, his stories "couched in decent language" were none the less "horribly scandalous in their subject," and Mme. de Genlis tolerated them. His Highness was delighted with his confidante, and invited her to stay a few days at Villers-Cotterets; and when she returned after two weeks' visit, during which she was chaperoned by Mme. de Puysieulx, he opened a correspondence with her.

Mme. de Genlis says her august friend "was never tired of singing my praises." He wrote "many very tender letters" to her at Sillery, and she does not hide the fact that if a certain pretty lady had wished to take the place of the absentee, there would have been nothing easier in the world. Sainte-Beuve has written: "There are certain things which must always be believed of women when they say them." Let us follow this advice. In any case, the Prince reinstated the Marquise in his affections upon her return. The good soldier resumed his duties; and if there was any delay in the marriage, at least it was duly celebrated.

Faithful to her programme of prudence, Mme. de Montesson sent him away for two years, giving him the time to calm the Duke of Chartres' susceptibilities and to obtain the royal sanction. This did not amount to much, for Louis xv., not wishing to have to legitimise the issue of such a union later, would not consent—on the advice of Mme. du Barry—to anything but a morganatic marriage. The essential fact is that the marriage took place, for the Archbishop of Paris, Mgr. de Beaumont, celebrated the marriage of the first prince of the blood with the Marquise de Montesson on 28th July 1778.

Meanwhile, Mme. de Genlis was appointed to the Palais Royal, to the court of Mme. la Duchesse de Chartres, and all biographers agree in attributing this nomination to Mme. de Montesson's influence. Every one of them, on the supposition that the success of her aunt's ambitions was due to the young Countess's part in them, has supposed that the position at the Palais Royal rewarded "her extraordinary dexterity" in "retiring in time from her double-dealing game."[1] All these opinions are based on an apparent coincidence of dates.

In the absence of reliable documents to the contrary, we must believe Mme. de Genlis when she says in her *Memoirs*, "I entered the Palais Royal a month before my aunt's marriage." The two events would appear from this to be

[1] Cf. Billault de Gérainville, *Histoire de Louis Philippe*, i. 15.

thirty days apart, the one logically the result of the other. However, it is certain now that Mme. de Genlis's memory was evidently confused, and she is mistaken by one year. She was undoubtedly at the Palais Royal before July 1772.[1]

When she asserts that her appointment to the suite of the Duchess of Chartres had nothing whatever to do with Mme. de Montesson, she is near enough to the truth. Undoubtedly there is a connection between the marriage of the one and the accession to a position of honour of the other, but it is more indirect than one imagines. Undoubtedly, too, since the aunt is not yet married, she thinks it opportune to introduce her niece into the family; it looks like excellent diplomacy. But could she rely blindly upon this niece?

As a matter of fact, at the time of the marriage, and even for several months beforehand, peace did not exactly reign between the two women; each was looking after her own interests. They were merely reconciled on the eve of the wedding for the benefit of the gallery. In addition, have we not just seen, during the absence at Barèges, the curious manner in which this niece takes care of her aunt's love-affairs? Was she not exploiting the Duke of Orleans' interest in herself for her own ends?

Then, in speaking of her appointment, Mme. de Genlis says: "My aunt had no reason to take credit for it. M. le duc d'Orléans personally desired it, for I pleased him, and he thought that I would add to the enjoyment of the long journeys to Villers-Cotterets."

The right to appoint his son's household did indeed belong to the Duke of Orleans, and in her heart Mme. de Genlis had been longing for some time to occupy a position in the Palais Royal. She had forced her way to it under Mme. de Montesson's wing in the beginning, no doubt; but she was not placed there as a reward. Herein lies a vast

---

[1] According to another version, the marriage, declared officially on 28th July, had already been entered into on 23rd April. The Prince's correspondence permits of assuming with a certain amount of security that 28th July is correct. In any case, Mme. de Genlis's appointment to the Palais Royal took place eight or nine months before the event.

difference, inasmuch as it would not have cost her a single one of her many flirtations and overtures to have attained the desired post.

Was she not already thinking of it when the Comte de Provence married and there was a talk of appointing her to Madame ? Louis xv. promised this favour to M. de Puysieulx, who thanked him in public. People were not very astonished to learn that under the pretext of finding it impossible to conform to the necessary visit to Mme. du Barry,[1] the lady elect refused to go to Versailles.

When the suggestion that she should enter the Palais Royal was finally officially made to her, she knew how to behave under the circumstances, as a good pupil of Mme. de Montesson's should.

The preliminary overtures came at an inopportune moment. M. de Puysieulx had just died, and the Genlis household, which was established on the ground floor of the magnificent hotel in the rue de Grenelle, overwhelmed the widow with affectionate attentions.

Mme. de Genlis replies that "gratitude decided her to remain with Mme. de Puysieulx." She thinks, however, of nothing but how to fly away to the paradise of her dreams. She pictures herself a shining star at the youthful court of the de Chartres.

Her friend, the clairvoyant Vicomtesse de Custine, who had early guessed the secret of her ambition, was dismayed. No one could possibly blind themselves to the difficulties which would be met with in safeguarding—where the Duke of Chartres was concerned—the reputation of a young woman as beautiful and attractive as Mme. de Genlis was. However respected she might be, the gentle Duchess had by no means overcome the old Adam in her august husband, and his exploits were notorious in Paris.

Mme. de Custine was a sensible and prudent woman, and she used all her persuasion as a friend to deter Mme. de Genlis from taking heedless action, and she was successful in obtaining her promise not to enter the Palais Royal.

[1] According to Billault de Gérainville, Mme. de Genlis did not have the chance of refusing to visit Mme. du Barry (*Histoire de Louis Philippe*, i. 15).

Unfortunately, the Vicomtesse died of a mysterious illness soon after, and Mme. de Genlis considered herself absolved. Scarcely three months passed before she allows herself to be influenced into going to Raincy, and to the Palais Royal or anywhere where her ambition is likely to be encouraged. She makes use of every opportunity, here a word and there an attention or a call, with her eyes fixed upon the end which justifies the means. Those about her have guessed her object; they speak about it to her and try to sound her, but she prudently retires to a distance, temporises and delays her answer, for Mme. de Puysieulx as yet knows nothing about it. When at length she decides to inform the old lady, she cannot do so without acting a most artificial part. She pretends the greatest unhappiness at leaving the Marquise, and begs for her advice, apparently placing herself entirely in her hands.

Mme. de Puysieulx, in whom that sense of protection had been appealed to which is so easy to arouse in mothers, considered first of all the young people's interest. To have her nephew and niece in positions near to royalty was to be sure of their favour. She felt it almost a duty to persuade the deceitful girl, who wept at present " but would offer no resistance," to accept the offer. The good lady did not know the convert to whom she appealed. She even went so far as to urge M. de Genlis, who was not at all anxious, to apply to the Duke of Orleans for a position for his wife in the Duke of Chartres' household.

To tell the truth, M. de Genlis did not go without a great deal of persuasion. He was only induced to do so by Mme. de Genlis's assurance that she would refuse to enter the Palais Royal without him. Then he yielded and asked for two places. He was given them—a captaincy in the Guards for himself, " one of the first in the household and worth 5000 francs," and for his wife the position of lady-in-waiting, which was worth 4000 francs.

With what delight Félicité du Crest hailed her new dignities! The unhappy days of her youth were far behind now. However, the joy of success was not without its remorse. Her conscience was troubled by her hypocrisy, and Mme. de Genlis confesses to it in her *Memoirs* as " one of the greatest faults of my life." [1]

Therefore, when the day came, Mme. de Genlis was ashamed of herself and quite unable to keep up the false appearances which deceived poor Mme. de Puysieulx, who imagined her niece was in despair at having to leave her. She left at nine o'clock in the morning without saying good-bye to anyone, and wept like a culprit who has a sense of early punishment awaiting her. As if in answer to this presentiment, her coachman nearly upset her in turning the corner of the street, when he dashed against a post. " Good heavens ! " Mme. de Genlis cries in anguish, " what an omen ! "

But it is too late to look backwards. " With an indescribable heaviness of heart " she enters the gates of the Louvre, passes in front of the Palais Royal, dismounts before a little door opening on to the Rue de Richelieu and gains her apartments.

The repairs and alterations which are being made in those intended for her use are not yet finished. She is to occupy in the meantime a temporary room at the end of the large passage on the first floor which had been part of the Regent's former suite, which was connected to the rue Richelieu by a private staircase. The gilding and the profusion of mirrors, the libertine subjects of the paintings which covered the panels and ceilings shocked the newcomer, and she felt ill at ease.

Alas ! as Laure d'Abrantès says : " M. le Duc de Chartres bore these kinds of embarrassments easily."

---

[1] " I might say that it was only the interests of my children which decided me, that it was a maternal sacrifice which was painful to me: if it had been so, Heaven would have blessed this action. But God, who can read the depths of all our heart, knew the motives and has severely punished me. I merited it " (Genlis, *Memoirs*, ii. 161 and succeeding pages).

CHAPTER III

THE PALAIS ROYAL

THE Duke and Duchess of Chartres, but lately married, had just set up house like a happy young pair at the Palais Royal, and under the influence of the Prince the place had at once assumed an air of great elegance. But by a special arrangement there were few young women in the household. They were rather to be found at Versailles, to which the Dauphine, Marie Antoinette, had brought, like a ray of springtime, the wonderful beauty and the spontaneous youthful grace of her sixteen years.

The Duchess of Chartres was surrounded almost exclusively by solidly respectable ladies, incapable of arousing or exciting the least jealousy.

There were the old Comtesse de Rochambeau, formerly the governess of the Duke, whom she excused and made much of—kindly, indulgent, a regular grandmamma; the Comtesse de Montauban, of about the same age, a wild gambler, but rather dull-minded, and " a match for anyone at saying nothing "; the Dowager Marquise de Polignac, who, thanks to having spent all her life at Court, was allowed the privilege of uttering sweeping opinions which then went the round of gossip; the Marquise de Barbentane, a very great dame, imperious, somewhat haughty, and really the grand-mistress of the Palace; the Vicomtesse de Clermont-Gallerande, younger, but of a grave and somewhat sad aspect; the young Comtesse de Polignac, who was the only one of them all near the age of Mme. de Genlis; Mme. de Fleury, Mme. de Noailles, and Mme. de Belzunce;

and finally, the Comtesse de Blot. It was rather a dull kind of world.

The Duke did not care much for the studiously correct society of these ladies. Far from dallying in their company, he tried to lighten the time, during which etiquette required him to endure it, by walking up and down while he assailed the feminine circle with jests and sarcasms. To take the standpoint opposed to received opinions, to ridicule fashionable conversation, put forward paradoxes and offer to bet upon them,—this was the amusement of the "Égalité" of days to come, now the declared enemy of romance and sentiment. It was only the Marquise de Polignac who held her own against the sallies of His Highness, and made smart replies to them. Mme. de Blot, on the contrary, took the line of offended delicacy. The other ladies preferred to smile at the Prince's outbursts.

Before the coming of Mme. de Genlis the Comtesse de Blot was the angel of the Palais Royal. "Pretty, elegant, affecting fine feelings," she seemed to live in an azure realm of love, without troubling herself much about M. de Blot, a mortal of more earthly mould, quite without any pretension to intellectual ideas or even it seems to ordinary wit,—nor about the Marquis de Schomberg, whom she drove to despair by her coldness.

Mme. de Blot, it was afterwards known, hoped to make a conquest of the Prince himself, and quietly to bring him to her feet, but he detested the ethereal type of woman and obstinately avoided her.

Tall, vigorous, alert, with a proud, independent bearing, the Duke of Chartres "was then in all the flower of youth." His noble and lofty countenance, with its wide forehead, would have been handsome only that it was spoiled by a florid bourgeois complexion; his eyes, already sunk in their orbits, had a look that was at once *blasé* and capricious. There was a good deal of haughtiness in them, too, and their glance was disturbing, able to attract but not to captivate.

Like the Prince of Wales, whom he greatly admired, he gave the tone to masculine fashion.

His English tastes, the cut of his clothes, the shape of his hats, his carriages, his jockeys (for his thoroughly British zeal for horse-racing was extreme), were the law for the fickle world of men of fashion, some of whom went so far as to have the hair removed from their foreheads in imitation of his premature baldness.

When he was, so to say, hardly out of leading strings, he had posed as the chief of a number of licentious youths, who too often made it their boast to go beyond, if possible, the irregularities of their leader. But knowing that he was "inclined by character to independence and the hatred of all authority,"[1] the people, already hostile to the Court, were blind enough to attribute to him, in contrast to other royalties, the generous good qualities of a liberator, qualities with which, however, the Prince seems to have been very poorly endowed.

The Duchess of Chartres, Louise Marie Adélaide de Bourbon-Penthièvre, pretty, graceful and modest, was purity itself. To see her beside her husband, whom she loved with simple affection, one thought of the lily of Scripture, whose whiteness shone forth in the midst of thorns.

Kindly to the verge of weakness, somewhat soft in disposition, scrupulously attached to her duties, very pious, and, like her father the Duc de Penthièvre, inspired with the idea of perfection, the Princess would have nothing to do with the intrigues that are the life of courts, and without which they would often die of boredom. And except on state occasions, the days of the opera and the comedy, when there were crowds at the Palais Royal, because all who had once been presented could come without further invitation, the Duchess held few receptions. Her tastes were for quiet evenings, of which the chief occupations were conversation and little games, while she herself with her royal hands worked at some garment for the poor. As twelve o'clock struck she withdrew, leaving her household to the delights of gaming, cards or *tric-trac*, with the lady-of-honour who happened to be on duty presiding in the salon.

Only for its theatricals the elegant Palais Royal would have been but a dull background for this anything but

[1] Clermont-Gallerande, *Mémoires*, i. 64.

playful round of existence, amidst which there stood out in slight relief the affected and languishing airs of Mme. de Blot.

The Comtesse de Genlis made her appearance at the right time.

She was no sooner at the Palais Royal than there was seen to be "an immense change in its ordinary life." As if by enchantment, conversation there took a higher and more lively tone, that was very different from the usual insignificant small-talk of drawing-rooms.

Mme. de Genlis, who in her education and the culture of her mind was very superior to all the ladies about the Duchess, was able to lead the conversation to interesting subjects, and to make it amusing by her animation and sprightliness and her original ways. Her harp, which she played like a professional musician, inaugurated the era of a series of charming little musical parties, and, of course, theatricals, which were then all the rage, completed the work of bringing life and animation to the little Court. As if under this new influence, the Duchess began her "little days," when there were parties and regular suppers, at which sometimes as many as thirty sat down to table, and at first most people were quite delighted.

But the pretty Comtesse, having easily secured the leading place in all this, very soon aroused the jealousy of the rest. Before long all the women were her enemies, beginning with Mme. de Blot, whom she had dethroned.

The men no longer paid attention to anyone but Mme. de Genlis. "They vied with each other in their courtesies to me," she says, "but their gallantry is anything but encouraging when one has to fear the enmity of the women." And as she did not affect the humility of a dependent, war was declared against her, and a hundred malicious little persecutions were brought to bear upon her.

Mme. de Blot, belonging to a higher grade in the hierarchy of the Court—she was a "lady-of-honour" and Mme. de Genlis only a "lady-in-waiting"—did not hesitate to make her authority felt. She indulged in hectoring orders, needless commands, little affronts, all the guerrilla tactics of pitfalls for the unwary in which women excel.

Mme. de Genlis knew how to offer resistance. To conquer by tiring out the enemy was no new thing for her intelligent mind. She had given proof of this already. And she was not without a certain liking for a fight. Observant and persevering as she was, she had soon taken the measure of each one's strong and weak points, and could think with a smile that the last word would be hers. Henceforth she began to study a part in the drama of life that has often been played: she was apparently full of detachment, moderation, and integrity, but under this exterior passionately eager for success, imperious and ambitious. With undeniable cleverness, she concealed the game she was playing.

She might have taken advantage of her growing prestige with them and made the men her allies. But she preferred to seek the protection of the Duchess of Chartres.

Nothing could be more pleasing to Mme. de Chartres than a serious and cultivated young woman, occupied with learning and with educating herself; and Mme. de Genlis, with the remarkable industry that had become a habit of hers, devoted all her spare time to reading, writing, perfecting her talents, while the other ladies were idly passing their time in useless frivolities. There was nothing better calculated to win the pious and pure-minded Duchess than the protestations and discourses of her lady-in-waiting, who was always talking of virtue and piety, and eager to wage war against the passions in the name of morality and religion. So she freely gave her entire esteem and admiration to such an exceptional young person.

With the inexperience of youth, she thought she had found the happiness that is so rare even among princes—that of meeting with a devoted heart on which one can rely—and she soon abandoned herself to the ardent friendship that her new lady-in-waiting showed towards her.

This " marked protection," if it " in a short time destroyed all the petty social opposition that still survived,"[1] did not blind the envious eyes of the Palais Royal. These veteran

[1] Talleyrand, *Mémoires* (*loc. cit.*).

worldlings understood intrigue better than the gentle, simple-minded Duchess of Chartres. The difficulties of the début of Mlle. de St. Aubin, a late arrival in high society, made them mistrustful, and their watchful jealousy became all the keener in the half-light of the salons and corridors of the Palace. Meanwhile they saw how Mme. de Genlis was summoned to the private apartments of the Duchess at all hours even when she was not regularly on duty, and as they heard Her Highness herself proclaiming the merits of the new lady-in-waiting, they chafed under the effort to keep quiet.

But at the end of six months—whether it was a clever move or a mere yielding to fatigue — Mme. de Genlis suddenly left the field clear for the malcontents, and herself offered them an opportunity for disarming.[1]

She asked for leave of absence, wishing to accept the invitation of a friend at Brussels, the Comtesse de Mérode.

She was given leave for six weeks, and set off. It was a move that reminds one of the methods of De Montesson.

And this journey to Brussels was a fine triumph, a series of even more brilliant days in the life that had already been such a success. The Court of France enjoyed, as is well known, a privileged position with regard to foreign Courts, and these distinctions of etiquette ensured for Mme. de Genlis the most marked honours while she was with the Comtesse de Mérode. But apart from such conventional rights, the graceful manners of Paris everywhere won universal admiration, and Mme. de Genlis combined in herself all claims to such favours. Did she not on one occasion presume on this position to the extent of keeping all the most important people in Belgium waiting for several hours, and yet they did not complain of this breach of politeness? On this subject Mme. de Montesson wrote later on to the Duke of Orleans:—

" Just imagine, one day Madame de Mérode gave a dinner to the Stahrembergs, the Arenbergs, in a word all the most

[1] " My absence just as I began to be in favour would prove that I had no desire for domination " (Genlis, *Mémoires*, ii. 247).

important people, and she (Madame de Genlis) arrived wearing a jacket, after having kept them all waiting more than three hours, and instead of making excuses, she said that that was the way they dined at the Palais Royal!"[1]

So our Countess won uninterrupted success in Belgium, and the six weeks' leave lengthened out to three months. On the return of the De Genlis the attachment of the Duchess for Madame, increased by the privations of her absence, was all the stronger. And so was the hostility of the courtiers.

Relying on this all-important protection, the Countess passed through plenty of petty displays of ill-will with her mind at rest and her head carried high. She seemed no longer to care much for Court life, and was even more absorbed in study, always carrying about some book[2] with her, and reading it as she walked or drove in a carriage. She learned English, continued her famous collection of extracts, questioned everyone — foreigners, artists, travellers — and made notes of these conversations. In a word, she did not lose a minute, for she even utilised for writing a selection of verses the quarter of an hour during which the Duchess regularly kept her ladies waiting for her before dinner.

So much wisdom was a marvel to the Duchess of Chartres. "She attached herself to me," say the *Memoirs* of Mme. de Genlis, "with a kind of passion that lasted in full force for more than fifteen years."

Seeing the Countess possessed by this frantic zeal for knowledge—she used to go now to the Jardin du Roi to be initiated into the mysteries of natural history, and was painting flowers in miniature — Mme. de Chartres herself became anxious to learn. She had, it seems, "no education, and did not even know how to spell"—at least, according to Mme. de Genlis. But the teacher was at hand, and generously offered to give lessons. Had she not already persuaded Her Highness to study geography?

[1] Mme. de Montesson to the Duke of Orleans, 22nd May 1773 (A. E. France, 319).
[2] The Abbé des Aulnais, the royal librarian, lent her all she asked for, even manuscripts.

Orthography, history, mythology, regularly taught, soon furnished the mind of the august pupil, and made still more dear, more indispensable to her the studious friendship, the affectionate cares of her " lady-in-waiting." Almost imperceptibly she let her take a larger place in her daily life, made her really her confidante, her intimate adviser, and finally her secretary.[1] How could she, the Princess, round off a note or scribble a letter as elegantly as Mme. de Genlis? So the Comtesse drafted all Her Highness's correspondence, which the Princess then copied in her own handwriting.

Having so quickly become indispensable, Mme. de Genlis escaped the malignant enterprises of the courtiers, their slanders, and their venomous suggestions.

She took advantage of the fact also to extend her influence by organising at the Palais Royal—as, for the matter of that, she did wherever she went—a circle of wit and talent.

Twice a week the Comtesse de Genlis had a reception. On the Tuesday she held a kind of intellectual reunion of men of letters and men of the world. And though she claims that she never opened her door to men of letters with the exception of M. de Sauvigny and M. de Dorat, she knew and visited Buffon, who by his own account came to see her at the Palais Royal " at least once a month,"[2] and at his place she met Bailly, Héraut de Séchelles, and Lacépède; so it is most probable that these Tuesday conversations brought together literary men and a circle of amateurs—M. de Schomberg, the Comte de Fleurieu, the Chevalier de Durfort, etc. Soon La Harpe came to them regularly.

The Saturday was devoted to music. Mme. de Genlis on that day gave regular concerts with artists and composers of note, especially Gluck and Monsigny. During

---

[1] " Every day if anything out of the ordinary occurred to her she told me of it and sent for me to consult me or to confide to me what interested her. It very often happened that she sent me Mademoiselle Lefèvre, one of the ladies of her chamber, at two or three in the morning, when I had not been able to see her during the day " (Genlis, ii. 258).

[2] " I went," says Mme. de Genlis, " to dine with him every ten or twelve days. I came rather early in order to find him alone; we never talked of anything but literature " (Mémoires, ii. 279).

this winter of 1772-78 the quarrel between the Gluckists and the Piccinists was at its height. Mme. de Genlis, whose position as a musician was undeniable, owed it to herself to fight in the foremost rank.

Not only did she encourage Gluck by faithfully attending all the performances of his works, but she also missed none of the rehearsals of the orchestra. And moreover, her witty pen, her sarcastic speech, made the most of the thousand pointed railleries she shot off against the literary champions of Piccini.

As literary men are not necessarily experts in music, it sometimes happens that in musical matters they take sides without quite knowing why, or at least for reasons that have very little to do with music. Now, according to Mme. de Genlis, the literary partisans of Gluck " did not know a word " of music. She did not hesitate to tell them this cruel truth. And none of them pardoned her for it; Suard in particular cherished all his life a certain rancour for the too frankly ironical Comtesse.

But her own celebrity gained by all this. Criticising and judging with the authority that came from talent, Mme. de Genlis was asserting in a brilliant way her own pre-eminence as an artist. And with this view, to use the expression of a contemporary, " listlessness and indifference seemed to her always worthy of condemnation." [1] What a victory it was for her when the Gluckists carried all before them! But the opposing camp revenged itself by means of strange demonstrations. As soon as Mme. de Genlis arrived at the Opera there would be a great display of feeling, which was not entirely made up of admiration.

Then she only showed herself there on the days when she was on duty as lady-in-waiting; it was a sacrifice so painful to her musical disposition that she thought she would have to seal it with a vow. But, on the other hand, her talent was to receive the consecration of royal approval next year at Marly. The Princes, following the example of the youthful Louis XVI., went there to be vaccinated, and Mme. de Genlis accompanied the Duchess of Chartres. Here is how

[1] Toulotte, *La Cour et la Ville*, i. 3.

she tells us what happened: "When I came back to my rooms in the evening after supper, I generally played some music for two good hours before going to bed. One evening between eleven and midnight, when, according to my custom, I was playing the harp and practising a sonata, M. d'Avaray, to my great surprise, suddenly came into the room and whispered to me that the Queen was with Madame Valbelle (in the next room) to hear me play the harp." One can imagine how Mme. de Genlis would feel such an honour. Under her agile fingers the delightful Italian sonatas, or chaconnes and gavottes, mingled their lively rhythms with the "Graves" and "Largos"; displayed all their alluring charms; and the brilliant variations of their recurring cadences resounded triumphantly through the thin wall of the room, on the other side of which was the Queen, all ears, and all delight.

Romances followed the sonatas, for now the artist was singing. And for an hour and a half the unequalled talent of Mme. de Genlis excited the enthusiasm of Marie Antoinette. When, at last, Her Majesty withdrew, and respect no longer restrained the other listeners, the applause came ringing through the wall; at the same time M. d'Avaray brought the compliments of the young Queen to Mme. de Genlis, who stopped, wearied out with her performance. Next day Marie Antoinette deigned herself to compliment the artist-Countess, and told her she would be pleased to hear her at her private concerts. The Princesse de Lamballe strongly urged her to have herself included in them, and thus to be brought into closer relations with the royal family.

Strange to say, Mme. de Genlis showed herself indifferent in this matter. "I had," she says, "ties enough not to wish for others. This would have taken up an enormous amount of my time, and so would have upset my studies. . . . So I allowed no further steps to be taken in the affair."

That she should refuse such a chance of royal favour naturally seems surprising in the case of a woman who was so resolved to make herself a name. More than one in her position would have welcomed with smiling face such an augury of fortune, and would have hastened to bask in the great sunlight of Versailles.

But clearly Mme. de Genlis was better pleased to be at the Palais Royal. No doubt she had so much at heart the friendship of the Duchess of Chartres that even the patronage of Marie Antoinette could not stand the comparison.

We shall see what is to be thought of all this.

For we have come to the morrow of the visit to Forges, the first episode of a fresh romance, and a dramatic one. It was the second and the great romance of the life of Mme. de Genlis, and it lasted twenty years, beginning with a love duet and ending with a capital execution—namely, the guillotining of Philippe-Égalité.

CHAPTER IV

THE VISIT TO FORGES

THE biographers of Mme. de Genlis have all passed lightly over this journey to Forges, on the surface an insignificant event.

There could be nothing more natural than that in the first part of July 1772 Mme. de Chartres, weak in health, anæmic, and distressed at her childlessness, should go by the doctors' orders to the waters of Forges, as Queen Anne of Austria had gone there formerly for the same reasons; and that Mme. de Genlis (with Mme. de Blot and the Vicomtesse de Clermont-Gallerande) should accompany Her Highness; and that the Duke of Chartres, as an affectionate young husband, should not let his wife travel without him, and should himself preside over her temporary establishment at the watering-place.

And so certain unfriendly echoes, originating doubtless among the jealous folk of the Palais Royal, and current at the time among well-informed people, had, until quite recently, the look of calumnies, the air of being only the talk of evil tongues that one does not venture to transmit to posterity in the written record.

And not long ago a biographer could affirm that the friendship of Mme. de Genlis for the Duke of Chartres had nothing more in it than good comradeship.[1]

There was no precise fact known that could justify a directly contrary supposition. Besides, the *Memoirs* of the lady concerned make it impossible to fix the date of this journey on her testimony alone, for they speak of it very

[1] Cf. M. de Chabreul, *Gouverneur de Princes*, p. 200.

carelessly in the midst of the events of 1777, as it were a forgotten trifle of the past, and so take away from it any kind of importance.

Notwithstanding this clever confusing of details, there can be no possible doubt nowadays. The proof—alas! the famous irrefutable proof, that Mme. de Genlis herself used to require when judging of a woman—the proof exists. It consists of her own letters and those of the Duke of Chartres, discovered in the archives of the Ministry of Foreign Affairs, and published in 1904 by M. Gaston Maugras.[1]

According to this correspondence, the Duke went to Forges not only to instal the Duchess there, but also that he " might live in closer relations with Madame de Genlis,"[2] and to abandon himself for a few days to the delights of an ardent love that was returned.

He had hardly begun this new experience when on Saturday, 18th July 1772, he was called away to Chantilly on account of the condition of his young sister, the Duchesse de Bourbon, who was from one moment to another expecting the birth of an heir. Then he went back to the Palais Royal, whence he could easily go to see the Duchesse de Bourbon; and he consoled himself for the absence of his lady friend by exchanging affectionate letters with her. As a precaution, M. de Genlis had been sent to Charleville.

But these letters, which the post conveyed daily from Paris to Forges, and *vice versa*, were opened before they reached those for whom they were intended, and read by other eyes than theirs. Louis XV., whose secret police were hard at work, and amongst other intrigues kept a watch on those of his licentious cousin, certainly amused himself by having the first reading of them. He had copies kept in his *cabinet noir*. So they were preserved to our day mixed up with diplomatic secrets between the covers of a green portfolio at the Foreign Office. And it must be granted that they bring the element of romance into the place. *Billets doux* mixed up with diplomatic documents! Would even the late Ponson du Terrail have ventured to imagine such a thing! But anyhow, he could easily have imagined what

---

[1] Gaston Maugras, *L'Idylle d'un Gouverneur.*   [2] *Ibid.*, p. 9.

the letters themselves were like, for nothing resembles one love-letter so much as another.

Mme. de Genlis confirms the rule. She is wretched at the departure of the lover; she is consumed with the fires of passion. Thus, for example, she writes: "Oh, my love, I can really love only you! You are the one object of all my feelings, all my thoughts. I have accustomed myself to pass half my life in seeing you, and the rest of the time in waiting for you, hoping and longing to see you," etc.

Or again: "Yes, my dear friend, I have given myself to you, abandoned myself to you in a transport of delight. Never was friend or child loved like you," etc.

For the two lovers addressed each other as "Mon enfant" (My child), and perhaps Mme. de Genlis's tone was sometimes rather that of a protector, despite her imprudent declarations. As for the Duke, to prove the irrevocable character of his feelings, he had a device tattooed upon his arm; and, what was assuredly in better taste, he ordered from Fragonard two pictures with subjects taken from one of Madame de Genlis's stories. During this time the Duchess of Chartres was suffering with her teeth, and using ether as a remedy, the odour of which made her lady-in-waiting feel ill. And she received a letter from the husband with these edifying words: "I would like to hear from the Chevalier [1] to-morrow that all her jaw had been taken out And I would not even be sorry if the tongue went with it!" [2]

A touching expression of conjugal love!

After about a month—to be precise, on 14th August 1772—the Duchess ended her cure. On the 12th a last note reached the Duke: "I hear from Paris that M. de Genlis is to arrive there on the 14th. If this is so, he will know from Saint-Jean what day I am to arrive. I shall, I think, manage to get rid of him before half-past eleven on the pretext of fatigue. Come quietly, and if the door is closed, *mon enfant* will wait, and picture to himself that on the other side of it there is a heart as agitated and as impatient as his own." [3]

In October the flame was still burning.

[1] The Chevalier de Durfort.   [2] Maugras, *op. cit.* p. 19.
[3] *Ibid.* p. 51.

The Duke and Duchess of Chartres spent the autumn at Chantilly with the Prince of Condé, and the Countess seemed to take a pleasure in defying public opinion. She drove the ducal carriage, and " there was laughter among the courtiers at those carriage drives, which seemed symbolical, for the Duke and Duchess, seated side by side, were taken through the winding alleys of Chantilly at the whim of Madame de Genlis' fancy."[1] The Duchesse de Bourbon, who had seen through it all, died of horror. Did the illusions of her simple-minded sister-in-law last much longer?

Now a princess is seldom the first to discover secrets of this kind. But in this case the secret was so well kept that even the keenest of the sharp-minded onlookers thought only that there was some dangerous warmth. Everything was known at last, but they were only suspected in the following spring—in May 1778—and then on account of a false move on the part of Mme. de Genlis.

It was at the moment when Mme. de Montesson—having been obliged to put off her marriage for two years, an interval of delay that she had herself fixed—had gone to Spa to pass away the time. The Comtesse de Genlis was to have accompanied her aunt. But this would have been to give up, or at least to relax, her relations with the Duke of Chartres. At the last moment—when she was divided between two dangers: that of betraying her secret, and the risk her love-affair would run through absence—she chose to allege an illness of some kind of her daughter's—a poor pretext that deceived no one; and her cleverness broke down. She refused to leave Paris, insisted on her husband spreading the story about, and ceased to appear at the Palais Royal.

But there was incredulity everywhere. At once some mystery was suspected, and certain letters of the Duke of Orleans to his dear Montesson clear up the subject very well indeed.

" You ask me, dear friend," he writes on 22nd May, " what is the effect of this silly conduct of Madame de Genlis, and how long she will go on playing this comedy. As to the last point, I know nothing. As to the former, everyone is asking

[1] Cf. Vitrac, *Philippe-Égalité et Monsieur Chiappini*, p. 73.

what it means. It is regarded as bad form and something that has no sense in it. No one can say what her reason is, for there is not one who believes in her daughter's illness. . . ."

Before long "fat Philip" was better informed. Just after this Mme. de Blot, whose keen-sighted jealousy had half discovered, half imagined the existence of a romance, took it into her head to relate to him an interview between Mme. de Genlis and her aunt, in which the latter had offered, without any result, to put off her journey.[1]

Finally, the Dowager de Ségur had lost no time in telling the Duke of Orleans how on Sunday morning, the day before the start, M. de Pont-St. Maurice, calling upon Mme. de Genlis, had found her discussing the journey with the Vicomte de Pont, who was to accompany Mme. de Montesson. "It is absolutely necessary," said the Countess, "for me to be in Paris on 9th June. I have promised this to the Duke of Chartres and all his ladies." The Viscount urged that this was impossible. "But we need only shorten the stay at Brussels," she said. "It is for you, Madame," replied M. de Pont, "to obtain that from your aunt. But I doubt if you will succeed." "Well, if she won't cut short her visit, I am not afraid of riding. I shall get astride of a post-horse and come back from Brussels at full gallop, for I must be here on the 9th."

The Comte de Pont-St. Maurice went away after this peremptory statement of Mme. de Genlis, leaving her still disputing with the incredulous Viscount.

Mme. de Genlis, a hundred leagues away from the Palais Royal, was informed at Spa of the current talk, and expressed to her correspondents her pleasure in amusing herself with the gossip about her niece's conduct. But all the while the sagacious Marchioness was asking herself if the influence of this niece, who did not like her, might not do her harm in the opinion of the Duke of Chartres.

Meanwhile, only a few days after these events, Mme. de Genlis was laid up with a serious attack of measles, and at

[1] *Ibid.* See also *Le Duc Louis Philippe d'Orléans. Son mariage secret avec la Marquise de Montesson*, par A. Choppin de Janvry.

once the report spread abroad that the Prince's passion was declining and growing cool, and seemed about to disappear.

"Madame de Genlis has a fever," wrote the fat Duke of Orleans.[1] "It is said that she is not on such good terms with someone you know. It is even made out that they have parted. But we shall soon know all about that."

At the Palais Royal the jealous crowd, who had long marvelled at the constancy of the Duke de Chartres in his love-affair, were now secretly rejoicing. We learn this from another friend of Mme. de Montesson, the Marquis d'Entraygues, who liked to send her the small-talk of the Court. "It is said," he informed her on 27th May, "that she (Madame de Genlis) is threatened with trouble. At the moment she is ill with the measles. Before this latest illness of hers, she was very depressed. Perhaps she remembers the prediction once made to her that she would be greatly to be pitied. She will be unhappy, if she is abandoned and has no one to pity her. This is the event with which she has been menaced."

The envious people were rejoicing too soon over what they hoped for. But it must be recognised that just now a greater prudence directed the proceedings of the two lovers. When on the occasion of his father's secret marriage to the Marquise de Montesson, in July 1773, the Duke of Chartres, in order to show his disapproval the more strongly, left Paris and in his turn went to Brussels, it is true that he still corresponded with Mme. de Genlis, but it was in very reserved and almost ceremonious terms. "Monseigneur" and "Madame" had replaced the affectionate "Mon enfant." Perhaps it was only a pretence. Perhaps some rumour had put the two friends on their guard. But let there be no mistake: the Prince was for a long time under the empire of Mme. de Genlis. And he was never to free himself altogether from her sway. When the caprice of the libertine was satisfied—and this was indeed a trifling matter in the time with which we are dealing—the fair one knew how to substitute for the impulses of passion a friendship that was assiduous, all-subduing, warm still, but subjugating, by

[1] Cf. Maugras, *op. cit.*

which she ruled all the intelligence that the poor weak Duke possessed.

He did not know how to resist the woman who knew how to lead him, he said one day to his sister. And that woman was the Comtesse de Genlis. She excelled in the skill to hide behind the scenes, and work this poor puppet like a marionette.

Immensely his superior, she arrived at the point of ruling him even in the smallest details of his life, exerting her power even to tear him away from his despicable pleasures, and give him back to his simple, pure-minded Duchess. Soon Mme. de Genlis controlled the secrets of his policy as well as those of his household; before long she was to hold that position of "Governor" which is unique in history, and thus it was that, from the time of the visit to Forges, she ruled without resistance the future Philippe Égalité. It was to this she tended with all the force of her being. To rule was her business far more than to whisper words of love: this comes out indeed clearly enough in her letters. There is no doubt passion in them, but one looks in vain for those childish expressions, or the self-devotion of a heart enraptured with love and swayed by some sublime illusion.

So from 1772 the Palais Royal was in the hands of Mme. de Genlis. She was to reign there in secret for nearly twenty years; no longer probably by the sway of passion, but through the subtle intelligence of a mind that knew how to "animate that moral corpse,"[1] think for him, and inspire him with a line of policy, until the day when the more cunning and more daring Laclos supplanted this artful intriguer in the political field. Till then she remained the Prince's Egeria.

Under the date of 1st August 1778, three months after that famous attack of the measles, the *dossier* of the Foreign Office on which we have already drawn contains two curious letters that it is interesting to compare.

One is addressed to the Duchess of Chartres, who, still in Paris, is about to find herself for the first time in the embarrassing position of meeting her father-in-law and Mme. de Montesson, who five days before had, so far as

[1] Ferrières, *Mémoires*, p. 91.

MME. DE MONTESSON.

a morganatic marriage went, become Duchess of Orleans. The other reached Mme. de Genlis by the same post. The first—that of a husband giving his wife instructions as to the line of conduct to take—would seem quite natural, and would be of trifling interest, if we did not learn from the second that it was to a certain extent dictated by Mme. de Genlis.

"Set your mind quite at rest, and do not be at all anxious," writes the Duke to his wife. "He certainly will not speak to you of it [that is, of his recent marriage], but probably he will do what he can to give you some hint of it; and if you blush or seem embarrassed, it is very likely that he will suppose you have understood without his having actually said it, and he will go on to talk of it as if you knew all about it. This is just what you must try to avoid by calling up all the self-possession and even the effrontery that you are capable of, even if he takes you, for the time being only, to be the most stupid of creatures. You must not seem to understand him, whatever he says," etc.

Now here is the letter to Mme. de Genlis :—

"SPA, 1st *August* 1773.

"I have just written to M. la D. de C. [*i.e.* Madame la Duchesse de Chartres]. I tell her that I strongly approve of her having sent to Raincy, and that above all she must not show any affection towards her [Madame de Montesson], but that unhappily it is necessary that she should be prepared to do things that later on will be very displeasing to M.P. [*i.e. Mon Père*—my father]. You may be quite sure that I shall not change anything in my plan in case they write to me. I have worked the whole matter out with you, Madame, and I have too much confidence in your views and opinion of it to change anything whatever on which we have together decided. If they write to me, I shall reply with a very simple letter, as affectionate as possible, but in which this matter will not be touched upon. This is just what we decided upon—is it not?

"Do not fear that I shall forget anything that you have said to me. Adieu, Madame. I do not know how to thank you for all your kindness. I hope to hear again from you this evening or to-morrow at latest. Indeed you are too good to me."

So now the line is taken. Externally there is nothing to disclose the sovereignty of Mme. de Genlis; she is not to be seen in the guise of a favourite, an appearance she will never assume. But in reality the policy and the manner of life of the Palais Royal will depend on her.

And if the Duke of Orleans and Mme. de Montesson know what course to take, they will beware of compromising so useful an ally, even though the Countess has done nothing —but quite the contrary—to incline the Duke of Chartres to accept with good grace his father's second marriage.

Finally, out of consideration for the peace of mind of the Duchess of Chartres, whose eyes will remain closed for many years to come, they will be silent in her hearing.

Just then the Princess, wonderfully strengthened by the waters of Forges, was hoping soon to be a mother. And in fact, on 5th October in this same year, 1773, she brought into the world her first-born, the Duke of Valois, afterwards King Louis Philippe.

When later on her husband announced to her the plan he had formed of embarking for a " naval campaign "—in other words, a cruise—she listened with delight to the suggestion of Mme. de Genlis (whose jealous passion she did not suspect) that she should accompany the Duke as far as Toulon. Then leaving M. de Chartres at Toulon to continue his expedition (the first step to the post of Grand Admiral in which he hoped to succeed his father-in-law the Duc de Penthièvre), the two young women decided suddenly on the plan of pushing on into Italy without the previous permission of the Court.

The Duchess was to be supposed to be seized with an irresistible desire to go to visit her grandfather the Duke of Modena, and from Antibes she wrote her excuses to the King.

The journey was to Modena by way of Nice, Monaco, and the Corniche road, then to Mantua, Venice, Rome,

Parma, and Naples. For her suite the Duchess brought with her only her dear Countess and a young person hardly sixteen years of age, Mlle. de Rully.

Could one imagine that such an innocent escapade would give rise to one of the enigmas of history, which people are discussing to this day?

This was the Chiappini affair—a strange outcome of the journey to Forges, in which the name of Mme. de Genlis has been unpleasantly involved.

There was a well-known lawsuit at the beginning of the reign of Louis Philippe over which the enemies of the house of Orleans eagerly did their best to provoke a scandal.

The heroine of and the prime mover in the affair, Maria Stella Chiappini, the daughter of an obscure jailer of Modigliana, a little town in the neighbourhood of Ravenna, tried to make out that she had been changed at birth with a boy born on the same day in August 1774. She alleged that she was the daughter of a great French noble, the Comte de Joinville.

Now, by a curious coincidence it happened that the Duchess of Chartres actually travelled in Italy *incognita* under the name of the Comtesse de Joinville. Hence people were found to credit the story of Maria Stella, and gave it out as something certain that Mme. de Chartres had brought into the world at Modigliana a daughter, whom her husband, the pseudo-Comte de Joinville, had changed for the male child of Chiappini, bribing him with a fortune. Thus it was said the child of a poor Italian jailer became by fraudulent means Duke de Valois, and later King of France, while Maria Stella, born a Princess of royal blood, was condemned to poverty and a life of adventures, and these adventures were famous enough; first she was a singer, after which came her two marriages.[1]

At the time many writers championed this claim, of which historical documents have completely disposed. We may be pardoned if we here discuss it in anticipation.

---

[1] Maria Stella married first an English nobleman, very wealthy and of an old family, Lord Newborough. Then when she became a widow she was married again to a Russian noble, Baron Sternberg.

Though the Chiappini affair dates from 1824, it had all the same its origin in this journey in Italy, and by the theories to which it gave rise it is linked with the *liaison* which Mme. de Genlis began at Forges. But after all, if the memory of Louis Philippe emerged unharmed from the scandal, it must be admitted that the reputation of Mme. de Genlis had to endure further attacks on the part of certain narrators of the affair, not to talk of the extremities to which some went against her; and we owe it to her to recall these things if only to show that she had no reason to fear the discussion.

In the first place, she was formally accused of having herself effected the exchange of the children.[1]

Once public curiosity had been started on this track it did not stop. As the lawsuit began just at the moment when the Comtesse de Genlis was publishing her *Memoirs*, people turned to them, and not without suspicion, to seek there lights and details on the journey to Italy.

But, unfortunately, every time that there is any question of compromising events the *Memoirs*, far from clearing up the facts, seem purposely to confuse still further the tangled skein.

There is no clearly fixed date, no definite point from which one can argue with certainty. And it was asked why did Mme. de Genlis seem to take a pleasure in enveloping her narrative in obscurities and needless and uncalled-for digressions? Why does she represent the journey under the guise of a secret expedition, suddenly resolved upon? Why was she the only companion of the Duchess—for one can hardly count the young Comtesse de Rully as an expert witness? Why does she seem to have doubts about the Duchess being soon to become a mother?

The enemies of the house of Orleans compared these mysteries with another, that referring to his own birth which Philip-Égalité almost admitted, shamefacedly, before the Convention, and they suggested various doubts. The fact that Mme. de Genlis had been under serious suspicion since the Revolution gave a leverage to hostile opinion. Besides, certain rumours that had circulated in the old Court

[1] Cf. Paul Dumont, *Orléans et Chiappini*.

still haunted the ears of the Royalists. Although there were no actual proofs available, they held for certain the amorous relations of the Countess and Philip Égalité at the time when he was known as the Duke of Chartres, and this was a secret motive for not sparing her.

From this there was only a step to accusing her—only a step to the absurd fable of Mme. de Genlis hating the Duchess of Chartres, and wishing for nothing less than her death in order to take her place beside the Duke. That step malevolent writers deliberately took.[1]

Because, during the Italian journey, one fine day a wheel came off, and the travelling carriage upset, falling over to the side on which Mme. de Chartres was seated—then supposed by her friends to be in delicate health—the terrible charge of having intended to assassinate the Duchess hung over Mme. de Genlis.

It was a commonplace accident, such as happened hundreds of times in those days of carriages and post-chaises, and as for this pretended attempt at assassination, one need hardly say that it cannot stand honest examination. The sole cause of the accident was that the wheels were wrong—they were new ones, a present from Cardinal de Bernis, and not the proper size for the carriage.

As for the mystery of Modigliana—if mystery there be—how can Mme. de Genlis be shown to have been an accomplice in it, seeing that in the month of August 1778 she was undeniably at the Palais Royal,[2] as were the Duke and Duchess of Chartres ; and that the journey to Italy took place in reality not in the course of the year 1778, but three years later, in the summer of 1776.[3]

What remains of this obscure story ? Is there perhaps anything in it to explain the confused statements of Mme. de Genlis in her *Memoirs* ?

But when she related these events, some fifty years later,

---

[1] Cf. G. de Vautibault, Paul Dumont, *op. cit.*
[2] Cf. *Gazette de France*, 1773.
[3] See on this subject Billault de Gérainville, *op. cit.*, ii. 143, etc. ; Maurice Vitrac, *Philippe-Égalité et Monsieur Chiappini* ; the Vicomte de Reiset, *Belles du temps passé, Maria Stella.*

her memory had not always the clearness one would desire. No one will deny the disorder, the loose writing of these *Memoirs*, in which under what is meant to be a chronological order nothing or hardly anything is in its place.

And in this particular case Mme. de Genlis was thinking much more of communicating her impressions of Italy than of giving precise historical details. Her overflowing enthusiasm, her transports of delight, her tears of joy at treading the soil of the Eternal City; her disillusions at Venice, where "the gondolas, black all over, looked like coffins floating on waves of ink"; the account of her adventures at Naples, all give us evidence enough of her desire to describe with a certain artistic pride the state of her mind in this Latin land of glorious monuments. She acted as a traveller describing a picturesque country, not as a historian putting documents on record.

And if she does not speak of the pretended secret on which the Chiappini scandal was propped up, it is evidently because no such secret existed.

One would like to be able to pronounce with the same certainty upon another enigma, and this a more closely connected result of the visit to Forges.

There is indeed a certain coincidence of dates and events that leads one to the belief that the relations of the Duke of Chartres with Mme. de Genlis left some traces.

When, as a result of the epidemic of measles that raged at Paris, little Casimir de Genlis died, her sorrow brought the mother, who herself was ill, to the gates of death.[1] She fell into a kind of languid state of illness that was very serious, and thought herself doomed. It seemed to her that divine Justice was pursuing and chastising her, and she was haunted by gloomy remorse. The *Memoirs* in telling of this episode throw a strange light on the agitation of her conscience. One finds in them, under the form of sorrowful self-consciousness, the echo of the terrors of Mme. de Genlis.

She tells us how, believing that she was attacked by

[1] Mme. de Genlis says she had at this time an attack of the measles. Now we know she had been ill in this way already in 1773. Is she not confusing one date with the other, unless indeed she had this illness twice?

consumption of the lungs, she made her will, and wrote some verses on her malady ; how as her carriage drove through the Bois de Boulogne amid the scents of spring, by thickets perfumed with the rosy whiteness of the flowering hawthorns, her imagination was for a moment aroused again and built up a romance, of which notwithstanding her weakness she noted the outlines on paper as soon as she returned home.[1]

And at last she was making such a slow recovery that Tronchin le Jeune sent his patient to the waters of Spa.

But was this languor the consequence of symptoms of quite a different kind ?

Mme. de Genlis does not fail to inform us that her sadness and her state of collapse made it impossible for her to receive anyone during her stay at the Belgian watering-place, " except on two or three occasions when there was music."

She hardly saw anyone but an Englishman named Conway, whom she told of the breakdown of her health. And when, nine or ten years later, two little girls, who came from England, arrived at the Palais Royal, scandalous gossip did not hesitate to attribute their parentage to the Duke of Orleans and Mme. de Genlis.

But the absence of proof makes all these mysteries well-nigh impenetrable. And they are made only the more obscure by the confusion of dates that is introduced, as if at haphazard, into the *Memoirs* of Mme. de Genlis.

She places her stay at Spa in 1776. But the list of visitors shows that she arrived there on 12th June 1775. The Chevalier de Conway had been there since 1st June.[2]

And Mme. de Genlis goes on to say : " My health was perfectly restored by the end of six weeks," and a tour through Luxemburg, Germany, and Switzerland completed the cure. " I wrote to Paris to ask for an extension of leave, and to M. de Genlis for permission to make a journey in Switzerland," she adds. " I obtained all I wanted."

Now this tour, with halts at Luxemburg, where Mme.

---

[1] This romance appeared twenty years later under the title of *Les Vœux téméraires*.

[2] Cf. *Liste des Seigneurs et Dames venus aux eaux de Spa.*

de Genlis was the guest of the Prince of Hesse; at Strasburg, where she wrote her name on the silver bell of the Cathedral; at Colmar, where her father-in-law, Baron d'Andlau, lavished entertainments and presents upon her; at Bâle; at Lausanne, where she made the acquaintance of the Prince of Holstein and Mme. de Crouzas, whom she delighted with her playing on the harp,—this tour brought her to Ferney, a literary pilgrimage, which was inevitable for every foreign visitor to Switzerland.

But this visit of Mme. de Genlis to Voltaire is not noted in the philosopher's correspondence till August 1776.

Now, it will be remembered that the visit to Italy took place, without any possible doubt, precisely in this summer of 1776.

Did Mme. de Genlis make two journeys in this year? Or rather, as the cure at Spa was in 1775, must we not place the tour that followed it, ending with the visit to Ferney, in that same year?

But finally, as to the two little girls who came from England in 1785, though absolute certainty is not possible, the date of their birth seems to coincide exactly with that of Mme. de Genlis's absence. And who can say if the scandalous talk that was set going by the arrival of Paméla and Hermine was not founded in part on this coincidence?

CHAPTER V

BELLECHASSE

"For your sake I shall give up for a while my slippers and my dressing-gown," wrote Voltaire to Mme. de Genlis. The Comtesse, decked out with "all her flowers and feathers," arrived too soon, but was not sorry for it. The confusion of the domestics led her to make the amusing reflection that her unexpectedly early visit would prevent the patriarch from writing a few more impious or licentious lines. She had plenty of time to remark, in the rather darksome waiting-room, a magnificent Correggio, unworthily hidden away in the shade, while a frightful picture, "a regular ale-house sign, representing Voltaire in a blaze of glory with Calas at his knees, and trampling under foot his enemies Fréron and Pompignan, held the place of honour in the middle of the salon."

The sight of this strengthened all the more the resolution she had taken not to conform to "the etiquette of Ferney."

It appears it was a rule for visitors to Voltaire "to seem deeply moved, to turn pale, to be overcome" at his appearance, and finally to throw themselves into his arms. Mme. de Genlis promised herself that she would treat this rule as a dead letter, and took up an expectant attitude, which she had plenty of time to rehearse, for she was kept waiting.

At last there was a little noise and some excitement that seemed to herald the entry of the great man.

But it was only Mme. Denis and Mme. de St. Julien. They proposed to the visitor and her travelling companion—a German painter named Ott—to walk round the grounds while waiting for Voltaire.

But the terrace to which they took Mme. de Genlis to give her a view of the surrounding scene with the Alpine summits towering above it—this terrace, sheltered by an arcade of foliage with plants that were bent into low arches, was disastrous for fine toilettes. It was difficult to stand erect; everywhere one had to stoop a little, and the feathers caught in the branches, and broke and hung down; the dress and petticoats got mixed up with the tangle of twigs, and were held and torn by them. So the Countess appeared before her host "with headgear spoiled, everything disarranged, and with a really wretched appearance that took away all self-composure."

She never felt less inclined to embrace him.

Despite the discreet suggestions of Mme. de St. Julien, and notwithstanding her disordered costume, she assumed a grave look and went forward to meet Voltaire with the greatest respect and with all the dignity she could muster

Voltaire remembered that Mme. de Genlis belonged to the Court. So he played the gallant, took her hand and kissed it

"I don't know why," she says, "that very commonplace act touched me, as if this kind of homage was not as vulgar as it is unmeaning. But after all I was flattered at Monsieur de Voltaire having kissed my hand, and I embraced him with all my heart—in spirit."

On the other hand, the enthusiasm of the German painter absolutely lacked all discretion, and displayed itself to the point of extravagance. Ott, taking advantage of this exceptional occasion, eagerly tried to attract Voltaire's attention by showing him some miniatures done at Berne, which he at once took out of his pocket. One of them represented the Blessed Virgin and the Infant Jesus, and this the famous man made the occasion for "many impious remarks that were as stupid as they were revolting." Mme. de Genlis took no pains to conceal her displeasure, and Voltaire abruptly changed the subject of the conversation. He spoke of Italy and the fine arts, but in a rather mediocre way. When they rose from table, he asked Mme. de St. Julien to open the clavecin in honour of the visitor, and to play for her, in old-fashioned style, some of those airs that carry back the thoughts to the time of Louis XIV. "But this recollection," says Mme. de Genlis, "is not the most pleasant to recall." Finally, he accompanied the Countess as far as the village in her travelling carriage, passing on the way the alms-houses he had founded.

It was then only that Mme. de Genlis admired and felt herself better disposed towards Voltaire. From that moment the eyes of the philosopher seemed to her to be extraordinarily full of thought. "They had at the same time," she says, "something of velvet softness and an inexpressible mildness. The soul of *Zaïre* is all in those eyes." But she adds: "His smile and his extremely malicious laugh changed all at once this charming expression. He was very broken down. . . . When the talk was not of religion or of his enemies his conversation was simple and natural without any pretentiousness, and consequently, with an intelligence like his, perfectly pleasing. It seemed to me that he could not endure that on any point one should hold an opinion contrary to his own. If one contradicted him in the least thing, his tone became sharp and sarcastic." But in the opinion of the Comtesse de Genlis, who having very fully studied him knew his circle, Voltaire had, thanks to the unmeasured adulation of which he was the object, lost the manners of good society—of that society with which he was not now familiar, and to which she returned to resume her place in it, sure of herself, with her mind once more calm and brave, after five months' absence and her meeting with the "philosopher." Never had her zeal against immorality, vice, and the passions been so full of conscious vigour. But by a strange irony of fate these were just the devouring monsters that she found installed as masters in her own home.

M. de Genlis, who from what we know of him was a somewhat ridiculous figure, thought he was escaping ridicule by making free use of the excessive freedom of conduct that was the fashion at the time even in the best families of high society. A contemporary tells us how "he made a point of honour of showing himself to be giddy, frivolous, and debauched. By the mere fact that he was one of the frequenters of the Palais Royal he thought himself obliged by his own conduct to recall that of the *roués* of the Regency. In a word, he was one who made a boastful show of being vicious, and bad as he was in appearance, he was better in reality." [1]

One cannot say whether husband or wife was the first to be unfaithful, or if the relations of Mme. de Genlis with the Duke of Chartres were the determining cause of a serious rupture.

Perhaps the Countess, who was soon tired of the gaming-table, was not, as has been suggested, the first to be wronged. Her husband was indeed one of the wildest gamblers that ever lived. The story of the time finds frequent traces of him in the gaming-houses. And if he and his brother, the Marquis de Genlis, never openly kept such an establishment in the strict sense of the term, they nevertheless used to gather in private round the green table in their rooms the greatest gamblers in Paris, including Talleyrand, then merely the Abbé de Périgord. When, in February 1776, the Parlement de Paris, roused to action by current scandals involving considerable losses of money, directed the Lieutenant-General of Police to make an inquiry as to public and private gambling, and to look up the gaming resorts, several *lettres de cachet* followed. The brothers Genlis, who were proved to have kept a table for play " in a house situated in the Place Vendôme and in another in the Rue Bergère," [2] narrowly escaped one of these warrants, and their name was talked of on this occasion.

And when, in 1776, Mme. de Genlis met her husband again, it was to hear that he wanted to go abroad.

M. de Genlis was in fact trying to obtain the governorship of San Domingo. There is no doubt that just then the cards had made a serious breach in the family fortune, and it is probable that what made the Comte think of going abroad

---

[1] Cf. *Mémoires d'un émigré*, i. 420.
[2] Hector Monin, *Paris en 1789*, p. 410: A. N. X¹B. 8975. "Compte rendu fait au Parlement par le lieutenant général de Police de la quantité de jeux tant publics que particuliers des noms et qualités de ceux qui donnent à jouer et des banquiers des jeux " (Dulaure, *Histoire de Paris*, v. 507).

was rather the desire to repair these losses than that of putting some thousands of leagues between his wife and the Duke of Chartres. Thanks to the influence of the Princesse de Lamballe, the place was promised him as a favour to be expected. And in anticipation of the great establishment to be set up Mme. de Genlis hastened to provide herself with table linen, silver plate, dinner services, etc.

Suddenly the dismissal of the Minister of Marine, M. de Bômes, and the appointment as his successor of M. de Sartine, "a personal enemy of M. de Genlis," put an end to all these fine plans. At least this is the version of it supplied by Mme. de Genlis, who adds: "To tell the truth, I was not sorry for it,"—a light-hearted way of taking it, with which perhaps the influence of a certain Prince had something to do.

Besides, her active mind, always eager for occupation, was already busy with other plans. The Countess was purposely turning her energies in the direction of educational work.

First of all, she got up a course of physical science for fashionable people at M. Sigault de la Fond's. It was soon followed by a course of chemistry applied to the arts at Mittouart's, the King's chief apothecary. She succeeded in attracting regularly to these lectures more than twenty-five people belonging to the Court—the Comtesses d'Harville, de Jumilhac, and de Chastenet; the eldest daughter of Lazare du Crest, now Marquise d'Arcambal; Mme. de Meulan; the Chevaliers de Cossé and de Chastellux, M. de Guibert, the Comte de Custine, etc. etc., without forgetting M. de Genlis himself.

Then, by a remarkable happy inspiration, she prepared the way for that apostolate of education which within a few months she was to exercise in so brilliant a manner, by arranging for her daughters and their girl friends to give representations at her rooms of charming little comedies from her own pen. These were real gems of delicate art, truth to nature and tactful grace. They were masterpieces of moral teaching shown in action for the use of children, but with such an insight in the choice of subjects and such an unusual knowledge of theatrical expedients, that their scope was far beyond that of a play for children, and placed them far above the productions ordinarily intended for young people.

Nothing better in this style than these works of Mme. de Genlis has ever been done.

She had a genius for the theatre and for educational work, and from her earliest youth she had given evidence of both in her strange disposition. And now in her first attempt she reached perfection.

Even before an act of generosity was the occasion for their author having them published, these little dramas, played in Mme. de Genlis's salon, had delighted the society of the day, and the taste she had displayed in them called forth flattering echoes from the literary world.

On the occasion of the second representation a hall that could seat five hundred was found to be too small for the crowd of aristocratic lovers of the stage, who were moved to tears by Pulchérie and Caroline de Genlis, only eight years old and already pupils of Mlle. Sainval. In the audience literature was represented by Dalembert, Marmontel, La Harpe, Diderot, and the Abbé le Monnier, all brought by the Vicomte de la Tour du Pin. The friend of Julie de l'Espinasse expressed his emotion to Mme. de Genlis in an " obliging note." [1]

La Harpe, who now saw the Countess for the first time, had felt " one of the sweetest impressions I have ever experienced in my life," and celebrated it in lyric fashion in a set of wretched verses, which he sent next day to the Palais Royal. Here are two of his laboured stanzas:—

> "Non, ce que j'ai senti ne peut être un prestige,
> Non, j'ai su trop bien en jouir,
> Et si l'on doute d'un prodige
> Comment douter de son plaisir.
>
> . . . . . .
>
> Ton art, belle Genlis, l'emportant sur le nôtre,
> Ne fait parler qu'un sexe et charme l'un et l'autre

---

[1] Mme. de Genlis, under the impulse of political feeling, wrote later on: " M. Dalembert wrote me on the subject of education things that would make the hair of anyone who quoted them stand on end. They were pompous eulogies which good feeling, not modesty, prevents me from reproducing, for there was nothing in them to be proud of " (*Précis de ma conduite*, 274).

> Que tes tableaux sont vrais dans leur simplicité.
> Tu peins pour des enfants, mais la maturité
> Et se reconnaît et t'admire," etc.

In July 1779, Mme. de Genlis was deeply touched by the fate of four gentlemen of Bordeaux, the Messieurs de Queissat, who were condemned to pay 75,000 *livres* in damages to a business man of their city, and being unable to do so, were imprisoned with the prospect of remaining there for the rest of their days; and she had the idea of publishing her delightful comedies for their benefit. The venture had a triumphant success. The first five hundred copies were snatched up at unheard-of prices. Twice and three times the twenty-four *livres* asked for each volume were paid for them. The Queen and the Princesses headed the subscription list. The Empress of Russia and the Electress of Saxony caught the enthusiasm and had the little book translated, and the Electress even wrote to Mme. de Genlis to ask for her friendship.

All the papers of the time without exception praised the *Théâtre à l'usage des jeunes personnes*.[1]

La Harpe, in a letter to the Grand Duke, spoke of Mme. de Genlis as "the woman in all Paris who had perhaps the most brains," and said that her piece, entitled *La Mère rivale*, "would perhaps be worthy of the Théâtre Français if the author would incur the risk of producing it there."[2] Then, becoming quite excited on the subject, he began again to make rhymes in honour of the "fair Genlis," like an admiring and foppish young gallant. Now he dedicated to her his *Trois langages*; then, annoyed at a clumsily written eulogy of the Comtesse in the *Année littéraire*—"that rhapsody which for a long time has hardly been read anywhere except in the cafés"—he mended his pen and exclaimed—

> "Devant les Déités du Cnide et du Parnasse,
> Le don le plus grossier se mêle au pur encens.
> Un lourdaut (sic) peut sentir la grâce;[3]
> Un sot a loué les talents," etc.

---

[1] *Théâtre à l'usage des jeunes personnes*, Chez Panckouke, Hôtel de Thou, Rue des Poiterins, 8vo (1779–80).
[2] La Harpe, *Correspondance littéraire*, Lettre LXXXI.
[3] *Ibid.*, Lettre CXIV.

Or when Mme. de Genlis goes away to the country, he writes in Petrarchian fashion—

> "Ah ! Genlis, ne nous quittez plus !
> Nous sommes tous heureux du désir de vous plaire,
> D'un seul de vos regards nos soins sont trop payés.
> Vous voyez près de vous un époux, une mère,
> Vos enfants dans vos bras, et nous tous à vos pieds."

A little later Grimm[1] himself honoured the *Théâtre* with a long analytical review, in which, contrary to his custom, the criticism was interwoven with praise. In a word, there was no one more in fashion than Mme. de Genlis, who had become the object of a real enthusiasm.

It must be added that meanwhile an important event served to increase her importance and surround her name with respect and prestige.

On 23rd August 1777 the Duchess of Chartres had given birth to twins, and the little Princesses had been entrusted to Mme. de Rochambeau, until the time when their governess could undertake their education.

Then in the enclosure of the convent of Bellechasse the construction of a detached building was begun. The governess was to retire to it in order to devote herself completely to their education.

Now, this governess was to be no one else but Mme. de Genlis.

"It had been long settled between us,"[2] she says, "that if the Duchess of Chartres had a daughter, I would be her governess, and that instead of taking charge of her when she was fifteen, I would take her from the cradle."

She had made up her mind in advance, she tells us, not to educate her at the Palais Royal, but to place herself in a convent with her.

But could the Comtesse de Genlis thus desert the elegant Palais Royal ? Could she exchange her brilliant life at Court for life in a cloister, or at the very least for the merely scholastic and quasi-monastic life of a boarding-school teacher ?

---

[1] Grimm, *Correspondance*, July 1779.
[2] This promise, it seems, dated from the time of the visit to Italy.

Why should she retire from the world, in complete health, only thirty-one, with still youthful features and a graceful figure, and without any pecuniary gain; for notwithstanding the generous offers made by the Duke of Chartres, and although there were two Princesses, she would not accept anything more than the allowance of 6000 *livres* fixed by the regulations.

It seemed a colossal sacrifice.

But Mme. de Genlis liked winning wagers.

She had proved this already by giving up the use of rouge as soon as she was thirty. "It was," according to a contemporary, "the age when some women of the great world, out of affectation, ceased to dance or to wear flowers. It was a way of prolonging the youth of those who were pretty and well preserved."[1] When Mme. de Genlis announced her intention of marking the occasion by giving up rouge, the Duke of Chartres laughed at her, said it was only a piece of feminine coquetry, made a bet on it . . . and lost. On 26th January 1776 the Countess appeared at the Palais Royal without rouge. The next day she found seated at her writing-table a life-sized doll, pen in hand, before a quire of fine paper, and within reach were thirty-two octavos of blank paper bound in green morocco and twenty-four others bound in red morocco, displaying all the bright newness of their gilt edges. At the feet of the figure lay a large cardboard case furnished with notepaper, envelopes, sealing-wax, gold and silver powder; a penknife, a compass, a ruler and scissors completed the present. The Duke of Chartres had lost his bet and was paying his debt in a way that was both gallant and ingenious.

"It is strange," said Mme. de Genlis at a later date, "that though I always had religious feelings, yet all the devout sacrifices I have made were not inspired by religion, and it is a thing I am sorry for." We can therefore without doing her an injustice reckon up the advantages she would derive from her apparently claustral retirement at Bellechasse.

In quitting the Palais Royal Mme. de Genlis did not

[1] Comte de Trémont, *Notice inédite*.

really give up what was most valuable to her there, namely, her close friendship with the Duke and Duchess of Chartres, but she gained in so far as her conduct would no longer be subject to the unceasing and malevolent inspection of the courtiers, so that she would enjoy the freedom of action that she valued, and have the time and the quiet that were necessary if she was to pursue the literary career of which she had made such a brilliant beginning. She would no longer be the mark of ill-will, jealousy, and spiteful epigrams.

Instead of living continually on her guard, in a state of war that her smiles hardly disguised, Mme. de Genlis would regain her independence. She would be the mistress, and the absolute mistress, of the Princesses. Finally, there was the glorious thought that she was walking in the footsteps of Mme. de Maintenon.

Beautiful and younger than the widow of Scarron, she was, like her, about to rule over a little world of her own, withdrawing far from useless distractions, with the royal children and their nurses, and like her, too, devoting herself entirely to her new duties, moulding as she pleased these young minds and watching over them night and day.

Where Mme. de Genlis broke with the tradition left by her austere model was in reserving her appointment and her rooms at the Palais Royal for her daughter Caroline, for the days when, after her marriage, she could have the benefit of both.

But as Mme. de Maintenon had not a daughter, one cannot say what she would have done if the existence of children had forced her to take their future into consideration.

The convent of Bellechasse,[1] a house of the canonesses of the Holy Sepulchre, known also as the nuns of Lorraine, then occupied the large rectangle between the Rues St. Dominique, de Grenelle, de Bourgogne, and de Bellechasse—that is to say, very nearly the site now occupied by the basilica and the square of Sainte Clotilde and the Rue Las Cases. The front of the buildings looked upon the Rue de

---

[1] The community at the end of the eighteenth century was composed of twenty-four nuns and six lay sisters. It had an income of over 30,000 *livres* at the time of the Revolution (Arnaud, *Adélaïde d'Orléans*, p. 20).

Bellechasse, and on that side was the main entrance. But the gardens extended lengthwise between the Rues de Grenelle and St. Dominique as far as the Rue de Bourgogne. It was on the side looking out on the Rue St. Dominique, in the garden to the left of the convent, that the Duke of Chartres caused to be built for the young Princesses and their teacher a detached building, of which Mme. de Genlis, acting as an amateur architect, had drawn the plans.

It was a square house with one storey above the ground floor, in a simple and regular style without ornamentation. It was connected with the convent by an alley of trellis-work, roofed with oilcloth, along which a vine was trained. Before the front door, opening on the Rue St. Dominique, was an iron rail and gate, of which the nuns kept the key.

After the Revolution this building became a dwelling-house with a courtyard opening on the end of the present Rue de Solférino, and was numbered 18 (or, according to M. Lenôtre, 11 and 11 *bis*) in the Rue St. Dominique. And in our own days, before a great modern erection took its place, there was still to be seen, it appears, instead of the iron rail a screen of sheet-metal " painted to represent curtains falling in folds " flanked by two niches in which lightly draped figures of women seemed to invite the visitor— " one smiling with her little foot advancing as if in a gliding step of a dance ; the other turning her head away half pettishly, and with a sweeping gesture bringing an upraised finger to the corner of her lips."[1]

In the time of Mme. de Genlis the interior of the building, its arrangement and decoration, all, even to the smallest details, told of the educational purpose for which she had designed it.

It was so arranged that day and night she could watch over her pupils.

Her own room was hardly separated from that of the Princesses by a glass door without any frosting on the panes, and with no curtains. From her bed the governess could see all that happened in her pupils' room. She has described for us, with a touch of pride, this room for the children,

[1] Lenôtre, *Vieilles maisons, Vieux papiers* (*Temps*, 29th December 1909).

with its walls adorned with panels painted in oil, on which, on a background of sky-blue, medallions in monochrome represented the seven Kings of Rome and at least six dozen of the Emperors up to Constantine, with their Empresses, copied from Roman medals. From the dawn of their intelligence the twins could see above the door the chief exploits of celebrated men, on two large folding-screens the portraits of the Kings of France, and on hand-screens scenes from mythology. All the staircase was devoted to geography. The whole length of the walls was covered with hanging maps, which could be taken down for lessons—those of the southern countries at the lower end of the stair, those of northern lands higher up. Finally, an English maid and one who knew how to speak Italian perfectly were chosen for the Princesses.

Having thus organised the surroundings in which her teaching was to be carried on, the new governess, after having been fêted at a state dinner, given in her honour by the Duke and Duchess of Chartres, entered in triumph into Bellechasse, " that refuge where I was to exercise so sweet a sway." She was accompanied by her mother, now a widow, and her daughters, who followed her into her retirement.

One may ask, no doubt, with the latest biographer of Marie Adélaïde, what precisely she could do for Princesses so young as these ?

First of all, she had to share with the Duchess of Chartres, who came and spent a part of the day with her children, the sweet cares of motherhood, the smiling and kissing and singing by the cradle. But to talk about education, and discuss its various methods, was so much the fashion with mothers since Jean-Jacques, that this had to be a part of the programme till the Princesses were old enough for practical applications of the theory.

As there were no lessons to be done, no teaching to be given, the governess at least took care to show that she was a good housekeeper. A great lady now, she clung to her reputation for this practical business, " because it is ordinarily denied to women who like reading and cultivate literature and the arts." She therefore organised the household arrangements of Bellechasse, and examined each day the prices of supplies for the kitchen; but, refusing to handle the money, she sent those who brought the bills, after she had properly checked them, to be paid by the Duke's treasurer. And this very admirable method once more reminds us of Mme. de Maintenon.

But the monastic peace in which she lived in the midst of this district of great houses and convents allowed Mme. de Genlis to abandon herself undisturbed to her favourite studies. In the evening after eight o'clock her familiar friends came to see her—the Duke and Duchess of Chartres very often, also the Marquis du Crest, the Balincourts, three or four of her inner circle; but the Duke of Orleans was never seen there, or Mme. de Montesson. They never set foot in Bellechasse.

At ten o'clock no stranger was to stay any longer within the bounds of the convent, and the portress closed the gate. However, the servants had the key of a little door opening on the street, and no doubt in case of need use might be made of this.

But every Saturday, from six to half-past nine, the governess held a reception. Her favourite guests were men of letters and artists; for the greater was her own recognised success, the more she liked to meet celebrated people and deal with them like one great power treating with another. So we find that these Saturday gatherings had very learned elements in their composition.

The most notable guest was Buffon, now full of years and fame, venerable, illustrious, and yet always ready to burn incense before "his noble daughter." Other incense-bearers were Gaillard, the historian, an easy-going gentleman; the Abbé de Vauxelles, famous as a bibliographer; the Chevalier de Chastellux, enthusiastic and eager; M. de Sauvigny, more eager and ardent still; Marmontel; the sarcastic Rulhières: they formed her ordinary circle. To these must be added the names of two regular visitors, men of letters and rather inclined to pedantry—Bernardin de St. Pierre and La Harpe. The latter was misanthropic, a grumbler, suffering from his own ill-humour, and though a friend of Rousseau by no means a philosopher in his way of living. "He went away before the rest, and always in bad humour,"[1] for he was worrying about the expected success of his *Études de la Nature*. The former, a passionate admirer of the fair mistress of the house, came dressed with excessive care, was affected in his conversation, stiffly dignified in his bearing, and, says Mme. de Genlis, "made no secret of his own opinion of his pretensions being all-sufficient." He avenged himself for the coldness of the idol to which he offered incense by letting fly in the conversation a number of sarcastic and spiteful remarks.

Sometimes Mme. du Deffand would find her way to Bellechasse, and her sad scepticism, full of bitterness as it was, would break out in more irritable remarks than usual if Dalembert happened to be present. For he came often enough with M. de Schomberg, sending beforehand one of his essays fresh from the printing press,[2] an act of homage always appreciated by an authoress. But she gave him in return even less of literary praise than of the favour of her good graces. For she disliked the appearance, the falsetto voice, the acrid, mocking, burlesque, and caustic tone of the *philosophe*. Perhaps unwittingly he reminded her of a certain salon in the Rue Neuve St. Paul, where, it will be remembered, he had come to pay tactless compliments to a little harpist, poor but already famous. Alas! she was no longer the simple-minded débutante whose sallies and self-willed jests well suited her fresh, childish looks. A condescending dignity befitting her new and important post of instructor to Princesses of the royal race was now the all-pervading characteristic of Mme. de Genlis's manners and bearing. And it was from this time that she began to assume the austere mask under which those of later years generally saw her. It was since she had established herself at Bellechasse that there was noticed in her that touch of pedantry which, according to a contemporary, "took from her one of the charms of her sex, simplicity . . . and which irritated the captious, imposed on the foolish, amused those who saw

[1] Arnaud, *op. cit.*, p. 40.
[2] "D'Alembert sent me his essays as soon as they were printed" (Genlis, *Souvenirs de Félicie*, ii. 317).

through it, and took in those who had not time to look closely into it."[1] Of course the life of Mme. de Genlis at Bellechasse was not a cloistered retirement like that of the nuns. At certain times she left the convent, went about Paris, and visited her friends.

According to Lefeuve,[2] it even happened sometimes that she received them in the privacy of a charming place of refuge. The historian of the old houses of Paris tells us that M. de Genlis owned in the Rue des Amandiers Popincourt one of those luxuriously furnished mansions that were so numerous in the eighteenth century, and were then called "follies" after having been known under the Regency as "petites maisons." The house had been the scene of his bachelor dissipations. It was the "Folie Genlis," a large and fine mansion surrounded by a little park and gardens. "The interior was enriched with wonderful paintings and sculptures. A small Greek temple adorned with statues was among the outbuildings. There was a parlour with mirrors, the entrance to which was defended by the figure of an armed warrior; the warrior's lance, moved by a spring, was lowered and presented in salutation to the visitors as they entered." The house, we are told, had been placed by the Count at his wife's disposal, and she used to come there to enjoy the delights of conversation in company with her cousin M. de Tressan, and some famous men, especially Gluck and Buffon.

The story is not without its points of interest. It opens the way to more than one theory. But, unfortunately for it, the "Folie Genlis" really belonged not to the Count, but to his brother the Marquis, who gave it to his wife, *née* Villemeur, no doubt in partial restitution of her dowry, which he had squandered in his dissipations with La Duthé. So when Lefeuve hints at scandals connecting the authoress of the *Veillées du Château* with the "Folie Genlis," is he not confusing Mme. de Genlis with her sister-in-law, who was said to have taken reprisals on her husband by conduct even more lax than his own?

[1] Cf. *Galerie des Dames françaises*, Polixène.
[2] *Anciennes Maisons de Paris*, 1873.

There is nothing to show that even the fine description of the house is correct. Lefeuve tells us what it was like when he saw it in 1856. But the "Folie" had been rebuilt by the sculptor Carbonneau, who certainly must have changed its original arrangements. All these reasons must make us doubtful as to the presence of Mme. de Genlis at the mansion in the Quartier Popincourt. But there is reason to believe that besides Bellechasse the governess had another place in Paris. According to a tradition preserved in the Quatremère family, she lived for some time in rooms in one of the two houses, both of which are now numbered 6 Rue de St. Dominique. Perhaps this lodging was intended for a place for meeting politicians during the Revolution; perhaps it served for other purposes. In any case, it would seem that Mme. de Genlis had thus provided herself with a shelter outside Bellechasse, where she could go when she wished, and have more freedom than inside the walls of a convent.

Mme. de Genlis discharged the duties of governess during about five years.

The Duke of Chartres had engraved in London "in black and white" a print showing the teacher with her two daughters and the two Princesses. Below the print, which was entitled "The Governess," there were verses specially composed by La Harpe, celebrating the talents and the maternal love of the teacher.

And indeed this La Harpe, with his facile rhymes, had made himself indispensable. His pen was always ready for an appropriate verse. If the young Princesses presented the Duchess with a drawing on her birthday, La Harpe at once added a quatrain as its inscription.

The Duchess was present at the marriage supper of Caroline de Genlis, who married in 1779 a Belgian nobleman, the Marquis Becelaer de la Woestine, a rich match well regarded at Court: La Harpe addressed to Her Highness a couplet composed at the table. The young bride on the same occasion presented to the Duchess an allegorical drawing representing virtue surrounded by its attributes, and again it was La Harpe who versified its dedication and inscribed with his own hand its pompous phrases below the drawing.

He could hardly in decency be so troublesome as to present himself every day at Bellechasse : but are verses ever out of place ? So his were continually arriving there, full of exaggerated praise, and dull even to stupidity.

On 1st January 1780 he sent his " poetic tribute " with the *Maxims* of La Rochefoucauld, his New Year gift to Mme. de Genlis. This was what he said : [1]—

> "Voici du cœur humain ce sinistre interprète,
> Ce moraliste redouté,
> Qui médisait de tout auprès de La Fayette,
> Ce peintre sévère et vanté,
> Qui d'un triste crayon noircit l'humanité,
> Près de vous, ô Genlis, eut changé de palète (*sic*)
> Et vous voyant aussi parfaite, il eut peint la nature en beauté," etc.

As was anticipated, the young Marquise de la Woestine took possession of her mother's appointment and rooms at the Palais Royal.

As has been mentioned, Mme. de Genlis had invited Mme. d'Andlau, now a widow, to live with her at Bellechasse.

In the beginning of January 1782 the eldest of the little Orleans twins, Mlle. d'Orléans, was attacked with an illness " which was stated to be measles or scarlatina, but was really nothing less than smallpox," and there was grave anxiety about her.

The Duchess of Chartres came to stay beside her daughter, and would leave to no one else the duty of caring for her, while Mme. de Genlis took away to the château of St. Cloud the other Princess, whom it was necessary to remove from the danger of infection.

But in spite of the doctors and of the most devoted care, Mlle. d'Orléans succumbed on 6th February. Her sister Adélaïde, who had so far been known as Mlle. de Blois, then took the title of d'Orléans.

A month before this to the very day—on 6th January 1782—a surprising piece of news, which no one could credit,

---
[1] La Harpe, *Correspondance littéraire*, Lettre cxx.

flew from Paris to Versailles, and in the twinkling of an eye went the round of the salons. The Duke of Chartres, in some incomprehensible whim, " had just dismissed the governors and deputy-governors appointed ten years before for his two sons, the Duc de Valois and the Duc de Montpensier, in order to hand over for the future the entire care of their education to the gentle Comtesse de Genlis, already the instructress of his daughters the two Princesses." [1]

[1] *Journal du libraire Hardy*, 8th January 1782.

CHAPTER VI

THE GOVERNOR OF THE PRINCES

OF all the singular proceedings with which the Duke of Chartres from his youth upwards had been in the way of setting people talking, the appointment of Mme. de Genlis to the post of governor of his sons, the young Princes, was the most unexpected. If we are to believe the lady, she found herself unexpectedly the object of a choice which, she says, "nothing had ever led me to anticipate."

There was a curious scene at Bellechasse one evening between eight and nine o'clock. The Comtesse was all alone in her rooms, expecting her august friend, who generally paid her a visit at that hour. When he came, he was disturbed, excited, in a bad humour. He declared pointblank that he could no longer endure M. Bonnard, the "sub-governor" of his sons. In the way in which things were going on, they would soon have the manners of "shop-boys." Had not the eldest that very morning had the impudence to say that he had been regularly "drumming" at the door; and during a walk at St. Cloud that he was "very much tormented by his relations"—meaning the insects spoken of as *cousins!*

Really this was intolerable. So the Duke had come to consult Mme. de Genlis as to the choice of a governor, who would put the "sub-governor" in his proper place.

She proposed several names in succession. M. de Schomberg? He would make the boys into pedants.

The Chevalier de Durfort? He was too solemn; too emphatic. M. de Thiars? He was levity personified.

"Then," adds Mme. de Genlis, "I began to laugh, and I said to him, 'Well, what about me?'"

Strange to say, the Duke did not move a muscle. He seemed prepared to hear this wild proposal; one would have said that he had foreseen it. At once his lips murmured, "Why not?"

And, stranger still perhaps, Mme. de Genlis at once accepted. Anyone else would have played the part of being taken by surprise, would have pretended to think it was a jest, would have protested. She, on the contrary, was delighted, and took the chance as soon as it presented itself. "The manner and the tone of the Duke of Chartres," she says, "made a very strong impression on me. I saw the possibility of something quite out of the common, something famous, and I hoped that it might be possible for it to be realised. I told him quite frankly my thoughts. The Duke seemed charmed, and said to me, 'Well, it's done. You shall be their governor.'"

On the Epiphany all Paris learned the latest new departure of the Duke of Chartres—a regular *coup d'état*. It created an extraordinary sensation everywhere, an immense agitation of public opinion, the echoes of which went on for some months to come.

Nothing else but this event was discussed in conversation and in correspondence, in the newspapers and news-letters, among gossips and sensible people, in the Court and in the city.

And whatever Mme. de Genlis may say, the thing was not generally approved of—" rather it called forth general ill-will." [1]

It was whispered that, notwithstanding the Duke's well-known disregard for conventionalities, it might well be at Bellechasse that the idea had its origin. It was asked if the Duchess of Chartres had been consulted; and no one could say, because her maternal anxieties soon made Her Highness a prisoner at the bedside of her sick daughter, and cut her off from all relations with the outside world. But her friendship for Mme. de Genlis at this time does not permit any doubt of her approbation.

[1] Cf. Toulotte, *La Cour et la Ville*, i. 17.

MME. DE GENLIS.

When the Duke, in fulfilment of his duty, asked the opinion of the King, Louis XVI. replied, with a shrug of the shoulders, " Happily I have the Dauphin. The Comtesse d'Artois has her children. You have the right to do what you please with yours." [1]

Naturally the Court made the most of the royal ill-humour ; the Palais Royal, with its jealousy of the Genlis, was even more hostile. The bourgeoisie criticised a step which went beyond established usage, and the publisher Hardy, echoing its respectable feelings, did not think that " the example given by the Duke of Chartres ought ever to find any great number of imitators." Even foreigners mixed themselves up with the affair. " One cannot say," writes M. de Kageneck, " what new theory of education has led this father to entrust his sons to the hands of women so long after the time when all Princes take theirs away from them." [2]

As soon as the appointment was officially notified—in the last days of February 1782—there was a shower of songs, little poems, epigrams of all kinds.

" Here," says Garat, " they talk for two or three days about a battle won or lost, and then the success or failure of a comic opera soon makes people forget about it. It is not so with the adventure of Madame de Genlis. It has now for more than a month been the chief subject of conversation, and every day there is a renewed outburst of couplets, sarcasms, and puns." [3]

The jokers of Versailles started a report that the Duc de Luynes, whose stupidity was proverbial, had asked for the post of nurse to the little Dauphin. And the story went that, when His Majesty asked a nobleman of the Court about it, he got the reply, " Sire, however powerful the Duke of Chartres may be, I can hardly believe that he will ever succeed in changing a woman into a man." [4]

[1] The reply of Louis XVI. has been variously reported, but these variations do not change its sense. Cf. Kageneck, Garat, Prudhomme, *op. cit.*
[2] Letters of Kageneck to Baron Alströmer, 1782, p. 388. Cf. *Correspondance secrète inédite*, publiée par M. de Lescure, i. 455.
[3] Garat, *Précis historique de la vie de M. le Chevalier de Bonnard*, 103.
[4] *Ibid.*

Talleyrand, later on, attributed the event to the vanity of the Duke. But, after all, at that time it was an easy pretext for the " furbishing up of old stories that had been forgotten."

In Mme. de Montesson's circle they were humming—

> "Être prude, être galante,
> Mêler la gloire à l'erreur
> Fut l'art de la gouvernante
> Pourquoi pas du gouverneur ?
> De cette femme charmante,
> Ne plaignons point le Destin.
> On peut bien être pédante,
> Sans pour cela cesser d'aimer le genre humain."

There was undeniable truth in the gossip which alleged that feminine failings had prepared the way for this masculine appointment. Truth has sometimes ugly aspects. Besides, Mme. de Genlis herself thought it well to cast a veil over them. When her *Memoirs* appeared in 1825, and especially that charming account of the famous evening when the Duke seemed, as if on a sudden impulse, to have appointed her governor, the story was to be contradicted by the son of the Chevalier de Bonnard.

" One may be allowed," he wrote, " to regard as incorrect this account of the manner in which the Duke of Chartres suddenly decided to appoint Madame de Genlis governor to his children. The papers in my possession contain suggestions of very different circumstances, and point to the decision having been brought about by preparations made long in advance." [1]

At the same time the *Genlisiana* recalled the fact that the public in 1782 named La Harpe assistant governess, attributing, in a spirit of exaggeration, to the author of *Les Barmécides* " the greater part of the writings of Madame de Genlis." [2] And in fact there is to be found among the minor records of the period before 1789 an epigram that had been quietly handed round in this scandal-loving world, which is an attack on the critic and Mme. de Genlis.

Before this chorus of jest and sarcasm Mme. de Genlis did not for a moment lose her self-possession. She would

---

[1] *Journal des Débats*, 26th May 1825.
[2] Cousin d'Avallon, *Genlisiana*. Cf. also Nougaret, *Anecdotes*, ii. 190.

indeed have had little foresight if she had not anticipated all this clamour. The reality was, in fact, something less than she expected, and the outburst less terrible than she had feared.

She was not afraid of being talked about. It is opinion, says Pascal, that makes success. The Countess therefore took possession of her new post with incomparable assurance. By what mistaken sense of shame could she disguise her joy at it ? This title of " governor" was a superb triumph, a brilliant glory for her, a halo round her name.

Her pride exulted, and all her being glowed with a haughty sense of the intoxication of success. One can see it in the delightful miniature at Chantilly, that portrait with its daring charm which " has an expression of real triumph, and must be as good a likeness mentally as physically." [1] When one has seen it, one feels that Mme. de Genlis was the kind of woman to put the railers to silence.

Usually the governors, while nominally presiding over the education of their princely pupils, confided, for good reasons, the active part of their duties to subordinates. The Comtesse de Genlis, a governor in petticoats, did not mean to have the title without the duties, and was resolved on justifying her ambition by the knowledge she displayed.

Capable as she was of instructing and communicating science, she decided not to leave to anyone else the task of teaching her pupils what she had acquired with patience and resolution. A woman called to an office which till then had belonged only to men, she thought she could do better than any man; and at the price of her freedom and her repose, though not of her own personal likings, she assumed the task of educating the descendants of Henri IV.

It was she, then, who was to dole out to them each day instalments of history, mythology, grammar, literature, and the arts, without counting good advice and the incessant care such a duty required—a difficult, fatiguing, heroic task, worthy of a Fénelon and not of a Maurepas.

But since she had the toil, she must also have the honour

[1] Gruyer, *La Jeunesse du roi Louis Philippe*, 28 (this portrait is the frontispiece of the present work).

of it. Mme. de Genlis was intent on this above all else in the world, and she gave proof of it by once more refusing the salary of 20,000 francs offered her by the Duke.[1] In return she insisted upon full powers and an almost unlimited resignation of the father's authority into her hands. She meant to be " absolute mistress " of the education of the Princes. From the day when she took up her duties, " Madame le Gouverneur " made her authority felt, and let it be clearly understood that she placed in the first rank the virtue of obedience. To submit or to resign, such was implicitly the watchword of her joyous accession to her post; and the first victim of it was the gentle, upright, and methodical Chevalier de Bonnard.

Bernard de Bonnard was one of those men who are sensitive in heart and mind, and who direct to noble ideals the faculties of their soul and the aspirations of their life.

Affectionate, serious-minded, delicately scrupulous, " an agreeable poet, but above all distinguished by his moral character,"[2] full of gentleness and pleasantness, the Chevalier had none but friends.

Such natures seem made for quiet provincial life, with its narrow circle and its somewhat contemplative character; for family life, where their modest virtues can expand in the glow of the domestic hearth. But above all they are capable of deep and faithful attachment. They triumph in the accomplishment of long-enduring tasks, in which the example they give of continuous, persevering effort gradually wins esteem, and builds up stone by stone a solid edifice.

It was a task like this that Bonnard thought he was called by Heaven to accomplish with the Orleans Princes.

And since, according to custom, the governor—always a great noble—enjoyed his title as a distinction that gave him privileged rank at Court, and entrusted to his subordinates the care for the practical duties of his office, to be appointed sub-governor was to find oneself called to direct these young

---

[1] " The Duke of Chartres offered me 20,000 francs. I replied that such an engagement and so much care could only be repaid by friendship. He insisted in vain " (*Mémoires*, iii. 143).

[2] Michaud, *Biographie*, art. " Genlis."

minds; to guide, adorn, and develop them, and make them worthy of their name and their future. For the Chevalier "this post of sub-governor was his life, his aim, his honour. He had ardently desired it."[1]

Thanks to Guéneau de Montbéliard; to Buffon, whose disciple he had been, and to the excellent Mme. de Buffon; thanks also perhaps to Mme. de Genlis, who boasts of having been his patron,[2] Bernard de Bonnard obtained the realisation of his dream on 8th November 1778.[3]

The dream had lasted four years—for a dream here below that is something immense—when the sudden appointment of the Countess made it vanish.

According to Mme. de Genlis, the Duke of Chartres thought of leaving Bonnard his title of sub-governor for the sake of appearances. But one can well understand that to impose the rule of Mme. de Genlis on a man who had been exercising power for four years was to place that man in an impossible position. "M. de Bonnard," she says in her *Memoirs*, "felt that with me the honour of educating the Princes would not be left in his hands; that he would have to follow my ideas and not his own; it seemed to him very humiliating to obey a woman." The Chevalier gave in his resignation. It was equivalent to a dismissal.

Many have asserted that the dismissal preceded the appointment of the lady governor. This is hardly likely. The Countess herself, the son of Bonnard, and following them the latest biographer of the Chevalier, hold that the dismissal was a result of the appointment. They are certainly right.[4] In any case, the two events succeeded each other at an interval of a few hours, between the 5th and 6th of January. As soon as he heard that a governor was appointed, and that this unexpected governor was Mme. de Genlis, Bonnard retired. Both, far from attracting each other according to

---

[1] Martin-Dairvault, *Poésies du chevalier de Bonnard*, p. 12.

[2] "The Chevalier de Bonnard, who owed his place to me" (Genlis, *Mémoires*, iii. 145).

[3] He was appointed in December 1777, but did not enter upon his duties till 8th November 1778.

[4] Cf. Genlis. *Ibid.*, *Journal des Débats*, 24th May 1825. Martin-Dairvault, *op. cit.*

the laws of physics, mutually repelled each other. Too many divergences separated them. When one arrived, the other, judging that he had lost his master's confidence, went away. He enjoyed—and this, it would seem, at the request of his enemy—the same salary as if he had remained in office; moreover, an autograph letter from the Prince softened his disappointment at having to retire. The magnanimous Mme. de Genlis flattered herself that she had on this occasion obtained the highest approbation from Buffon—a mistake frankly pointed out by Nadault de Buffon in a note on his uncle's correspondence.[1]

We do not know why Mme. de Genlis was always extremely unfair towards the Chevalier, whose death came not long after.[2]

Forty-five years later she once more turns him into ridicule in her *Memoirs*, laughing at his ways, his "bad tone," his puerile poems, and his negligence. Already before this the *Journal d'éducation des princes*, published during the Revolution, contained several passages criticising the unfortunate habits that poor Bonnard had given to his pupils.

"It seems," says the son of Bonnard sadly, "that forty years after his death she could not pardon him the harm she had done him during his life."

Was it out of a kind of incomprehensible jealousy that she complained to the Duke of Chartres about the *Précis de la vie du chevalier*, published by Garat in 1785, as a homage to the memory of his friend; and that under the pretext that the Prince's letter to the sub-governor on his resignation was printed without his authority, she induced His Highness to bring the matter before the Keeper of the Seals? The latter being unable to touch an author whose work had not

---

[1] "The friendship of Buffon for Madame de Genlis cooled for a moment. He was a patron of the Chevalier de Bonnard, and with the help of the Count de Maillebois had got him a place in the Palais Royal. But he was very displeased with the conduct of Madame de Genlis towards the Chevalier. On the day when she was appointed Governor of the children of the Duke of Chartres, the Chevalier de Bonnard asked for his dismissal, and Buffon had some difficulty in forgiving Madame de Genlis for the injury she had done to his protégé" (*Correspondance inédite*, published by Nadault de Buffon, ii. 568).

[2] He died of the smallpox in 1784.

been issued for sale, turned upon the printer Didot, and sent him to spent two nights in the Bastille.[1]

We shall not try to clear up this problem of feminine antipathy. Perhaps the foundation of Mme. de Genlis's animosity was a feeling of awkward constraint. For it is said that Bonnard was a man "who was perfectly well informed as to the frivolities and failings of her youth,"[2] It would thus be of extreme importance for the Countess to send away to a distance from Bellechasse a witness who knew so much.

However this may be, the post of sub-governor fell to a M. Lebrun, formerly secretary to M. de Genlis, a good mathematician, an excellent administrator, and uprightness itself.

The Abbé Guyot remained as a tutor. "Madame the Governor," indeed, made some fun of his pretence to wit, his pedantry, his mania for repeating on every occasion, "If I may venture so to express myself." He armed himself with evangelical patience and remained. There were associated with him later, an Italian master, M. Mariottini; a chemist, M. Alyon; and a Polish painter, Myris.

M. Lebrun and the Abbé whose duty was to go over various lessons, the former in the exact sciences, the latter in religious instruction and Latin, brought their pupils every day to Bellechasse, and took them back to the Palais Royal at ten in the evening. Mme. de Genlis thus gave each day all the afternoon to the instruction and education of the Princes.

At this period only the two elder boys counted for the Governor. M. de Valois was eight, his brother, M. de Montpensier, seven. As for the youngest, M. de Beaujolais, he was still in the nursery.

Mme. de Genlis took it into her head to teach them all the knowledge of the time in all its branches. Having given her attention a little to everything in history, literature,

---

[1] Cf. Grimm, *Correspondance*, September 1785. Also at the same date a curious letter of Garat to Grouvelle, and the reply of Grouvelle. See also Rabbe, *Biographie*, art. "Genlis."

[2] Billault de Gérainville, *Histoire de Louis Philippe*, i. 11.

grammars, and dictionaries, she had enough of personal erudition, even with a tinge of theology, to form for herself an idea of the extent of such a programme of education. Her ambitious desire to surpass in this way everyone who before her had engaged in such work, her mind inspired by the writings of Rousseau and formed on the new ideas, did the rest. From the very outset her plan included those practical exercises that *Émile* had brought into fashion, notably manual work at carpentry, gardening, basket-making, etc., till then unknown to Princes of royal blood; and besides those gymnastic exercises and that physical hardening, for which, before her time and during it, reliance had been placed only on riding and hunting. Then there was the study of five or six living languages, botany, etc.

She managed it all, it must be admitted, in a splendid way, and we shall have detailed proof of this later.

But from outside, eyes inspired by ill-will were watching the college and its directress.

Although exceptional intellectual culture was not denied to Mme. de Genlis, many threw doubt upon her capacity for teaching.

She, on the contrary, felt she was illuminated with infinite light. The difficulties of her formidable task filled her with a glorious zeal. As Sainte-Beuve says: "She was something more than an authoress, she was a woman-teacher . . . born with the sign of it on her forehead." And without loss of time she proved it.

In the very month in which she became Governor, a book appeared: *Adèle et Théodore, ou Lettres sur l'éducation*. It was the reply—or the challenge—of Mme. de Genlis to public opinion. The choice, of which she had just been the object, "had, so to say, fixed all eyes upon her. It was impossible not to be curious to see whether her book would justify such an extraordinary appointment, or would make it appear more ridiculous."[1]

These familiar letters, written in an excellent style, contained, on the whole, an adaptation to practical life of the educational principles of Rousseau—who himself took them

[1] Grimm, *Correspondance*, January 1782.

from Locke—but this adaptation was so natural, so well brought down to the understanding and taste of the minds of that time, that it was hailed as if it were a miracle. People thought they recognised in it "Plato without chimerical ideas, and Fénelon under the guidance of his heart and his fine imagination."[1] No work of Mme. de Genlis, except perhaps the *Veillées du Château*, had a more successful sale than *Adèle et Théodore*.[2]

But it did not contain only a treatise on education. There were, besides, views on practical morality—morality founded on the Gospel; there was a romantic element mingling in it, with word-portraits in which, under supposed names, the author caricatured some of the ridiculous women of her acquaintance.

The intoxication of success carried away Mme. de Genlis a little. Hardly installed in her pulpit at Bellechasse, she settled herself in it and began to lay down the law in her own way. But in her imprudence she avenged herself thoroughly upon her numerous enemies for their stabs in the back. Certain caricatures were unfortunately so lifelike that the names of the victims were soon on every lip.

Mme. de Montesson, who was by this time very jealous of her clever niece, recognised herself easily in the character of Mme. de Surville, and, if we are to believe certain gossips, she bestirred herself to make things unpleasant for Mme. de Genlis.[3]

Mme. de la Reynière, scarcely concealed beneath the name of Mme. d'Olcy, had the mortification of seeing her despair of being nothing but a financier's wife advertised by the satirical Countess. However, against the "Governor's" ready sarcasm, she was able to compare the by no means

[1] Cf. Fr. Ad. de Lezay-Marnésia, *Plan de lecture pour une jeune dame*.

[2] *Adèle et Théodore, ou Lettres sur l'éducation* (Paris, Lambert, 1762, 3 vols. 8vo).

[3] Bachaumont, on whom the responsibility for the information must rest, echoes a rumour according to which Mlle. d'Orléans, who had died previously, did not succumb to measles, but to the consequences of a fall which Mme. de Genlis had carelessly omitted to mention. "Madame de Montesson," he says, "hoped in this way to alienate at any rate Madame la Duchesse de Chartres, which would make her lose her position as tutor." Hardy, the bookseller, records the same rumour.

distant time when the latter, "before her marriage with Monsieur de Genlis, was nothing but a poverty-stricken canoness, who went about playing the harp in great houses," and to whom "she had formerly had the impertinence on twenty occasions to offer dresses which were all accepted."

By this time everyone was indignant, the more so since the author of *Adèle et Théodore*, with a suggestion of very feminine conceit, appeared herself under the name of Baronne d'Almane, "in combination with every virtue and perfection."

Quite suddenly a song appeared which was commonly attributed to Mme. de la Reynière's son Grimod, better known as a gourmet than as a literary man.

It was a tissue of such offensive allusions that Bachaumont, himself a lover of gossip and spicy anecdotes, felt obliged to censure them.

A second song followed, of which the last verse run:—

> "Le matin ma tête est sensée,
> Elle devient folle le soir.
> Je suis Monsieur dans le lycée,
> Et Madame dans le boudoir."

As we see, the same accusations of intrigue were always made, but they were not of much importance at that time, being raised only by the Épinays, Boufflers, Coignys, and Houdetots. Nevertheless, they became more serious, or hit harder, when the philosophers took part in them. *Adèle et Théodore* began the open warfare which was to last for half a century between Mme. de Genlis and the *Encyclopédie*.

The philosophers, authors by profession, finding themselves held up to scorn in the name of religion and morality by a woman who could both teach and fight, felt it wrong that this woman should defend in good style opinions contrary to their own. They called it prudery and "revolting hypocrisy," and pretended to have discovered not only that the educational part of the work was a mere infusion of Locke, Rousseau, Fénelon, and Nicole, but that in addition the romantic episodes came from English and German sources, and were borrowed by Mme. de Genlis, who afterwards translated them.

The songs began afresh. Every day a pile of anonymous papers arrived at Bellechasse, and there were not wanting many little ribald verses. In fact, "all the echoes of Paris were in accord" on the score of Mme. de Genlis.

Public opinion had not subsided four months later, when it showed its indignation on Tuesday, 10th April 1782, in the Théâtre-Français. *Les Femmes Savantes* was being played that night for the second time in the new house.

The arrival of Mme. de Genlis with the Princes, her pupils, who also accompanied their father, the Duke of Chartres, was the signal for the outburst of a tempest of whistling and hooting which went on for ten minutes. The storm had scarcely stopped when the Duke of Orleans and Mme. de Montesson appeared in their box, which was opposite the Duke of Chartres, and in violent contrast, the whole house breaks out into applause. During the whole performance, the allusions—"obvious to the point of indecency"—are greeted noisily. These two lines:—

"They wish to write and to become authors,
And in this house more than in any other spot in the world"...

were met particularly by cries, stamping, exclamations, and satirical applause.

In fact, "everything that is ridiculous in the rôle of Philaminte was applied to Madame de Genlis, and everything that is virtuous and ingenuous in the rôle of Henriette was applied to Madame de Montesson, to whom people turned with much clapping of hands, while nothing but scornful and indignant glances were cast upon the other."

The following day, and for many days after, there were new verses, songs, and parodies. Paris once more made merry at Mme. de Genlis's expense, as an authoress, instructress, and blue-stocking.

Again she raised her head and braved the storm. She replied to the bursts of ironic laughter and jeers by the publication of crushing diatribes against "impiety and false philosophy."

This was perhaps hardly putting the struggle upon its proper footing. The friends of Voltaire, if they took part among the scoffers, met with many sensible, noble men, and virtuous women, at Versailles or at Mme. de Montesson's. However, one must defend oneself as best one can. It was a plucky thing for a woman to attempt to defend herself against so many enemies.

And although the epigrams and indecent songs which ran from salon to salon made public opinion doubt her virtue, Mme. de Genlis went beyond the moralists and Christian teachers in raising the religious standard, and proved that she knew more of moral philosophy than anyone! Her ardent convictions, defended with head held high and with the daring of sincerity, gained for her at any rate the Church's protection and the esteem of pious souls, against the denials of Voltaire, the atheistic sensualism of Holbach, and the licence of Diderot.

CHAPTER VII

A CELEBRATED WOMAN IN 1782

DIDEROT learned through M. de Schomberg that Mme. de Genlis was about to publish a sensational book against the philosophers, and the Encyclopædic circle became alarmed. In spite of all the epigrams, Mme. de Genlis's prestige was growing. Her name was famous abroad as well as in Paris, and her influence, principally in matters of religion and morality, could not fail to win " the opinion of the great world and the Court at the Palais-Royal." [1]

The philosophers, aware that " the bishops and parliamentarians only awaited an opportunity to proceed against the *Encyclopédie*," [2] became frightened and thought of how to prevent such a disaster.

Mme. de Montesson's opinion, on the other hand, was of equal importance. The Marquise kept house for the fat Duke of Orleans with infinite charm and good taste. The most eminent and most respected people at Court and among the writers and artists visited her salon in the Chaussée d'Antin in the winter, and the Château de Sainte-Assise in the summer.

People found it impossible to conciliate the aunt and her niece at the same time, since neither of them forgave the other for her recent elevation, and both kept each other at a distance; although, in the case of any dispute involving philosophy or religion, the two enemies would certainly have joined forces against the *Encyclopédie*—as that circle well knew.

A medium for agreement was looked for, and finally

---

[1] *Souvenirs of the Marquise de Créquy*, iii. 94.   [2] *Ibid.*

Dalembert took it upon himself to treat with the feminine powers. As he was often a visitor at Bellechasse, it was easy for him to begin with Mme. de Genlis. An excellent means of winning the consent of both ladies occurred to him, for both Mme. de Genlis and Mme. de Montesson, while differing greatly, presented the same vulnerable spot to a penetrating observer—that of their vanity as authoresses.

Dalembert, like a clever mathematician, submitted the two vanities to the same calculation, believing that the operation would infallibly bring forth the same result in both cases.

His idea was none other than to open the doors of the French Academy to their feminine talents. Dalembert would very courteously lead them towards immortality. He began with Mme. de Genlis, and invited her before anyone else to sit in the glorious arm-chair of the Forty, providing she would not attack the *Encyclopédie* and " would not intrigue with the bigots." [1] After her would come Mme. de Montesson, and then—so as to " frame " them—Mme. Necker, Mme. d'Angivilliers, and the Marquise de Créquy. This was all right so far as it concerned Mme. de Genlis, who was a woman of great promise, but as to her foolish aunt, with her insipid collection of dull, unplayable comedies, unskilfully imitated from those by Marivaux, and drawn, it is said, from twelve models—could he have seriously thought of it?

Dalembert, who was secretary for life of the French Academy, was for the moment busy only with the persuasion of Mme. de Genlis, which he undertook with great eloquence. It was a game at which he had often played, and in which he excelled.

Alas! Mme. de Genlis remained insensible to the charmer and his honeyed words. The glory of attaining immortality—when, moreover, she would have to share it with other women—did not attract her under such conditions. She wished also—and this does her honour—to preserve her freedom of thought and belief, and to be able to speak and write according to her conscience.

[1] *Souvenirs of the Marquise de Créquy*, iii. 94.

An hour and a half of arguing did not convince her, and, besides, Dalembert was the last to whom she would have yielded. He finished by saying with a touch of spite : " You will always have charm on your side, Madame, but you will not have force." " Monsieur," she replied, with an ironic smile, as she showed him out, " women have no need of it."

In this way Mme. de Genlis saved the French Academy from the feminine peril. Or so she assures us. But the anecdote is an amusing one, and Courchamps, who probably had it from the Comtesse when, during the Consulate, he visited her frequently, is the only one who confirms it, so the responsibility rests with him.

Since then, the idea of an Academy in which women might have been included has often exercised our writers. It is a remarkable thing that Mme. de Genlis has always appeared worthy of being a member of it, and quite recently the eminent critic, M. Emile Faguet, placed her in the same rank with Mme. de Sévigné and Mme. de Stael. However, at the period when (if she did as she asserts) she refused with some haughtiness the honour of a seat among the Immortals, the philosophers paid her out in return, and the opportunity was not long in coming.

In June 1782—the same year—she was imprudent enough to solicit one of the Monthyon prizes for *Adèle et Théodore*. The success of the work, the discussions of which it was everywhere the subject, the approbation and praise which it received, seemed to ensure its being crowned. The philosophic clique thereupon ostensibly interested itself in the second volume of *Conversations d'Émilie* which had recently appeared, and which was particularly dear to it more on account of Mme. d'Épinay's name than on account of the work itself.

On the whole, the two books were of much the same importance.

Mme. d'Épinay, whose book dealt merely with the education of earliest infancy, wrote in general of appropriate subjects, neatly expressed in the natural style of dialogues between mother and daughter. As became a disciple of

Jean-Jacques, the basis of the whole doctrine was the beauty and glorification of Nature.

Mme. de Genlis was more scientific. Her book was broader, more learned, and was a better treatise on education. It roused at once the reader's interest and allowed him to assist in detail in the special education which the Baronne d'Almane, an excellent instructress and authoress of a *Théâtre à l'usage des jeunes personnes*, gave to her pupils. But it firmly disputed the principles of the philosophers and the excellence of human nature as extolled by Rousseau.

Mme. de Genlis had not the slightest doubt that the Academy would feel obliged to award the prize to her. Once more she hoped to break down all barriers and enter among people in spite of their resistance. A very amusing letter from Mme. de Genlis to her cousin, the Comte de Tressan, who had lately been elected to the French Academy, shows very clearly how she went to work. Here is the essential passage from this curious epistle:—

" . . . As you speak to me with deep interest about the Academy and the judgment which it is going to pronounce, I am going to answer you with frankness. There is only one medal which could flatter me: it is the one which they are going to give; if I do not have it, they will do well not to offer me any other afterwards. I know that there is a little plot to give it to the *Conversations d'Émilie*, a little work which is known only because I praised it, and which I praised only because it is by a woman. However, this work, abounding in faults of language, without interest, full of expressions in the worst taste, is not in a position to compete.

"The first volume, the only one which can be read, and the only one which I praised, appeared four years ago. This second edition of this year offers nothing newer than a second volume, and upon the acknowledgment of everyone this second volume is detestable. Supposing it were excellent, it is not in a position to compete, since it is not a complete work. This is what you can say as coming from yourself; and, moreover, suggest to them that they read, if they can, these insipid conversations, and promise to show them at least twenty pages of phrases which are not French and of words which only chambermaids use (words in the mouth of the mother), taken from this work, which I will pledge myself to furnish you with when you want it, quoting volume and page. . . . I wish you could induce Monsieur Gaillard to attend the meeting which will decide this matter. I count greatly on his justice. As for the rest, I leave it to you to make the best of *Adèle et Théodore*, this work being above all by the author of *Le Théâtre d'Éducation*, and this author a woman. To tell you the truth, this medal will give me pleasure; but if I do not have it the injustice will be too obvious to humiliate me. I shall lose no glory and I shall gain my freedom of speech. I shall ridicule them all quite at my ease, and I know how to ridicule with sufficient grace; incapable of malice, I am one to revenge myself by piquant raillery which would attack the honour of no one, but which could bring ridicule upon some. I have a pretty little story *ready against every event, the page is prepared*; however, do not think that I have prepared this story with any design, etc. . . .

" From Saint-Leu, this Tuesday, 17th June 1782." [1]

Did the Comte de Tressan act as ambassador? He did, and acquitted himself perfectly, bestirring himself zealously in the interests of his beautiful cousin. He paid " numerous visits to gain votes "; [2] Mme. de Genlis, on her side, exerted herself in every way by " visits and overtures which were not at all customary."

The Academy naturally resented the intrigues and petty threats with which Mme. de Genlis made herself ridiculous. Some of the Immortals defended her through friendship—Buffon, Gaillard, M. de Chastellux, La Harpe, and Tressan—but the philosophers carried the day and the prize was awarded to Mme. d'Épinay!

The author of the *Conversations d'Émilie*, as La Harpe says later, " against my advice and, I believe, against that of the

---

[1] Saint-Leu-Taverny, a magnificent château surrounded by a park, which was crossed by a stream, and adjoining the forest of Montmorency, was acquired by the Duke of Orleans in 1780 to serve as a summer residence for his children. It was this château, says Mlle. Bader, which was decorated by Queen Hortense.

[2] Cf. Michaud, *Biography*.

public, has prevailed over Madame de Genlis. It is true that the latter is foolishly waging war against the philosophers. But what does that matter? Let them reply to her if she is worth the trouble, and let them crown her if she merits it. I am perhaps the one whom she has treated the worst, and I know why. . . ."

La Harpe's opinion is a valuable one to have. Tired of burning incense at the feet of an inaccessible divinity, this devotee was not long in putting it aside and taking up his sharp and bitter pen again. For the author of *Adèle et Théodore* kept her word. Her famous story, *Les Deux Réputations*, directed against the French Academy, appeared in 1784 in the *Veillées du Château*, and spared neither Voltaire, Fontenelle, Dalembert, nor even Marmontel and La Harpe. The latter, with extreme annoyance, saw himself exposed to public contumely under the name of Damoville, the type of an intriguing author, and his judgment and feelings towards yesterday's idol underwent an understandable change, of which he hastened to give proof by unmercifully criticising *Adèle et Théodore* in the *Mercure*.

In this way the Comtesse de Genlis, one of the most eminent women in France by reason of her work and position, became in a short time also one of the most criticised.

One of the slightest of the inconveniences attendant on celebrity is to find oneself a target on every occasion and to see oneself exposed daily as an object of curiosity to the multitude.

Mme. de Genlis laid herself open to gossip more than anyone else; but she continued on her way with the most perfect freedom, an enemy to obscurity in every sense. She took no heed of public opinion; on the contrary, she loved to provoke it without intermission, and during the fifteen years which are to follow people never stopped talking of her.

The excitement caused by *Adèle et Théodore* had scarcely subsided when people were gossiping again. This time it was over the marriage between Pulchérie de Genlis and the Vicomte de Valence,[1] who was supposed to be very attentive

[1] Jean-Baptiste-Cyrus-Marie-Adélaide de Timbrune-Thiembrone, Comte de Valence (1757–1822), colonel and first equerry to the Duke of Orleans, lieutenant-

to Mme. de Montesson. People insinuated that the Marquise was anxious to keep her Sigisbée, and took " the only means of attaching permanently to her person the man she loved." They wondered spitefully how Mme. de Genlis could so lightly and selfishly endanger Péky's (as she was called by her intimates) happiness, knowing the motives.

The unhappy woman has accused herself and lamented her lack of foresight. " I admit," she says, " with the sincerity which I have promised myself always to have, . . . that my ambition for my daughter in this case overcame my foresight and judgment: in principle, the motive which decided me should have prevented me from thinking of that union."

However, the Marquise, who was now a widow,[1] did more for this marriage " than anyone could have imagined." She had Pulchérie near her, and gave the young people 600,000 francs—in fact, Mlle. de Genlis did not receive any dowry from her parents—and she was able to raise her to the greatest honours. In short, if she loved " that fool Valence " we can imagine how far she would go, for she was forty-seven and he was barely twenty-nine. Pulchérie's seventeen summers had to take the chance of comparison, with disastrous results.

Should not the Comte de Genlis, however, bear the same responsibilities as his wife in this matter ?

We do not know whether he was much interested in the marriage of his daughter, marriages at that period being such flimsy ties that no one bothered much about them, save for personal advantage in high families; and M. de Genlis appeared to be very much engrossed by other matters. His love affairs and luck at cards were the subject of much scandal at that time.

He was then living as a bachelor in the Place Vendôme. Separated from his wife, he used to walk gaily along the

general in 1792, afterwards commander-in-chief of the army in the Ardennes, took the side of Dumouriez. Napoleon appointed him senator. Louis XVIII. created him a peer of France.

[1] The Duke of Orleans died on 18th November 1785. According to custom the Duke of Chartres took the title of Orleans, and that of Chartres went to his eldest son.

streets, conspicuous still for " the very courteous manners which he kept even in the worst company," and for a scepticism common to those who are quick to laugh at everything for fear of being forced to weep. According to a contemporary " he had a passion for gambling, and for every woman except his wife, with whom he lived as a mere acquaintance; he even made fun of her, and called her Mme. Livre. He enjoyed relating how different were her private life and character from those which she exhorted in her works,"[1] and he sang of his happy lot in ribald verse.

The household, founded upon one of those loves-at-first-sight of which girls dream—the fragile foundation of a still more fragile union—was now broken up entirely.

Its already precarious existence had been destroyed by Mme. de Genlis's resolution to retire to Bellechasse; a resolution which did not meet with any apparent opposition from her husband, the two having lived separate lives, in fact, for some time past. M. de Genlis was too much a man of his world and the period not to know how to save appearances. Every day, or nearly every day, he visited his wife; and this regular visit, paid between the hours of eight and ten in the evening, coincided with those of their relatives and intimates who came to join Mme. de Genlis's circle after supper, and sufficed to give the impression of a perfect understanding between husband and wife. Genlis, it has been said, hoped to find in the wife who inspired him with the noblest sentiments a more tender affection and a deeper attachment than those of which she was so lavish in speech. He was mistaken, and consoled himself after the manner of the age. Mme. de Genlis does not appear to have suffered by this state of affairs, and from this point of view she is entirely a woman of her time. She has the outward appearance of it—the big words, the deep-seated insincerity, the " religion of sentiment," the " romantic imagination," and that indescribable artificiality and verbosity which are so skilled in hiding the heart's indifference.

Wonderfully intelligent, she is at the same time truly *intellectual* because of her endless curiosity and thirst for

[1] *Mémoires d'un Émigré*, i. 420.

understanding, but although she talks unceasingly of tenderness she is little gifted in that direction; the wife of Alexis Brûlart was, rather, cold and unfeeling.

The Genlis household is licentious frivolity allied to intelligent ambition, subjected to the dissolvent influence of the Palais Royal. But it is not an exception in a society where family life is unknown, where the events which disturb it do not count outside the official register except for personal gain and self-conceit.

It was therefore not astonishing that M. de Genlis did not interfere with Pulchérie's marriage. Valence was of good family; he belonged to the Palais Royal, and his future promised to be brilliant; everything was satisfactory. Her father made no more objection than he did when, in 1785, the arrival at the Palais Royal of two mysterious little girls from England excited the greatest curiosity, as indeed it does to this day. We fall again among the enigmas of history.

In order to accustom her pupils to speak English very correctly, Mme. de Genlis had the brilliant idea of giving them as companions a little English girl of their own age. It was not as though there were no English girls in Paris, but she would have none of them. Then the Duke of Chartres wrote to London " and commissioned his correspondent, Mr. Forth (ex-secretary to the British Ambassador in Paris), to send him a pretty little English girl of about five or six years, after having had her vaccinated." A month later, Forth confided the child to the care of a horse-dealer named Saint-Denis, who was bringing the Duke a thoroughbred, with this brief letter: " I have the honour to send your Serene Highness the prettiest mare and the prettiest little girl in England."

The Duchesse de Gontaut speaks in her *Mémoires* of a charming little girl who could not speak a word of French, whom the Chevalier de Grave, First Equerry, had brought from England. Mme. de Genlis had promised to look after the future of this child, on the condition that she was never reclaimed.

She went by the name of Nancy Sims. It sounded too

common, and Mme. de Genlis gave her the more distinguished one of Pamela. "However," Mme. de Gontaut adds, "this was not enough; we looked for a family name, and that of Seymour was chosen and made known."

What was the true origin of this child? To speak frankly, it is lost in a very romantic obscurity. The mother, Mary Sims, a poor English working-girl, seduced by a young nobleman named Guillaume de Brixey, and taken by him to Fogo in Newfoundland, had given birth to it in the icy regions of that island. Later, fallen back into poverty after the death of the father, she had returned to England, and had become a washerwoman at Christchurch, in the county of Hampshire, when Forth discovered her, and offered her a small annuity, provided that Mary did not see her daughter again until her majority.

This unlikely story, which was whispered of in secret, was not credited. When, on 24th May 1785, the *Correspondance secrète* announced the arrival of Pamela and the other little girl, Hermine, its author wrote without pretence: "That they are both the daughters of Madame de Genlis, who has had them brought up under fictitious names . . . these young ladies believed themselves orphans, when suddenly they have found their parents."[1] Grimm said the same thing at greater length, and just as bluntly. He even added unpublished details: namely, that the Comte de Genlis had recognised the two children, that Mme. de Montesson took it upon herself to provide their dowries, and that the Duke of Chartres gave M. de Genlis a hundred thousand *écus* "for having so well guarded the secret which had been exacted of his paternal affection."[2]

And Mme. de Genlis might well remark that Pamela favourably resembled the Duchesse de Polignac; others also saw the hereditary dark eyes of the Orleans. Since that time, this historical enigma has never ceased to interest searchers.

According to one of them, Pamela was born in Paris in the greatest mystery on 28th February 1774; Hermine two

[1] *Correspondance secrète*, published by Monsieur de Lescure.
[2] Cf. Grimm, *Correspondance littéraire*, 17th May 1785.

years later, about 1776.¹ Now, if one remembers, certain relations begun by the journey to Forges were still continued in May 1778.

However, an impenetrable secrecy surrounds everything, so that we have to fall back on conjecture in default of documents.

Investigations, nevertheless, have been made in England. There is no official registry of births in Newfoundland to refer to, but a family of planters named Sims has been discovered in Fogo Island. A member of this family, Henry Sims, who died in 1786 at the age of eighty-five, relates that his grandfather, an Englishman living in Fogo, had a daughter. This girl, Mary Sims, had a child at Gander Bay, and sailed for Bristol the following summer on a ship captained by a Frenchman named Brixey. Since then the Sims had heard nothing of her.²

Yet more recently, Southey's Commonplace Book has given the result of researches made in Christchurch at the period when the incident was still fresh in the memory of the inhabitants of the little town.

Mary Sims was known there as a Bristol woman, living at Christchurch with her only daughter, a natural child, aged five or six years, of extreme beauty. She had consented to allow her to be sent to France to the Duke of Orleans in return for a small annuity, the amount of which is unknown to us. The business is said to have been transacted by a clergyman of the same name as the Duke of Chartres's correspondent.³ It is said that Mme. de Genlis made sure of Mary Sims's renunciation of her child, the unfortunate mother promising by a deed duly signed and registered, for the sum of twenty-four guineas once paid, never to reclaim her child unless she paid back all the money which her education might have cost up to the day when her mother's love might attempt to claim its rights.

This deed, however, remains very hypothetical, since in

[1] Nauroy, *Le Curieux; Deux sœurs de Louis-Philippe.*
[2] *Dictionary of National Biography.* Pamela Fitz-Gerald. Cf. also Lenôtre, *Vieilles Raisons, Vieux papiers* (loc. cit.).
[3] Ida A. Taylor, *The Life of Lord Edward Fitz-Gerald.*

spite of research no trace of it has been found. Among all those who have been engaged in clearing up the question, one writer alone—Monsieur Nauroy—states that he has seen an authentic copy of a deed of 1784, giving the rights to Mme. de Genlis. However, he has it that Stephanie-Caroline-Anne Sims[1] passed from the control of her mother, Mary, to Mme. de Genlis on 4th February 1780. The *Correspondance secrète*, which was usually well informed, did not announce Paméla's arrival until 1785, as we have seen, when the event was intended, it appears, to cover the introduction of Hermine to the Palais Royal. This child who, in consequence, benefited by the favours of the Orleans family, was born at Spa or Paris, according to different accounts.

Mme. de Genlis's stay in the Belgian watering-place, at a time which her *Memoirs* do not permit of being accurately determined, but which, according to the visitors' list, is found to begin on 12th June 1775, will doubtless be remembered.

We know, too, from the Countess herself what " sadness " and " affliction " she suffered at Spa.

She has taken care to make a note that she received no one, with the exception of " an Englishman of my acquaintance, Mr. Conway," to whom she confided the wretched state of her health. (Later on she saw the Comtesse Potoçka there also.)

Ought we to put the birth of Hermine down to this date —the June of 1775?

The child was, like Paméla, brought up in England and, coming mysteriously to Paris, passed for a young relation of Mme. de Genlis, Hermine de X——, whose father was supposed to have been a certain Colonel Campton. The Englishman, Conway, who was at that time a cavalry major in the service of the King of England, might well have been there providentially. Could not he or his wife, who accompanied him to Spa, have taken the child across the Channel and kept her until she was of an age to go to the Palais Royal?

---

[1] The Christian names—Stéphanie-Caroline—which appear on the official deeds, are by a curious coincidence those of Mme. de Genlis and her eldest daughter respectively.

If, on the contrary, she was born secretly in Paris, in 1776,[1] she might have been taken by a third person to Major Conway, who was again in Spa with his wife from 6th June of that very year.[2] Georgette du Crest, one of Mme. de Genlis's nieces, will say that Hermine is the daughter of an English major who died leaving his widow and child without means.

We may mention further this recent opinion that " Hermine could lay claim to an illustrious albeit irregular origin on which Mme. de Genlis was alone the very discreet confident,"[3] and await the happy chance which will discover the birth certificates of these two children. Finally, we may say that, rightly or wrongly, Pamela passed everywhere—even in Mme. de Genlis's family—for the daughter of the Duke of Chartres.[4] Later on she remembered clearly her arrival at the Palais Royal, when the Duke took her in his arms, kissed her, and himself carried her across the dark corridors to Mme. de Genlis, to whom he said, " Here is our little darling."

In those days, Bellechasse was a veritable colony of learning. Not only had Mousieur de Beaujolais, who was a delightful little man, an aristocrat to the tips of his fingers, joined the princes, their brothers and Mademoiselle, but César du Crest—the son of the Marquis du Crest, who had lost his mother and was confided to his aunt's care[5]—and Henriette be Sercey, Mme. de Genlis's niece, lived at Bellechasse and took part in the Princes' lessons.

The arrival of Paméla and Hermine therefore brought the number of students at this miniature college, which Mme. de Genlis directed with great happiness, up to eight. She was in her element. No trouble or pains were spared where her mission as teacher was concerned.

---

[1] Cf. Nauroy, *op. cit.*

[2] *Liste des Seigneurs et Dames venus aux Eaux de Spa.*   [3] Lenôtre, *op. cit.*

[4] Cf. Comte de Neuilly, *Dix années d'émigration* : Cs. A.N.F.' 6221, no. 1291 : Mlle. Paméla described as the natural daughter of Mme. de Genlis and the late Duke of Orleans, etc.

[5] The Marquis du Crest had married at Versailles, on 12th February 1775, Marie-Louise-Bonne-Alexandrine de Canouville de Raffetot. Their Majesties signed the contract. The young Marquise died prematurely on 24th October 1782, leaving a son, of whom Mme. de Genlis took charge.

It is certain that few ladies of her rank and position would have taken up such duties; especially as since the deaths of M. de Puysieulx and the Maréchale d'Éstrées, which followed each other at short distance, had made the Genlis heirs to the name and marquisate of Sillery, and to more than a hundred thousand *livres* income. Sillery was that considerable property in Champagne, in the neighbourhood of Rheims, which produced an effervescing wine that is famous to-day.

Its historian, according to a document found in the National Archives, brings the total value at that period up to 1,859,920 *livres*, without counting several buildings; the manor, lands, seigneurial rights representing about 153,000 *livres*.[1] M. and Mme. de Genlis therefore entered into a large fortune. The Countess took the title of Marquise de Sillery-Genlis, but did not change her mode of life in any way.

In December 1786, Mme. de la Woestine died in turn, and this unlooked-for catastrophe plunged all her family into grief. Mme. de Genlis felt her loss profoundly, but this did not prevent La Harpe from writing to the Comte de Montmorin-Saint-Heren on 22nd December that: " Mme. de Genlis's daughter has been universally regretted and deserved it. People talk a great deal of the grief of her relatives, of the sorrow of Mme. la Duchesse d'Orléans, in a word, of all those who knew her: but what is curious is that no one has said a word of Mme. de Genlis: it is as though Mme. de la Woestine had no mother." [2]

This soured writer has changed his incense of former days to gall and vinegar.

Posterity which has not the same reason for doubting Mme. de Genlis's maternal love will not do her that injustice. She rants of her sorrow in her *Memoirs*, it is true, and this characteristic shows clearly the depth of the imprint of theatricality which she had received when she was young, and she showed at every moment in her writings; she could not express herself with simplicity. Did she suffer? Her

---

[1] Pêchenart, *Sillery et ses Seigneurs*, p. 183. *Vide* also Young, *Voyage en France*, i. 417.

[2] Cf. *Amateur d'Autographes*, November 1866, No. 117.

pen itched to transcribe " Reflections on Grief " or to build up a chapter on resignation.

She redoubled her work and ardous studies,[1] but her affliction was none the less real—so real, indeed, that her health suffered from it. She was so shocked by the death of Mme. de la Woestine that the doctors ordered another cure at Spa.

" I did not wish to do this," says Mme. de Genlis, " on account of leaving my pupils." The Duke and Duchess therefore decided to stay at Spa with their children, out of friendship for the governess. It is during this stay that the Princes, at Mme. de Genlis's instigation, celebrated their royal mother's name-day in the Sauvinière thickets, which they had cleared, by erecting an altar to Gratitude among the heather and flowers, on which they placed sheaves, while they recited verses composed for the occasion by their governess; it was a little stage effect that was quite in keeping with the " sensitive " tastes of the period, which delighted their highnesses and proved to them Mme. de Genlis's sentiments.

The soothing effect of the waters and climate of Spa refreshed the latter after the work she had set herself while under the influence of grief which her daughter's death had caused her.

She had, in fact, just published the famous book against the philosophers, the mere announcement of which alone had frightened that society five years before.

It appeared during the month of March 1787, bearing—according to the fashion of that day—the formidable title of : *La Religion considérée comme l'unique base du bonheur et de la véritable philosophie. Ouvrage fait pour servir à l'éducation des enfants de S.A.S. Mgr. le duc d'Orléans et dans lequel on expose et l'on refute les principes des prétendus philosophes modernes*—and the preface apprised the reader that this work, written especially for the young Duke of Chartres, had been read to him in manuscript as a preparation for his first communion.

[1] Mme. de Genlis set herself to learn Spanish and Portuguese after the death of Mme. de Puysieulx.

Mme. de Genlis had, in fact, considered herself better qualified than any ecclesiastic to prepare her pupil for this important religious duty, and the Abbé Guyot had been informed that she intended not only to give religious instruction herself, but also to reserve to herself the right of authority over the mind and conscience of Louis-Philippe.

The Abbé permitted himself to make some remarks: the governess retaliated. The diary of the Princes bears the trace of these disagreements. Both stood their ground in writing, and suavely acid reproofs covered innumerable pages. " If I believe myself to possess the talent for representing religion as it is, consoling, indulgent, and necessary to happiness, may I have," says the governess, " the patience that Monsieur l'Abbé demands of me ! " (read : to leave the catechism to the Abbé !) Monsieur l'Abbé insists on saying it is for the good of education. I shall reply, with as little modesty since he forces me to it, that my works have proved that I know how to talk of religion in a manner to make it liked. I know how to do so perfectly : I have already in my life prepared two children—my own—for their first communion. I have since acquired a great deal of experience ... etc." [1] In witness whereof the Abbé Guyot, who was obviously wrong in believing himself appointed by his office to teach the principles of religion, gave in to the imperious governess, and, like Bonnard of old, sent in his resignation (November 1786). A few months previously, the young Abbé Mariottini had, for the same reasons, left Bellechasse, the " flowery inn where dwells the goddess without whom the earth would be a vast horror." And in a scathing and somewhat unedifying pamphlet, embellished with those various metaphors to which the Italian language lends itself so easily, he has left us an amusing picture of the governess's relations with her collaborators.[2] According to him, they lived under the most despotic rule imaginable at Bellechasse.

Mme. de Genlis is " a lady of excitable and brilliant imagination and of too sensitive and impetuous a heart ... "

---

[1] *Leçons d'une gouvernante à ses élèves*, i.

[2] *Alla signora di Sillery-Brûlart* (per lo innanzi Contessa di Genlis), Lettera dell' abate Felice Mariottini.

She treats everyone with the same tyranny. She makes no difference between the under-governor, the tutors, the masters for drawing, foreign languages, dancing, the dispenser or the servants. They had all to bow the head, and the more humbly they inclined, the more they enjoyed the friendship of Madame the governess. The Abbé boasts with humorous self-conceit that he possessed it to some extent. The letters addressed to him by Mme. de Genlis and published by him show evidence of a sympathetic disposition, a certain preference somewhat haughtily accorded, and of many courtly phrases and pretty words, friendly expressions of esteem for " the beautiful mind " of the young ecclesiastic, all of which mean nothing, and it is useless looking for anything deeper.

But at the least remark, the least attempt to discuss the principles of education, there came the call to order, squabbles by letter, explanations, replies without end, and the complete cessation of respect in the presence of the pupils and strangers. If they patched it up and renewed their service, her favours returned with warnings like these :

" I am always interested in my duties, firm to keep up my rights when the good of the family requires it ; unable to permit or tolerate that anyone should want the respect due to my position, my sex, and I dare say to my person, but, despising little things, incapable of taking revenge, knowing the value of friendship, and always ready to serve those who hate me." [1]

Nevertheless—again according to the Abbé Mariottini—Mme. de Genlis was very exacting as to the privileges of her sex. He complains of the " distaste " which he felt in pandering to the governess's caprices, the madrigals and love-letters which he had to write, the servile adulation and flirtations, the " maniérosa morbidezza del bel mondo Parigino, e della corte " which he had to conciliate with his serious duties as tutor. And he declares it impossible for him to be " sybarite at night and Spartan in the morning."

Without attaching too much importance to these suggestions, it must be stated that at the beginning of 1787, Mme.

[1] *Alla signora di Sillery-Brûlart* (per lo innanzi Contessa di Genlis), Lettera dell' abate Felice Mariottini.

Desrois, under-governess, was dismissed for incompatability of temper; she also left Bellechasse and retired to the Convent of the Visitation, Rue de Chaillot.

But let us return to Mme. de Genlis as a theologian. The uncomplaining departure of the Abbé Guyot left the field clear for her.

Those who, from curiosity, may read *La Religion considérée, etc.*, will doubtless wonder what influence this extraordinary instruction had on the mind of a little boy of ten. Louis-Philippe's Voltairianism is in consequence recalled to mind. The religious substance of this book is really very slight; one would say that it had all been taken from some abridged volume of apologetics.

The remainder, a long and violent attack based on copious quotations touching the existence of God, original sin, the immortality of the soul, forgiveness, etc., taken from Bourdaloue, Malebranche, Pascal, and principally from the Abbé Gauchat's letters against Voltaire, appears to be aimed at personal enemies rather than at evil principles. The tone is especially deplorable.

Mme. de Genlis fancied she was writing a theological work, and instead she strayed into controversy. Her method was more like giving Voltaire, Helvetius, Diderot, Raynal and others a number of smacks in the face, than discussing their work in a serious way. It was a curious manner in which to carry on the debate, if debate there was, since with the exception of Condorcet and Raynal, all the philosophers stigmatised by Mme. Livre were dead, Dalembert included. Of course, their disciples and their works lived to annoy the morality and piety of catholic tradition. Their friends were numerous in the literary world, and one can imagine how they rose against the self-constituted theologian!

A great deal of adverse criticism was levelled at her, and Mme. de Genlis found less support around her than when *Adèle et Théodore* was published. Grimm spitefully gave her the nickname of "Mother of the Church," and the name "caught on" wonderfully. He reflected upon "the principles hazarded with as much assurance as frivolity" in the book, and denounced with sly humour at the Sorbonne "this new method of defending religion."[1] His long article aroused many echoes. Although Mme. de Genlis lived at Bellechasse, people always considered that she lived with the Duchess of Orleans, and it seemed amusing that a religious thesis should come "from the boudoirs of the Palais Royal." And as five years' earlier gossip had named La Harpe the "father" of *Adèle et Théodore*, so the theological paternity of *La Religion considérée* was attributed to the Abbé Gauchat and the Abbé Lamourette.[2] Mme. de Genlis received at any rate the distinguished support of Buffon, who wrote her a dithyrambic letter which she did not allow to remain overlooked.[3]

However, this token of respect from the great naturalist was entirely personal; it did not influence public opinion, and Mme. de Genlis was greatly disappointed. The public would not obey her orders like the Princes at Bellechasse, where she was listened to, admired and obeyed with an unequalled veneration. Here she reigned in truth, and everything she did was the object of an ardent, almost passionate worship on the part of the Orleans children.

Mademoiselle, of delicate and nervous constitution and of extreme sensitiveness, expressed her feelings in tears and sighs. The Princes were more fervid; Mme. de Gontaut

---

[1] Grimm, *Correspondance*, April 1787.

[2] Cs. *Galerie historique des Contemporains*. Michaud, *Biographie*.

[3] In the King's garden, 21st March 1787. " My noble daughter, I have just read your new book with all the interest of friendship and that love which is renewed with every paragraph in a book written by a master's hand. A preacher both persuasive and eloquent, when you present religion and all the virtues with the style of a Fénelon and the majesty of books inspired by God Himself, you are an angel of light; and when you descend to earthly things you are the first of women and the most pleasant of philosophers. I have read with emotion the praise with which you overwhelm me, and I accept with much gratitude the place which you have created for me alone. But I view with reverence this friendship, which is my glory and the despair of my rivals. When you drew certain sham philosophers, you did not allow a single trick which characterises them to escape you; you have combined delicacy of colouring with boldness of drawing, and you have placed in the shadow all that should be there. This is what, my adorable and noble daughter, I think of your work. I congratulate you with that sincerity and that tender and respectful affection which I have vowed to you for life" (Le Comte de Buffon, *Correspondance inédite*, ii. 221).

has left recorded for us the moods of exaltation that made these children kiss Mme. de Genlis's footprints. "I had almost blushed to be left behind in the romantic devotion which everyone sought to show her," she says; "... and I confess to my shame that wishing one day to distinguish myself in affection, I precipitated myself upon the armchair from which she had just risen, and having kissed it with fervour, I found my mouth filled with dust, which calmed my devotion."[1]

We may smile at the recital of this devout and certainly blameless love, which was yet disquieting because it encroached upon the affection due to parents, and principally to the mother. The Duchess of Orleans loved her children very much more than most aristocratic mothers of the age. She clung to the outward marks of respect because her rank exacted them, but her maternal affection was profound. She would never have suffered her son to be left to the care of any valet, as, for example, the sons of Mesdames de Tilly and de Biron.

And yet the real mother of the Princes is Mme. de Genlis: "Maman" Genlis. To her their young hearts unreservedly belong, to the extent of blind submission and the subjection of their individuality, which they accepted with joy—hanging on the least word that escapes from her lips, happy at the slightest caress, the lightest kiss on the forehead, the faintest words of praise, as though they were priceless favours. Truly, this "smacked of sorcery," for Mme. de Genlis ruled by severity: "the fear with which she inspired us then doubled our desire to please her by showing admiration," says Mme. de Gontaut.

But she also ruled by justice, and she governed these children through their conscience. We have innate in us in our youth so great a repulsion to injustice, and we understand the relations of things so little, that our esteem is sure to be gained by equity.

In the innocent eyes of her pupils, Mme. de Genlis seemed as inflexible as Truth itself. When Mme. de Genlis, informed on the most varied subjects as she was,

[1] Duchesse de Gontaut, *op. cit.*, p. 6.

started the school of universal learning, their youthful intelligence was amazed and saw in her a woman of vast knowledge. It was not astonishing that she had won the hearts of these gifted children.

With the implacable and summary logic of their years, the Princes, though full of respect for their august mother, did not feel for her the same warmth of affection that they had for Mme. de Genlis, who kept it alive at every moment. They had no intercourse with the Duchess which was not semi-officially ordered. She could not fail to notice it. Fundamentally she was so timid, lacking both will power and initiative; never daring to displease the husband whom she adored in spite of his vices and dissipation, and who swore by Mme. de Genlis that she endured this impossible state of affairs in a spirit of Christian resignation.

The Duke ostensibly attached himself to Mme. de Buffon, whom it appeared his Egeria had chosen for him; but he was still to be met with at Neuilly, in the "Parc Saint-James," in amorous conversation with the governess.

"They were reputed to have quarrelled, out of respect for Madame la Duchesse d'Orléans, who had obtained this much by force of weeping," says Mme. d'Oberkirch, "and they were very much astonished to see me there. His Serene Highness had asked for the exclusion of the public from the garden, and Monsieur de Saint-James had promised it to him, but the concierge had misunderstood. . . . The Prince bowed to us without animation. The lady adopted a supercilious attitude and raised her head, looking at us like an empress. I saw her again in the evening, I no longer remember where, with her eternal harp which she dragged about with her everywhere; she pretended not to recognise me, and her haughtiness did not decrease after this."[1]

Finally, the Duchess, faithful to her beliefs as to her duties, and attached to the King as to her God, was to see the governess estrange the Duke and the Princes from these

---

[1] Baronne d'Oberkirch, *Mémoires*, ii. 376. Lamartine says: "The outraged Duchess's complaints did nothing but change the inclination into obstinacy" (*Girodins*, i. Book xi.).

secular principles, which was as great a grievance as the other, if it were possible.

The new ideas which her traditional royalism could not accept, the Duke was to make his own, and vigorously aided by Mme. de Genlis, he was to transmit them to his sons. The Princess, no doubt, had not the mind for great political schemes that Mme. de Genlis had.

However, the Revolution approaches, and it will not take the governess by surprise.

PART III

MME. DE GENLIS AS A REVOLUTIONARY

WE catch fleeting glimpses of Mme. de Genlis every now and again as we see the events of the revolutionary period passing before us in quick succession.

We become momentarily conscious of her presence following in the wake of the gods of the hour, now of Mirabeau, now of Talleyrand or Camille Desmoulins. It is, of course, no secret to anyone that she is mixed up in the operations of the party of Philippe-Égalité.

But everything she does seems clothed in mystery—to such a degree, indeed, that she herself is able to deny, sometimes in a fashion both maladroit and inopportune, that she took any part whatever in the politics of the time. This attitude of hers has helped to strengthen the view of her as a subtle and sinister figure, to be reckoned among the prime movers of the Revolution. The general belief in regard to her has come to be that she played a part in regard to Philippe-Égalité similar to that of Mme. de Maintenon, in regard to Louis XIV.

What really was her rôle? Had she really a definite plan of campaign in the politics of the time? Or did she merely drift with the ebb and flow of events, falling in with the varying currents of public opinion and the intrigues and manœuvrings of parties, without committing herself any more deeply than other philosophical onlookers and chroniclers

All we know for certain is that she was to be found

among the Revolutionaries—whether animated by the wish to see the Duke of Orleans on the throne, or whether working in the interests rather of his son, her pupil, the Duke of Chartres, we cannot say. She had long been aware of the incapacity of the father.

CHAPTER I

THE PRELIMINARIES

ONE is not a little surprised to find Mme. de Genlis formally denying in detail in her *Mémoires* that she took any part in the revolutionary intrigues, when one knows her past life—her courage, her ambition, for " there never was a woman perhaps less able to endure the slightest competition, nor more tormented by the desire to be first in everything, nor more eager to annex for herself every kind of glory."[1]

Her denials are significant to such a degree that, apart from all documentary evidence, they show clearly her political rôle

Let us therefore take her declarations; it is right to hear her defence first.

She flatly denies that:

(1) She mixed herself up in politics.

(2) That the Duke of Orleans ever spoke to her concerning his own policy, except vaguely.

(3) That, once the Revolution began, he ceased entirely to speak to her of his affairs.

(4) That she knew any of his political agents, even by sight.

(5) That she had any knowledge of the printed memoranda until they had been published.

" I add in this same matter that in order to be scrupulously truthful I must say that since the Revolution began he has consulted me on one single matter: this was relative to the regency at the time when they talked of proclaiming the King dethroned after his return from Varennes."

[1] Toulotte, *La Cour et la Ville*, i. 18.

She could not well be more explicit: she had been accused of having directed the Duke of Orleans and his party. She denies it; it is false. She continues: "Will they say I took part in politics by other means and ties? It would be as unfounded an accusation, as (in a word) I never left Bellechasse."

It is true that all her time seemed given to the education of the Orleans children, and behind the iron gates of the Rue Saint Dominique her life might be compared with that of the superintendent of a boarding-school. But with admirable foresight the governess had known how to take precautions for keeping her finger in all the politics at the Palais Royal.

The Duke of Orleans was surrounded by members of the Genlis family or their creatures.

His favourite, the confidant of his thoughts and amusements, was Sillery, otherwise Comte de Genlis, the captain of his Guards.

His chancellor was the Marquis du Crest, brother of the Countess-Governor, who had been introduced into the Palais Royal since 24th November 1785, at the annual stipend of a hundred thousand *livres*, with the use of a magnificent house opposite the Palais Royal.

His first equerry was the Comte de Valence, Mme. de Genlis's son-in-law, who in addition had just been entrusted with the military education of the young Duke of Chartres.

His business manager, Limon, decorated with the title of Superintendent of Finance, owed his position to Mme. de Genlis, through the Abbé de Cabre: this intriguer, her future intimate, became the Prince's also, through her influence, and Talleyrand speaks of his "extraordinary effrontery, his fascinating imagination, his eloquence, rich in style, extravagant and fertile in insult!"[1]

These men controlled both the Duke and his money. They gathered about them at the Palais Royal a band of ambitious and discontented people, dissolute courtiers in need of places, "people without morals or principles,"[2]

[1] Talleyrand, *Mémoires*, i. 179.
[2] Clermont-Gallerande, *Mémoires*, i. 64.

among whom were Biron, Liancourt, d'Aiguillon, La Marck, Talleyrand, Noailles, etc.

Such was the society which surrounded the Duke of Orleans in 1787, when the first signs of Mme. de Genlis's political influence were seen. Following the example of the Prince, she cherished a deep hatred for the Queen, the Polignacs, and the Comte d'Artois. In this matter she followed the traditional feud between the younger and elder branches of the Bourbon family. One created difficulties for the other, which weakened its power; and without going back to Louis XII.,[1] as Barère does, we may say that the Duke's opposition " to the abuses of the old régime and ministerial tyranny was a family inheritance."[2] It was, however, strengthened by numerous personal grievances which were notorious and more or less justified. Let us recall them briefly to memory: The refusal to give him the post of Grand Admiral of France, which should have gone to him by right on the death of his father-in-law, the Duc de Penthièvre, but which the Queen awarded to the eldest son of the Comte d'Artois, the Duc d'Angoulême; calumnies at Court after the battle of Ushant (27th July 1788), and after an excursion in a balloon; accusations concerning the premature death of the Prince de Lamballe, brother of the Duchess of Orleans; insults received at the time of the journey of Maxmilian of Austria; frequent reproaches from the King on the subject of the Duke's morals, and the opposition of His Majesty to his cousin's travels in England, where, under the pretext of keeping an eye on his capital which was for the greater part invested across the Channel, he acquired the too independent habits of his friend, the Prince of Wales, " an insubordinate son and a factious citizen ";[3] and finally, the last humiliation, the failure of the marriage recently proposed between the Duc d'Angoulême and Mlle. d'Orléans, a blow of which Marie-Antoinette was not entirely innocent, without counting the innumerable hurts to his

---

[1] Barère compares Philippe-Égalité to Louis XII., who, when he was Duke of Orleans, was calumniated, slighted, and persecuted at the Court in the same way.

[2] Toulotte, *op. cit.*, i. 49.

[3] Lamartine, *Les Girondins*, book xi. chap. iv.

self-respect which she delighted to inflict, or the sale of the estate of Saint-Cloud, which he had coveted.

The Duke hid his resentment the less as his popularity with the public increased, as it was known he was in sympathy with the general trend of its opinion. Indeed, the people began to denounce with louder voices the abuses and foolish expense at Court. Versailles was the object of general contempt. Whether they lamented more or less sincerely the people's sufferings, or whether they applauded Figaro or ranted against the ministers who came and went according to feminine caprice and never ameliorated the state of affairs —the people never ceased to decry the Court.

For the moment they made the most of the Queen, whose influence had brought Brienne into power (April 1787).

The Duke of Orleans is the personification of public discontent. Being a great lord, he commands the people's respect, and liked because of his enmity with the Court.

That which assured him preference, however, not only from the Versailles mud-slingers, but from the middle classes and the moderate party, was that great financial power which he wielded—for it is believed that he was the richest man in the kingdom by his marriage with the daughter of the Duc de Penthièvre.

In comparison with the state of the Treasury, this great monetary lever could raise the masses against royalty, more especially as their grievances, the bad administration and disorder of finances, and, finally, the new philosophy, excited their contempt for the monarchy.

Mme. de Genlis noticed all these signs of agitation. She was too intelligent and too ambitious to assist blindly at these preliminaries to the great upheaval.

Was she the first to prompt the Duke?

Was it the Prince himself who, exasperated by injustice at Court, feeling himself backed by public opinion and the popularity of which every day brought him fresh proof, took the first opportunity of his own accord to checkmate the King?

The question must remain in abeyance.

It is true that in 1787 " they did not know what they

wanted; they had always been so far from exerting an influence on the government, and they were so much accustomed to doing nothing but complain, that they complained without conceiving an idea how to act or how to make a revolution."[1] Who dreamed, therefore, of putting the Duke of Orleans at the head of the state?

He was a lover of pleasure and ease, indifferent, inconstant, of feeble and contradictory mind, happy so long as his eccentricities were flattered, but he could not be a leader; for in order to lead a party you must have a firm will, decision, courage, perseverance, and he had none of these necessary virtues. However, it would appear that Mme. de Genlis made up for it.

Though it might have been " the fashionable thing,"[2] for the Duke to pronounce himself against the Maupeou parliament, though, on 15th May 1781, he takes part in the acclamations which greeted the fallen minister (Necker), yet when he intervened in parliament on 20th September 1787, and opposed, in the presence of the King, the bill for the creation of a successive loan—he who had never taken any part in politics until now, he who could not speak in public without losing countenance at the end of three words—there must have been a stronger will to spur him on, or give him a lead, as we say to-day. This first excursion of his into the political fields has therefore been attributed to the influence of Mme. de Genlis.

Everyone who is interested in the Duke of Orleans has attempted to find the counter-party, the political complement of the Palais Royal, in the salon at Bellechasse. Not that the Comtesse's weekly receptions had taken a revolutionary colour two years before the convocation of the States-General; and the writings of Barère, upon which we rely for the description of the famous salon, do not by any means apply to the period which preceded 1789.[3]

If these gatherings constituted for the moment the principal means of Madame de Genlis's influence, they were

---

[1] Thiers, *Révolution française*, i. chap. i. (1787).
[2] A. Britsch, *Philippe-Égalité avant la Révolution*.
[3] Barère, *Mémoires*, i. 42.

attended only by literary and artistic people, and were held on Saturdays. They did not become openly political until after 1789, or, in fact, from the beginning of 1789, and took place on Sundays, without our knowing whether the Sundays put a stop to the Saturdays. Therefore, everything that has been stated concerning Mme. de Genlis's guests, her political gatherings and club at Bellechasse can only refer to the time immediately after the convocation of the States-General.

From that time, however, art and literature furnished Mme. de Genlis with opportunities for devoting herself to the process of approaching people in a skilful manner, in view of recruiting partisans for her friend the Duke of Orleans, and Bernardin de Saint-Pierre was among those who were caught with the bait of a pension.

The success of *Études de la nature* had only recently transformed the shabby, poverty-stricken philosopher into a great man.

Soon after, Necker, the Archbishop of Aix, and the Abbé Fauchet hastened to enlist him in their service, and Madame de Genlis had also fixed her choice on him. She was better able than anyone to succeed and to gain him over to the Orleans' party. "Cajolery, attentions, love-letters, kindness—all were employed in making her conquest," says her biographer; "never had she shown such skill and charm, never had she acted with such strong and subtle motives; he was caught, and received an annuity from the prince."[1] However, on the occasion of an insinuation which he had not understood, M. de Genlis laughingly told him one day that he was the greatest fool in the world, and that princes did not give something for nothing. M. de Saint-Pierre was so struck by this argument that he returned his brevet to the Duke of Orleans the very next day.[2]

According to Saint-Pierre's correspondence, Mme. de Genlis had paid him a visit with her pupils on 26th December 1786, and the pension was given to him on the 81st.

---

[1] It was an annuity of 800 *livres*, to date from 1st July 1786.
[2] L. Aimé-Martin, *Correspondance de J. H. Bernardin de Saint-Pierre, précédée d'une supplément aux Mémoires de sa vie*, i. Apologue, p. 109.

Mme. de Genlis's pre-revolutionary activity extended at the same time to the feminine society which surrounded the Duke. She jealously superintended it, and did not intend to allow her own supremacy to be taken from her; but by a subtle circuit of her self-respect, for which we should esteem her after all, she gave her ambitions an admirable moral motive—that of bringing some sort of dignity into the life of the Prince. It was her mission to reform people and to correct their faults, and she knew how to preach so eloquently of duty, honesty, and virtue that the licentious Duke ended by giving in to her.

We find him renouncing in that year, 1787, the degrading orgies which undermined and weakened his character, and attaching himself to young Mme. de Buffon, daughter-in-law of the great naturalist, on the advice of his far-seeing Egeria. "From that time one ceased to see women at Monceaux, and there never appeared any again." [1]

Agnes de Buffon, a pretty, gracious society woman, tender and frivolous, was to amuse the Duke without influencing him. She would take account of rivalry in love-affairs, and she never, so we are told by the Comte de la Marck, "tried to separate Monsieur the Duc d'Orléans from Madame de Genlis, whom she looked up to as a superior woman, capable of advising her well."

In short, it is curious to note at this period in Mme. de Genlis the beginning of an evolution towards new ideas.

Although she always remained an enemy to the Encyclopædic philosophers because of their impiety, she became impregnated with the democratic influences of the moment. The hatred of the Court with its abuses and privileges was crowned with doctrines of liberty and equality. These doctrines were in the air, and people breathed them in more and more every day "with a weariness and an impatience of rules and social yokes, judged to be too heavy, narrow and inflexible," [2] and with a spirit of reform and renovation which were goaded and harassed by

[1] *Correspondance entre le Comte de Mirabeau, et le Comte de la March*, i. 74.
[2] E. Faguet, *Dix-huitième siècle*, p. 291.

the newspapers, pamphlets, and manifestos now being issued in swarms.

Mme. de Genlis, while apparently revolutionary, was in reality practising the doctrine of opportunism, and she could adapt herself without the slightest repugnance to these new ideas.

Apart from any hope of royalty for the Duke of Orleans, she loved using big words, talking constitution, law, humanity, justice, and liberty; to write of them, to flatter herself that she was regenerating the State and exercising on men and the government of her country a ruling influence—this seemed to her a glorious task, and suited her bent for teaching. It is this that no one seems to have considered when they make it a grievance that she, the irreconcilable enemy of the philosophers, " did not look upon this revolution, the fruit and consequence of their doctrines, with horror." [1]

In truth, wherever there is manna for her vanity to pick up, we shall find Mme. de Genlis. This is the reason why she follows each fluctuation of opinion, and is always at the front, because the first arrivals are often the first rewarded.

" Every period," says Capefigue, " has its salon of *femmes savantes*. Molière has held up the type to ridicule for all time; it is only the shade of pedantry that changes or modifies with the generations." [2]

Would Mme. de Genlis permit Mme. Necker to be the only regent of the constitution? Certainly not—she would fight her for the glory of saving the State.

Did she not think of getting the best of that solemn, bourgeoise rival, whom she treated as a newcomer on account of her riches, and a dragon of virtue?

It may be objected that Mme. de Genlis's rôle was by no means so platonic, and that she was actuated by very ambitious motives. But it must be remembered that we are dealing with a complex nature.

The fact of being attached to the Duke of Orleans—

---

[1] Billault de Gérainville, *op. cit.*
[2] Capefigue, *Déesses de la Liberté*, p. 47.

Heaven knows how deeply—binds her to his fortunes and dictates to her in a sense the way she shall act and think. If would be surprising if it were different.

Because the Duke is an enemy of the Court, Mme. de Genlis follows him. He is—or is going to be—the idol of the people, so Mme. de Genlis must be democratic. The throne is tottering, and she looks about for one who will hold it firm—the Duke is the obvious one, so long as he is helped. Here is reason for her acting the part of an "Orleans conspirator," proclaiming it with a sincerity of accent, an enthusiasm, and such a spirit of republicanism that Brissot, for instance, did not hesitate to vouch for it.[1]

So, continuing to hate the philosophers, but more from personal animosity than horror of their doctrines, Mme. de Genlis embraced, with the exception of the question of religion, their anti-aristocratic liberalism, taught it to her pupils, and won their father over to it. She was successful in showing them how glorious it would be to sacrifice their titles and fortunes for the good of the people, and this is why she was called both "Mother of the Church," and "Goddess of Liberty."

If she thought of the good of the people, however, she did not lose sight of her own; and the future of the Duke of Orleans was her own at that moment.

She therefore manœuvred this pitiful creature, "who had not the least little shred of a political conviction,"[2] and who, as she knew, was incapable of following a serious question for a quarter of an hour. The Duke, blinded by his hatred of Marie-Antoinette, permitted her to manage him without the shadow of resistance.

For the rest, it must be stated that his friends at the Palais Royal, and more especially Laclos, were soon to take the responsibility of him, happily relegating Mme. de Genlis to a back place. To them, certainly, is due the greater number of the actions of the Orleans party.

However, it is obvious that the first steps were taken

---

[1] Brissot-Varville, *Mémoires*, ii. 263.
[2] Barbey d'Aurevilly, *Les oeuvres et les hommes*.

by the Comtesse. It was she who urged the Prince into the road where he fought with bent head, and at the end of which the scaffold reared its grisly silhouette.

Thus we have seen him intervene in the parliament on 20th November 1787.

CHAPTER II

THE *DRAMATIS PERSONÆ*

To these first indications of a revolutionary tendency on the part of the Duke of Orleans, the King replied, as will be remembered, by exiling him to Villers-Cotterets.

Mme. de Genlis, who, hidden away in retirement at Bellechasse, was undoubtedly the instigator of the scene in parliament, had not been *en évidence*. But the Marquis du Crest, her brother, who was under suspicion from the first, and who presently was accused of being the author of the intrigue, was soon to pay the penalty.

Charles Louis du Crest, a man whose brain was ever teeming with new projects and ideas, had been absorbed, before he began to exercise the functions of chancellor to the Duke of Orleans, in innumerable inventions, every one of which he expected to make his fame and fortune. In his youth he had attached himself to "Diderot, Helvétius, and others of that kidney," M. de Neuilly tells us; brought up in their school and much disposed like them to take things easily, he was very careless of his person. A man of parts, however, and devoured by a fierce anxiety to distinguish himself, the Marquis du Crest, in addition to his originality, could lay claim to be a person of genuine worth and good sense.

He it was who originated the idea of transforming the magnificent gardens of the Palais Royal into galleries of shops, the rents of which served to re-establish the Duke's finances, so deeply involved through his gambling and unlucky speculations.

This move, of course, set the entire fashionable world of Paris in arms against both the Duke and his chancellor, for it had been the thing to stroll and loiter beneath the famous rows of chestnut trees leading to the Orangery; but what did that matter to the Duke. His coffers began to refill, and soon we have du Crest talking of replacing Necker!

On 20th August 1787, he addressed to the King a naïve epistle accompanying a memorandum in which he affirmed that he alone could save the State without new taxes and without convoking the States-General, provided His Majesty appointed him Prime Minister. "This piece of madness was his undoing," comments Brissot; the chancellor enhanced his *faux pas* by having his memorandum printed and distributed broadcast throughout Paris and in the provinces. But how true a prophet he showed himself! "No one knows better than I," he had written two days earlier, "what must be the outcome of the fermentation now going on in every brain. The convocation of the States-General will be the tomb of the royal authority." He did not indeed realise the full truth of his prediction. Public opinion, however, refused to take Du Crest seriously, and he became a target for ridicule. On the occasion of the Prince's intervention in the Assembly, there had been talk of " certain secret conclaves held behind locked doors in a house owned by the Marquis du Crest at Gennevilliers." Unmasked now by his own hand, du Crest began to be alternately sneered at and threatened by the Royalists as a conspirator. And instead of presiding over the destinies of the State, he has to content himself with a vague mission to England upon which the Duke sends him in company with his friend Brissot, another (but less ingenuous) angler in unquiet waters.

The Prince exiled, du Crest out of the country, the Court believed itself to have foiled a conspiracy triumphantly. But behind the harmless and sanguine Marquis was to be descried the more impressive figure of Mme. de Genlis. Well-informed people began to say that the disgrace of the brother would presently involve that of the sister. The *Correspondance Secrète* went so far as to add (making no secret of its delight), when announcing du Crest's departure: "Mme. de Genlis might very well follow him. The reign of the *femme-gouverneur* is over no less than that of the chancellor."

Once again a succession of pamphlets attacking her began to appear.

One of the first of these was a satirical parody of no merit, entitled *Le Songe d'Athalie*, preceded by a dedicatory letter to M. le Marquis du Crest, signed with the initials, "G. D. L. R."—standing for Grinod de la Reynière. But the sponsorship by an amateur whose methods derived from Lucullus rather than from Juvenal seemed out of keeping with the style of the pamphlet, and there were some who attributed the work to either Rivarol or his imitator Champrenetz. In the catalogue of the *Bibliothèque Nationale*, the pamphlet is ascribed to the latter.

Besides railing at Mme. de Genlis, *Le Songe d'Athalie* contained attacks upon her supposed principal allies, the Abbé Gauchat, Gaillard, La Harpe, and it heaped ridicule on Buffon. Even Condorcet came in for some hard knocks.

The insolence of this brochure was accentuated by one which followed under the title *Désaveu du sieur Grimod de la Reynière*.

Another publication in which Mme. de Genlis was ridiculed was the companion volume to *La Petit Almanach de nos Grand Hommes* dealing with "grande femmes." In this she is alluded to as "the most learned of all the learned ladies, past, present, and probably to come," and La Harpe and Gaillard are twitted with being her collaborators. The screed ends with the malicious sentence: "We may say that there has come into our possession a letter of Mme. de Sillery's, written and signed by herself and in which we have found the precise style of her other works, save for some faults of grammar and orthography such as are commonly to be met with and overlooked in the writings of women authors." And in a series of *Predictions for the year* 1789, appended to the *Almanach*, satirical references are made to new works alleged to be forthcoming from the pen of the famous authoress.

Perhaps these attacks served as a warning to Mme. de Genlis, showing her the need of prudence?

In any case, she left Bellechasse with her pupils to take up her residence at Lamothe while the Prince was in exile.

Here she remained until the Duke of Orleans, by dint of continual entreaties and even a letter to Marie Antoinette, his enemy, at last succeeded in obtaining permission to return to Paris.

It is thought—and it would redound nicely to her credit—that she had some part in inspiring the truly royal gifts bestowed on the poor by the Duke and Duchess during the terrible winter of 1788—gifts which at Versailles were looked upon askance as "munificence with a motive."

Certain it is that the *Comtesse-Gouverneur* displayed much zeal in charitable work at this time, being at pains to bring the young Princes, and more particularly the Duke of Chartres, into contact with the people by means of visits to workshops and manufactories. She sought to accustom the Duke of Chartres to intercourse with the people, so that he might keep them in mind in everything he said and did, and thus win their confidence.

When in June 1786 the Duke of Chartres put these principles into practice by destroying, while at Lamothe, the famous iron cage of Mont St. Michel, he had the appearance of acting as a demagogue.

Meanwhile, the opening of the States-General is fixed for 1st May 17'9. Throughout France people are getting ready to prepare the *cahiers*, the Duke of Orleans publishes his *Instructions aux Bailliages*, those fourteen articles demanding all kinds of rights, even that of divorce, and destined to serve as a model for a great number of other *cahiers*. These are the famous "instructions" which Mme. de Genlis is accused of having inspired, but with which she protests—apparently with truth—she had nothing to do. Moreover, it was just at this moment that an intriguing individual made his way into the confidence of the Duke of Orleans. This was a captain in the engineers named Choderlor de Laclos, better known through a scandalous romance which served as a more effective recommendation to the good graces of the future Philippe-Égalité.

Laclos soon got the Duke's political affairs into his hands, beginning with the drawing up of these instructions, Madame de Genlis doing all she could to oppose him. She even went so far as to threaten to resign her post if the Duke accorded to Laclos a post which the Vicomte de Segur had sought to secure for him.

The rivalry between these two skilled players becomes from this out a subject of much interest to historians of the Orleans' *clique*; and if Laclos apparently triumphs and acquires the predominance, Mme. de Genlis, at least, never gives in but continues to foil so far as possible her opponent's schemes and plans.

Was it he who persuaded the Duke to allow Sieyès to amend the *Instructions aux Bailliages*? As the Abbé is believed to have been in the habit of visiting at Bellechasse, this has been supposed, but the fact has not been ascertained. She undoubtedly judged it opportune to applaud the ideas of the Third Party and—perhaps won over at heart to the popular cause—to give a political tendency to her salon.

Dating from 1789, it begins to be frequented by gazetteers, deputies, publicists of all kinds; and this change in its nature —for hitherto it had been essentially a literary salon—encourages the idea that Mme. de Genlis, far from being discouraged by her defeat at the hands of Laclos, was stimulated into new energy, veering towards the side of public opinion as a natural consequence of being ousted from her rôle of political guide to the Palais Royal.

Now begin her famous Sunday receptions in that salon at Bellechasse, and to which the Goncourts refer as her " *salon bleu*," confusing it apparently with her reception rooms at the Palais Royal, of which she took possession seventeen years previously. These latter were noted for their blue damask hangings and their profusion of mirrors. When she betook herself to Belleville, however, Mme. de Genlis handed over her suite of rooms at the Palais to her eldest daughter, and on the latter's death the furniture is not likely to have come back into her hands. There is no record of the salon at Bellechasse being a " blue salon." If, indeed, blue was its dominating colour up to 1789, red and white soon were added. The tricolor was to be the note alike of its outward appearance and of its social atmosphere.

The Goncourts says also: "This salon derives its importance, not from the woman who conducts it but from the man by whose wish she does so." In a sense, of course, this is true; Mme. de Genlis was on sentinel duty, and Bellechasse was primarily an antechamber to the Palais Royal. But the Comtesse herself was a sufficiently notable personality to win fame for her salon. She knew how to make the most of her conversational powers, reinforced by a melodious voice and her skill as a harpist, and "the grace that emanated from her whole person, and the fresh and ravishing charm of her countenance."[1]

There is no exaggeration in this description of her. Amidst all the bitter criticisms from which her reputation still suffers, there is a chorus of admiring tributes to her fascinations. They arouse a keen regret in us of the twentieth century to whom conversation is a lost art. How pleasant it would be to lend ear to those witty sallies and wise reflections which Bouilly admired so much, which so astonished Barère, and which Mme. Vigée Lebrun tells us she would like to have made notes of. "Within half an hour," she says, "friends and enemies alike were enthralled by the brilliancy of her conversation."

It is easy to picture her presiding over her flock of reformers, attired in her bluish-grey dress with its fichu of lawn crossed over her breast; her hair, with the merest sprinkling of powder on it, raised high on the forehead, is fastened with a narrow blue ribbon, two long curls *à l'Anglaise* framing the delicate oval face. Her brown eyes sparkle with intelligence, and the suspicion of a smile curves her sensitive upper lip as in that charming portrait of Vestier, which tells rather of the citoyenne Brûlart than of the Marquise de Sillery.

With tact and confidence she initiates and directs the conversation, drawing it into new channels when topics are reached in any way dangerous to her supremacy. Throughout it all she remains the centre of admiration by reason of the distinction of her bearing and "a charm of manner which seems the product of kindly feeling and which wins

---

[1] Bouilly, *Des Récapitulations*, p. 251.

our affection by ministering to our self-esteem."[1] And as she is entirely free from the arrogance of the great, she has no difficulty in convincing the representative of the Third Party that she is a genuine anti-aristocrat. It is not surprising to find the lions of the Assembly, properly tamed, assembled at her gatherings—Barère and Brissot conspicuous among them; the former a young and ardent son of the Pyrenees, "fresh from his provincial home, yet endowed with manners well fitted for high society and the Court," his somewhat boyish, southern vanity flattered to the extreme by his welcome into such famous company; the latter, taken from the Bastille by Mme. de Genlis in 1784, at the instance of the geographer, Mentelle, and married to Mlle. Dupont, lady of the bedchamber to Mlle. d'Orleans, who perhaps acted as an intermediary between the Comtesse and Pétion. Here is Pétion himself, " the pure and incorruptible," whose intimacy with the Comtesse is a matter for whispered comment and speculation even in Jacobin conclaves. Here is a group of able men: Talleyrand, Mathieu de Montauron, the Abbé de Cabre; Alexandre Lameth, of whom later our hostess will declare " that she never spoke to him in her life." There are some hot-heads: Volney, Barnave, Alquié, the painter David, and possibly (but this is not certain) Camille Desmoulins, as yet an obscure young lawyer. The " Procureur de la Lanterne " will be one of Mme. de Genlis's most intimate associates later, but he does not appear to have been much of a frequenter of Bellechasse.

Barère will rub elbows here with the Vicomte de Beauharnais, and at times with the Duke of Orleans and the Duchesse de Bourbon, and last but not least with his hostess's husband.

The latter, for his part, is wont to receive Brissot, Laclos, the Marquis de Clermont-Tonnerre; Danton, of whom he said that he was " one of those creatures that you set to do the dirty work, but with something out of the common about him "; Lechapelier; and presently he will be welcoming Manuel and Robespierre.

[1] Hélène-Marie Williams, *Lettres écrites de France à une amie d'Angleterre pendant l'année*, 1790. *Lettre* v. p. 37.

Were the doors of the salon opened habitually to the young Orleans' Princes? To have them listening to discussions of public affairs and *la haute politique* would have been to push even the advanced educational theories of Rousseau to extremes. From the following passage in the *Memoirs* of Mme. de Genlis it would seem that the children were not admitted to the Sunday receptions. " We entertained at Belleville on Saturdays with a view to forming the manners of the young Princes and so enabling them to get into the way of listening to conversation. I wrote down in my diary the things in which they were at fault and which they ought to have done or said." But we know that they were initiated into the doings of the Assembly, and that they often came across some of the deputies either in the Parc de Monceaux or in the Parc du Raincy, where their father invited them to dinner.

Barère boasts of " delicious days " thus spent, and the Duchesse de Gontaut recalls an afternoon in 1789 when she was present as a child at such a dinner at Monceaux, followed by Blind Man's Buff, and when she saw the Duke of Orleans, Biron, and Mirabeau conferring with a group of men who were unknown to her. Mme. de Genlis was of the party also.

It is interesting to note how, dating from 1789, the Palais Royal and Bellechasse compete with each other in their efforts to control the actions of the weak and vacillating Duke of Orleans, posing now as the saviour of his people, and with a Party of his own in the Assembly—a Party, as Clermont-Gallerande said, " with their usurper all ready for use "—this usurper being of course the Duke himself. He had contrived to make himself something of a power by means of the *Instructions des Bailliages*, and by the agents appointed everywhere in his domains. Other subordinate agents, recruited doubtless by Laclos, " excited and directed the actions of the populace or else sought to corrupt the troops by bribes in his name." And the tribe of unemployed who turned the gardens of the Palais Royal into one of the lowest and most infamous spots in Paris, acclaimed wildly and frantically this sworn enemy of the Court and of the Queen, this Prince of the Blood Royal who had abandoned his rank to please them, substituting for it the status of a mere *député!*

The gardens of the Palais Royal became now the centre whence went forth the signal for all the mad and wicked follies of the town.

All day long they were filled by a restless shouting mob, shoving now this way, now that, as one speaker after another took up his position on chair or table to harangue them.

To the gardens came the earliest tidings always of everything happening at the Assembly or at Versailles, or elsewhere. "You knew nothing of what was going on," says Pasquier, "unless you made your way through the gardens at least twice in the course of the day."

It was from the gardens that the mob set out, which rushed to the Abbaye on the 20th of June, to set free the undisciplined soldiers; and hence also issued that other mob on 12th February which, at the instigation of Camille Desmoulins, tore down the leaves of the trees and twisted them into cocades, and which, carrying the busts of Necker and the Duke of Orleans in triumph, came into collision with the *Royal Allemand* in the Place Vendôme.

We do not hear of Mme. de Genlis putting in an appearance in the gardens, but it is questionable whether she had not something to say to these violent proceedings.

If she did not take part in them herself, apparently she was represented by Pamela, whose striking beauty combined with her mysterious origin to inflame the imagination of the crowd.

It is Mme. Vigée-Lebrun who relates how she saw the beautiful young girl attired in a riding habit, and wearing a hat decorated with black feathers, proceeding from one end of the gardens to the other, followed by two attendants in the blue and yellow uniform of the Orleans household, the crowd dividing into two sections to let her pass, and yelling at the tops of their voices—"Voilà! Voilà! There is she whom we must have as queen!" And we hear of her again on the 14th of July, dressed in red, making a triumphal progress through the excited populace.

It seems that Pamela ought to have been attending to

her studies on that day with her governess. Now, Mme. de Genlis was not at Bellechasse. Some days earlier she had taken her pupils to Saint-Leu. And Sillery, who spent Sunday the 12th of July at Saint-Leu with his wife, received a message there announcing the dismissal of Necker. He set out at eight o'clock that evening, and, reaching Paris at the Clichy barrier in the midst of fusillades of musketry, he waited for daybreak before proceeding to Versailles. On the morning of the 14th he carried to the tribune of the Assembly an address, "the object of which seemed to be to egg on the populace to new excesses." [1]

At the outbreak of these disturbances a messenger hastened to Saint-Leu. Mme. de Genlis and her pupils are engaged in theatricals. They abandon this occupation without a moment's delay and, without delaying to change their attire, start for Paris at once, on horseback or by carriage.

Beaumarchais, friend and frequent guest of the Duke of Orleans, invites them to the terrace of the new gardens which he has had built not long since, and from this splendid vantage point they look on at the assault on the Bastille, as are doing many of the aristocrats and many fashionably dressed ladies, a-foot among the crowd, "having left their carriages at a distance in order to get there more easily." [2]

Mme. de Genlis, observers noted, made no concealment of her delight and enthusiasm. It is said that not only Louis-Philippe and his brothers, but also Mademoiselle, were witnesses of this brutal demonstration, a portent of the impending fall of the monarchy. Mme. de Genlis came to be spoken of as a Revolutionary and a Terrorist. She herself admitted her imprudence, but she did not deny her feeling of satisfaction, and the hands of the Parisian who broke down the feudal monument seemed to her the "avenging hands of Providence."

Was she ignorant of the fact that the destruction of the Bastille had for a long time been part of the Revolutionary programme?

In his famous letter to the King the Marquis du Crest

[1] E. Dard, *op. cit.*, 183.
[2] Chancelier Pasquier, *op. cit.*, 53.

had called out for the destruction of the Bastille as an urgent measure. It was only natural, therefore, that Mme. de Genlis should be a joyful and conspicuous witness of the actual event.

She did not, however, dare to avow another step which she took,—one which was much more rash. On this same night of tumult she conducts her pupils to the Palais Royal, and she and the young Prince take part in the wild dance, hand in hand with the drunken viragoes who are making the gardens re-echo with their frenzied songs and obscene yells.[1]

On the following day she returned to Saint-Leu, retracing her steps on the 2nd of September in order to instal her pupils at Passy, so that they might be within reach of the National Assembly.

Throughout this period the Duke takes no part in what is happening. He had but to present himself before the King and his Council, who were quite terrorised.

Popular as he is at this moment of unrest, he is in truth the uncrowned King of Paris, supported by his lieutenants: Laclos, Gillery, Sieyès, Latouche, watched over by Mirabeau, from Montrouge, where he is waiting; backed up by crowds of mercenaries; the hope of the famished mob which throngs the Palais Royal. A single word from him and he is lieutenant-general of the kingdom, with power to nominate ministers, to dispose of the royal treasure, etc. etc.

But he dares not utter this word. In the royal antichamber, where he knocks up against the Baron de Breteuil, he loses countenance, forgets the part which has been composed for him by the plotters of Montrouge, stammers out some banal inquiry, and capitulates without striking a blow.

It would be idle to enter into details on this subject, for the historians of the Revolution have dealt with the matter fully.

Coming back to Mme. de Genlis, it is important to note that she had nothing to do with the Montrouge schemings. She was not inactive, however. Her name recurs several times at this period.

[1] Cf. A. Nettement, *loc. cit.* Touchard-Lafosse, *Souvenir d'un demi-siècle*, 26.

First of all, on the 17th of August at Rouen, in connection with the Bordier affair. This Bordier, an actor from the Variétés, was a ringleader in the outbreak at Rouen. A sum of 74,000 livres was found upon him. Particulars of the charge against him were forwarded to the Châtelet, but the matter was hushed up, Bordier himself being executed without any fuss. It was known only that in his pleadings he had mentioned the Duke of Orleans and Mme. de Genlis.

The Orleans party was believed at this juncture to be working to prevent supplies of corn from arriving and the bakers from baking (it is said to have cost them 150,000 francs a week to contrive this), besides endeavouring to corrupt the troops. A witness saw " Mme. de Genlis going about the barracks of the Gardes Françaises with the Duchesse d'Aiguillon, Mme. Necker and her daughter, addressing the soldiers or giving them brandy."[1] And there are similar statements about her visiting other barracks and garrisons and camps. But this kind of gossip is not to be credited. What is known, however, is that she now gave Mirabeau that single interview of which he was to boast so fatuously to Sophie Monnier.

On the 16th of September, when the Assembly was discussing the question of the succession to the throne and the eventual right of the King of Spain, a Bourbon, to reign in France, Sillery intervened suddenly and unexpectedly.

The Duke of Orleans had just left his place as though to refuse all responsibility for what was being done, and was standing conspicuously near a door, when M. de Genlis, who was known to have been ill and in bed, made his unlooked for appearance, and took out of his pocket, where somehow they had found their way, the letters patent of 1713 (resulting from the Treaty of Utrecht), and the renunciation of the throne of France by the Royal House of Spain.

This incident indicates to what an extent the political future of the Duke of Orleans and the possibility of his becoming Regent were engaging the energies of the Party.

It would not be rash to recognise in this step the influence of Mme. de Genlis, whose memory for historical dates and

[1] Touchard-Lafosse, *op. cit.*, 26.

incidents were wonderful. She was more likely than her husband to remember the Spanish renunciation, and it was she probably who supplied him with the necessary documents at the right moment.

The fateful days of October now approached.

Recent histories of the Revolution show that it is no longer possible to impute any responsibility for the events of those days to the Duke of Orleans. It is even doubted now whether he was at Versailles on the 6th of October.

All that can be charged against Mme. de Genlis is that she was staying within reach in that Maison Boulainvilliers where Rivarol would have us believe that emissaries of the Party continually arrived with news. It is not known whether she was present on the 5th at that stormy meeting of the Assembly, when the mob of frantic women led by Maillard made their way in : the meeting at which Mirabeau broke out into violence, and at which Puget de Barbentane cried out: " It can be seen that these gentlemen want some *lanternes*—they shall have them!" The Duke of Chartres was present with his brother, Montpensier, but apparently they were not accompanied by Mme. de Genlis. The young Duke took up Puget's words and repeated: " Yes, gentlemen, yes,—we must have more *lanternes!* "

" When we reflect," Billault de Gérainville comments upon this, " that the Prince who uttered these words was barely sixteen years old, and that the horde of cannibals with whom he seemed to threaten the King's friends were only a few yards away, it is difficult not to believe that he had been initiated into the dreadful plot which was about to do its work. "

A courier rushes up now and whispers into the ear of the Duke of Chartres a message from his father, who immediately hastens away with his young brother and makes for Passy and the Maison Boulainvilliers.

Night falls. In the darkness, rain falling heavily, cries, shouts, yells, and the clash of sabres and pikes are to be heard unceasingly all round the castle.

The ragged mob, made ferocious by hunger, swarms up against the iron railings. The guard cannot keep them back

—they succumb before the wild onslaught. The attackers are hungry for blood as well as bread. In a moment blood begins to pour, heads are cut off and raised aloft on pikes. Now the castle is broken into and sacked—the Queen's own apartment invaded and sullied, Marie Antoinette herself taking flight in her nightdress and by a miracle escaping the mob.

Such were the facts in brief. We are all familiar with them. We all know, minute by minute, the terrible story of those twenty-four hours, during which the knell of the unfortunate Louis XVI. tolled in every heart.

When at last the Royal Family are taken to Paris as prisoners, surrounded by its terrible escort, it passes in front of the terrace of this Boulainvilliers mansion, from the height of which, as from a box in a theatre, Mme. de Genlis and her pupils, with the Duke of Orleans and Laclos, are looking down with smiles upon their lips.

At the sight of the Duke, conspicuous in his grey coat and with a gigantic cocade in his hat, the mob is said to have burst out into shouts and cheers, the while Mme. de Genlis " indulged in the most offensive comments upon the Queen and Mme. de Lamballe." [1]

She herself declared afterwards that she took no part in these proceedings, but numerous witnesses establish the fact of her presence. " I saw her," records the Comte de Neuilly. " I can certify to this."

On the morning of the 6th the French Guard said to La Fayette: " If the King is too weak, let him put aside the crown. We shall nominate his son. We shall have a Council of Regency, and all will be well."

A Council of Regency! This meant the triumph of the Duke of Orleans.

And we are set thinking sadly of Lamartine's saying: " It is more fitting for a king to abdicate than to be overthrown; from the moment he ceases to be king, the throne is the lowest place in the kingdom." [2]

---

[1] Cf. Clermont-Gallerande, *op. cit.*, i. 191. Comte de Neuilly, *op. cit.*; Ducoin, *op. cit.*, etc.

[2] Lamartine, *Girondins*, L. vi. ch. xi.

CHAPTER III

POPULARITY OF THE YOUNG ORLEANS PRINCES

In Paris public opinion, in the nervous fit that followed the disorders of the 5th and 6th October, blamed the Duke of Orleans and Mirabeau. Baron de Stael shared the general opinion, though he was in a good position for obtaining information, for his wife and Mme. Necker were with the Queen at the Œil-de-Bœuf and had not seen the Duke of Orleans at the palace. Writing on the 22nd to Gustavus III., to inform him of the outbreak, De Stael explicitly indicated the Duke and his friends, Latouche, Biron and Sillery as the authors of the plot.[1]

Further, the Court directed the tribunal of the Châtelet to open an official enquiry involving the Prince and Mirabeau, and there were rumours that the faction, though its plans had been upset by Louis XVI. having come to Paris, was preparing for a new attempt.

As for Mirabeau, he was the man to get out of an awkward situation, for he knew thoroughly well how to make himself feared, especially by La Fayette. Now, if he sided with the Prince he could, by making a scene in the Assembly, draw the people on to new disorders, and ruin the rising glory of the general, who was supposed to have saved the King and defeated the Duke of Orleans on 6th October.

It is well known that La Fayette sent the Duke away to England—whether by alarming him as to the proceedings that might be taken against him as the instigator of the disturbances,[2] or dazzling him with the prospect of the

[1] Cf. E. Dard, *op. cit.*, 187.
[2] The Comte de Quélen writes to the President de St. Luc, October 18, 1789:

Regency and the Duchy of Brabant, if he could intervene efficaciously in the Low Countries, now in revolt against Austria (this last prospect a mere Utopia, a dry bone that M. de Montemorin threw to the Orleans party, and which the Prince gnawed at persistently for nine long months).

As for Mme. de Genlis, she tried, it seems, to regain her influence. A fine opportunity presented itself for throwing the responsibility for the events of October on Laclos. But she had to encounter the preconceived ideas of her august friend, and the Marquis de Luzerne, the ambassador at London, was able to write on 10th October:—
" I know by private reports that the Duke is on bad terms with Mme. de Sillery, that she has done everything in the world to induce him to dispense with the services of Laclos, whom she cannot bear; but that notwithstanding her efforts the latter has succeeded in maintaining himself in favour. . . ."[1] Then she thought of retiring from the scene, and prepared to go with her pupils to Nice. "Unfortunately," she says, "I had announced my intention, and the idea was so censured by the newspapers, and seemed to be so damaging to the fragile and fatal popularity of the House of Orleans, that it had to be given up,—at least for the moment."[2]

Gorsas confirmed this statement of the Governess in his newspaper,[3] and Mme. de Genlis at once replied to him in a long letter which Gorsas published next day, and which was reproduced in the Orleanist papers. At the same time a pamphlet issued in the form of an open letter to the Duke of Orleans said: " It is reported, Monseigneur, that yielding to the advice of the female Governor whom you have placed over your children you are thinking about, nay, you have

---

—" Mischievous people—and there are some of them about—are spreading the report that M. de la Fayette said to Monseigneur in the presence of the King, ' I have handed His Majesty a written statement containing the proofs of your influence on the rising of the people and your desire to get me assassinated. This just lets one see how far the malice of men will go. . . ." (P. de Valssière, *Lettres d'aristocates*).

[1] Cf. E. Dard., *op. cit.*, 157.
[2] Genlis, *Mémoires*, iv. 87.
[3] *Le Courrier de Versailles à Paris et de Paris à Versailles*, October 15, 1789.

decided on, removing them from the Kingdom, on sending them to Italy. . . .

" Is it an ambitious over-bearing woman trying to involve in and identify with her teachings all your thoughts, all your plans,—is it a woman who has only a certain wit, extravagant ideas and no principles but those of getting everything into her own hands—is it, I say, a woman 'Governor' who will be able to inspire them with the virtues they require ?

"Delay, or rather abandon at once, Monseigneur, this projected journey, this separation from your family. The People has taken alarm at it, and nowadays the People is swift to murmur, to be angered, to proscribe and condemn. . . ."

It is true that Mme. de Genlis fixes these preparations for a journey in the autumn of 1790, but it seems clear that they were the outcome of the events of 5th and 6th October 1789—events of which she could not for the present escape the after effects in Paris. In fact, the Prince himself started off suddenly like a fugitive on 14th October, accompanied by Laclos. Mme. de Buffon followed him, keeping just one stage behind him on the way. And next day the King informed the Assembly that he had entrusted the Duke of Orleans with a special mission to the King of England.

It was the sign of the times that George III. did not grant him an audience till November, and then only after giving him a weary wait of three-quarters of an hour in the anti-chamber. In the Prince's own circle there had been nothing to make anyone expect this sudden departure.

"I thought," relates Mme. de Genlis, "that we would start in a couple of days, when one evening M. de Valence came to tell me that he knew for certain that M. d'Orleans was setting out that very night for England. He found it impossible to persuade me of the matter that was so unexpected and so strange, but it was nevertheless absolutely true. M. d'Orleans set off at five o'clock in the morning.

"They gave me a note from him in which he said that

he would be back *at the end of a month*, yet he remained in London for nearly a year."[1] But he left Mme. de Genlis *full power over his children.*

This event made a most disastrous impression on the public. Then, in concert with the Duchess of Orleans, the deserted Egeria drew up "a short statement of about a page announcing this strange journey," and Mme. d'Orleans had this short statement inserted in all the newspapers.

Nevertheless there came showering down on Paris a cloud of pamphlets and anonymous fly-sheets on the departure of Monseigneur the Duke, on the motives of his journey, on his pretended embassy, etc. . . . Friendly publications, the work of the Prince's adherents, put forward lengthy explanations of his conduct, defended him from the charge of criminal ambition, and further assured the public that "he was entrusted with the purchase of wheat in England." The anti-Orleanist pamphleteers jeered at these explanations, indulged in epigrams, or said flatly that the Prince had run away.

The Palais Royal was utterly depressed, and Mirabeau, turning contemptuously away from his ally of yesterday, with a shrug of his shoulders applied to him an epithet too grossly emphatic to be reproduced here. Mme. de Genlis was in a fury at finding herself tied to Paris, for she says: "This journey, inconceivable from every point of view, made it impossible for my pupils to leave France. The people, already in ill humour at the departure of their father, kept an eye on them, and would have stopped them at the frontier,"[1] — as they had nearly stopped the Duke at Boulogne.

Now that the Duke of Orleans had gone and had abandoned himself without resistance to Laclos, his cause evidently ceased to be of much interest to Mme. de Genlis. M. Dard goes so far as to say, "that cause was in her opinion a lost one, since she had been supplanted by Laclos."

But while the Prince, after having more than once allowed the chance of sitting in the place of Louis XVI. to slip through his irresolute hands, seemed thus to abandon the struggle

---

[1] Genlis, *Précis de ma conduite depuis la Révolution*, p. 12; *Mémoires*, iv. 89.

and his party, the Revolution none the less pursued its course.

Why should Mme. de Genlis, well known for her Republicanism, slacken in her zeal?

Why should she lose for nothing the results of her activity and all her efforts?

Is there not another left to her—young, enthusiastic, formed and fashioned by herself even to the inmost recesses of his conscience, submissive to her in heart and soul, whose will she can sway as she chooses, who eagerly drinks in the slightest word that falls from her thin lips, and who with an excess of veneration speaks of her as "his beloved friend," "his mother"—the Duke of Chartres!

We shall have to say more of the affection of the pupil for his Governess, a passionate affection, but as she would have it, *entirely blameless*,—of this there is no possible doubt. Meanwhile let us note that she had literally applied the principle of Rousseau: "Émile will love and respect his parents, but he must obey only me."

For the present she thought it opportune to bring the Duke of Chartres forward, keep him before the people, bring him to take his father's place in public opinion, and try to attract to this grave youth of seventeen the popular favour. And strange to say, the practical and encyclopædic education that Mme. de Genlis had given the young Prince was so well adapted to his new destiny, that it seemed as if she had long foreseen the actual situation. Not only was M. de Chartres subjected to a rigid rule of life, austere enough to rival that of a monk, punished, put on bread and water for eight days for the slightest outbreak, but he had been taught, contrary to tradition, democratic habits, and the principles of absolute equality.

He must rise at six in the morning, in winter as well as in summer, after having slept on a plank; for breakfast he had a raw apple and a little dry bread and cherries; his only nourishment was milk, roast meat and fruit, without ever being given even the least dainties, and sweets never or hardly ever. Here certainly was a severe regimen. And one cannot deny that the Duke of Chartres was trained to be a strong man, if one remembers the enormous amount of physical exertion that Mme. de Genlis's varied programme imposed upon him—manual work as a mason, a carpenter, a smith, and even as a groom; physical exercise that included the handling of heavy jars of water, weight lifting, hauling on pulleys, wearing leaden soles to his shoes; visits to factories, and the medical as well as charitable task of tending the sick in the Hôtel-Dieu, and with all this his intellectual studies!

But he was also trained to be a free man.

This son of the first Prince of the Blood Royal takes no account of birth and rank; he despises decorations, distinctions, titles and other baubles of vanity; he values only personal merits; and be it said, by the way, that all this is quite in harmony with the precepts of the Gospel. But he believes firmly in the equality of all men, in the sovereignty of the people, which is outraged by privileges and abuses. Moreover, he is used to keep account for himself of his own affairs, study the character of those around him, exercise a minute supervision over his subordinates, keep a watch on himself, master himself, give under all circumstances an example of acting as if his slightest movements were subject to the criticism of all the world. Finally, his political ideal—at the age of eighteen—is the Republic.

Honourable, courageous, pure, pious, well educated, the Duke of Chartres, wonderfully gifted and besides of a charming presence, rises so high above the average of mankind and of the generality of princes, that he seems a hero, an exceptional man.

"A democrat Prince," exclaims Miss Helena Williams, in a transport of admiration at the grave and somewhat Puritan manners of Chartres, " is in itself something strange enough!" Pitt's fellow-countrywoman is full of admiration for this " warm partisan of the new Constitution of France, who is determined with all the enthusiasm of a youthful mind and an ardent soul to sacrifice the splendour of his titles to the general good of his country."[1]

[1] Helena Maria Williams, *Letters written from France* to a friend in England during the year 1790, p. 38.

THE DUKE OF CHARTRES
(SON OF PHILIPPE-ÉGALITÉ).

How could he fail to tread deliberately the path in which he was preceded by Mme. de Genlis—that unwearying panegyrist of the Constitution—seeing that with Montpensier he carefully followed the debates of the Assembly, made written summaries of the discussions of its orators, and several times each week submitted these reports to the criticism of the deputy Biauzat, whom the Governess had charged with the duty of teaching politics to the two princes under the guise of a course of law.

How could he fail to be popular, he who since the 14th of July wore habitually, like his brothers, the uniform of the National Guard, though it was something of an encumbrance for little eleven-year-old M. de Beaujolais? He used also to frequent the public swimming school, established since July 1789, at the point of the Ile Saint-Louis, wearing, however, a swimming costume that differed in colour and material from that of ordinary mortals.

And the popular enthusiasm for the young Duke broke out especially at the theatre.

While he was a child he had not been taken to the theatre more than eight or ten times each winter. Now things were different, and the three princes were often in the audience at those tragedies, at which the clamorous applause of the people emphasised the lines that lent themselves to political allusions, thus interpreting certain passages in a sence that neither Corneille, nor Racine, nor even Voltaire had ever dreamed of.

On Wednesday, 4th November, they were to be seen at the representation of Chénier's *Charles IX.*, and the whole audience applauded the princes with persistent enthusiasm.

The popularity of the Duke of Chartres increased rapidly. In this excitable, inflammable Paris, where the least spark produced explosions, the Dames de la Halle were prominent in their effervescence. In this same month of November, meeting a very well dressed young man, and doubtless mistaking him for the Prince, they make him come down from his carriage, kiss him, decorate him with a beautiful rose, and " invite him to go to meet the Duke of Orleans, who they declared was to arrive that day." [1]

Then it is M. de Chartres himself who takes fire. One day in March 1790 he reads Marat's paper. In it some anonymous penny-a-liner likens the people to a wild beast, and further speaks " with much contempt of the new Constitution and of the National Assembly." [1] In a fit of indignation he sends by post to the newspaper a protest. He does not sign it. But the article fell into the hands—or was sent to —the Duchess of Orleans, who recognised her son's style. Sent for by his mother, the young prince blushed, lied, and denied its authorship. And he had a sharp reprimand from Mme. de Genlis, but only because he had not dared to avow himself the author of the protest.

Some days before this, on 9th February, with his brothers, and in the uniform of the National Guard, he took the civic oath, in the district of St. Roch, an act to which, Billault de Gérainville notes, " they were in no way obliged, and from which their age dispensed them." On the page of the district register the Prince struck out all his titles and dignities, which had been inscribed there beforehand, and signed himself, " Citizen Chartres."

On 81st March the abolition of the right of primogeniture filled him with joy.

On 19th June a decree abolished titles of nobility. At once the Duke assembled his people, forbade them to address him as " Monseigneur," or even as " Monsieur le Duc," made them put off their livery, " unfrocking coachmen, lackeys, footmen and the rest."

On the day of the Fête of the Federation, his arrival at the Champ de Mars caused a great sensation. The people lavished their applause upon him.

To such an extent that the enthusiasm of M. de Chartres became touched with fanaticism, and Mme. de Genlis, fearing with her accustomed prudence the excesses to which a young head might lead them, held forth to her pupils on 28rd April in a discourse full of edifying restraint :—

" I have taught you," she said to them, " to despise

[1] *Journal de la Cour et de la Ville*, November 8, 1789.

ridiculous outward show, and really to honour only merit and virtue . . . I read the Game Laws for you to make you detest them. I asked you to promise that you would renounce all these horrible rights; I taught you to despise pomp, and to seek the love of the people, the only foundation of the renown of Princes. . . . Thus you never received from me an aristocratic education, . . . but as I hate excess, which is the characteristic of limited intelligences, I desire that you should go nowhere else but to the National Assembly —otherwise you will commit many follies and sheer absurdities." [1]

This episode shows that the teacher felt scruples that did her honour, but that were somewhat belated. For some time Mme. d'Oberkirch had remarked that the young princes were losing all respect for their name and race, and, at the risk of repetition, let us add that for some time Mme. de Genlis was giving them the example. She too has renounced all her titles and the "*de*" to become plain "Citizeness Brûlart; she too wears in her own fashion the patriot uniform—a tricolour dress trimmed with an immense profusion of blue, white and red ribbons. She proudly displays a piece of jewellery, made out of a bit of stone from the Bastille, bought no doubt from the famous Palloy, and mounted in a revolutionary medallion that deserves description.

In the very centre the word "Liberté," written in diamonds, sparkled on a moon, represented in its phase of the Fourteenth of July, while in smaller diamonds the name of the planet that shone that day was inscribed above it. All round, forming a frame for the medallion, a wreath of laurels in emeralds, closing upon a cockade of gems on three colours, through which passed the chain that suspended the jewel on the graceful neck of the Countess.[2]

To complete her collection of revolutionary jewellery she had, besides the medallion, half a dozen rings cut out of a flinty agate that also came from the Bastille. On each ring was engraved the date "14th July 1789," and the inscription, "For one of the six best patriots."

[1] *Leçons d'une gouvernante*, April 23, 1790.   [2] Miss Williams, *Letters*, 11.

Of those six distinguished beings one only, Alexander Lameth, is known to us. Those who came to visit the lady, friends on the Saturday, politicians on the Sunday, found her in her rooms " so bedizened with the three colours that their crude contrasts tired one's eyes."

In this appropriate setting Miss Williams heard her talk with disdain of distinctions of rank, and of " the silly English Constitution with its hereditary peerage and its two houses instead of a single chamber."

Rings, jewels, inscriptions, trifles that had a meaning, anathemas and prophecies uttered by a pretty woman—what a love the close of the eighteenth century had for such amusements! How they bring back to us the time with its sensitive beings in pannier skirts and powdered hair!

But we must come to graver matters; let us see the *Discours*.

Mme. de Genlis publishes two of these discourses in this same year 1790.

The first, the one that made the most sensation, appeared in the month of July. It was the *Discourse on the Education of the Dauphin*,[1] intended to prove that the happiness of a people depends on the education of the heir to the throne; that under a free Government the interests of the King can never be separated from those of the people; that a free nation had therefore the right to supervise the education of the prince who is to govern it.

Consequently the plan for his education ought to be printed in full detail and made public; an *Education Journal*, issued each month, should record hour by hour, his studies, his physical and mental exercises, with bulletins of his health, notable remarks made by the prince, and a general account of his progress. Thus the people will follow moment by moment the life of " a child so precious to them."

The leading part in this programme belongs naturally to the " Governor," whom Mme. de Genlis indicates by a boldly outlined characterisation of what he should be. Under

---

[1] *Discours sur l'éducation du Dauphin et sur l'adoption*, par Mme. de Brûlart ci-devant Madame Sillery, gouvernante des enfants de la maison d'Orléans (1790).

her pen the Dauphin's Governor appears as an exceptional being, an unheard-of assemblage of all the virtues, all the sciences, a saint and a phenomenon. She promises him in advance the hatred of envious men and the persecutions of the wicked; she predicts for him solitude and abandonment, for he will find it impossible to cultivate his friends; the enmity of those below him, who will always consider his vigilance excessive—in a word, all that it was of public notoriety that she herself had experienced.

In the presence of these explicit utterances, the Court at first began to ask if Mme. de Genlis herself was aspiring to the post of Governor of the Dauphin. But there was a certain passage in which she described a pupil "of lofty soul, superior intelligence, intrepid courage, extraordinary genius," of whom his Governor, "especially at the moment when a new Constitution had been created, should not make either a conqueror or a despot." This significant passage, which could not in any way whatever be applied to poor little Louis XVII., pointed plainly enough to the Duke of Chartres.

The Royalists, on second thoughts, made no mistake about it, and in the *Mercure* La Harpe—whose intervention in the affair one would hardly have expected—frankly told the author of the *Discours* to mind her own business.[1]

But the *Discourse on Adoption*, published shortly after the former pamphlet, pressed the point, if one may say so, and showed the course to be followed.

Adoption enabled one to give to merit the rights and distinctions unjustly bestowed on mere birth and nobility without virtue or talent. Mme. de Genlis reminded her hearers that the historic names of Trajan, Marcus Aurelius, Childebert, were those of adopted sons.

[1] La Harpe wrote ironically: "I am very far from suspecting Madame de Sillery of that self-centred way of thinking which, when it dictates the opinions to be given to the public, leads only to the revelation of secret egotism and of the delusions of self-love. . . . I do not think that anyone will ever give practical effect to Madame de Sillery's idea. One might for her own sake advise her not to treat of political questions. She will not succeed any better in these matters than she succeeded when she tried to treat of theology," etc. (*Mercure de France*, September–October 1790).

And there was some support for the idea that in the presence of the unpleasant rumours, the imputations and the calumnies that were current about the Queen and the birth of the Dauphin, Louis XVI. might "disavow the son of the Austrian woman," and adopt as his successor a Prince of the younger branch, a descendant of Henry IV.—in a word, the Duke of Chartres.[1]

And we may take it that there is a further emphasising of this idea in a note added by Mme. de Genlis in the second edition of the *Discours sur l'Adoption*, in 1802, in which she says: "While entirely disapproving of hereditary distinctions, I by no means wish to argue that royalty should not be hereditary"—a pointless explanation if there was nothing to call for it.

But after all the *Discours* seems to have been a two-edged weapon. It tended, by one at least of its paragraphs,[2] to assist in the realisation of a personal plan of its author—the adoption of a charming girl, the idol of her reputed parents: the adoption of Paméla or of Hermine. And this seems to be confirmed by a pressing letter of our Countess to Camille Desmoulins, dated 11th July 1790:—

". . . Allow me to make a request of you, which is not prompted by self-love, but in which I have a heartfelt interest of the most tender and lively kind. It is that you will strongly advocate with your eloquence and your admirable logic my proposal relating to adoption, with this condition—that one may adopt a daughter in addition to other children.

"If the law is passed in this form, I shall give the first example of the happiness it can procure. I conjure you to do everything in your power, by your writings and with your friends, to have this law passed. Another in your place would ask me what right a person unknown to you can have to expect such zeal on your part, but this zeal will

---

[1] Cf. E. Dard, *op. cit.*, p. 295.
[2] "Whatever number of children one may have, there ought to be permission to adopt besides a daughter on condition only of securing her an annuity for life."

contribute to the happiness of two people, and no doubt to that of many others. It will cost you nothing; and if your writings indicate your way of thinking, they justify the confidence I am reposing in you. You see, sir, how frankly I speak to you; I hope my motive will excuse me with a soul such as yours, and I swear that I shall feel towards you faithful friendship and real gratitude if, in a matter so dear to me, and touching me so deeply, you help me with all the zeal and activity of which you are capable.

"I am your most humble and obedient servant,
"DUCRET-BRÔLARD.

"SAINT-LEU, 11*th July* 1790."[1]

Taken literally, the request would indeed seem to have been inspired by the desire to adopt Paméla, whom she so petted, and treated with greater tenderness than all else; but the other plan—that which was concerned with a possible adoption of the Duke of Chartres—might after all be hidden away under the disguise of that which was openly avowed, and Mme. de Genlis was not the woman to reveal herself completely in a note in her handwriting addressed to Camille Desmoulins, who just before this was unknown to her except by reputation.

Their relations seem, in fact, to date from the publication of the *Discours sur l'Education du Dauphin*, as a frontispiece to which the publisher had inserted an engraving—the portrait of the author, sitting at her writing-table, in a pannier skirt and a little hat *à la Paméla*, with her hair dressed in youthful fashion with very full puffs.

Below in a medallion was shown a lamp burning with a band bearing the inscription: "Pour éclairer tu te consumes" (You consume yourself in giving us light).

And the portrait was accompanied by these verses of M. de Sauvigny :—

> "Vertus, grâces, talens, esprit juste, enchanteur,
> Elle a tout ce qu'il faut pour embellir la vie,
> C'est le charme des yeux, de l'oreille, du cœur,
> Et le désespoir de l'envie."

---

[1] *Correspondance de Camille Desmoulins*, publiée par Matton, p. 73.

Feeling her modest love of equality offended, Mme. de Genlis raised an outcry, "broke out into invectives against the engraving," and sent a protest to Camille Desmoulins, who published it in full in his *Révolutions de France et de Brabant*. It must have been shortly afterwards that, charmed at his action, and anxious to have a near view of the fiery Revolutionist, she sent him the note on the adoption question. It throws an interesting light on the obscurity in which Mme. de Genlis's proceedings are lost to sight at this period; and lights of the epistolary kind are rare. It also shows us something of the quiet independence of this busy woman, who was now content to dispense with the once necessary support of the Orleans name.

For the moment the Duke was not an ally that could count for much. He had returned from England on 20th July, but was living and lodging no one knows where, probably at Mme. de Buffon's. He nowhere showed himself in public, did not go to the Palais Royal, and met the attacks of the journalists with complete silence. Apparently he had returned to his former apathy, his pleasures, and, left to himself, was taking no interest in current events. It was said that he was abandoned by all, even by Mme. de Genlis, whose enemies, ever on the alert, proclaimed her ingratitude in an anonymous pamphlet.

This insulting publication, taking the Governess directly to task, reproaches her with "the incredible proceedings of the Prince, his irrational conduct, and the discredit into which he has fallen," and ironically invites her "to give some explanation as to the line she intends to take or induce her old pupil to take."[1]

Mme. de Genlis's only reply was to assert herself all the more on the popular side. We have proof of this in her assiduous visits — sometimes with Mlle. d'Orléans — to the sittings of the Assembly, to several meetings of the Jacobin Club,[2] and even to that of the Cordeliers,[3] where she

---

[1] *Vie privée de Madame de Sillery.*
[2] Cf. Toulotte, *op. cit.*, i. 77.
[3] Mme. de Genlis has left us a picturesque account of the meetings of the Cordeliers in her novel *Les Parvenus.*

found a piquant excitement for her curiosity in the fierce excitement of the mixed audience, with its contingent of fishwives ever ready to interrupt. Amid such surroundings she met her husband again

On 3rd March 1791 Sillery wrote to Camille Desmoulins :—

"Madame de Sillery is coming to dine at my place with Péthion and Robespierre, and I venture to ask your amiable and pretty wife to do me the same honour. Madame de Sillery tells me to say to you that she is as fond of you as ever, but she is afraid that you may be childish enough to be sulky towards her.[1] Come, my dear Camille, and if ever you find yourself amidst pure democracy it will be next Sunday at eight, when I hope to grasp your hand. Send me a word in reply. "SILLERY."[2]

Was it on this Sunday, or some other day, that in M. de Genlis's yellow salon in the Rue des Mathurins she sang, for the Attorney-General of the Lanterne, accompanying herself on the harp, a song in praise of inconstancy ?—It was, alas! a seasonable subject for the Genlis, but well calculated to make Lucile Desmoulins anxious. Meanwhile Paméla danced for him a Russian dance "so voluptuous," he says, "and performed in such a way, that I don't think young Herodias can have danced for her uncle anything more calculated to turn his head."

The ungrateful Revolutionist! He will remember it all, but only to use these recollections of a fête day as points of accusation. Nevertheless, at the moment he inspires the *Livre Rouge* to celebrate with highest praise the merits of Genlis the Siren.[3]

[1] In the original of this letter, in possession of the learned Dr. Pol Gosset of Rheims, one can read in the margin opposite this passage these words in the handwriting of Lucile Desmoulins : "You have not made a bad guess."

[2] *Correspondance de Camille Desmoulins.*

[3] "If she had been content with certain social talents ; if she had been an exquisite nobody, or if she had been nothing more than a good, useless, kindly woman, praise would not have been spared to her ; but when it is a case of an extraordinary career, of successes won in various departments, the human race rises in anger, multiplies obstacles, conspires against reputations, and tries to destroy them before they have reached the summit. It is then that equality

But how after all could they omit the praise of a Governess whose favourite pupil had just been received into the Jacobin Club!

In fact, he had for long months been all eagerness to become a member of this society of the "Friends of the Constitution," in which he would find scope for his patriotism and his impatience for action.

Mme. de Genlis took care to write for the sake of posterity: "The Duke of Chartres was received into the Jacobin Club by desire of the Duke of Orleans, and assuredly not by any wish of mine." Yes, it is true that she made the young Prince defer this step till he had received his father's authorisation.[1] But this merely formal delay is no set-off against the enthusiastic encouragement which she lavished on her pupil. And indeed she does not deny this.

Besides, Chartres could not be received into this subversive assembly without the nomination of a member, and it so happened that the member who nominated him was Sillery.

On the day—2nd November 1790—Mme. de Genlis was not so far away from the Jacobin Club as she afterwards pretended, and the tumultuous applause, the re-echoing din, that marked the reception as something different from all the rest, did not teach him anything that she had not long since made perfectly acceptable to him.

Though the newspapers dilated upon the excited scene, and the Court expressed its strong disapproval, and a letter, that certainly came from the royal circle, attempted to enlighten the Duke of Chartres on the character of his detestable advisers,[2] it was all waste of trouble. The political con-

is a real necessity; but try as one will to create it, there is an aristocracy which will endure. It is that of talent" (*Mémoires historiques sur les Pensions*, 11th supplement, 41).

[1] *Précis de ma conduite depuis la Révolution*, p. 36: "The eldest of my pupils, the Duke of Chartres, became a member of the Jacobins, but I had no part in this matter. The Duke of Orleans wished it, and took him there."

[2] "Young Prince, your first teachers must certainly have told you that wisdom is a gift of Heaven, for all comes from on High. Those who replaced them have inspired you with contrary principles. I who have no interest in deceiving you . . . I tell you that truth will no more approach young princes, than young maidens who are pretty will come to them. Everyone around you flatters you; and they flatter you only to deceive you; and they

victions of Chartres were of too old a date and too deeply rooted.

deceive you only to take advantage of your weaknesses. The school of Pythagoras would have been more useful to you than the Club of the Jacobins," etc. (*Lettre à M. le ci-devant Duc de Chartres*, no date or place of publication).

CHAPTER IV

A FAMILY DRAMA

WHETHER the Duke of Chartres' membership of the Jacobin Club was due to Mme. de Genlis or not, it had woeful results besides those it entailed in the sphere of politics. It made a mother's heart overflow with grief till then suppressed.

What a path the innocent Duchess had traversed since the time when she unreservedly bestowed her confidence on a newcomer, who was both talented and attractive!

How many illusions had vanished since the day when, without hesitation, she had entrusted to her her dearest possession—her children!

When, and by what chance, did she discover the masterful interference of Mme. de Genlis, her domination over the Duke, and, through this, over the whole life of the august household? We cannot say.

Neglect had come first, then disunion. She found herself forestalled with her children, and there was the humiliating sorrow of not being, from the secondary position to which Mme. de Genlis had quietly reduced her, able to intervene even in the slightest way in the education of her sons and her daughter.

Even if she could still possess the affection of her children —but every time she met them she found them more distant, more unresponsive and colder to her—she no longer knew the way to their hearts. She had to abdicate all rights over them, and remain outside of their lives to such a point that she never—or so rarely—heard from them a word of affection, a thought of filial attachment to her.

Of this fact there is deplorable evidence in the *Diary of*

the Princes; of themselves these children never give a thought to their parents. During the summer visits to Lamothe and St. Leu, where the stay of the Duke and Duchess sometimes extended over more than a month, this separation does not weigh upon them. It never even occurs to them—naturally affectionate though they are—to lighten this absence by letter-writing. They never write to the Palais Royal unless by order of their Governor, and then as if it were a difficult duty or a task imposed as a punishment.

Thus forced into a mournful self-effacement, which she accepted with most noble resignation, the helpless Princess had been for ten years suffering without a murmur.

No doubt it was a long time before she knew the whole truth. No doubt she was too obsequious to the commands of a husband who was unworthy of her. She was wanting in firmness, and then in her wounded pride she judged it unbecoming to demand from her children an affection which they owed her, but did not accord her.

At present, in the heart of the three Princes there was nothing that could withstand the influence of the Governess. The most that could be said was that M. de Beaujolais, the youngest, but already the most reserved, showed some indifference towards her; but this was amply compensated by the assiduous and demonstrative fidelity of the Duke of Chartres.

And the incredible spell thus cast over her eldest son by Mme. de Genlis was not the least of the Duchess of Orleans' reasons for complaint. That the Governess was very superior to the mother, everyone agreed. But what right had she to alienate so completely from the latter the heart of the young Prince?

Why should she claim, under the cover of a mere pretence, to leave her his respect and filial attachment, while she kept him to herself in all that regarded heartfelt affection, admiration, and personal confidence?

There has been much talk about the relations between Chartres and his teacher. Some, relying on an anecdote of doubtful authenticity and an unfavourable interpretation of the private diary of the Prince, have been ready to attribute to these relations more or less of a disgraceful character. They have gone so far as to say of Mme. de Genlis: "She was the lover of the father and of the son."

Now we have to put an end to this allegation, since, after a serious examination of the matter, no mistake about it is possible. We shall be therefore excused if we go into some detail, at the risk of seeming to dwell somewhat insistently on this delicate subject.

At the period when the Duke of Chartres ceased to be a child, he confided his thoughts to a private diary. Throughout these pages written by the young man, and which one can compare with the *Diary of the Princes*, kept day by day by Mme. de Genlis, his state of mind appears clear as a crystal.

He reveals it to us in his continual desire to be with Mme. de Genlis; in his overwhelming distress at being separated from her; in his excessive joy in her presence When he spends a day at Bellechasse, the Prince writes, "A good day," or "This day has done me more good than I can say."

He is more pleased to escort on foot his Governess on her donkey through muddy and stony lanes rather than go for a ride with his brothers. He cannot conceal an outbreak of vexation or a fit of melancholy if on a carriage drive he is not placed beside Mme. de Genlis.

He devotes himself to listening to, looking to her only. He writes her *tenderly affectionate* letters—as his teacher herself testifies—and he takes for their composition time set apart for his studies.

Finally, all his happiness centres on certain private conversations he has with her, some of which—on two or three occasions—are prolonged after midnight. And here is the passage from his private diary which has chiefly excited the suspicion of the malevolent:—

"*8th February* 1790.

"After supper went back to my friend. I remained alone with her; she treated me with infinite kindness, and I came away the happiest of men."[1]

[1] Cf. *Correspondance de L. P. J. d'Orléans*, publiée par L.C.R.

What was the conduct of Mme. de Genlis in this matter? Assuredly the *Diary of the Princes* shows that she thought there was nothing more puerile and stupid than the exclusive and unwelcome preference for her of this young fellow " who dares not be away from his Mentor for a minute." On several occasions she intimated to him an order not to be always running after her, and " to put himself in his pocket." [1]

As for those *tenderly affectionate* letters, the pupil ventures to address the Governess as . . . what? " My dear friend! my mother!" Yes, and sometimes as " My real mother! " as she permitted him to do. One of the letters contains the words, " What I love best in the world is the new Constitution and you! " And one may well grant, with a smile, that a passion which unites in the same ardour the Constitution and the beloved object is hardly a dangerous one. Moreover, the other Princes and Mademoiselle had also permission to write to Mme. de Genlis; they availed themselves of it from time to time, and might have written oftener if their hearts prompted them.

There remains the question of those famous private meetings.

Why be startled at a woman of about fifty granting her pupil the privilege of an hour's conversation? Rather late in the evening, it is true! But the occupations of both left them no free time except in the evening, after supper. And if one tries to find fault with such conversations, why suppose that Mme. de Genlis did not keep to those serious subjects that were, after all, the topics generally selected with precocious gravity by the Duke of Chartres, and in which this youth, older than his years, took special pleasure!

But it will be said, what were the feelings of the Prince?

And was not love the source of these preferences, these joys and sorrows, of which Mme. de Genlis was the mainspring.

" King Louis Philippe said to me the other day," relates Victor Hugo, " ' I was never in love with anyone but once in my life.' ' And who was it, Sire?' ' It was Madame de Genlis.' "—Granted that there was love—it was love of the

[1] *Leçons d'une gouvernante*, i. (April 19, 1790).

head, not the heart; love of the disciple for the teacher; docile, obedient love, bearing joyfully the yoke of recognised and venerated superiority; which indulges in admiring contemplation; takes delight in a word, a note; is satisfied with talk, and lives in feelings, not realities. Can one see anything else in it but schoolboy simplicity?

Let us look more closely at the private diary—those little confessions of a heart of seventeen. It is impossible to be mistaken about it. There is not a trace of sensuality. What one does find there is a scrupulous uprightness, great loftiness of feeling, remarkable piety, instead of the anxious emotions and excited superlatives of transports of passion.

A word from Mme. de Genlis would have been enough to transform this critical mood of a studious and retiring youth into reality. But she scrupulously refrained from it. One can find still clearer proof of this in two significant passages, taken the one from the *Diary of the Princes*, the other from the private diary. The more one reflects on the matter, the less one gives credit to that anecdote—a piece of thorough gossip—so very complacently accepted by Michaud, and of which, by his own account, the painter Myris was a witness at the château of Anet.[1] Mme. de Genlis notes on 18th June 1790 : " I see with great satisfaction that as the Duc de Chartres and the Duc de Montpensier increase in age, they at the same time become all the more firmly fixed in feelings of true piety, and in the love of modesty, chastity, and virtue. I venture to say that there are no young people of their age of purer lives than theirs."[2]

Nearly a year later, on 22nd May 1791, the Duke of Chartres has some idea of marriage—perhaps one might say with Paméla—and makes an ingenuous confession of it : " I know well that this moment is still far off, but at last it will arrive. And this is what supports me, and failing which I would succumb and abandon myself to all the irregularities of young men. O my mother, how I bless you for having

---

[1] Visiting the château of Anet with her pupils, the Governess is said to have exclaimed before the tomb of Diana of Poitiers, " How fortunate she was in having been loved by the father and the son ! "

[2] *Leçons d'une gouvernante*, i. (June 28, 1790).

preserved me from all these evils by inspiring me with those religious sentiments that are my strength, giving me the certitude of a life to come, and the knowledge that a fault of this kind would be like the stab of a dagger."[1]

And further, we may rely upon the very proper letter written by Mme. de Genlis to the Duchess of Orleans at the moment when the eldest of the Princes, having completed his seventeen years, was leaving the hands of his " Governor " to become his own master :—

"*For yourself only, Madame, this letter concerning the Duke of Chartres exclusively* :—

". . . I would wish, Madame, that at this moment, when he is being given his freedom, you would have immediately an interview with him, in which you would say : That he can make you happy only by conducting himself in an irreproachable manner ; that you hope he will maintain his religious principles, and that if he abandons them, and allows the purity of his morals to be corrupted, he will make you very unhappy ; while on the contrary, if he preserves his morals and principles, he will make you the happiest of mothers and will be passionately loved by you."

But Mme. de Genlis adds, coming to the substance of the letter: " In order to strengthen him and keep him in the right way, you must exert that predominant influence over the Prince that I myself have had over him, and which can be the result only of a perfect knowledge of his defects, his virtues, and the bent of his mind. I will therefore tell you the line to take, and it is important that your influence in this direction should be quickly established, for the most dangerous year for him is that which is about to begin. I cannot watch over him in the world ; that office is that of his good and thoughtful mother," etc.[2]

And finally, we have the testimony of Louis Philippe when he was King, as reported by Victor Hugo. In a few words he gives us a pleasing impression : " When I was

---

[1] *Correspondance de L. P. J. d'Orléans*, publiée par L.C.R.
[2] *Leçons d'une gouvernante*, ibid.

quite little," says the King, "I was afraid of Madame de Genlis. I was a weak, idle, timid boy. . . . She made of me a fairly courageous man with a heart. As I grew up I began to see that she was very pretty. I did not know what my feelings in her presence meant. She noticed it, understood me, and saw her way at once. She treated me very harshly."

On which Victor Hugo concludes that she absolutely refused " to complete her work by the supreme education of love."

It is now sufficiently demonstrated that the conduct of Mme. de Genlis in this matter was altogether to her honour.

Doubtless she considered it necessary to obtain a commanding influence over her pupil, and she succeeded only too well. Her empire over him had banished the very image of his parents from the Prince's heart, and it was of this that the Duchess of Orleans complained as a just cause of offence.

But now it was too late to resume her rights, and Mme. de Genlis, despite her letter of resignation, knew this well. The flame of filial love no longer burned in the Duke of Chartres. He never really loved his mother.

He was not happy when with her.

He was ill at ease on account of the divergence of their opinions. If he dined three or four times a week at the Palais Royal, and this without any particular enthusiasm, he escaped as soon as the meal was over, to run off to the Jacobins or to return to Bellechasse.

Besides, the conversation of his mother's guests grated on his patriotic feeling. "She went astray"—these are the very words of the young Prince—"in the frivolities of a disgusting aristocracy."

The Duke of Chartres preferred to dine at Monceaux, where his father invited some of the deputies to meet his sons and Mme. de Genlis, and better still at Bellechasse, where such guests as Voidel, Sillery, Barère, Volney, Péthion set on fire his ardour for equality.

So on 25th March 1790 we find him informing the Duchess that henceforth he can only dine twice a week with her.

Mme. d'Orléans agrees to this. She does not wish to

displease her son. But can one doubt that this caused a cruel wound to her heart?

Doubtless at first she had not taken the political tendencies of her eldest son at all seriously.

They were the outcome of the excitement of youth and impatience for action; and with everyone in Paris saving France or the throne twenty times a day since the States-General, she attached no great importance to his ideas. But when the talk of the Court and the newspapers announced that Chartres had become a novice of the Jacobins, the granddaughter of Louis XIV. revolted with all her sincere Royalism.

Mme. d'Orléans could not endure that her son should be made to renounce august traditions, that in her eyes were something sacred. And if she had not been able to bring up the heirs of the first Prince of the Blood Royal in respect for these traditions, at least she desired at any cost to save them from Jacobinism. The well-known letter which she wrote on this occasion to her husband might be worthy of a saint. It was a gentle, plaintive, supplicating letter, full of concessions to this husband who had wandered so far from his duty; a letter in which her goodness, her tender conjugal fidelity, her indulgent forgetfulness of the wrongs she had suffered from her husband, call forth our admiration, and in which, as it were in spite of herself, the deep grief of this broken heart breaks out in every line.

The unhappy Princess makes an appeal to respect for the throne and for religion. Prepared for the greatest sacrifices, provided only she can save her son, she yields easily on the question of Mme. de Buffon.[1]

As for Mme. de Genlis, she despises her, for she has seen and heard those things of which she complains: "You tell me," she writes to the Duke of Orleans, "that Madame de Sillery is a source of happiness to you, and that she loves

---

[1] "So everything was arranged. Madame de Genlis and Madame de Buffon had each their share of authority: one skilfully and decently, the other with public scandal; and thus everything combined to rend the heart of the Duchess of Orleans, and fill her life with bitterness and suffering" (Laurentie, *Histoire des Ducs d'Orléans*, iv. 249).

me. I confess to you that when you say things like this to me, it kills me." [1]

Nevertheless, if her husband considers it necessary for the education of the children, she will endure this woman. But do not let them put Chartres on a false track. Let him learn politics at the Assembly and nowhere else. At his age, indeed, it is hardly yet time for his being initiated in politics. . . .

This touching letter received only an evasive reply.

The Duchess insists, renews her complaints, and the Duke replies to her in brief notes, without any frankness, without opening his heart to her, and with shifty expressions.

The Duchess, who had at last shaken off something of her apathy, and at last was capable of an effort, relying on the support—weak and out-of-date as it was—of her father, the Duc de Penthièvre, began to attempt something against the astute Governess, the cause of all her troubles. But besides we must note that behind the poor Princess, whose tears were often her best resource, there was manœuvring a feminine *deus ex machina*, the Comtesse de Chastellux, who had been appointed a lady of honour on the retirement of Mme. de Genlis, and, admitted like her to deal with confidential matters, was carrying on a struggle against her predecessor. She was an Irishwoman, Miss Jenny Plunkett, and Mme. de Genlis had arranged her marriage with the Marquis de Chastellux, and installed her at the Palais Royal, where she repaid her benefactress with ingratitude and jealousy. She was working to get her dismissed. And this was the critical point of the business.

For throughout all his embarrassed replies one sees clearly that the Duke is pleading for Mme. de Genlis.

In the first place, she is his Egeria, his Minerva, to whom he returns as to a port of refuge; she comes before everything else.[2]

[1] *Correspondance de L. P. J. d'Orléans.*
[2] When Mme. Desrols, dismissed by the Governess, left Bellechasse, she wrote to the Abbé Mariottini: "The Duke of Orleans will give me a pension of 1800 *livres* on condition that I do not talk; but if I say a word I am to be deprived of it for ever" (*Lettera di Madamigella Nonon all'abate Mariottini*, March 2, 1787; *op. cit.*, p. 90).

Mme. de Genlis has ideas that accord with his own, with liberty for their first principle, and he, the Duke of Orleans, considers her an admirable woman.

Mme. de Genlis will not bring up his children in old-fashioned prejudices; she will make them new men, men of the future, and he, the Duke of Orleans, approves of this, utterly rejecting the childish fears of his wife.

It is therefore the Governess herself that the Duchess will have to attack.

And here we come to an infinitely sorrowful story—that of a mother trying to regain her children. And it matters little that her motherly love may have been mingled with something of feminine pride. Every right was on her side, against Mme. de Genlis.

As to this sad episode—perhaps the most pathetic of all those that darken the story of the Palais Royal—one of the most important pieces of evidence we possess is that of the Governess herself.

She had just then the idea of making the public the judge of her dissensions with the Duchess—an unfortunate and indiscreet idea if there ever was one, but by which we gain something, for it led the Governess to provide herself with proofs to be laid before her contemporaries.

The *Diary of the Princes*, a defence prepared well in advance for the justification of their Governess, contains in fact a long statement of her wretched quarrel with the Duchess of Orleans.

"More especially in a free State," exclaims Mme. de Genlis, "when a citizen lays his defence before the public, he has the right to be heard. The public is the august tribunal that alone can vindicate virtue from a host of calumnies that the laws do not punish; its opinion formulates decrees that must be respected. . . ."[1]

So we find in this *Diary* the minute, detailed record—hour by hour, one may say—of the relations of Mme. de Genlis with her pupils and with their mother; of her acts and deeds, her discourses, her reprimands. The teacher is throughout in the forefront of everything.

[1] *Leçons d'une gouvernante*, Paris, 1791, 2 vols. 12mo.

But the Duchess, notwithstanding the requests of Mme de Genlis, and of her sons, would never read the *Diary*, though she accepted that which his *valet de chambre*, Barrois, kept for M. de Beaujolais. This refusal indeed marked the opening of hostilities, or at least served as a pretext for them after the outbreak of the Duke of Chartres in Marat's newspaper.

It was in March 1790, then, that the Duchess, making Mme. de Genlis responsible for the imprudent conduct of her eldest son, showed mistrust and coldness towards her. But for some time before she had made only brief visits to Bellechasse. On 15th March, Mme. de Genlis, anxious to give proof of her good intentions, had asked Madame d'Orléans to be so good as to read the *Diary*, and received this negative reply: "I have no reason for reading the *Diary*. I trust my children."

At once the Governess scented danger.

She was not the woman to let herself be surprised, and she foresaw the blow that was coming. The hostile attitude of the Duchess showed that she was well informed. As the Comte de Moriolles said afterwards, she had suddenly learned "a thousand things that everyone but herself had long known." And already Mme. de Genlis was preparing for resistance. She was making weapons, gaining allies, and preparing for an appeal even to public opinion, for she had at once thought of a possible publication of the *Diary*.

From 2nd April onwards she secures a verification of its authenticity by making the Princes themselves henceforth attach their signatures to each entry. And to begin with, they approve with their signatures a long defence, a regular state paper, in which she insidiously puts on record the shortness of the Duchess's visits to Bellechasse, always made at moments when she knew she would not meet the Governess there.[1]

[1] "There is one thing to which I attach a very great value, namely, to put myself in a position to be able one day to give an exact account, minute by minute, of the whole of the education of Monseigneur to Madame . . . and *perhaps to the public*, if I judge this necessary." Then comes a long statement as to the authenticity of the *Diary*, which the Princes approve as follows: "I have just read this entry, on this 2nd of April at 10 p.m., and I recognise

Thus it would seem that Mme. de Genlis had the treacherous purpose of, in a way, making the children ratify a charge against their mother, a complaint supported by proofs against the conduct of the Duchess towards them.

And the endless piece of special pleading, including copies of letters exchanged between the Duchess and the Governess on this occasion, which closes the first volume, is proof enough that if Mme. de Genlis wished to inform the public of the method of education of the Princes, she was at the same time making an indictment against the Duchess of Orleans before the bar of public opinion.

But all these arguments nevertheless did not prevent even the most prejudiced minds from believing firmly that the more persecuted of the two, and the real victim of injustice, was not Mme. de Genlis.

In fact, she could not deny that she had taken an unfair possession of the children, and after Chartres had thus secured Mademoiselle, his sister.

Even in the *Diary* itself one can see how the Princess had been alienated from her mother. On various occasions the Duchess makes a complaint; she suffered still more at the moment when the Duke of Chartres no longer concealed his impetuous zeal for the Jacobins, at the moment when, after the noisy reception of her eldest son into the sect, she was led in an agony of fear to write to her husband.

After letters on letters that had no result but the clumsy equivocations of the Duke, Mme. d'Orléans at last made up her mind to question the children herself as to their feelings.

"Is it true that you love Mme. de Sillery so much?" she asked of her daughter, of Chartres, and of Montpensier. And Mademoiselle replied, "I would be very ungrateful not to love her with all my soul."

The two boys made much the same reply.

There was no longer room for doubt. On her side, Mme.

with the greatest pleasure that all its contents are of the most exact and most scrupulous veracity: A.P.L. d'Orléans (the Duc de Chartres). Rue de Provence, Chaussée d'Antin, this April 3rd, 1790; I give the same testimony as my brother and with the same feelings: A.P.L. d'Orléans (the Duc de Montpensier)." Then come the signatures of Adèle d'Orléans, Beaujolais, Henriette Sercey, Paméla, Olimpe (?), and César Ducrest.

de Genlis, to whom the children told everything, was all rejoicing. "Add to this," she writes, "that they see the Duchess of Orleans only for a few minutes at a time; that they are treated with extreme coldness by her; that they see that I am entirely devoted to them; that they think that such care as mine ought to inspire such gratitude as one gives to a mother. . . . Certainly they will not say that I am in the wrong, and such conduct cannot fail deeply to embitter them." [1]

Meanwhile the Duchess of Orleans no longer concealed her displeasure, and ceased to receive the Governess at the Palais Royal. She refrained almost entirely from going to see her children at Bellechasse, and gave them to understand that she had withdrawn from them, if not her affection, at least her confidence.

It was then Mme. de Genlis's turn to play the part of an injured woman. So on 10th September she throws her resignation in the face of the Duke,—unless "within three days I am given the reparation I have a right to. . . . Let Madame d'Orléans resume her friendly relations with me, and let this be followed by a *decent treatment* of me, and let her come here in the evenings as she used to do . . . in that case I shall remain and forget everything. . . ." [2]

The Duke refuses the resignation, and promises to obtain from his wife satisfaction for Mme. de Genlis.

Then these matters come to the ears of Mademoiselle, who is known to have been of an extremely, almost unhealthily, sensitive disposition. The fear of being separated from her dear teacher throws her into such a terrible agony that she loses consciousness and faints out in the garden at Bellechasse. They take her into the house " in the most frightful convulsions ! " [3]

It is not possible to think of abandoning Mademoiselle in this state. In fact, the young Princess only recovers from her attack of the nerves when she gets from Mme. de

---

[1] Genlis, *Mémoires*, iv. 16.
[2] *Ibid.*, Letter of Mme. de Genlis to the Duke of Orleans, Bellechasse, Friday, September 10, 1790.
[3] *Ibid.*

THE DUCHESS OF ORLEANS
(LOUISE MARIE ADELAIDE DE BOURBON-PENTHIÈVRE
WIFE OF PHILIPPE-ÉGALITÉ).

Genlis a formal promise that the latter will remain with her till she has completed her education, and will never voluntarily leave her.

The Governess then finds herself so much at her ease as herself to write a letter to the Duchess of Orleans—the letter of an injured innocent, who nevertheless is anxious to enter into explanations. She reminds the Duchess that she as well as the Duke begged her to take charge of the education of the Princes, that she has more than a hundred and fifty letters of the Princess in support of this statement. Mme. de Genlis purposely insists on these proofs, on the multitude of letters, portraits, keepsakes, pledges of friendship she has received from Mme. d'Orléans. Then she goes on to speak of her zeal as a teacher, her disinterestedness, and the exceeding danger of violent emotions " for the extremely sensitive nature of Mademoiselle." Finally, she protests her good faith and her keen desire for an understanding, even offering to educate Mademoiselle at the Palais Royal.[1]

But this masterpiece did not touch the Duchess; she perceived its threats, disguised though they were as concessions. But, in her love for peace, she diplomatically lent herself to a kind of compromise, hoping thereby to gain the heart of her daughter.

So Mme. de Genlis received a note in which the Duchess announced that she would come three times a week to take out Mademoiselle, and keep her with her each time for about an hour and a half. She would also come and take the children each Sunday at three o'clock, and after the dinner, at which the Governess might be a guest with her pupils at the Palais Royal, Mademoiselle would be taken back to Bellechasse. Things went on in this way for three weeks.

The Duchess lavished caresses and affectionate care on her daughter, and Mme. de Genlis dined on the Sundays at the Palais Royal with her pupils.

Then, at the end of this time, without apparently anything in particular having happened, the Duchess felt that she had no longer the courage to receive her enemy at table.

She informed her husband that she felt an " invincible

[1] *Leçons d'une gouvernante*, Letter of October 3, 1790; *Mémoires*, iv. 22-31.

repugnance" for Mme. de Genlis, and that by her desire the young Princes were to come to her on the following Sunday without their Governess. After that day the latter never again set foot in the Palais Royal.

But Her Highness failed in her attempts to regain her daughter. Whatever she did, Mademoiselle could not be tamed. No sign of reviving affection gave warmth to word or gesture on her part. It was no longer possible for mother and daughter to abandon themselves to affectionate confidences, Mme. de Genlis having long before this cut off the current. And each of them had in her heart a secret thought that closed all access to it and chilled their intimacy.

The Duchess tried to brighten their interviews with the presence of the lively lady-of-honour, Mme. de Chastellux. But this only made things worse, Mme. de Chastellux railing at Mme. de Genlis, and Mademoiselle complaining of this. So the utter defeat of the mother's love was completed.

At the beginning of 1791, as the Duke of Chartres was fulfilling the office of porter—or "censor"—at the Jacobin Club, Mme. d'Orléans ceased her visits to Bellechasse and broke absolutely with Mme. de Genlis—a decision which, rightly or wrongly, the latter attributed to the influence of Mme. de Chastellux.

The Duke thought he might make his wife more tractable by arranging meetings on neutral ground, so he invited her with her children to dine at Monceaux. But as Mme. de Genlis was to be present the Duchess kept away.

At the time of the carnival Mademoiselle gave four little dances with refreshments—children's parties, where there was a dance to the tune of *Ça ira!* The Duke came without the Duchess, and Mme. de Genlis in a tricolour dress presided at these gaieties.

At last, to put an end to this false situation, the Duke insisted on his wife coming to a frank explanation with Mme. de Genlis.

The timid inferiority of the Duchess pitted against the cleverness of Mme. de Genlis would guarantee the success of the latter at the interview, for which, as the Governess herself confesses, she had been long preparing. "I thought," she explains, "of saying to her: 'I have promised Mademoiselle not to give in my resignation, so I shall not do so. You will not ask me for it, because M. d'Orléans controls the arrangements for his children and you would not take a step opposed to his wishes, and therefore to your duty.'" Finally, she would suggest, very diplomatically, that it would be better to come to a mutual understanding, avoid annoying the Duke, meet Mademoiselle's wishes, and at any rate put off the question of the resignation till the next winter.

But the Duchess had taken into account in advance her own weak points; and when, one morning in March 1791, she presented herself at Bellechasse, it was to read to the Governess a statement of what she wanted set down in writing, and to signify to her her dismissal.

"She came in brusquely," relates Mme. de Genlis, "sat down, bade me be silent, and took a paper out of her pocket, telling me in a most imperious tone that she was about to declare to me her intentions. Then she proceeded at once to read to me in a loud voice and with great volubility the most surprising document in the world.

"The Duchess of Orleans signified to me in this written statement that, considering our differences of opinion, I had no other course to take, *if I were an honourable woman*, but to go away without further delay."

In the presence of such a positive order she could only submit and depart. Mme. de Genlis immediately declared that she would go in a month, "unless," as she told the Duke, who was anxiously awaiting the result of the interview, "Mme. d'Orléans herself should ask me to stay."

But the Duchess stood firm.

In vain her husband exhausted every means of persuasion; pleading the unfinished education of his daughter, public opinion, the health of Mademoiselle. In vain he sent his son, the Duke of Chartres, to add tears to entreaties. Mme. d'Orléans would not yield.

Suddenly, on 5th April, there came the news that she

had gone away unexpectedly to Eu. Mme. de Genlis would have it that she was merely putting herself beyond the reach of those who were arguing with her. But later revelations told of more cruel incidents, and if we are to believe the Comte de Moriolles the Duchess was brutally driven out of the Palais Royal by her husband himself in his fury at her resistance.[1]

From Eu the poor woman applied to the courts for a separation, or rather this formality was carried through for her, for she would never have been strong enough to take the step herself.

The wrongs pleaded by the Duchess were the squandering of her fortune, the unfaithfulness of the Duke, notably his guilty relations with Mme. de Genlis, the difference between his and her political and religious opinions, and finally the anti-traditional education given by the "Governor" to the children.

The Prince at once replied by expelling Mme. de Chastellux from the Palais Royal, giving her a written order to hand over the keys of her rooms within fifteen days. Finally, on 19th April, a process-server summoned the Duchess to return to her husband's home—a mere formality, says one of his biographers, by which the Duke expressed his satisfaction "at getting rid of an inconvenient and yet too generous witness of his way of life."[2]

And on 26th April, in the early morning, Mme. de Genlis departed from Bellechasse, taking Paméla with her, for a tour in Franche Comté. She left three notes addressed to Mademoiselle, and to be given to her at intervals of twelve hours. The young Princess did not know the truth. It had been thought prudent to conceal it from her.

What a sorrowful surprise these three notes must have caused her! One may judge of it by their contents, which we purposely reproduce here. They throw a clear light on this family episode, and satisfy our curiosity as to the

---

[1] "The Duchess of Orleans, whom her husband had driven from the Palais Royal, sending her away with only the clothes she wore" (Comte de Moriolles, *Mémoires*, p. 32).

[2] Ducoin, *Philippe-Égalité*, p. 148.

strangely exaggerated tone of her Governess's affection for Mademoiselle.

First Letter

"*April 25th*, 1791, 8 *p.m.*

"Mme. de Genlis to Mlle. d'Orléans.

"DEAR CHILD,—I am forced to leave you at least for a time; but I hope that we shall meet each other again. In the name of your affection for me, be reasonable and take care of your health.

"The Duchess of Orleans has forced me to go away from you. But my heart remains with you. Remember, my dear friend, that you must submit to a mother's will. . . ."

Second Letter

"*The 25th. Midnight.*

"You felt, dear child, that violent palpitation of the heart that I noticed when you lay down in bed.[1]

"I leave your room. I have just kissed you once more. . . . My dear child, I would never have asked to leave you, whatever treatment was inflicted on me; but the Duchess of Orleans herself has positively required it of me. I had to obey. I shall write you a long letter to-morrow morning; but it will not be handed to you till you are again calm and reasonable.

"Dear child, I love you more than my life—a thousand times more; take care of your health if you want me to live.

"Be quite sure that we shall meet again."

Third Letter

"*The 26th. Morning.*

"MY DEAR CHILD,—I am going to write to you more in detail. I promised you that I would never ask to leave you, no matter what treatment I experienced. I have kept my word. I have suffered all that you have seen in the last two

---

[1] Mademoiselle had had sad presentiments; without having been told anything, she feared misfortune was near; she cried without any reason, and was ill when she went to bed. To calm her, Mme. de Genlis had to play the harp for her, and assure her that her fears had no foundation.

years. I have been treated as they would not treat a servant-girl, since the Duchess of Orleans forbade me to go to the Palais Royal even with you. I have suffered many other things that you have witnessed. If I had not loved you, as they never love, I would have asked for, I would have been bound to ask for, my dismissal at the very outset of this conduct. But to keep you with me nothing was too great a price for me. . . .

"The Duke of Orleans has not left you in ignorance of his fears as to the petition for a separation made by the Duchess of Orleans,—terrible, heart-rending fears for you and your brothers. . . . Thank Heaven, I am not even made the pretext for this last outbreak of the Duchess of Orleans; she insisted on my going away the day she came here by herself. It was in my room, a month ago. And I replied that I would go. So she has gained what she wanted. Our separation is very cruel, my affectionate friend; but a misfortune like this is not unprecedented. Remember the story of Fénelon and his pupil the Duke of Burgundy. (Mme. de Genlis adds in a note in her *Memoirs*: "I had on purpose read this story for her some days before our separation.") They were parted in much the same way . . ." etc.

As one can see, there is not in these letters a single word to open the eyes of Mademoiselle to the real reasons for the resolution taken by her mother.

Thirty-five years later, Mme. de Genlis ventured at last to do partial justice to the Duchess of Orleans. She did it awkwardly, alleging as the explanation the "false philosophy"[1] which misled so many minds at the period of the Revolution, but between the lines one can easily read a desire to make some reparation, inspired by some beginning of repentance; it was, it is true, a belated reparation. Public opinion had long before this given the example to Mme. de Genlis.

[1] "The motive for the sudden breaking off of the Duchess of Orleans from me was plainly the difference of our political opinions; but I recognise now that all her fears, which then seemed to me so exaggerated and even so unjust, were only too well founded. Such had to be the inevitable results of the odious principles that had been propagated for more than half a century in Europe, and above all in France, by a false philosophy" (*Mémoires*, iv. 81).

CHAPTER V

THE JOURNEY TO ENGLAND

MADEMOISELLE bore these saddening events badly. This sudden departure was the cruel breaking of a thousand dear bonds of affection; it was as though an abyss had opened around her heart and soul. The presence of Henriette de Sercey, whom Mme. de Genlis had left with her to lessen the shock, was but a poor palliative, and did not console her for the loss of her dear Governess.

Extremely impressionable as she was, Mademoiselle gave way to despair, and her weak health suffered in consequence.

And her relatives, seeing her suddenly reduced to such a wretched state, hastily recalled her tutelary genius.

When the first alarming news reached Mme. de Genlis, she was at Lyons.

Without losing an instant, and all the while secretly rejoicing, she turned back.

She was only about six leagues from Auxerre when she was met by an express courier sent after her with a bundle of pressing letters.

And, good Heavens, what letters! Did they really believe the Governess would persist in taking her dismissal as final?

There were letters from the Duke of Orleans, from the three Princes, from M. Pieyre, from Mme. de Valence, from M. de Genlis himself.

All Bellechasse was imploring her, adjuring her with clasped hands to return, "to save the poor little thing from death or from a state a hundred times worse."

The Duke of Orleans had even thought it right to add to

his epistle a copy of that which he had sent to inform his wife, and the reply of the latter addressed to Montpensier.

As the Duchess declares that "she has no rights over her daughter, that she wishes to have no part in the affair, and that she leaves it absolutely to the Prince to take any precautions required for her,"[1] and as Sillery adds, "The Duke of Orleans has formally stated to me that your return depends on yourself alone," Mme. de Genlis could consider that her self-respect was satisfied, and that she could say she was authorised to reappear at Bellechasse.

Swiftly—doing the last stages at full gallop—she arrives, and in fact finds her dear pupil "in a heart-breaking state."

But like a young plant beaten down by a stormy wind but revived by the least drop of water, Mademoiselle at once regains strength under the fond looks of her dear mistress. "My care and my affection soon restored her to health," says Mme. de Genlis. The Duke of Chartres, too, who has been severely tried by this crisis in the family, and has also been ill, regains his normal condition.

As for the Duchess, she is at Eu.

She did not appear at her daughter's bedside—a fact that lends some confirmation to the report that she had been brutally driven away by the Duke—nor beside the rival who though dismissed a few days ago had now returned to the precincts of Bellechasse as their immutable and predestined guardian.

All in tears, the Duchess of Orleans, now staying with her father, awaits the result of the suit for a separation. She has the esteem and sympathy of others, although gossip runs on and dilates upon the interrupted journey of the Governess. The least malicious report is that in fact she went into the provinces to recruit from club after club partisans for the Orleanist faction.[2] But nothing that happened afterwards confirms this improbable story, this fancy of over-excited

[1] Cf. M. de Chabreul, *Gouverneur de Princes*, p. 273.

[2] "Meanwhile Madame Brûlard has just gone with her Paméla to rekindle the zeal of all the societies of 'Friends of the Constitution' on the road between Lyons and Paris. They make out that the eloquence of the mother and the beauty of the daughter have worked marvels, and won many servants for Philippe Capet, who is hiding, as far as he can, under the mask of a Friend of

brains, and Heaven knows if just then Orleans had any supporters in Paris or in France, either on the side of the Aristocrats or in the grasping, hate-inspired crowd of which the Jacobins were the leaders. And it so happened that one May day this People, on whom Mme. de Genlis lavished so much affection in her writings, was so good as to let her experience the sweets of its vigilance.

It was during a carriage-drive that the teacher took to Colombes with Mademoiselle and the two youngest of the Princes—the Duke of Chartres was at Vendôme with his regiment. Some Sansculottes, thinking the party were Madame Elisabeth, Madame Royale, and the Dauphin, stopped the carriage and took them under a strong escort to the *mairie*, despite the protests and democratic harangues of Mme. de Genlis. They were kept prisoners there until the return of an old servant, whom they sent in haste to Bellechasse to bring their "papers of identity," at last extricated them from this awkward situation.

On 21st June came the flight to Varennes.

Intrigues were once more busy around the Palais Royal, now known as the Palais-Orléans. Laclos conducted them.

Rumours of the deposition of the King and rumours of a Regency were in circulation and found credit.

The tribunes of the Clubs, the newspapers, resounded with the name of Orleans.

Certain papers devoted to his faction—notably Perlet's *Assemblée nationale*—published "regular Orleanist manifestoes."

At the Jacobin Club, Laclos, Brissot, Danton, and the rest did the oratorical part of the business.

For the third time the Duke of Orleans had only to say a word and the throne of France would fall to him—he would first be Regent, then King—this would come as a matter of course, considering the feeble health of the Dauphin.

To the indignant surprise of some, to the utter stupefaction of others, he refused to say the word.

He rejected the throne in a speech at the Jacobin Club,

the Constitution" (*Correspondance secrète*, published by Lescure, May 21, 1791).

at the sitting of 25th June 1791, the very evening the King was brought back from Varennes; and in a letter to Mme. de Genlis next morning, 26th June. The letter appeared in the *Assemblée Nationale* of 28th June in the form of a reply to Perlet's manifesto.[1]

Was Mme. de Genlis responsible for this determination, which was as tactless as it was unexpected ?

If we are to believe her *Memoirs*, all that she did was to draw up the note for the newspapers by order of the Duke.

"I imagine," she suggests, "that he got me to draw up this declaration because his recognised counsellors did not approve of the step."[2]

It would seem that at this point her recollections are wanting in accuracy.

This refusal by the Duke of Orleans would seem to have been nothing more or less than the revenge of Mme. de Genlis on Laclos.

And the learned biographer of Laclos does not hesitate to write : "This treacherous woman saw with fury the efforts of her old adversary Laclos. . . . With the Dauphin crowned and the Duke of Orleans Regent, there would for the present be an end of all hope for the Duc de Chartres. In fact, his father was an obstacle in the way of Madame de Genlis. She resolved to get rid at once of the barrier and of her master. . . . On the 27th Madame de Genlis frightened and persuaded him into signing this letter addressed to Perlet, but which appeared in all the newspapers next day."[3]

These papers, which were so enthusiastic for the Duke of Orleans the day before, now suddenly took to repeating in honour of the Duke of Chartres the enthusiastic eulogies which the cause of his father inspired but yesterday. And

---

[1] "To the Editor.—Paris, June 26, 1791.—Having read in your issue No. 689, your opinion as to the steps to be taken after the return of the King, and all that your justice and impartiality dictate in my regard, I must repeat, what I have already publicly declared on the 21st and 22nd of this month to several members of the National Assembly, namely, that I am ready to serve my country on land, on sea, in the diplomatic service, in a word in any position that requires unbounded zeal and devotion to the public welfare; but that if it is a question of governing, I renounce now and for ever the rights the Constitution gives me" (*Assemblée nationale*, No. 692, Tuesday, June 28, 1791).

[2] Genlis, *Mémoires*, iv. 92, 93.   [3] E. Dard, *op. cit.*, 302–303.

the young Prince gave an example of patriotism to the nation by hurrying from Vendôme, where he had received the civic crown, to mount guard at the Tuileries.

What a hero was this young Duke of Chartres—patriotic, brave, enlightened!

Mme. de Genlis was triumphant. She took advantage of this exceptionally favourable moment to publish the *Leçons d'une gouvernante*, which have been already mentioned. This enabled her not only to let the world know what an admirable education she had given to her pupil, but also publicly to renew her profession of democratic faith.

From the summit of this pedestal she shows herself teaching, day by day, hour by hour, contempt for the order of things founded upon old prejudices, training her pupil "to sympathise with the oppressed People, to detest arbitrary power and all the abuses of the *ancien régime*, to despise pomp and empty distinctions . . . and to regard as sacred and inviolable every engagement, public or private, and therefore a solemn oath pronounced in the presence of the whole nation. . . ."

But the civic virtue of Chartres, undoubted and remarkable though it be, seems to fall to the second rank compared with the proclamations of Revolutionary doctrine put forth by his Governess, in her preface, which was obviously inspired by recent events. Brissot could hardly be suspected of Royalism, and even he after the event was startled by these utterances.

"One may ask," he says, "if it was possible to invoke more artfully—I would almost say more perfidiously, if this word could be applied to an act of loyalty—the Constitution to which the King had taken the oath; one may ask if it was possible . . . to bring Louis XVI. more directly before the tribunal of the nation in case he violated the law; and it was at the very time when by his flight to Varennes he had just violated it.

"It is perhaps in this piece of writing that one can trace the first word that seems to suggest his deposition uttered as if by prophetic inspiration—a word that others merely repeated."[1]

But Brissot judged all this from his own point of view,

---

[1] Brissot, *Mémoires*, ii. 329–330.

and Brissot was not trusted, and so was kept in ignorance of the latest intrigues of the moment.

There was Laclos, refusing to acknowledge his defeat, and pretending not to believe that the Duke of Orleans had renounced his claim to the Regency. Elected secretary of the Jacobin Club, Laclos was manœuvring in the dark to uphold the constitutional monarchy, by hook or by crook, to the advantage of his patron.

Following with the biographer of Laclos the course he took as a leader in this affair, one discovers how, on 18th July, he instigated the petition of the Champ-de-Mars; how by a skilful addition made by this master of intrigue the text of the petition "implied the proclamation of the Dauphin and the Regency of the Duke of Orleans"; how, on 16th July, Mme. de Genlis sent her husband to warn Bailly, while Laclos with his printing-press was preparing to send the text of the petition all over France; how when Danton solemnly read the petition at the "altar of the fatherland" on the Champ-de-Mars, the Cordeliers protested, and had the petition referred back to the Jacobins; how finally, after a long discussion, Laclos succeeded in maintaining the original text, when at that very moment a deputy ran in with the news that the Assembly formally recognised Louis XVI. as King.[1] This time Laclos had clearly lost the game.

And granted that his failure was due rather to the decision of the Assembly than to the work of Mme. de Genlis, all the same she had won; it was merely a victory for her personal pride, it is true, for from the political point of view she had gained nothing.

Unfortunately, her successes were won only over the Duchess of Orleans.

For the Duke, ill provided with cash, and even in some difficulty, did not want to spend his money on the support of his four children. He had lately entered into negotiations with his wife, asking her to provide an annual allowance of 100,000 *livres* (francs) for each of them. The Princess, whose dowry he had squandered, was not rich enough "to satisfy such an exorbitant demand."[2]

[1] E. Dard, *op. cit.*, 324. [2] Ducoin, *Philippe-Égalité*, 149.

All that she could do was to provide for the present and the future for Mademoiselle and Beaujolais, on condition that these two children were at once sent to her.

By the advice of Mme. de Genlis, who could overcome even his cupidity, the Duke treated this offer with disdain, and kept possession of his children, and on 11th October 1791 the Governess took Mademoiselle to England, together with Paméla, and Henriette de Sercey, and her granddaughter Eglantine de Lawœstine.[1]

Pétion and Voidel accompanied the ladies.

The presence of the future Mayor of Paris with Mme. de Genlis in the familiar association of the inside of a travelling carriage, where the Governess and Paméla " sat knee to knee with the worthy man," seemed very suspicious to the " men of the Mountain " in 1792. And Camille Desmoulins, Robespierre, and especially Marat, violently reproached the incorruptible Pétion with this expedition, for which they could see no good reason. It remains puzzling enough so far as he is concerned.

Mme. de Genlis in her Memoirs relates that she was led to accept the offer of Pétion's escort because she feared the journey might excite disagreeable suspicions " if she had not a man who could harangue the people and the municipalities in case of need." [2]

But Pétion knew that he was on the eve of being elected, by the favour of the Duke of Orleans, Mayor of Paris. Should not his interests have led him to remain there ?

The following letter of Mme. de Genlis to the Duke of Orleans, published long after, shows that this journey was arranged between them, but for a later date.

"BATH, *Thursday evening, 3rd November* 1791.

" . . . I had agreed with Pétion to take him to London, and then when I suddenly decided to start I thought he would not come, for I had settled not to start till the 4th or

---

[1] A week before Mme. de Genlis, Mademoiselle and Paméla visited the Louvre, where in the Salon of 1791 Giroust exhibited his "Leçon de harpe." All three wore the red cap and called forth wild enthusiasm.

[2] Genlis, *Mémoires*, iv. 99.

5th of this month. I thought of M. de Voidel, and M. de Sillery answered for him, on condition that I would take him in the carriage as far as Bath, and bring him back to London, and that, further, a carriage should be found for him from Calais to Paris. This having been settled one evening, and having to start next day, I wrote to Pétion to tell him I was going, that he was not now necessary to me, but that I would take him with pleasure. He took me at my word, and I was not sorry to have two instead of one to extricate me from the fearful perils that I foresaw. This is how I came to take them with me. I parted from Pétion in London while we were changing horses. I brought Voidel here. I am sending him back in a chaise which Dufour will pay for."[1]

It is still said that the incorruptible Jerome courted the fair Countess. She does not deny that she felt "a real esteem" for him, and we have Brissot's word for it that it was reciprocated.[2]

Was this journey only a proof of polite attention, an excursion in pleasant and charming company?

The presence of Voidel and of Mademoiselle forbids any suspicion of gallantry. But were not those terrible politics hidden away in the background of it all?

May not Pétion have gone to London to get into touch with agents or emissaries of the Duke, who was so well known and popular there? Perhaps to come to an understanding with the Marquis du Crest, who since 1789, that is, since his second marriage, with Mlle. Parisot, a younger daughter of the President de Minute, was living in a French hotel in London? But of all this nothing has been made public.

Mme. de Genlis remained a fortnight in the British capital, and then went to stay at Bath, the fashionable watering-place, and a centre of the most elegant society.

But her sudden departure from France is proof enough that she meant to remain mistress of Mademoiselle.

A little while ago Laclos lost his game. Now the Duchess had lost her daughter. From Eu, whither she had followed

---

[1] *Correspondance de L. P. J. d'Orléans*, 196.   [2] Brissot, *Mémoires*, ii. 322.

her father, she wrote to " an old and humble friend, M. Le Roi, who was a true sympathiser with the unfortunate," these lines as to Mme. de Genlis: " This wicked and haughty woman, who in my regard dispenses with the simplest forms of courtesy and respect, and who considers it necessary to withdraw my daughter from ' *my dangerous influence* ' . . . this woman to whom I have never done any harm, and of whom I cannot speak without weeping. . . ."[1]

When after seven years of separation she saw Mademoiselle again, a painful incompatibility, a deep chasm that had been dug long ago, formed, alas! a barrier for ever between her and her daughter.

It was not the first time that the Governess had travelled in England.

Six years before, in 1785, she had gone there with Paméla, winning everywhere the greatest success in the higher circles of English society. It was then that she received the degree of Doctor from one of the Universities; it was then that she met Horace Walpole, the enemy of women-authors, the enemy of Rousseau, the enemy of Mme. de Genlis, on account of her theories of education, or from hearsay—a mere prejudice on his part.

These unfriendly dispositions towards this " hen-Rousseau," this " schoolmistress," did not however prevent the dryly aggressive satirist from surrendering to the charms of Mme. de Genlis, notwithstanding a certain bourgeois air which he asserts hung about her. She made such an excellent impression on him that he invited her to lunch.

As for Paméla, he says: " Mme. de Genlis had educated her to be very like herself in the face."[2]

At Bath in 1791 the Governess, the Princess and their companions lived a somewhat retired life. They seemed to be giving all their attention to the study of the English language, and with a view to this they took a box for the season at the local theatre.

Mme. de Genlis mentions six people—among them an Irish priest, and the doctor in charge of the waters—who

---
[1] Baron de Maricourt, *La Duchesse d'Orléans*.
[2] Ida A. Taylor, *Life of Lord Edward Fitzgerald*, 123.

made up their circle of acquaintances. But their resources would not allow them to follow the round of wealthy social life. Living at Bath was dear, and for her entire fortune the Governess had a hundred louis in her pocket. After a few weeks reasons of economy made a less expensive place of residence advisable, and Bury, a country town in Suffolk, gave the shelter of one of its cottages to their unpretentious housekeeping. Victor Hugo has told how, in order to spare the hundred louis, Mademoiselle and Paméla had to sleep in the same room. There were two beds in it, but only one woollen bedcover, and this Mme. de Genlis authoritatively allotted to Paméla. Mademoiselle had "to be content to shiver through every night."[1] It is curious that the house soon obtained a singular reputation in the neighbourhood. Men, who seemed odd-looking to the inhabitants of the little town, appeared to have some business with the French ladies, and were treated now on the footing of equals, now on that of servants.

The Governess passed for an oddity. Her so-called caprices were the subject of local gossip, and it is said led to a forecast that she would go away before long.

The truth is that whilst devoting herself with incredible ardour to literary work, and literally devouring English dictionaries, histories and dramas, she never ceased her watch on the affairs of France, and on this account she was receiving political visitors at Bury. She certainly spent there the spring and summer of 1792.

It is also said, on the strength of one of the Governess's letters to the Duke of Orleans, that while in England she was engaged in drawing up a diary of events intended to represent the Duke as a model husband and father. But people have misinterpreted a passage in the letter as indicating a new publication. She does indeed allude to a diary she has written, but this diary is nothing else but that of the Princes, those *Leçons d'une gouvernante*, which were just then causing so much talk at Paris.[2]

[1] V. Hugo, *Le roi Louis-Philippe*.
[2] Cf. Genlis, *Mém.*, iv. " I am charmed, dear friend, at your having heard such good opinions of my Diary," etc. See also *Les mères rivales*, Preface, xii.

But she was too clever to defend before, and against, every one a lost cause, and such was the cause of constitutional royalty after the dismissal of the Girondins. After the 10th of August—or at any rate during the events that led up to the 10th of August, she sent her husband an imperative warning :—

"I see that the good cause is very nearly lost," she says to him. . . . "You can take one of two courses; either that of supporting the Constitution and perishing in its defence; or that of accepting the changes that are proposed, but at the same time laying down conditions which will make the change as lasting and as solemn as possible. Then everything will go on for five or six months without proscriptions. France will not be the freest country in the world, but it will not be under such a despotical government as before the Revolution. Some things will be abolished for ever—*lettres de cachet*, the tyrannical game laws, and feudal rights, and that is always a gain. And in course of time everything really good in the Constitution will be re-established. These things have been debated and put into print, and they will assuredly be established again. I have never thought that people went too far, but I have thought that they went too fast. The scheme of ideas and principles is generally excellent, but the plan of conduct was absurd. . . . Do not count upon Luckner," she adds, " he has no knowledge of politics, and don't dream of being able to turn out Lafayette. For that one should be able to point to some misdeed, not against the Jacobins, but against the Constitution, and there is none." Her last piece of advice is this : " Supposing there is talk of negotiations with the enemy, look to your means of leaving France. Give our landed property to Mme. de Montesson, on condition of her paying us an annuity; but take proper precautions, and try to have a secure contract in legal form."[1] Certainly this was prudent advice. But no one will be surprised that Sillery took no notice of it.

His political faith attached him to the Duke of Orleans, and with reckless audacity he disdained to cling to life. At

[1] *Correspondance de L. J. P. d'Orléans*, 210.

Paris, for some time people had been playing with danger, dancing on a volcano without being swallowed up. Naturally daring, and with his feelings dulled by habit to the danger of death, Sillery braved it without showing anything of the braggart. But all the while the volcano was becoming more dangerously menacing and pouring out lava on all sides.

After the September massacres, Philippe-Égalité, knowing that the law against the *émigrés* was in preparation, asked Mme. de Genlis to send his daughter back to him. But the girl, rightly alarmed at the idea of returning to her native land at such a moment, refused to come. Was there a fair wind blowing for home ? Was there not on the contrary the rising Terror driving Frenchmen across their frontiers ?

Like a torrent swollen by a storm, aristocrats and "suspects" came pouring into England. They had a fierce hatred for the Orleanist party, and contemptuously called Mme. de Genlis the *Jacobine*.

Then she had to face the greatest alarms.

Anonymous letters insulted and threatened her, spoke of burning down her house in the night; of carrying off Mademoiselle by force "to hand her over to a foreign sovereign."

Under the stress of these menaces we find her attempting a defence of the royal family in a letter for which a kind of semi-theatrical advertisement seems to have been organised. Mme. de Genlis addressed it to Pétion with the design of forwarding it to him through Fox and Sheridan, to whom she sent it unsealed, after having sent it round to a number of people in London. The letter appeared without a signature in the *Patriote Français*, and Gorsas reproduced it in his newspaper on 3rd October,[1] "and this," writes Mme. de Genlis, "secured for me henceforth the hatred of the party of Marat and Robespierre."[2]

All the same, the Royalists continued to shower upon her the most insulting anonymous letters. One of them, written in English, called her "a savage furie" (*sic*), and added such

[1] *Annales patriotiques*. [2] Genlis, *Mémoires*, iv. 125.

serious threats that the Governess in a fright sent off a pressing appeal to Fox begging him to send her without delay a legal adviser.

She hardly knew the great opponent of Pitt, having only met him at the house of John Hurford Stone,[1] an enthusiastic Revolutionist and a faithful friend of Miss Williams, who also knew Sheridan. But in a situation of such danger—at least in her opinion—the views and the influence of Fox seemed to her, with some reason, to suggest that it would be useful to have recourse to him, and she addressed to him a suppliant request :—" I am uneasy," she wrote, " sick, unhappy, and surrounded by the most dreadful snares of fraud and wickedness."

The reply of the English statesman has not reached us, but we know that he at once sent Sheridan to the Governess to give her his assistance and advice.

In the beginning of October Sheridan took the little party of Frenchwomen to a hotel in London, where their presence was at once known.

For London was full of *émigrés*, nobles who had brought across the Channel the feelings and the manners of their class.

And they were as divided as they had been at Paris.

But nothing was easier for Mme. de Genlis than to find old acquaintances among them. Always sociable and ready to bestir herself, she soon succeeded in getting together a little circle of her own shade of politics, and Mademoiselle presided in the evenings at its quiet social gatherings.

Old friends of the Duke of Orleans, whom Walsh calls " the colleagues and accomplices of Égalité," refugees who lately frequented the Palais Royal, Narbonne, Mme. de la Châtre, Mme. de Flahault, the inevitable Abbé de Cabre, met each other there. But " the star of this little coterie " was Talleyrand. Escaped by a miracle and by great efforts from the claws of Robespierre, he never better understood the value of freedom.

---

[1] Stone, accused of high treason, went to live in France. But in 1790 he was one of the most active propagandists of the Society of the Friends of the Revolution in London. It is said that Stone secretly married Miss Williams.

With Mme. de Genlis he found himself among people of his own way of thinking, and far from those Jacobins whose excesses he denounced in those forms of words of which he had the secret, epigrams that told, and that he had carefully prepared beforehand.

" Sociable and brilliant, he is lavish of his cheerfulness and his polished amiability." [1] He is the most welcome guest, the one they like to see by himself. Every evening he brings books, and partakes of a supper of which he praises " the inestimable frugality."

These two aristocrats, the unfrocked prelate and the Governess, have more than one point in common. Old habitués of the Palais Royal, influenced by the same political ideas, both had more or less helped to bring about this awful state of things, and both were silently awaiting better days for their ambitions.

At an early date they had understood each other's minds, and their first meeting had been long since. It dated almost from Mme. de Genlis's first entry into the social world, from 1770 or 1771. She had seen at Sillery, in the salon of Mme. de Puysieulx, Maurice de Périgord, accompanying his uncle the archbishop. He was then thirteen, and, being intended for the Church, he already wore the soutane. The pale face of the delicate youth, his silence, his slight limp, and above all his observant looks made a deep impression on the fair Countess. Later on she remembered the young cleric, when the gaming tables of the Comte de Genlis were at least as great an attraction for the Abbé de Périgord as the charms of the wife. And it is not to be denied that if he often risked a stake with Genlis, he was said to have also paid assiduous court to the Governess.

Their common interests attached them to the Orleanist party.

One meant to be a minister in the Government; the other had, it might be, still higher projects. Henceforth a real attachment united these two ambitions, these two clever, attractive people, the offspring of the same century, brought up in the same school of refined corruption, and who had

[1] Bernard de Lacombe, *Vie privée de Talleyrand.*

early learned in an unhappy childhood to busy themselves with making the way easy for good fortune.

The fierce whirlwind that swept over France in 1792 had just brought them together again for a while in London. But they will find a way to meet again even after the widest of separations, and notwithstanding the worst vicissitudes keep faithfully a mutual remembrance and friendship. We shall see them again on more than one occasion.

Meanwhile the decree against the *émigrés* was being got ready.

In his anxiety on his daughter's account the Duke of Orleans put into circulation a note in which he explained the departure of Mademoiselle on the plea of " a fear that my wife, in my absence, would come and take possession of my daughter and change her education,"[1] and alleged the health of the Princess as the reason for her prolonged stay in England, and in which, finally, he made much of the sound principles of Mme. de Genlis.

This note did not prevent the Commune from entering the names of the Princess and the Governess on the list of the *émigrés*.

Hoping to obtain their removal from this list on condition of their returning, Philippe-Égalité, in the beginning of November, sent Maret—the future Duc de Bassano—to Mme. de Genlis with a power of attorney, with a view to bringing back Mademoiselle to her father, in case she was not herself willing to escort her immediately to France.

Maret found that they were no longer in London.

Alarmed by the threats of an Irish gentleman named Rice, who talked of nothing less than forcibly embarking her for America, or taking her away to be shut up on his property in Ireland, and frightened half out of her mind by the accusations of the newspapers, which made out that she was in political correspondence with Calonne, Mme. de Genlis had been only too happy to accept for herself and her pupils the hospitality of Sheridan at Isleworth, near Richmond.

The dramatist had fallen madly in love with Paméla, and asked for nothing better than to entertain his muse, or

[1] *Correspondance de L. P. J. d'Orléans.*

rather his fiancée. He was a widower, and the charming Paméla bore such a striking likeness to the late Mrs. Sheridan that he thought he saw his wife living again in her. He loved her, and was only too happy to invite her to the house he had just taken at Isleworth, because he could not pay the rent of his rooms in London.

Walpole makes sarcastic remarks about the balls and parties given by Sheridan for his French friends. A month was thus spent in amusements; but the prospect of happy days to come was suddenly interrupted by the arrival of Maret. . . .

The action taken by the Duke of Orleans was a severe blow to Mme. de Genlis. She was "in a desperate state as to either sending Mademoiselle to France or escorting her thither." However, Sheridan's advice led her to decide on returning.

She would take the Princess back to her father, hand in her own resignation, and return in a fortnight to be present at the marriage of Paméla—this was her programme, and it showed a great haste to part with both Mademoiselle and her father.

It would seem, indeed, that from this day, considering that the Orleans family had become "suspect," and that she herself was compromised by Philippe-Égalité, whom Jacobins intended to get rid of very shortly, Mme. de Genlis meant to separate her fortunes from those of the House of Orleans.

Moralists will perhaps recall the familiar comparison that a certain King of Prussia once mentioned to Voltaire in connection with a sucked orange, but assuredly at this period Mme. de Genlis regarded her own safety as above every other consideration.

At 10 a.m. on 20th October she got into the carriage with her pupils. By a strange coincidence she would have arrived at Paris on the very day on which the decree of the Assembly ordered Louis XVI. to be brought to trial. But she did not even go as far as Dover, on account of a strange adventure, a regular episode of brigandage, of which she was the victim.

The postilions on the carriage horses suddenly took an unexpected direction. Refusing to reply to the questions of the travellers, they had put the horses to full gallop and would not stop. Was she being carried off ?

Thanks to a faithful servant and the providential help of two passers-by, this surprising attempt was brought to an end. Mme. de Genlis, all alarm, had herself taken back to the house of Sheridan, who began an investigation. Strange to say, the matter ended there, and Mme. de Genlis confesses that the mystery was never cleared up. It was not, and for a very good reason; for this tragi-comic adventure was the work of Sheridan himself, who wanted to keep his fiancée with him for awhile. And it was a complete success, for the departure of Mademoiselle was put off until the English dramatist could accompany the French ladies as far as Dover, that is to say for four weeks.

Mme. de Genlis and her pupils were not able to start until 17th November. On the 20th they reached Calais. If the Countess speaks truly, a great crowd cheered the Princess as she landed. Sillery, returning from the Argonne, where he had been sent with Prieur and Carra as a delegate to proclaim the Republic, met them at the jetty. They arrived just in time to be a first offering to the law against *émigrés*. They were coming, one might say, to throw themselves into the jaws of the wolf.

The Duke of Orleans, knowing the danger, had sent a courier to meet the travellers. He ordered them to retrace their steps at once, instead of coming on to Paris. But they had already reached Chantilly, and Mme. de Genlis, in a hurry to get rid of Mademoiselle, went on. "I took no notice of that order," she says, "and in the evening I arrived at Bellechasse. They were expecting me there."

They were expecting her in an agony of anxiety.

Every face bore a look of consternation. Neither Chartres nor Montpensier, nor Beaujolais (who had all gone to the army of Dumouriez), were there to do anything to lighten the ill-omened reception.

The Duke, with dark and anxious looks, "and a kind of wandering expression that had something really sinister in it,"[1] and Sillery looking hardly any better, notwithstanding his habitual recklessness, spoke of disasters to come in a way that made Mademoiselle burst out into a fit of sobbing.

Mme. de Genlis, cool and dignified, formally handed over Mademoiselle to her father in the presence of all, gave him her famous resignation, and announced that she would go away again next morning. Then Philippe-Égalité became alarmed, led the Governess into a neighbouring room, and adjured her not to desert his daughter.

Was it not the fault of Mme. de Genlis that Mademoiselle had returned too late?

Why not have brought her back at the time when he ordered it?

Nevertheless he will ask as a favour to both himself and his daughter only this—let Mme. de Genlis consent to go and wait for her in some neutral territory. Will she be so cruel as to refuse this last proof of affection to the child she has educated?

"I replied coldly," says the Countess in her Memoirs, "that I would take Mademoiselle to Tournay, but on condition that unless a decree of exemption was published within fifteen days, he would send some person to Tournay to replace me in the charge of Mademoiselle. He gave me his word of honour for this."[2]

Next morning Barère, on going to see Mme. de Genlis, found with her Guadet, whom Sillery had asked to draw up the petition for exemption and to present it, and who had already consulted their colleagues in the Convention on the subject.

The same day the Prince spoke from its tribune. His speech reminded the Jacobin legislators of the motives of his daughter's journey to England, without omitting to allude to the principles of the Duchess of Orleans, and contrast them with the "Republican virtues" of Mme. de Genlis.[3]

The Convention exempted, in general, from the law against

---

[1] Genlis, *Mémoires*, iv. 143. [2] Genlis, *Mémoires*, iv. 143.
[3] Cf. *Moniteur*, 23rd November 1792. See also, "Envoi par la Convention Nationale au Comité de législation d'une motion du citoyen Égalité en faveur de sa fille." 21st Nov. 1792.

émigrés, " children sent abroad for their education," but this decree was never put in force.

The Commune, without taking any account of Mademoiselle having renounced the name of Orleans for that of Égalité, gave her notice of " the order that she must leave Paris within twenty-four hours, and go and await the decision of the Convention outside the territory of the Republic." [1]

A stormy interview between the Duke and the Governess followed.

After the sitting of the Assembly, Philippe-Égalité had returned to Bellechasse. He came and went from room to room without stopping, seeming very nervous, and " as if anxious to avoid conversation." Mademoiselle, Henriette, and Paméla were present. With an authoritative order Mme. de Genlis sent them into the gardens, and with a glance of her eyes told her husband to follow them. Sillery understood the look. He left the Prince and his Egeria alone. It was she who started the hunt by a few words on the political situation. He sharply interrupted her, for she was getting on to dangerous ground; he was a Jacobin—that word summed up everything.[2] Then as in old times, when she used to address him as " *mon enfant*," Mme. de Genlis rated the Prince. His conduct was a crime, a folly; the Jacobins were making a tool of him only to ruin him; he would be their victim; the decree against the *émigrés* had been passed only to strike at his daughter. . . .

Let him go away and seek a refuge in America with his family; this was the only course to take. But it is all in vain that his friend of old times exhausts herself in representing to the Duke how irrational his conduct is; he looks away, shrugs his shoulders, and keeps silent. Having used up all her arguments she suddenly goes towards the mantelpiece; with a wave of her hand she points out to him the royal emblem still glittering on the smoke-blackened tablet, the

---

[1] Ducoin, *op. cit.*, 253.
[2] " Orleanists," says Billault de Gérainville, " meant the same thing as Montagnards, though they always pretended not to know each other. Marat lavished abuse on Philippe-Égalité and was in agreement with him " (*Hist. de Louis-Philippe*, i. 115).

three fleurs-de-lis heraldically displayed there with the princely coronet of Orleans, notwithstanding the Jacobin decrees.[1]

Surprised and taken aback, Philippe-Égalité stares at it. The argument is like the cut of a whip. He starts up, he is in revolt, he becomes again for the moment a Prince of the Blood Royal. "I left them there," he exclaims, "because it would have been a piece of cowardice to remove them!"

Having risen to this higher tone he thinks it well to keep to it. The listless, easy-going *enfant* is now holding his own against the former lover. He lets the conversation change from a discussion to a dispute. The debate becomes excited, bitter expressions are exchanged, and suddenly the Duke cuts it short by leaving the room.

And now it is Sillery's turn.

What precisely passed at this last interview between wife and husband?

We shall probably never know. Sillery's diary would perhaps have told us, if he had not unfortunately burned it, when the first attacks on the Girondins began in the Convention.

Mme. de Genlis relates that she "conjured her husband, with tears in her eyes, to leave France. He had," she says, "enough money in his possession, about 200,000 francs." But he refused, for he hoped for the fall of Robespierre at an early date, and did not want to desert the master whom he knew to be ruined, and "whom the Jacobins took a pleasure in degrading so that they might be able later on to sacrifice him more surely."

Mme. de Genlis did not press the matter, or did not press it far enough; for, after the execution of Sillery, she felt great remorse, and keenly reproached herself with her conduct on this occasion.

Next day she started for Tournay with Mademoiselle, Henriette, and Paméla.

And then there came another moving scene, that passes

---

[1] Sevelinges asserts that this was not so, and that after the close of the sitting, at which nobility was abolished, the coats-of-arms with the fleur-de-lis were broken by well-known hands (*op. cit.*, 235).

before our eyes like a tragic picture on the dark and sinister background of the threatening future.

We see the travelling carriage waiting at the gate of Bellechasse; the Duke, whose fit of anger has passed off and is now regretted, is standing there, pale, ill at ease, his thoughts given up to the emotions of a parting, the harassing anxieties of the present, and above all the revival of half-vanished memories.

Now on the eve of the great Terror a very little thing would have been enough to re-establish the influence of his friend of the past after its temporary eclipse.

But she felt herself all of a tremble.

Let us hear what she says: " The Duke of Orleans, more depressed than ever, gave me his arm to escort me to the carriage. I was greatly agitated. Mademoiselle burst into tears. Her father was pale and trembling. When I was in the carriage he stood motionless by its door, with his eyes fixed on me. His look of sorrow and pain seemed to implore pity! 'Adieu, Madame,' he said to me. The broken tone of his voice brought my agitation to a climax. Unable to utter a word I held out my hand to him. He took it, pressed it with a strong grasp, then turning and going quickly towards the postilions he made a sign to them and we started." [1]

Never perhaps did the unknown that broods in the background over every parting, contain more of agonising pain and mournful surprises than at this sad separation.

Of the actors in the sorrowful scene two were very soon to lose their heads on the scaffold. And of the four women not one was to see France again for many a day.

[1] Genlis, *Mémoires*, iv. 146.

PART IV

THE EMIGRATION

CHAPTER I

WITH DUMOURIEZ

"MME. DE GENLIS found herself, like Dr. Pangloss, in the best of all possible worlds, when the blast of political tempests swept her, so to say, from the hall of the Jacobins and cast her into the lands of the emigration."

These words—slightly exaggerated though they may be—in which the chronicler Toulotte expresses his opinion on the departure of our celebrated lady, sum up the situation accurately enough.

For the present, notwithstanding their provisional passports,[1] Mme. de Genlis and Mademoiselle are fairly launched on the way of exile. They are practically *émigrés*.

Having dried the tears of their departure, they meet at one of the first stages a young Irish nobleman who begins to follow Sheridan's example, and politely escorts them as far as Tournay.

Lord Edward Fitzgerald, a son of the Duke of Leinster, had fallen madly in love with Paméla, and this with most serious intentions. The affair dated from only three days ago, from 21st November 1792. That day after dinner at White's Hotel, in the rue des Petits Pères, he took a fancy

---

[1] "Those they gave us stated that we were going away only in obedience to the law, and further eulogised our civic virtues" (Genlis, *Précis de ma conduite*, 62).

to spend the rest of the evening at the theatre. They were playing *Lodoïska* to a rather thin audience, but in one of the boxes his attention was attracted by some ladies of charming figure, bright eyes, fine and winning features, and a wonderful chance would have it that a friend of his was there, like himself bitten with Rousseau and the Revolution, and who knew these enchantresses, and presented our young dandy to Mme. de Genlis and Paméla. It was John Hurford Stone.

By a piquant coincidence, Fitzgerald had been the object of the last love affair of Mrs. Sheridan. She loved him to the extent of leaving her husband to follow him, and then die of remorse for it. Paméla's likeness to her, which had so agitated Sheridan, electrified Lord Edward in the same way. Next day he dined at Bellechasse, and the day after that he was galloping along the Tournay road, and at the first halt presented himself as a suitor of Paméla.

And when, comfortably installed with Mme. de Valence and Hermine, who had already joined the *émigrés* at Tournay, the four ladies had resumed their usual occupations, the old round of life as it was at Bellechasse, all kinds of little industries, such as Mme. de Genlis, the enemy of idleness, excelled in, Lord Edward was there to amuse them as they busied themselves with embroidery, water colours, straw plaiting, and to listen to the harp, or read for them. The Orleans Princes were serving on the staff of Dumouriez, but César du Crest had just arrived.

The susceptible Irishman made rapid progress.

In less than three weeks he had gone on from the betrothal to the marriage; this included the time for crossing the Channel to obtain—as Mme. de Genlis required—the written consent of the Duchess of Leinster, his mother, "whom he led to believe that Paméla was a natural daughter of one of the Seymours."[1]

The marriage ceremony was celebrated at Tournay, on 27th December 1792. Did Philippe-Égalité accompany to the altar, in the character of her father, his reputed

---

[1] Forneron, *Hist. générale des émigrés*, i. 406.

PAMELA, LADY FITZGERALD.

daughter, who instead of a bridal veil wore the red cap under her wreath of orange blossoms? This has been asserted.

He had given her in 1791 an allowance of 6000 francs, in addition to another allowance of 1500 francs, this being the price at which he bought Mme. de Genlis's library.[1] And on the other hand, the latter speaks of having agreed to renounce in favour of Paméla her retiring pension as Governess, which amounted to 6000 francs.

It seems that the Duke of Orleans was present at least as a witness for Paméla, together with the painter Myris. Besides, he signed the marriage contract, as well as the Duke of Chartres, Mademoiselle, César du Crest, Mme. de Valence, Henriette de Sercey, Hermine, and finally Mme. de Genlis, and old General O'Moran, the Governor of Tournay. Immediately after the wedding breakfast, Lord Edward took his young wife away to Ireland.

And this was the last time that Mademoiselle and the Duke of Chartres saw their father.

In the midst of all these rejoicings, the poor young Princess was having a trying time. She endured the continual misery of knowing that she was a trouble to others, that she was compromising those around her.

Notwithstanding her "repeated letters," no substitute came to set Mme. de Genlis free. On the contrary, the Duke, every time he wrote to her, entreated her, as a favour, to wait a few days longer.

Mademoiselle, so delicate, so impressionable, was in misery at the sight of the impatience of her Governess.

Attached from the depth of her heart to Mme. de Genlis, and with the whole of her delicate nature under her influence, she, who believed that she held the first rank in her affections, now saw herself on the eve of being abandoned by her to the first hireling that came along. It was, in fact, quite clear that Mme. de Genlis was thinking only of extricating herself from the whole affair.

The Princess had seen this. Silent, discreet, wrapped up in herself, she hid her sorrow. But her feeble constitution

[1] Barère, *Mémoires*.

could not bear up against it. She fell sick. It was a bilious fever, the result of anxiety.

"To leave her at such a moment," says Mme. de Genlis, "would have been to send her to her death." She remained therefore a little while longer, consenting thus to a provisional prolongation of her engagement.

In January 1793 the Duke of Orleans sent news of the condemnation and death of Louis XVI., in a letter in which he explained stupidly enough his own unworthy vote. Sillery wrote also. His letter enclosed a large number of printed copies of his "opinion"—the pamphlet beginning with the words, "I do not vote for death. . . ." He asked his wife to have them sent over to England, and said to her plainly, "I am perfectly well aware that in pronouncing this opinion I have pronounced my own sentence of death."

Mme. de Genlis seems to have received her husband's letter with a certain amount of apathy. She had persuaded herself that he would get off with a few months' imprisonment, and being besides unable to do anything, since her return to France was forbidden under the penalty of being at once sent to prison, she did not trouble herself very much, knowing that Sillery was clever enough to get away if he wished, and believing that he would find support enough among his political friends. But the trial of the King and the conduct of Philippe-Égalité filled her "with horror and consternation." The Duke of Chartres did not conceal his disgust. He expressed it some weeks later to his father, in that letter which the Committee of Public Safety found when it searched Philippe-Égalité's papers after the defection of Dumouriez, and which served as a pretext for the arrest of the regicide Prince.

In March 1793 all Europe was in league against France, and Belgium, on the point of being invaded by the Austrians, was about to rise, everything indicating an immediate revolt. In a fortnight Tournay might be in the hands of the enemy—and not only of the Imperial troops, but also of the thousands of Royalists who swelled the army of Condé.

Mme. de Genlis was distracted! Caught in Tournay

as in a mouse-trap, connected with the Orleanist party, and, to add to it all, accused of having contributed to the death of the King, what fate could she expect? She literally lost her head! She formed a thousand impracticable plans. To be in France, in the country, in one of the provinces which she knew well, seemed to her by far the most preferable position. She thought of taking refuge in Burgundy, with an uncle of hers, and eagerly asked for leave to return. The reply was that "the recall of Mademoiselle would be obtained, but that hers was again deferred."

Then she began to anticipate, with terror, misfortunes like those of Lafayette. To hide herself in a convent and pass herself off as an Englishwoman seemed to her a reasonable plan. She would perhaps have decided upon it, if the want of money did not forbid it to her. Mademoiselle is no better off, and the Governess, who has had to make her an advance of one hundred and thirty-two louis, spends days of terror and of indescribable panic. Mme. de Valence, for her part, has preferred to return to Paris, where Mme. de Montesson offers her hospitality.

However, Sillery and Valence sent a courier with some money, and Mme. de Genlis could now escape. But she was no longer disposed that way. This was because Dumouriez, forced to evacuate Holland and retire before the Austrians, had come and camped in the neighbourhood of Tournay. The negotiations at Ath soon showed precisely what his real intentions were. To unite his army with the Austrian troops, march on Paris, make himself master of the Convention and establish a constitutional monarchy, such was the plan arranged by Dumouriez, in concert with General Mack, representing the Prince of Coburg. And what King but the Duke of Chartres would have occupied the throne. It is well known that Dumouriez gave this to be understood. Accompanied by his staff officers, the Duke of Chartres, Valence, and Montjoie, he came to Tournay to pay his homage to Mademoiselle, and had military honours rendered to her, thus posing as the champion of the House of Orleans and the powerful protector of the persecuted Princess.

Mme. de Genlis was "charmed at seeing Dumouriez,

that celebrated man," [1] charmed, above all, at being able to leave Tournay and all its dangers, and go and place herself under the immediate protection of the General, moving to his very camp at Boues de St. Amand.

The Ath negotiations lasted four days, and the conspirators had every facility for meeting each day at the Governess's quarters. Lamartine believed firmly in her influence on "these corps commanders who had to be excited and won over to turn against the Republic." [2] And Camille Desmoulins did not hesitate to say flatly that "the Republic was betrayed . . . through the complaisance of Mme. Sillery for an old man-of-straw" [3]—a supposition that came naturally to the mind of such crude psychologists. Mme. de Genlis, in her *Mémoires*, has defended herself on this point as well as she could, perhaps, some will say, too well. But in such matters the makers of hypotheses have the game in their hands.

Because the Commissioners sent to Dumouriez did not meet the General in his camp, but at the lodgings of Mme. de Genlis, can this sole fact—and there is no other alleged against her—be taken as sufficient proof of a mere possibility?

When Proly—according to Mme. de Genlis it was Dubuisson—went to order Dumouriez back to Tournay, he found the latter in the midst of a numerous circle, which included Mme. de Genlis, Mlle. Henriette de Sercey, Valence, the Duke of Chartres, and some of the staff officers. The General was not afraid to give the "Representative of the People" a most unbecoming and most "uncivic" reception, "and the Governess smiled malignantly." Of all this the angry representative complained to the Convention. Result: on 2nd April, that is to say, on the eve of the seizure of the three Commissioners, the Committee of Public Safety issues a warrant of arrest against the Citizeness Sillery, the two sons of Égalité, Valence, and some others.

On 3rd April, Robespierre demands from the tribune that the members of the Orleans and Égalité family shall be

---
[1] Genlis, *Mémoires*, iv.   [2] *Girondins*, i. 37.
[3] Camille Desmoulins, quoted by Ducoin.

brought before the Revolutionary Tribunal, as well as Sillery, his wife, Valence, and all those who are specially attached to the House of Orleans.

That same Wednesday, 3rd April, Dumouriez intercepted the package of warrants of arrest issued against himself and his officers—among them the Duke of Chartres—made prisoners of the three envoys of the Convention, and handed them over to the Imperialists.

If we are to believe Mme. de Genlis, she heard the news only at midnight, and by rumours current in the camp. Already "suspecting some very terrible designs and plots," and in every way disapproving of them, "I no longer had," she says, "but the one desire, that of flight from St. Amand, but the difficulty of procuring horses kept me there in spite of myself."[1]

That is to say, that since 1st April she had been on the alert, because the French troops were on the verge of revolt,[2] and on the 3rd, at that late hour, the general increase of disorder, or some officer, perhaps Montjoie, told her of the probable failure of the conspiracy.

She lost no time, did not go to bed, got a promise of horses, and passed the rest of the night preparing for flight. She would start in the morning. Dumouriez, she says, offered her passports, which she refused, "knowing his conduct." But was it only that night in the course of a conversation with the General that she became aware of it?

And is it not more likely that Dumouriez had offered her these passports at an earlier date, and while he expected a successful result? For they could be of no use after a failure.

At this anxious moment Mme. de Genlis is in a hurry to get away from the armies of the Convention. She has also decided as to Mademoiselle "to leave her in the hands of her brother, as I was no longer her Governess, and not to involve her in my own dangers and misery."

[1] Genlis, *Mémoires*, iv. 171.
[2] *Lettre de Mademoiselle d'Orléans à la princesse de Conti* (Genlis, *Mémoires*, iv. 233).

The unfortunate girl suspects this. Weak as a bent reed she accepts without a word this sad destiny, having, alas! only her tears with which to oppose it. And this sad night, when anxiety deprives her of sleep, she lies down uttering dull moanings and weeping, with her heart torn with grief.

At dawn, about five in the morning, she is exhausted, her poor strength has broken down, and Mademoiselle falls into a dull slumber. The Governess was waiting only for this moment. With tears in her eyes, but in great haste, she pays a silent farewell to her pupil " with all a mother's affection and blessings," and goes out of the room to pray till it is time for starting.

At seven o'clock the Duke of Chartres arrives. He has seen a carriage at the door. Henriette is already seated in it with Montjoie. Mme. de Genlis, brought face to face with him, begins a farewell.

Hardly capable of understanding the hurried explanation given by the friend of the family of why she wishes to avoid a heart-rending leave-taking of Mademoiselle, the young Prince looks round for his sister.

But the Governess is not taking with her the child she has brought up, dear Adèle, of whom she has so often declared herself the second mother. What a strange affair! Chartres thinks he must be dreaming!

He conjures her to return to another state of mind. Can she really expect him to expose his sister to the dangers of a soldier's life? How can he take care of this weak child in the midst of the toils of his profession, and when he must defend his own head against the Republicans!

Mme. de Genlis brings up against him equally pressing arguments; the general reprobation of the name of Orleans, the danger of arrest. It would be better for Mademoiselle to go alone to Valenciennes. Then they would not dare to take any rigorous measures in her regard; at most they would send her across the frontier.

No doubt Mme. de Genlis was still ignorant of the fact that some time before this Mademoiselle had been condemned to death *en contumace*, for failing to appear before the

Revolutionary Tribunal. Finally, she refuses to be moved from her refusal She goes out. She gets into the carriage.

The Duke of Chartres has hurried to his sister's room. Suddenly, at the very moment when the coachman is about to start his horses, the Prince is seen rushing out of the house, carrying in his arms, enveloped in only a muslin gown, the whiteness of which contrasts with his General's uniform, a fragile female form, all collapsed, and as it were crushed, which he quickly lays down on the knees of Mme. de Genlis.

It is Mademoiselle! Desperate, carried away by an impulse of impetuous and romantic youth, her brother can think only of this violent means of saving her. To go and take her from her bed, and almost undressed as she was, hand her to the fugitive Governess, slam the carriage door, and make a sign to the coachman to drive off, such is his conduct, worthy indeed of the romances of Mme. de Genlis. One would have thought they were running away with her. He saved indeed the life of the Princess, but he saved only that . . . and her harp. Jewels, dresses, clothes, headgear, nothing ever reached her. They seem not to have known what to do with the harp, and a servant put it into a car that later on found its way to Mademoiselle; but it did not bring her " even a dress, even a piece of underwear."

However, even now the situation was a very anxious one. Three women and a man, in flight, at the beginning of winter, without passports, and travelling over awful by-roads, all mud and ruts, in a frontier district infested with Republican volunteers and deserters—what a miserable journey!

The first patriot they met might question them, arrest them, and send them to the Committee of Public Safety at Lille or Valenciennes, and then it was certain death.

It had been agreed that Montjoie alone was to speak at the posting-houses, and he was to represent his companions as three English ladies on the way to Ostend. The ill-health of Mademoiselle might help to support this explanation, but the three women did not conceal from themselves that it was a lame story. Their trials were only beginning. They were hardly two hours on the way when the carriage broke down.

While it was being repaired they had to wait for an hour and a half in a drinking bar full of volunteers. Before they could get away, they had to meet a thousand questions, and answer without betraying themselves. And very soon night began to come on. It begins early in the north at that time of the year. With the twilight an icy fog rose from the damp earth towards the low-lying clouds that covered the sky. In sticky quagmires the carriage sinks to its axles.

To avoid having to stop they get out and walk, shivering with cold, while a guide with a lantern shows the way to the coachman.

After dragging along thus for a league, at a walk, the lantern betrays the presence of the fugitives. A captain of volunteers, making his rounds, has the idea that there is something suspicious in this way of travelling. The replies he gets only confirm his suspicions. Evidently these people are *émigrés*. He is so sure of it that he decides on taking them to Valenciennes, under a strong escort.

At this moment the four fugitives must have imagined they saw the blood-stained blade of the guillotine outlined above their heads. Its terrible menace stimulated the energy of Mme. de Genlis like a formidable spur. Then staking everything on a bold stroke, and with wonderful presence of mind, she took the officer's arm with a sprightly air, and as if he has been suggesting a pleasant party, she takes him in hand, talking volubly in broken French with an irresistible English accent, smiling all the time, and in the drollest way " making a thousand jests," so that presently he had no longer any doubt about the thoroughly British character of this " Lady Verzenay and her nieces." Charmed by the adventure, he pushed his politeness so far as show them a safe road to Quiévrain, which was held by the Austrian outposts. They were saved !

At Quiévrain there was another adventure, this time pleasant enough and even comical. Mme. de Genlis has given an amusing account of the mistake of Baron de Vounianski, the Austrian commandant, who was absolutely convinced that he recognised in the pretended Lady Verzenay, the Princess von Lansberg, his Dulcinea, and acted accordingly. A splendid supper and an escort to Mons, closed, in the happiest way, this episode worthy of Cervantes.[1]

But the Princess and Henriette felt the effects of so many trying experiences. Mademoiselle, in her light muslin, had caught cold at the very outset, and during the night journey through the half-frozen mud of Hainault she never ceased shivering.

At Mons a severe attack of fever and scarlatina prostrated her as well as Henriette, and forced the two girls to remain shut up in a wretched inn, of which the better rooms were already engaged by others

Mme. de Genlis installed herself as their nurse, passed the nights beside their beds, and went out only to buy medicines, keeping all the time a strict incognito, for Mons was crowded with Royalist *émigrés*.

Ill-luck would have it that one day, when she " went to get some drugs at an apothecary's," she found herself face to face with one of the most ardent partisans of Marie Antoinette, namely, her relative the Prince de Lambesc. Lambesc, at once recognising the "*Jacobine*" Genlis, rushed off to denounce her to the Austrian commandant. It so happened that he was General Mack.

Could he be ignorant of the intended result of the conspiracy, the co-operation of Dumouriez and the Duke of Chartres with the Austrian troops? However this may be, the memory of Ath was still too recent for him to act otherwise than as a friendly gentleman.

General Mack, accordingly, went in person to the lodging of Mme. de Genlis and Mademoiselle, who were trembling with fright. But he came to reassure them, and to procure for them passports from the Prince of Coburg, which would allow them to travel through Germany without interruption.

Provided with these, the three women were able to leave Mons on 18th April, and cross the German frontier. Montjoie

---

[1] The existence of the Princess von Lansberg has been disputed, although Mme. de Genlis refers to the testimony of two young nobles of Moravia, whom unfortunately she does not name. The anecdote, in any case, has no importance, and we leave her all responsibility for it. Cf. Toulotte, *op. cit.*, and Sevelinges, *Madame de Genlis en miniature*, p. 252.

had left them for some private reason at Quiévrain, but he now rejoined them. They reached Wiesbaden on the 20th, and went up the Rhine as far as Schaffhausen, where they arrived on the 26th, after having run some serious risks. "We were obliged," say the *Mémoires*, "to pass close to the Hessian camp, which lay along the Rhine on our side of it, while on the other we could see Cassel, where the French were. Mayence was burning and there was a cannonade in progress."[1] In these circumstances Mme. de Genlis did not feel her conscience quite at ease, as she lets us know later on. "Seeing myself in the midst of the enemies of my country," she writes, "my reason in vain repelled a kind of involuntary remorse, as painful as it was groundless. For assuredly I had nothing with which to reproach myself. . . ."

This way of thinking was, however, not generally accepted. The name of Mme. de Genlis was commonly associated with the conspiracy of Dumouriez.

When on 4th April the news of the General's revolt called forth an outburst in the Convention, and led to the arrest of Philippe-Égalité, hardly six months before the terrible shearing off of the heads of the Girondins, Mme. de Genlis, luckily for her, was out of the reach of the party of the Mountain.

At the moment when the search among the Prince's papers led to the discovery of the famous letter from the Duke of Chartres,[2] a lady's-maid of Mademoiselle's arrived from Tournay with a story that the Governess still treated Chartres as a little boy, "making him sing vespers from morning to night, describing his father to him in the most fearful colours," and even having recourse to tears "to induce him to follow Dumouriez."[3]

This same Thursday, 4th April, the Committee of Public Safety issues its warrant of arrest, signed by Santerre, not only against Philippe-Égalité, Sillery and the Duchess of Orleans, but also against Mme. de Valence and her children

---

[1] Genlis, *Mémoires*, iv. 195.
[2] It contained the words: "I see liberty lost. I see the National Convention utterly ruining France, by forgetting every right principle."
[3] Cf. Brissot, *Mémoires*, ii. 335.

THE DUKE OF ORLEANS
(PHILIPPE-ÉGALITÉ).

and Mme. de Montesson. At midnight—still on this 4th April—the two women were arrested and their effects put under seal, while Santerre's underlings escorted them to the prison of the Abbaye.[1]

Valence, of whom Sillery had once said, " I will punish him myself like Brutus if he is guilty," [2] followed Dumouriez, thus escaping from the Sansculottes. But their hatred was more violent against the Bourbons, and Marat soon demanded that a price should be put upon the head of the Duke of Chartres. Such were the more immediate results of the conspiracy of Dumouriez.

Can we hold Mme. de Genlis responsible for it ?

The ambitious General had no need of her advice. If she had some part in his plan, if she knew of his hesitations, if, perhaps, she hastened the hour of rebellion, that hour would have struck without her.

Mme. de Genlis may have helped plans that were already ripe, but she did not inspire them.

As for the Duke of Chartres, he refused to fight against his country. Leaving Dumouriez and the Austrians, he made an adventurous journey through Germany, accompanied by a single servant, the faithful Beaudoin. He travelled in a chaise, and on 4th May rejoined his sister at Schaffhausen. Barthélemy mentions his having passed through Basel the evening before, 3rd May. Montjoie was there already, living with his family. He was a native of the canton.

But Basel, a dangerous city, united to France since 7th April, Basel which is now a part of the Department of Mont Terrible, and where members of the Convention, Monnot, Ritter, and Laurent, are recruiting victims for the Revolutionary Tribunal, and where the famous inn of the " Three Kings " " has been metamorphised into a branch of the Jacobin Club,"—Basel, one may imagine, has no attractions for the Prince.

---

[1] A.N.F.', 4619.
[2] He wrote also: " I have forgotten the services which he (Valence) has rendered to the country, and I only recall his name to inform my fellow-citizens that my daughter divorced herself from him on hearing of his crime." (Sillery, *À ses concitoyens.*)

Besides, it is his duty to protect his sister, and he does not know what are the intentions of Mme. de Genlis.

These two unfortunate young people, poor remnants of a broken family, are henceforth to lead a wandering life. Hated by the Royalist *émigrés*, hunted down by the Revolutionists, innocent victims against whom these opposing parties rage furiously, they seem destined to pay the price of their father's errors. If the Governess indeed shares their dangers, their hours of bitterness, the insults they daily endured, she at least was responsible through her own actions. Escaped from the talons of the Convention, and now beyond the frontiers of France, she began to take a juster view of her duties, and continued to link her life with that of her pupils,—princely victims of a birth that in a moment of frank devotion to equality they refused to regard as a privilege, and which for the present brought them only the privilege of persecution.

On 7th May the whole party left Schaffhausen, and put up at Zurich at the hôtel de l'Epée, until they could find in the city or its neighbourhood a suitable refuge in which to install themselves.

"They soon saw," says Barthélemy, "that this was not possible, for soon after their arrival the magistrates of Zurich sent to ask them when they would go away."

Four days later the Senate of Berne informed them that it had decided not to allow them to enter its territory if they presented themselves there. At the same time several of the *émigrés*, nobles of minor rank and poor education, who once they passed the frontier made the most of their titles, recognised the fugitives at Zurich, and expressed evil intentions regarding the "Jacobin women." Again they took to flight. On 12th May, Kilchsperger, the burgomaster of Basel, reports the passing through the place of M. Égalité, Mme. de Sillery, etc. . . . "who gave out that they were Irish, and seemed to be on the way to the St. Gothard and Italy."

But as secretly as possible they made their way to Zug.

A lonely little house on the margin of the lake sheltered them under assumed names. They hardly went out even to go to church, being always in danger of denunciation. A month went by—a month of truce. Then what they feared came to pass. A party of *émigrés*, passing through the place, recognised the Duke of Chartres. The same day Zug learned the real names of the mysterious dwellers in the little house by the lake. On 12th June the news appeared in the *Moniteur*. The magistrates of Zug were only waiting a chance of verifying the identity of the so-called Irish visitors. This publication of the news gave them what they wanted, and was made the reason for an order of expulsion. They used a little more formality than those of Zurich, but nevertheless they requested their visitors to leave the canton " as soon as they could do so without exposing themselves to the hazards of the future."

Mme. de Genlis insinuates that this order was directed against the name of Orleans, but not against her own, and that they offered to allow her to remain at Zug if she wished. "Bound to Mademoiselle d'Orléans," she refused, and summoned up all her courage. Young as she was, Mlle. du Crest had tasted the bitterness of misfortune. If she has passed through days as trying as these, she has learned also how one can tire out ill-fortune by resisting it. Without home or friends, and driven from two of the most tolerant cantons of Switzerland, she thought now of the august lady who had been ill-treated a while ago, and who was the natural protectress of the children she had helped to take from her,—the Duchess of Orleans,—and she made Mademoiselle and the Duke of Chartres write to her. At all risks she added a letter of her own to theirs.

The unfortunate Princess made no reply. Did she ever receive these tidings of her children, at Vernon, where Robespierre was keeping her a prisoner? Was not her separation from them one of the most cruel sources of sorrow to her? Did not the Comte de Moriolles see her, during a short stay at the château of Anet, always in tears, with her eyes " red and bloodshot " ? did he not hear her complain that she was a lonely woman, the victim of treachery . . . with her children " running about Switzerland with Mme. de Genlis " ?

And can one doubt that, if it had been possible, she would at least have replied to Chartres and to Mademoiselle, considering that, worn as she was by sorrow and privation, she was nevertheless sending some of what she herself needed to Montpensier and Beaujolais, and giving it to the poor?

The Duke of Chartres and his sister were now living in the most harassing uncertainty as to the future. The young hero of Valmy strained at the curb in inaction that weighed heavily on his youthful energies. With his usual clearness of judgment, and the seriousness of his thoughtful mind, he did not shut his eyes to the fact that, of them all, he was the one whose presence was the most compromising. And his will, acting on reason, inspired him with the noble resolution of facing all alone the dangers which everywhere lay in wait for the name of Orleans. By this means Mademoiselle and her Governess might be able to live in security. Who would venture to attack weak women?

But where could they find a refuge? where hide themselves in this country of Switzerland, which was traversed in every direction by the *émigrés?*

In the midst of these cruel circumstances Montjoie came from Basel to see them. He had met, when passing through Bremgarten, a fellow-countryman, who had secured a great position in the country by his birth, his fortune, his valour, and his chivalrous courtesy. Maintaining excellent relations with the Senate of Berne and the magistrates of the neighbouring cantons, obliging and generous, General the Comte de Montesquiou possessed real influence.

Mme. de Genlis wrote to him, laying before him the wretched position of the children of the House of Orleans, and asked as a favour that he would arrange for herself, her niece Henriette, and Mademoiselle to be given a refuge in the convent of St. Clare near Bremgarten.

M. de Montesquiou at once showed admirable zeal on their behalf, and to such good effect that on 27th June, at ten in the morning, the four proscribed travellers made their way to this home of piety. It was high time. The position at Zug was becoming untenable. The evening before, some unknown persons had thrown heavy stones into the little drawing-room where Mademoiselle generally passed her time. By a fortunate chance the Princess had just gone up to the room of Mme. de Genlis, and so escaped this attack.

The Duke of Chartres accompanied the three women as far as the convent parlour. There he embraced the weeping Princess, bade farewell to Mme. de Genlis and Henriette, and then went away, without a guide, to the Swiss Alps, to wander from summit to summit, finding in the pure mountain air a means of renewing his courage, and among the peaks and rocks a refuge inaccessible to the hatred of men.

It is on record that, on 6th July, when, as he passed by the Lake of Sempach, he prepared to bathe in it, he was driven away with showers of stones and narrowly escaped being stoned to death.

At the Convent of St. Clare the registers mention the arrival of three Irish ladies, "Madame Lennox and her nieces Mesdemoiselles Stuart."

CHAPTER II

BREMGARTEN AND ALTONA

BECAUSE it did not completely isolate her from the agitation of the world, the shelter of the convent, welcome though it might be amid great misfortunes, seemed something that had not kept its promise to Mme. de Genlis.

The walls of St. Clare's did not secure peace for her. At Bremgarten she was too near France, where the Terror was in its full fury, and where noble blood flowed each day and cried for vengeance. At Bremgarten she was within reach of the Royalist *émigrés*, a crowd of whom had settled in the neighbourhood and were attempting reprisals, so far as they could, against everything that was Jacobin, or had even a trace of it.

Mme. de Genlis, classed among the executioners of the Royal Family, and "so despised," excited in the highest degree those feelings of resentment that rose to a frenzy after the execution of Marie Antoinette. It was then that to persecute a Mme. de Genlis seemed—alas for human nature!—by just comparison almost an act of piety, the paying of a debt of hatred contracted under the most atrocious conditions, and augmented by the proscriptions, confiscations, executions and massacres of the time. Doubtless, compared to these horrors, the exiling of a woman count for very little. When, in December 1793, secret intrigues secured the issue of a decree of expulsion against all the foreigners residing at Bremgarten, this order included not only Mme. de Genlis and Montesquiou, but also the Duke of Chartres, who was believed, and believed for certain, to be hiding with the latter.

When the Governess was informed of it she was suffering from the shock of terrible news. She was a widow—Sillery had been executed on 31st October, and her crape was the symbol of a double sorrow, for Philippe-Égalité had just been guillotined on 6th November, and in the charges against him the Revolutionary Tribunal had linked together the two names—that of the Prince and of Mme. de Genlis. She was in fact treated as his accomplice, not indeed his accomplice in the Revolution, but, contrary to what one might expect, his accomplice on the side of the Aristocrats. By a strange irony of events the accusers remembered her religious opinions to impute them to her as a crime, but forgot her political opinions, that had so effectively aided her to lead on the Duke, govern his children and annihilate the Duchess. Pétion and Dumouriez were also implicated in the affair.[1]

Voidel, the defender of Philippe-Égalité, and but lately the friend of Mme. de Genlis, made an unsparing attack upon her and Dumouriez, declaring that they had both prepared and consummated the ruin of the Prince by perverting his children, notably the Duke of Chartres, and deliberately taking them away from their father.[2]

Shortly before Louvet had harped upon nearly the same strain as to "the fanaticism of every kind of the Governess and of her writings."[3]

[1] Extract from the examination of Philippe-Égalité:—
Q.: "Why did you consent to put your daughter into the hands of that traitor (Pétion) and of de Genlis, a clever and treacherous woman who has since emigrated?"
A.: "I did indeed consent to hand over my daughter to the woman Sillery, who did not deserve my confidence. She associated Pétion with herself, and I undesignedly gave my approval to his accompanying her to England."
Q.: "But you could not but know that this woman, Sillery, was an intriguer."
A.: "I was absolutely ignorant of it."

[2] While the monster was gaining possession of the mind of this young man by politic proceedings and by the ascendency over him that his military reputation gave him, Mme. de Sillery, his teacher, acted on his heart by superstitious ideas and by exciting his pity, and under the name of reason and virtue made error and crime enter his soul" (J. G. C. Voidel, *A ses concitoyens sur l'affaire de L. P. J. d'Orléans*).

[3] Louvet de Cauvrai, *Mémoires sur la Révolution française*, ed. Aulard, ii. 221.

Mme. de Genlis did not know these details. But the catastrophe with all its horrors, nevertheless, deeply affected her. For the first time since leaving Paris she fell sick. And if the Comte de Montesquiou had not taken energetic, prompt and successful steps to have the order of expulsion withdrawn, one cannot say to what extremity she would have been reduced—perhaps to that romantic flight on foot, or in a country cart disguised as a peasant—a plan she had been considering. Thanks to Montesquiou, the two proscribed women were able then to remain at St. Clare's, an uncertain place of refuge, uncomfortable and poor enough, but after all a roof under which they could rest their heads.

Besides this, Mme. de Genlis was paying out of her own money for the board and lodging of Mademoiselle, and keeping the young Princess—then suffering from dysentery—ignorant of her father's death.

The Duke of Chartres must have been better informed. The change of feeling which he soon after manifested towards his former "Governor," and which is generally attributed to the emancipation of his mind in solitude and misfortune, clearly dates from this period. No doubt the newspapers informed him of the execution of his father, and of the way in which the name of the Prince was everywhere connected with that of the ex-Countess. The cleverness of the latter, the weakness of the former, were known to him. And the adventurous flight from St. Amand must assuredly have dealt a heavy blow to the unbounded veneration for the Governess that he had formerly professed.

Besides, had not some one intervened in this matter? Had not some one undertaken to open the eyes of the Prince, and to represent to him certain recent events, especially the judicial separation between the Duke and his wife and the taking away of Mademoiselle from her mother, as crushing charges against Mme. de Genlis? But if we may believe that Mme. de Flahault—who had little liking for the Governess—had something to do with the unfavourable opinion of the young Prince (now Duke of Orleans), with regard to his instructress, it is not all the same probable that she inspired his resolve to take Mademoiselle away from her, for, according to Madame's biographer, she was not now resident at Bremgarten.[1]

In fact, the Princess Adélaide was about to leave Mme. de Genlis and go to live with her aunt, Mme. de Conti, at Freiburg.

We are not very fully informed as to the real motives that led to the parting, this time a final one, between the Governess and her dear pupil. Mme. de Flahault, in her letters to Governor Morris, attributes to her eldest brother the initiative in withdrawing his sister from the hands of Mme. de Genlis. Mme. de Boigne, imagining like many other of the *émigrés* that Mme. de Genlis kept the Princess as a prisoner, writes that " after the catastrophe of her father's death, and her mother the Duchess being still in prison, the family reclaimed possession of the young Princess."[2] But what does " the family " mean here ?

Montpensier and Beaujolais were at Fort St. Jean ; the Prince de Conti and the Duchess de Bourbon on their way to Spain, and the Duke of Modena did not trouble himself about his granddaughter. There remains the Princess de Conti. She was believed to be with her father at the Court of Modena, but she was residing at Freiburg.

Was it she that demanded back—or as Barthélemy will have it, carried off—her niece ?

But at this moment the question—and a very imperious question—was whether the pretended Mme. Lennox and the pretended Misses Stuart could stay on at St. Clare's. The want of money had become urgent. Mme. de Genlis, who had already advanced 200 louis on Mademoiselle's account, was thinking about finding a printer as soon as possible to publish some work, in the hope of refilling her purse, now three-fourths empty.

The young Princess had already, in a long and very touching letter, begged for shelter and support with her grandfather. But he, being of a selfish disposition, limited his help to sending her exactly 180 louis, not quite enough to repay the advance made by her Governess.

Then, as Mme. de Genlis tells us, having learned by

---

[1] Cf. Baron de Maricourt, *op. cit.*, 176–178.
[2] Comtesse de Boigne, *Mémoires*, i. 427.

chance that the Princess de Conti was in Switzerland, "I made Mademoiselle write to her, asking to be received by her, and she wrote thus notwithstanding her sorrow at leaving me."

Mademoiselle's letter settles the question. It was she who first approached Mme. de Conti. Now, was this only at the suggestion of the Governess, and did not the young Duke of Orleans direct her to take this step? It is very possible.

However this may be, ten days later the answer arrived. Mme. de Conti would send for her niece in a month; and, on 12th May 1794, the Comtesse de Pont St. Maurice, her envoy for this purpose, drove up to the convent gate.

According to her custom, Mme. de Genlis avoided a farewell scene. Eight days before she had handed her dear pupil certain religious and moral exhortations, and a portrait of Paméla. On the arrival of Mme. de Pont St. Maurice she gave the latter written and detailed instructions as to Mademoiselle, "as to her character, talents, health, and way of living," etc. Then at the moment of her departure she stayed in her own room, and the Princess was told that Mme. de Genlis had gone out before daybreak.

So there was no "heartrending scene" between the young girl and her second mother. But the sorrow of both was not the less real, though it was more acute on Mademoiselle's side. Mme. de Genlis has left us in her *Memoirs* a pathetic account of the event, which is not wanting in sincerity.

Apart from all ambitious views, she had a real affection for the delicate Princess. Had she not brought her up?

She speaks the truth in this respect when she repeats: "One must be a mother, to imagine what I felt at such a moment."

This time their separation was to be a long one. It lasted till 1814. Mademoiselle wrote to her Governess during her journey. She wrote to her again from Freiburg, that letter dated 1794, so full of grief, so weighed down with all the burden of her sorrowful life, and in which she dwells upon their friendship and their mutual affection.

But the correspondence soon became infrequent—and

besides, it might prove dangerous for the security of the two friends—till one day there came a formal order from the Princess de Conti, who did not like it, that it must cease, at least openly.[1]

The young girl was then with her aunt at Landshut in Bavaria, whence they were driven by the armies of the Directory. They had to take to flight and made for Austria, where they stopped on the banks of the Danube at the celebrated and picturesque Hungarian city of Poszôny, otherwise known as Pressburg.

There Mademoiselle had recourse to her confessor to communicate with Mme. de Genlis, but the death of the priest in 1800 put an end to this secret correspondence.

These letters if published would definitely clear up the question of the real feelings of the august pupil for her Governess, feelings which have been supposed to be favourable to Mme. de Genlis or the reverse, according to the opinions of various writers.

We would then know if her feelings towards her remained those of confidence and affection, or if they changed to coldness and aversion under the hostile influence of Mme. de Conti, and much later of the Duchess of Orleans.

These letters are in the possession of the Orleans family, and till they are published—if ever—we have to be content with doubtful conjectures.

After the departure of Mademoiselle, Mme. de Genlis thought only of putting an end to her stay at Bremgarten, which had become an unpleasant place for her. Assailed with anonymous letters, and insulted in the French and foreign newspapers, she received blows from all sides.

Condemned to silence—she had been so imprudent as send a reply one day to the *Gazette de Leyde*,[2] whose editor refused to retract—and, hard pressed by want of money,

---

[1] A futile pretext was the motive for this interdict. Madame de Genlis had sent Mademoiselle on her name day a water-colour sketch of a red rose in a blue vase, the background being naturally white. Madame de Conti took offence at this tricoloured design.

[2] The *Gazette de Leyde* of 26th April 1793 announced that Dumouriez had started for Germany by way of Aix-la-Chapelle in company with the Duke of Orleans, M. de Valence, Mademoiselle, Paméla and Mme. de Genlis.

she was anxious to be away from Bremgarten and Switzerland.

And then she had to think of making a living with her pen, and though the spur of hard times was a powerful stimulant to her desire to be writing again, she must have a publisher and a printer somewhere near her. To send away her manuscripts would be a means of putting the Royalists on her track, the very thing she wanted to avoid.

It was just then that Talleyrand wrote to her offering her 12,000 francs. Since they met in London he had lost sight of her, but at the end of 1798 he was enquiring for her of Mme. de Flahault. She would be able to give the ex-bishop precise information. Mme. de Genlis refused the generous offer—an offer less surprising than one might imagine on the part of this man, who calculated every step, and who, when he thought it was the right moment, could be charitable in a lordly way.

But amid the cruel difficulties with which she was struggling, such a sum would have filled her purse abundantly, and cleared away most of her embarrassments. To refuse it was indeed to push self-respect to the verge of heroism.

The poor woman must have passports, and she only secured them after unheard-of difficulties, under assumed names. To mislead her enemies she procured two passports —one under the name of Mme. Brown which she did not use, the other under another pseudonym.

As soon as she was provided with these precious papers she left St. Clare's—" to her inexpressible relief "—on 19th May 1794, a week to the day after the departure of Mademoiselle. César du Crest had come to Bremgarten shortly before this. She left him to get away at his own risk and peril,—a mere boy of fourteen would excite no one's suspicions. She took her niece Henriette with her. They reached the Rhine, and went down it without stopping anywhere till they were at Utrecht, where M. de Valence had taken up his abode for a time.

But when she left Bremgarten she had broken with the Duke of Orleans.

Did they see each other at this time? Had they an explanation face to face?

If we are to believe a former chaplain of the Duc de Penthièvre, of whose sincerity there can be no doubt, we might ask if the date of May 19th given by Mme. de Genlis as that of her departure is correct?

Four months later, on 19th September, the Abbé Lambert thought he saw her leaning on the arm of her pupil, the young Duke.

The Abbé arrived that morning—a Monday—at Bremgarten in the hope of seeing the Duke, who, he had heard, was staying there with M. de Montesquiou. The bells were ringing for Mass, and he hastened to the church.

"I had hardly knelt down," he writes, "when I saw the Duke of Orleans come in with a lady on his arm whom I thought to be Mme. de Sillery."[1]

The Abbé had seen Mme. de Genlis only once, and that was on the occasion of the Prince's first Communion at Anet. After so many years would the Governess have been anything like his recollection of her, or rather would she not have disguised her general appearance, as it was her interest to put her enemies off her track.

In any case neither the Prince nor the lady wanted to be recognised, and when after Mass the Abbé, following their steps, rang at the door of M. de Montesquiou, where they had just gone in, a servant peremptorily dismissed him: "Monseigneur was no longer at Bremgarten. Monseigneur had gone away to the Grisons." And the poor chaplain took his departure sadly discomfited.

Can it be then that Mme. de Genlis was staying at Bremgarten in September? May one suppose that now that the *coup d'état* of Thermidor had changed the situation in France, she had an idea of coming to an arrangement with the Duke in view of some political move being attempted? This would be quite erroneous.

However, Mme. de Flahault—an enemy of Mme. de Genlis, partly through jealousy of her as an author, and still more on account of Talleyrand,—Mme. de Flahault, chosen by

[1] Abbé Lambert, *Mémoires de Famille*, L. iv. 180.

the Prince " as the confidante of his moral solitude and of his ardent desire to throw off the yoke,"[1] was writing a little later from Bremgarten to Governor Morris (the American diplomatist, who after having been such a frequent guest at the Palais Royal and in her salon showed himself so finely devoted to the children of the House of Orleans) a well known letter, which we must reproduce here in order to make our story clear :—

"I have seen the young Duke of Orleans in Switzerland. He has had a serious quarrel with Mme. de Sillery, of whom he has had so much reason to complain. But do not repeat this, for if she knew he had been talking about her she would persecute him even in his retirement. He will now have nothing whatever to do with that lady and her principles.

"Could you not do him the welcome service of informing his mother of his noble conduct, of his veneration for herself, and of his hatred for Mme. de Sillery, whose folly was the ruin of his father ? . . .

"He remembers having seen you, and admits that he was so much under the influence of the bad principles and the prejudices of his Governess, that you could not form a fair opinion of him . . . etc."

All this leads one to believe in a " quarrel."

But must we place it at about 19th May or 19th September.

The *Memoirs* of Mme. de Genlis formally oppose the latter hypothesis. And may not the lady whom the Abbé Lambert took for Mme. de Genlis have been Mme. de Flahault, who clearly was mixed up with the Prince's affairs, and, as a recent writer says, " threw as much oil as she could on the fire." But then, according to the biographer of Mme. de Flahault, she would not be at Bremgarten till the month of October. Who, then, was the lady seen by the Abbé Lambert ?

But it must be admitted that the letters written at this time by the Prince to Morris make no allusion good or bad

[1] Maricourt, *op. cit.*, 182.

to Mme. de Genlis.[1] At the beginning of 1795 he was anxious to get away to the United States, and he thought of that only. But then (January 1795) Mme. de Genlis was at Altona. She had had a rough journey. After having reached Schaffhausen, she and Henriette at Mayence took what she jestingly calls a "private gondola" to go down the Rhine to Cologne, whence they travelled in a carriage to Utrecht.

There M. de Valence was waiting for them; he took them to Naarden on the Zuyder Zee, where he had rented a little country house. There they could wait for better times.

At the end of five weeks Mme. de Genlis, wishing not to be an expense to her son-in-law, and to procure a more settled place of abode, set off for Denmark, the Government of which had shown itself friendly to the French exiles.

The expedition was not such an easy matter. There were not many roads between the province of Utrecht and Holstein, and these were difficult and in anything but good condition. Anyone else but the intrepid Mme. de Genlis would have lost heart at the outset, and abandoned the idea of using them.

But her old hardihood, her long-continued habit of physical exercise, enabled her bravely to undergo this new Odyssey. She astonished everyone by her persistence, by her wonderful endurance. And who else, indeed, would have thought it "a fine thing" to travel through Hanover in a post-chaise that was a miserable vehicle, hardly covered in, heavy, primitive, of a thoroughly German type of construction, in which one was lumbered up with bundles and baskets, and which took three days and three nights to go only from Utrecht to Osnabrück? What delicate *émigrée* dame from the French Court would have ventured to embark at Hamburg under a deluge of rain, to cross the Elbe in a poor, little, open boat, and arrive at Altona soaked to the skin and in a state rivalling that of a gipsy tramp? It was an expedition worthy of a writer of romances!

[1] On the other hand, Madame de Genlis says that the Prince wrote her a friendly letter in October 1794.

Mme. de Genlis had run these risks in the company of an old Jewess, a shopkeeper from Hanover, talkative, obliging, and ready to share with her the cost of the ferry boat on the Elbe. Our Countess got from the Jewess some information about Altona. She asked her, " At which of the inns of the place was the innkeeper most friendly to the French Revolution ? " And one need not be surprised at the question.

Altona, besides being, as is well known, the headquarters of the emigration properly so-called, also entertained opinions favourable to the Revolution. Altona, as indeed the rest of Europe, revered Robespierre. Since Klopstock wrote his emphatic ode on the taking of the Bastille, the richer classes —at a safe distance—had been taken with " a lively enthusiasm for the great movement in France." [1]

So a Red inn—in the political sense of course—ought to be easy to find in the town. And the best of all from this point of view was that of Master Pflock, in the Rathhausmarkt, in the Grund quarter of Altona.

The *Adressbuch* or Directory of Altona for the year 1794 mentions the house : " *Pflock (Christo), innkeeper,—wines & mineral waters—Grund, No.* 98,"—but does not count it among the hotels of the town. And as for the date at which our countess arrived, it is impossible for us to fix it. In the default of exact information we hesitate between July and October 1794.

Madame de Genlis found in Master Pflock the jewel of inn-keepers. A fine fellow, and though a Revolutionist a man of patriarchal manners, courteous, and absolutely honourable, he paid every attention to his new lodger, whose distinguished manners were in somewhat sharp contrast with the tone of his usual clients.

He gave her no rest till she accepted his invitation to dine at " the host's table,"—still a *table d'hôte* in more than name. And when Madame de Genlis had been assured that she would meet no unwelcome guest there, she would come into the room and take her place each day—generally after

[1] Cf. Charlotte Niese, *Die Gräfin von Genlis, Grenzboten*, No. for Dec. 3, 1903.

the first courses, for it was a solid meal—among the Danish or German officials, the business men and the other regular diners, who sat at the family table side by side with all the Pflocks.

Did it remind her of the Grand Vainqueur Inn, or the bar of the Porcherons, where, in disguise, one evening in 1778 she made a conquest of the courier of M. de Brancas ?

The comparison would certainly not have pleased honest Pflock. But here, as there, Mme. de Genlis exerted her usual charming influence. In a few days she had—as was her way—won all present, beginning with Mlle. Pflock, the innkeeper's daughter, who prided herself on literary culture.

She was known to them all as Miss Clarke, an Irish lady, educated in France. And as she hardly left her small room looking out on the courtyard except to go to church, it was thought she must be religious and an exile for it. Meanwhile her modest lodging was like a little temple of the arts. " I had," she tells us, " a fairly good piano, a harp, a guitar, water colours and pencils, a writing-desk, some books and a collection of dried plants that had been lent to me. My days went by with unimaginable rapidity."

She enjoyed also the consolation of talking about her dear France with two compatriots, a lady, Mme. Gudin, and an *émigré* gentleman, M. de Kercy, who was not too much of an aristocrat. Both were lodging at Pflocks. Madame Gudin, inspired with friendship for this interesting foreign lady, liked to practise music with her. But Kercy, who had the next room to Madame de Genlis, was even more friendly. He rendered Miss Clarke various little services. He helped her in her work, for, obliged to earn her daily bread, she had looked for and found employment. She designed and painted patterns of flowers and arabesques for a neighbouring factory of printed cottons.

M. de Kercy was useful in another way. He was always well supplied with news from France. He went regularly to Hamburg, only divided from Altona by a long avenue of fine trees, to look for news at a street corner café founded by an ex-duke, where the Paris newspapers were to be seen.

Finally, at a later date, he corrected her printer's proofs for his friendly neighbour.

Besides these two compatriots, Miss Clarke made acquaintance at Pflock's with two men whose friendship was very useful to her. One was a Danish official of good position, Pierre Joseph Texier, Councillor of Legation and Director of the Fisheries. The other was Dr. Unzer, a professor, district medical officer, and poet, a brother-in-law of Louis Schröder, Klopstock's friend, and a member of several literary societies. He had chosen the inn as his abode, and consoled himself for his desertion by his wife, Dorothea Ackermann, by devoting himself to painting. He it was who obtained for Mme. de Genlis work as a designer of patterns for the factory.

But above all, she rejoiced at being in safety. Her incognito seemed to her to be marvellously secure here within the walls of Altona. Two travellers only, Frenchmen, who passed through the inn recognised her, but they respected her secret. Amongst the *émigrés* living in the town, who were estimated at four thousand, she was, she says, quite unnoticed. But it would be astonishing enough if our Countess was not recognised at Altona, this rendezvous of Royalists, where the Princess de Vaudremont gave her famous evening parties, where all the *émigrés* were eager to be invited, among them the two brothers De Caraman, Maurice and Joseph, the latter the future Prince de Chimay — M. Clermont Tonnerre, the Marchioness de Pardaillan, Garat and the rest. It is more likely that they were aware of her presence, but pretended not to remember her. Besides, Mme. de Flahault — only to mention one — knew perfectly well where to find Mme. de Genlis.

But the natives of the place who frequented Pflock's inn certainly did not suspect the real identity of Miss Clarke.

Thus she had the piquant amusement of hearing her fellow-guests talk about a certain Marquise de Sillery living over in Hamburg, who they said had installed herself in that city with Dumouriez, and had been seen there and actually recognised. She could secretly give way to her amusement when one day, after she had changed her work from designing patterns for muslins to writing manuscripts, they looked at each other with a puzzled expression, and Mme. Gudin exclaimed: " Miss Clarke an authoress! I can answer for it that except her prayer-book she has never looked into a book of any kind."

Another treat of the same kind was reserved for her—to listen to criticisms of one of her dramatic works and go to see it played.

A travelling party of English actors, " Williamson's Theatrical Company," came to Altona and played several of Mme. de Genlis's pieces in an English translation. According to Professor Harkensee, the programmes of the local theatre which still exist in the town library of Altona mention only one with certainty, namely—*The Child of Nature, Comedy in four acts. From the French of the Marquise de Sillery by Mrs. Inchbald*, which was played at the Old Comedy Theatre of Altona on 18th November 1794, and on the stage of the Great Newmarket Theatre at Hamburg on 17th February 1795. This must have been her *Zélie ou l'Ingénue*. The translators did what they liked with titles, and besides Mme. de Genlis mentions this piece as having been the subject of conversation at the dinner table at Pflock's.

Let us add that the critics there were enthusiastic, and lavished their flowery praise on Mme. de Genlis.

These good people were not entirely ignorant as to French theatrical matters. Even though the Princess de Vaudremont sent them no invitations, they could go to the performances given by the *Schauspielergesellschaft*, the French company at Hamburg, and their critical judgments were not uninteresting. Miss Clarke took much pleasure in their friendly incense. But she had foreseen the possibility of something different, and for the sake of her literary honour she had made up her mind beforehand that, if they indulged in offensive censures, she would say who she was and leave the table.

She had not to proceed to this extremity, because her self-esteem as an author reaped only a harvest of praise.

Soon after this, Kercy knocked at her door at midnight. At this late hour the Countess was still writing by the light of her lamp. She did not open. Kercy knocked again.

Still she took no notice. Then he called to her: "Robespierre is dead!" and at last the door opened. In a transport of joy Mme. de Genlis embraced her worthy neighbour, and then knelt with him to offer a thanksgiving.

But the good people of Altona did not take the news so well. They seemed quite upset by it. It would appear even that one of the adorers of the virtuous Maximilien fell down in a fit at the news, for at Altona they almost believed that the man with the green eyes was as immortal as a god.

Robespierre being dead, it seemed that all Terrorism had vanished with him, and that the sun was shining again in the sky of France.

Mme. de Genlis, living thus hidden, had not met any of her own people for eight months, with the exception of her son-in-law, M. de la Woestine, then living at Cleves, who had come to stay with her for a fortnight. She now thought with a lighter heart of leaving her hiding-place. And just then Master Pflock died. The good man had carried his interest in her so far as to find a fiancé for the worthy Miss Clarke, a rich widower, a master-baker at Altona.

This suitor, whose best reason was that the delicate sounds of her harp had made him fall desperately in love with her, played his part so seriously that he died, it would seem, shortly after the refusal with which the unfeeling Genlis dismissed him. So this was one more victim of the French Revolution.

But the Comtesse was about to leave Altona. Her niece Henriette and M. de Valence had both arrived at Hamburg with a party of Dutch *émigrés*, and had come to look for her. Valence was about to establish himself in a farm not far from Hamburg, and Mme. de Genlis preferred to reside in that city, to be nearer her son-in-law.

Before leaving her friends at Pflock's she revealed her real name, in order that, as she says in her *Memoirs*, "all the French people whom I had seen during nine months might know, beyond the possibility of a doubt, that it was false that Madame de Genlis was living with M. Dumouriez." As a matter of fact, the General had attached himself to Mme.

de Beauvert, the sister of Rivarol; and some time ago that lady had rejoined him in his exile.

It may be well to note that the Duke of Orleans left Hamburg just at the time when his Governess arrived there. Thanks to a hundred *louis d'or* lent him by Governor Morris, he had, under the escort of Mme. de Flahault, been able to reach Hamburg, or rather the village of Neuenstadt at the gates of that city, and was preparing to travel on to Denmark and Norway. But during his stay there he carefully avoided Altona and all that had anything to do with Mme. de Genlis.

A letter from Mme. de Flahault to Morris, written, not without some bitterness of feeling, in February 1795, states this quite plainly.

Other considerations still enforced on the future Louis-Philippe the strictest incognito.

He did not wish to—and he could not—play any public part. Whatever may have been said to the contrary, he had no political party at Hamburg. And the most recent historians of the Revolution have so far not shown that any such party existed. But the mere presence of the young Duke in Europe excited to such a degree the suspicions and the fears of the party that had conquered in Thermidor, that they still kept his brothers Montpensier and Beaujolais as hostages, ready to sacrifice them on the first news that the young chief of the House of Orleans was at the head of an agitation. Louis-Philippe knew this through Morris. He lived as much unknown as possible at Hamburg, and this to such an extent that Dampmartin, meeting him one day with Montjoie, did not know for years after that his friend's " excellent young companion " was the Prince.

And then his departure for the lands of northern ice put an end to all the fables in circulation as to his alleged political ambition, and as to the equally mythical revival of the old Orleans faction. This made possible at last the liberation of Montpensier and Beaujolais, which Morris accelerated with all his intelligently directed enthusiasm. It was followed by the embarkation for Philadelphia, and the reunion of the three brothers.

Now it is quite possible that Mme. de Flahault pressed Louis-Philippe to get away from Hamburg as soon as possible. In removing him from the neighbourhood of Mme. de Genlis, she probably would not be sorry to give a lesson to her enemy, and would hope thus to deprive her eventually of the fruits of many years of intrigue.

CHAPTER III

HAMBURG

In her *Memoirs* Mme de Genlis says that she arrived at Hamburg on 1st April 1795. We must respectfully remark that she is wrong to the extent of a fortnight, for her letters of the time enabled us to assert that she arrived there on the 17th.

For the first few days the Comtess and Henriette put up at the house of a certain M. Braasch in the centre of the city and on one of the finest of the quays of the Alster, the Jungfernstieg. Thence they soon removed to the house of the Pastor Wolters,—Michel Wolters, second deacon of St. Catherine's, residing at No. 86 St. Catherine's Cemetery. Their bright and pleasant rooms on the first storey looked out upon the Alster, whose little green waves rippled against the walls of the house.

Mme. de Genlis soon forgot her homely existence in the Pflock household when she found herself on the sunlit quays, amid the traffic of this beautiful and populous city, teeming with life, with its port and its gardens, the open-air meeting-place of a rich and elegant crowd.

Her mind, which had stored up many things during the inactive days of a prolonged exile, suddenly awoke and began to sparkle, as soon as she found herself once more in touch with those of her own class and her own country. For Hamburg was crowded with *émigrés*. Though there might be a lack of luxury and even of comfortable ease, Mme. de Genlis found herself once more in the midst of a polished society, full of taste, and of the love of conversation, literature, and pleasure. She found herself again among

Frenchmen of noble birth, with their easy, polished, bright, and yet haughty, manners—and one must add—with their whims, their recklessness, and their habitual vices. In a word there was all the tone of Parisian social life—salons, gaming tables, supper parties, theatres. For if one must keep shop during the day, one became an aristocrat again in the evening,—one dressed, cultivated the arts, amused oneself. At once she tried to organise a little circle of her own.

Two very definitely separated parties divided this society into two camps. Between the Republicans who wore the tricolour cockade and the Royalists who had no cockade, there was not room for any shade of opinion. Now Mme. de Genlis stood at about an even distance from the one and the other, suspected by the former and an object of aversion to the latter. Nevertheless she tried to set up a rallying point. She could, at least, count upon her relatives—her son-in-law, General de Valence, and her brother, the Marquis du Crest.

M. de Valence was somewhat isolated. He was generally to be found in the little group, half-patriot, half-Constitutionalist, formed out of the wreckage of the old Orleanist faction, in which one met the brothers Lameth, the Duke d'Aiguillon, and a few others, "the Comte de Ricé, Beaumarchais, etc." He was of a melancholy turn, as is often the case with a man away from his family. Mme. de Valence, whom he had always neglected, and to whom he had been unfaithful, had, after the arrest in April 1793, taken advantage of the new law to sue for a divorce, and at this cost saved her life and that of her three children, and of young Hermine, whom she called her adopted daughter.[1] Thanks to a petition, in which she expressed her detestation of "arristocratie" (*sic*), and which she signed "P. Brûlard, divorced woman," she obtained from the Convention an authorisation to retire to Mme. de Montesson's house at Neuilly. Since then Mme. de Genlis had heard nothing of her.

More successful were the Marquis du Crest and his witty young wife, whose talents as a musician, but even more her

[1] The decree of divorce is dated 20th May 1793.

slanting, Chinese-looking eyes, her air of a little girl fresh from school, and her look of an Oriental, attracted many admirers. Their salon gathered together a society that was ready to be friendly, and not very strict in its morals, and this group formed the nucleus of the salon of Mme. de Genlis. It was soon reinforced by some Hamburghers of good standing, brought in by the influence of her Altona friends, Councillor Texier and Dr. Unzer.

The two salons, that of the brother and the sister, mutually helped each other. Their guests passed from one to the other. Music was the leading feature with du Crest, and literary matters at the social gatherings of Mme. de Genlis. Both of them were better used than most people to extricating themselves from the most trying situations, so these resourceful minds and thoroughly experienced characters triumphed over the prevailing disease of impecuniosity. They kept up appearances by dint of unceasing effort, she with her pen, he, the indefatigable inventor, the man of projects, by building boats and carriages half of wood, half of papier maché, and by winning, it seems, at the gaming tables, enough to be able several times each week to invite his friends to that "roast joint of modest proportions accompanied by a wretched salad," of which the biographer of Mme. de Souza gives us an amusing account.

The ex-chancellor of the Palais Royal had, like his sister, the art of pleasing and a wide erudition. He had never set great store on fine manners, or on the elegance of his costume, about which he was rather careless. But what of that! It was no longer the time for Court dress, and his guests preferred Mme. du Crest's sonatas and the anecdotes the Marquis had collected in old days in the society of Diderot, the Marquis d'Holbach, and Helvetius, rather than the baser delights of a well-spread table and the vanities of costly toilets. Poverty is not a vice! And Du Crest, perhaps less discredited than his sister, was able to attract, now here, now there, some young nobles, who, at twenty years of age, had enough of careless philosophy to keep politics apart from pleasure.

Amongst these the Comte de Neuilly, at some risk of compromising himself, went also to the salon of Mme. de Genlis. To speak frankly, she excited rather his sprightly raillery than his admiration. He admits her charms, but speaks of them in the past tense, or even in the pluperfect. "She *had been* very pretty," he says, "and even more piquantly interesting; and when her expression became animated, one saw that she *must have been* very attractive." He thus finishes his portrait of her, the most complete that we have of Mme. de Genlis at fifty: "Her mind, which was undoubtedly very remarkable, was spoiled by pedantry and a want of naturalness. Her tone, her manners, were affected. Everything about her, even her dress, had something pretentious in it. She was thin and rather short of stature, and she strutted about in high-heeled shoes. By the same token she trod on my foot with them one day, and with such force that I let go an exclamation that was quite soldierlike in its energy."[1] M. de Neuilly does not err on the side of indulgence. But even more than the formal literary and dramatic soirées of Mme. de Genlis, even more than "the little morning invitations with attractions that got talked about and won some useful recruits,"[2] the star that drew so many guests to her—patriots, citizens of Hamburg, writers, artists, and some young deserters from the *émigré* party, was the pretty brunette Paméla, who was staying in the home of her adopted mother while Lord Edward was preparing the Irish insurrection of '98. Whatever may have been said, she did not yet welcome any consolers. She was expecting the birth of her second child. But those on whom she did not smile took their homage to the star of the second magnitude, Henriette de Sercey. She had the ruddy complexion of a Rubens. A premature *embonpoint* showed itself in her shoulders, her arms, and her shapely hands, and touched with rosy red the round cheeks that contrasted with her ebony black hair. Her mouth, with full lips, showed pearly white teeth, and her eyes with their black velvety pupils shone as she listened to the rapid exchange of merry jests.

[1] Comte de Neuilly, *Dix ans d'émigration*, p. 138.
[2] De Lescure, *Rivarol et la Société française*, 435.

For the sake of the smiles of these two bright young women, the guests were ready to pay all the more admiration to the Comtesse, make more of the success of her talents, endure her sometimes pedantic moral maxims, or her lectures on politics. They welcomed her readings in the salon of choice passages, fresh from her pen, of that famous novel, the *Chevaliers du Cygne*—that, for instance, in which, with a strange lack of feeling, she described the execution of Marie Antoinette. They flattered her with exaggerated praise, and mercilessly ridiculed the little weaknesses, the small successes, of the would-be grand master of the intellectual world of Hamburg—Rivarol, the sworn enemy of Mme. de Genlis.

It is well known how, for a long time, "as a man, as a critic, and as a Royalist," he had hated her.[1] The horror Rivarol felt for Philippe-Égalité was of public notoriety. It quite naturally included Mme. de Genlis, and never was their hatred more persevering and more vindictive.

Whilst affecting mutually to ignore each other, the two opponents vied with one another in the exchange of epigrams, allusions, malicious witticisms, behaving like a pair of wolves that have fallen out. Rivarol was, beyond contradiction, the stronger of the two at this game.

Supported by the pugnacious aristocratic crowd of the *émigrés*, who circulated the slightest of his smart sayings as if it were an oracle, he could, with one sally, one peppery phrase, fire the hostility of the party against Mme. de Genlis, and he never hesitated to do so. With his scoffs, his insults, and his calumnies he set up a general boycott of the salon of the ex-Governess. When, in the month of July 1795, she went away to the home of her son-in-law, the Comte de Valence, at Silk in Holstein, she was in flight from Hamburg, which the discourteous manœuvres of Rivarol had made uninhabitable for her.

Silk, five leagues from the city, and half-way between Rheinbeck and Friedrichsruhe, was only a farm or country house that M. de Valence had rented. Mme. de Genlis —extricated from her troubles by the sale of the *Chevaliers du*

---

[1] De Lescure, *Rivarol et la Société française*, p. 253.

Cygne (which the publisher Fauche had just bought for 300 gold Fredericks, or 6600 francs), paid her son-in-law for her board and lodging. Here she was within reach of her friends at Hamburg, and she went back there from time to time, although, since the first days of her arrival there, her enemies in the city had given her the worst of reputations. They declared that they had seen Mme. de Genlis, disguised as a groom, in the company of Count Potocki. They announced that she was starting for Switzerland to marry Necker. Such were the absurd stories in circulation! In a wretched paper that appeared at Hamburg under the name of the *Spectateur de Paris*, she was described as the " ex-Comtess Flahault-Genlis," in ignorance of the fact that, as she notes in the *Memoirs*, these were the names of two different persons, who had no kind of connection or relation with each other. This gossip penetrated even to German social circles. Notwithstanding the fame of Klopstock's visit to the famous Countess, certain Hamburgers of note showed anything but a friendly feeling towards her. Such, for example, were Frau Doktor Reimarus and Herr Piter Poel. Mme. Reimarus wrote to a friend, soon after the publication of the *Chevaliers du Cygne*, " You have no doubt seen the new novel by Mme. de Genlis, and noticed her disregard of all decency and honour. And this worthy lady talks only of modesty and virtue. She plays the devotee " (an allusion to the pious habits of Mme. de Genlis, who, it seems, had been seen even in Protestant churches), " and yet she is certainly worthless. But she is splendidly clever." As for M. Piter Poel, he described the "thorough-going malice" of the Comtesse and her son-in-law, of which he said he had had proof.

On the other hand, Dampmartin considered himself " happy and complimented " in having been allowed to visit her.

And Talleyrand, who had returned from America and just landed at Cuxhaven (July 1795), and meant to stay in Hamburg long enough to find out what was going on there, eagerly hastened to visit Mme. de Genlis, with whom he had never ceased to keep up a correspondence. Mme. Flahault, then at Altona, and much occupied with her coming marriage with "that good M. de Souza," was quite mistaken in her fears that the old friend would avail himself of rights that had been in desuetude since 1792.

He had quite different things in his head. He could present himself without disturbing the admirably regulated plans, to which it would be a mistake to suppose he was in any way opposed. He went straight to the intelligent ally, whose well-tried energy would be of more use to him than the retrospective recollections of Mme. de Flahault. "I found Mme. de Genlis," he says, "just the same as I had known her at Sillery, at Bellechasse, and in England. The steadiness of such self-composed characters is a part of their adaptability." [1]

One may penetrate at one's leisure the significance of these words of the ironical diplomatist.

We must keep in mind the obscure agitations of the moment,—the rise of the Directory, the intrigues of the so-called Constitutionalists, the proceedings of the Royalists, and, finally, the disturbances in Ireland, of which some believe they can trace a reaction upon France. Considering all this, we cannot be surprised that Mme. de Genlis tried to give some support to movements so well calculated to bring the intriguing ex-bishop again to the front,—and promote her own interests at the same time. It is certain that she was not altogether a stranger to the insurrectionary movement in Ireland, with which Talleyrand was mixed up more or less actively.

Since the month of May 1798, negotiations had been in progress between the United Irishmen and the French Government. In accordance with the patriotic feeling of the nation the Directory had, in principle, decided to support Ireland in its revolt against England, the old enemy of France, and had declared itself ready to send troops to assist an enterprise for the establishment of the Republican form of government in Ireland. Lord Edward Fitzgerald and Arthur O'Connor, sent as delegates by their compatriots to arrange the details of a Franco-Irish convention, began by opening up communications with Reinhard, the French

[1] Talleyrand, *Mémoires*, i. 248.

Minister at Hamburg, and this was how Lord Edward came to that city with Paméla. Naturally, O'Connor too was a visitor of Mme. de Genlis, and it has been stated that Talleyrand, during his stay at Hamburg, had several interviews with her, M. de Valence, Fitzgerald, and O'Connor.

After this the two Irish gentlemen set out for Switzerland. They were to meet Hoche at Basel, and then go to Paris to negotiate with the Directory, which felt some mistrust of an insurrection to be organised by the husband of a supposed daughter of the late Duke of Orleans. Paméla stayed behind with Mme. de Genlis, and Talleyrand started for Berlin on a secret mission, in which his latest biographer refuses to believe,[1] but which, according to other historians, had for its object to inform Barras of the situation in Ireland.

Meanwhile, Reinhard, by his position at Hamburg, "the headquarters of the malcontents of England and Ireland," was better placed than anyone else for keeping the Directory well informed. And it seems that there was some kind of connection between the proceedings of Talleyrand and those of Mme. de Genlis, of whom John Murray—full of ill-will as usual, but with good information—does not hesitate to write that "She was the intermediary between Republican France and disloyal Ireland."[2]

On the other hand, an unpublished document, certainly of English origin, accuses Mme. de Genlis, "the Revolutionary pedant," of having drawn her son-in-law, M. de Valence, into the Irish insurrectionary movement, after having ruined him, and goes so far as to say: "After the ruin of M. de Valence, Mme. de Genlis was the only one that had pity on his misfortunes, and she gave him a few *louis* to enable that gentleman to pass over to England and equip himself with a view to fighting as a comrade of the Irish." These, however, are statements which there is not the least reason to take seriously, and they are only another proof of the animosity which the enemies of our Countess could not help showing towards her.

[1] Bernard de Lacombe, *Vie privée de Talleyrand*.
[2] John Murray, *The Female Revolutionary Plutarch*.

M. DE VALENCE.

Following Talleyrand's example, she tried to make herself useful to the Directory. This would be the safest method of preparing the way for her return to France, that happy return to which one can easily imagine that she must have looked forward as to the entry into the Promised Land.

So we need not look for any other explanation of her conduct, or for any other reasons for the famous open letter to the Duke of Orleans, published by Mme. de Genlis in March 1796, and known as the "Letter from Silk,"[1] and which echoed like a cannon-shot in Paris, where, on the least pretext, and without any pretext, there was talk of the Orleanist faction.

In this epistle, and in a tone of maternal dignity that well became a teacher abandoned by her august pupil, the Governess begins by a long dissertation on the mystery with which young Louis-Philippe surrounds his proceedings, and on his desire to keep Mme. de Genlis in ignorance of the place of his residence, forbidding even his correspondents to reveal it. Then she goes on to dissuade the youthful head of the House of Orleans from claiming the throne, and even defies him to do so. "You," she says, "a candidate for the crown! You, to be a usurper, to abolish a Republic which you have recognised, which you have loved, and for which you have fought valiantly! And at what a time! When France has been reorganised and a Government established, which appears to be based on solid foundations of morality and justice!"

"The throne," Mme. de Genlis declares, "if it is ever to be re-established—legitimately belongs to the brother of Louis XVI. And besides, you could not give peace to France, and except courage and probity you have none of those needful virtues that go to the making of a king."

Reading this pronouncement in the Letter, one asks oneself if its author really believed seriously that Louis-Philippe was unfit to occupy a throne; and to admit the sincerity of the "Letter from Silk," one must remember with what

[1] It was at first printed and circulated separately from the *Précis de ma conduite*, to which it was added after the appearance of the latter in July 1796.

singular persistence she defended the same opinion even in 1880.

It was a strange thing that in France she was thought to be a dangerous woman and capable of exciting a conspiracy.

And the more Mme. de Genlis turned her coat—so to say—the more she proclaimed her quarrel with Monseigneur, the more she seemed to renounce her former hopes, the more people were inclined to suspect the Duke of Orleans and his instructress. The men of the Directory did not realise that she was, above all, anxious to prove that she had no part in the acts of her pupil from the day when, as she says, " On his taking up friends who have never been mine, an end was put to a correspondence, the sole value of which was its mutual confidence." [1] They were hallucinated by the spectre of the Orleanist faction, and one finds echoes of this state of mind in the newspapers of the time, amongst others in the *Censeur* and the *Éclair*. The *Journal de Paris* alone ventures to judge the letter to be " in conformity with the principles of the Duc de Chartres " and to call the Orleanist faction a chimera.

No doubt the conduct of Mme. de Genlis seems self-contradictory, if we remember certain principles set forth and upheld in 1790 in the *Discours sur l'éducation du Dauphin et sur l'adoption*. But one must not forget that circumstances were no longer the same, and that the interest of the moment—the basis of all practical politics—imposed this attitude on her.

In her pressing need of getting rid of the awful clog of being counted as a Jacobin *émigrée*, which hampered her continually at Hamburg, anything that could hasten her recall to France seemed to her to be justifiable. This was why she published the " Letter from Silk," and sent it straightway to the Minister of Justice at Paris, on 14th July 1796 (25 Messidor, Year IV), adding to it a regular dossier—letter, petition, memorial, protests, and finally the manuscript of a pamphlet soon to be published under the title of *Précis de ma conduite depuis la Révolution* (" A summary of my conduct since the Revolution ").

[1] *Précis de ma Conduite*, 217.

There is nothing out of the way in the petition, unless it be that Mme. de Genlis brings forward as a claim to the goodwill of the Directory that for three years she has had no correspondence with her daughter, Mme. de Valence. There runs through it the usual tone of petitions, with the obligatory formula of respect and admiration for the Government and esteem for the Minister.

The letter to the Duke of Orleans and the *Précis* have for introduction a kind of preface, in which Mme. de Genlis seeks to clear herself of all charges of complicity with Dumouriez.[1]

But the Memorial is more interesting. It is presented as "a frank confession without any reserve." For those who like to draw parallels it suggests more than one instructive comparison. In this manifestation of herself the Countess, no doubt, tones down a good many things. Like the bat of the fable she excells in saying—and with full sincerity—

"Je suis oiseau, voyez mes ailes,
Je suis souris, vivent les rats."[2]

We may judge of how she pleaded her case by the following passage:—

"I hold some opinions that may be unpleasing. Here they all are—

"1. I have sincerely regretted all that has been done against religion, and this on account of my feelings, my

---

[1] "The fresh calumnies with which an attempt is made to blacken me in the *Gazette Nationale*, have decided me to have printed separately and immediately the letter addressed to the Duc de Chartres. If you will deign to read this letter, you will see if I took any part in the intrigues that they denounce. Assuredly this letter cannot leave the shadow of a doubt on the matter, but this is unnecessary in the country in which I have resided for the last two years. Here every one knows that I have lived in the most profound retirement, that MM. Dumouriez and De Montjoye are my bitterest enemies, as also are the small number of partisans they have in this country; that M. de Chartres broke with me three years ago; that I have never sought to meet M. Dumouriez and his associates, and I may add that I do not even know the name of the place where he lives. . . ." (*Mémoire et Réclamations de la Citoyenne Genlis*, "Archives Nationales" F⁷ 6521, No. 1291.)

[2] "I am a bird—see my wings,
I am a mouse—long live the rats."

persuasions, and because I hold that without religion a nation can have neither morals nor manners.

"2. I have regarded the deaths of Louis XVI., of his wife, and of his sister as cruelties that were not only useless but also impolitic.

"3. I would have wished that the monarchy had been preserved, because people had sworn to maintain it, and because this form of government is milder and less turbulent than the Republican, and I prefer peace to all else, but at the same time *I do not belong and I have never for an instant belonged to the party which is called Constitutionalist,* for from the moment that the French Republic was proclaimed I have desired from the depth of my soul that it should be maintained; this great step once taken, it seemed to me that the nation, for the honour of its character, should support it, and I think this all the more strongly since the war; *I have always persistently said, written, and repeated that the French nation, after all that it has done, would be the last people in the world if it resumed royalty.*

"This is the real state of my mind, but I will add (and my word can be relied on), that if my rights are restored to me, no French citizeness will show or entertain a more sincere attachment than mine for the actual government. . . ."

The Minister—it was Merlin de Douai, once a guest at the table of the Palais Royal and the companion of Laclos—received, every day, documents like this. As soon as he got them, he sent them off to the central police office, and thought no more about them. The Brûlard-Genlis dossier shared the common lot. Merlin wrote at the top of its first page—"Referred to the Minister of Police (for his personal information) 25 Messidor, Year IV," and signed the note. And the clever prose of Mme. de Genlis was buried in the portfolios of the police records, until, not long after, it was claimed again by its author. As we have seen, the publication of the *Précis de ma conduite* followed in four months that of the letter to the Duke of Orleans. Mme. de Genlis, in this pamphlet, while deploring "the excesses that tarnished the triumph of the people," dwells mainly on her attachment to the Revolution; and on the joy with which she saw the new Constitution " destroy horrible abuses and despotism "; but she earnestly repudiated the allegation that she had had any relations with the Revolutionists whose names had now become compromising.

Thus she makes out that she never met Laclos; that she never in her life spoke to Lameth or Sieyès; that she hardly saw Brissot, and that only with reference to matters that had nothing to do with politics; that she refused to receive Mirabeau; and that she called Barrère " a wretch and a scoundrel." The most she ventures to admit is her sincere esteem for Pétion, and that she had been *sometimes* at the National Assembly, twice at the Jacobin Club, and once only at the Cordeliers. Finally, she protests that, living shut up at Bellechasse—like the wise man in his tower of ivory—and occupied *solely* with literary work, she never mixed in public affairs, politics, and matters of ambition.

One can see that Mme. de Genlis would have made a splendid special pleader at the bar!

Meanwhile the Duke of Orleans had heard of the open letter his former " Governor " had addressed to him, as well as of the *Précis*. He read it at the beginning of August 1796, and thought it right to make a public reply to it, in a pamphlet of his own (now no longer to be found), with the title of *Quelques observations sur la dernière brochure de Madame de Genlis*, and signed *L.-P. d'Orléans*.[1]

This was not a direct reply to Madame de Genlis, for whom he no longer felt any affection, nor was it a political move. It was simply a correction of the errors, voluntary or involuntary, that he had noted in the *Précis*.

Louis Philippe informed his mother of this, and though the *Observations* are lost, the letter at least has reached us—

" For a long time," he writes to the Duchess of Orleans, " I have had no relations with Mme. de Genlis; she has lately had printed at Hamburg a letter addressed to me, accompanied by a summary (a very incorrect one) of her conduct during the Revolution, in which she does not respect even the memory of my unfortunate father. I

[1] Hamburg, 17th August 1796.

certainly have no idea of replying to the letter she has written me; but I think it my duty to set forth in their integrity some of the facts that she has misrepresented. I shall have this little piece of writing printed at Hamburg, and I will take care that a copy is addressed to the Minister of Police in the hope that he will be so good as to forward it to you."

The young Prince's pamphlet, which revived latent feelings of hatred for her, made a stay at Silk or Hamburg still more disagreeable for Mme. de Genlis. She made preparations for going away. Besides, there was no longer anything to keep her there. Fitzgerald was negotiating with Barras at Paris, and Paméla was living with her friend Henriette de Sercey, whom Mme. de Genlis had meanwhile married to a rich Hamburger, the banker Matthiessen. "I don't know how she took to him," says Neuilly.

Johann Conrad Matthiessen, hunchbacked, very ugly and already of mature age—he was forty-six—but head of the important firm of Matthiessen and Sillem, one of the foremost in the city, attracted by the elegant and subtle charms of the salon of Mme. de Genlis, had offered his hand, and a fortune of the first class, to the delightful Henriette.

Mme. de Genlis, after subjecting the banker's suit to the test of time, accepted him for her niece. She was only too happy thus solidly to secure her future. The wedding was celebrated at the family mansion of the Matthiessens in the Grosse Reichenstrasse, on 19th May 1796. The bridegroom being of the Reformed religion, the marriage was simultaneously blessed by Pastor Willerding of St. Peter's, and by Father Hovestadt of the Catholic Chapel, now the Kaiserlichen Herrn Ministers' Capelle.

Then the newly married couple set up housekeeping in brilliant style in a new house on the Speersort, and their receptions were soon the talk of all Hamburg.

The young wife threw herself into the whirl of life and devoted herself to fashionable amusements. Matthiessen, who was kindness itself, played beside her the part of a husband who was open handed but counted for little. He only half-understood the fine points of literary conversation, and he left his wife to the dozen of admiring cavaliers, bright-witted young fellows who did not hesitate to pay court to her, and in the first rank of whom glittered the son of the great Swiss banker, Baron de Finguerlin, the " model of dandyism." Henriette was to make a marriage with him that was famous, after five years of conjugal bitterness had tired out the kindly patience of Matthiessen and made a rupture inevitable.

The stout burgher deserved a better fate. Under an unpleasing exterior he really hid treasures of good feeling and generosity.

Had he not, when he married, offered hospitality to Mme. de Genlis ?

Out of a sense of dignity, the love of independence, and the fear perhaps of exposing the newly wedded pair to the attacks of the *émigrés*, she refused. For a long time she had been thinking of going away to seek a new refuge, and she felt attracted towards Prussian territory. Berlin then enjoyed—quite undeservedly—a reputation for giving a generous welcome to the French *émigrés*, though these soon found little it was worth despite misleading appearances. But its hypocritical selfishness was only found out by actual experience of it, and Mme. de Genlis, after so many adventures, was not likely to be influenced by mere omens or the anxious fears of a weak woman, so she set out in careless good spirits, counting on her celebrity as a writer [1] to provide her with a living in Prussia as well as at Hamburg.

Besides, she knew in advance where to put up. There was just then, in Berlin, an old maid who was the directress of a girls' boarding-school. She was a wild admirer of the French Revolution, and, by her own account, of the works of the Comtesse de Genlis. She gladly received *émigrée* ladies of " patriotic " opinions. It was Mlle. Bocquet.

At her place one was best treated at the outset. If new arrivals were received with violent enthusiasm, it soon declined as their bill lengthened. At the end of a short time Mademoiselle showed that she had an unbearable

[1] The *Précis de ma conduite* had been sold for 10 *louis*, and various minor writings for 30 *louis*.

temper, and one had to leave her house after a thousand annoyances of the domestic order. Mme. de Genlis had to learn this at her own expense. For the moment she met with nothing but demonstrations of friendship on the part of her hostess, at whose house moreover she met fellow-countrywomen, French ladies. Sieyès, too, is said to have been a visitor at the Pension Bocquet, which is surprising enough, for at this time he should have been at the National Assembly, for he was not appointed Ambassador to Berlin until July 1798.

And meanwhile, according to Mme. de Genlis, people were accusing her of reviving the zeal for the Republic among the French refugees in Berlin, and they tried to make out that she had gone to Prussia in order to be again in communication with the " patriot " element, that was so largely represented in its capital.

Did she think that she would thus get into touch with the French Government and obtain her recall? Had she made the mistake of supposing that Talleyrand, who she knew had lately been at Berlin, was preparing the way for her? On this point a beginner in politics might have been misled by simple want of knowledge, but not our experienced Countess. Even if she did not know that as soon as he reached Paris the ex-Bishop of Autun forgot the little circle at Hamburg, she must have guessed it. Talleyrand, in fact, was at this moment on the look out for a ministerial portfolio, and was cultivating with remarkable assiduity the influential salons and the women who were leaders of the current fashion —Mme. de Stael, whose intellectual gifts influenced the two Assemblies, and through them public affairs; Mme. de Beauharnais; Mme. Tallien; and besides, that last refuge of the polished grace of the *ancien régime*, the hôtel Montesson, where the name of Mme. de Genlis was not precisely popular.

In fact, she had hardly anything but enemies, either in Berlin or in Paris. It was not much use her protesting that she had never seen Sieyès—no one would believe her; and indeed it seems very surprising that in the days of Bellechasse she had never had occasion to meet the Abbé-deputy, whose relations with the Orleanists were well known. And it is certain she had seen him, at least at the National Assembly.

Well, at Berlin it was asserted that one day, by the most unlucky of chances, he was recognised going into the Pension Bocquet. Surely he must have been paying a visit to Mme. de Genlis! "No," she said. "Yes, certainly," thought the Royalist *émigrés*, who were in high favour with King Frederick William.

This was enough. Someone, "a lady," says Mme. de Genlis, without further identifying her, took it upon herself to send at once to the King of Prussia a memorial, in which the Countess was described as "having largely contributed to bring about the Revolution, and as being capable of disturbing Brandenburg and Prussia." The writer of the memorial was the more insistent upon the inconvenience of Mme. de Genlis's presence at Berlin because Frederick William, himself an excellent musician, knew by repute that Mme. de Genlis was famous for her talent with the harp, and had, it seems, expressed a wish to hear her.

In the eyes of the maliciously disposed *émigrés*, the harp suddenly appeared to be a formidable instrument of intrigue. They feared its seductive powers, and would not rest until the royal ears had been made safe against these melodious philtres.

One fine day, as twelve o'clock was striking, Mme. de Genlis received the visit of a police official, and heard that she was ordered to leave Berlin within two hours.

Frederick William had a tendency to cruel jests. "I shall never exile Mme. de Genlis from my library," he had said, "but I shall not tolerate her in my dominions." Already many a subject of Prussia, who had suddenly fallen under suspicion, had been sent in this summary fashion to the fortress of Landau, whence it was not easy to get away. The King even carried his incivility to the point of expelling people at their own expense. Mme. de Genlis, who still had 80 *louis* but no carriage, had hurriedly to borrow one from an obliging neighbour, " a kind of little *calèche*, entirely open, and seated for four."

Mlle. Bocquet and her nephew, full of the gloomiest apprehensions, got into it with her and the police officer, and they drove off at a gallop between two lines of the Berlin crowd, that had gathered in the street. It was some consolation that the police official did not know one word of French, so the prisoner could exchange her impressions with her friends. These, after the first stage of the journey, knew what they had to expect; they had turned their backs on the direction of Bavaria, and were not travelling towards that terrible Landau. Mme. de Genlis was being simply taken back to the frontier. As it happened, the frontier town that was nearest was Rathenow, on the borders of Saxony. The *Memoirs* of Mme. de Genlis inform us that the night was passed in travelling, and they arrived at the frontier early next morning. Now, the distance between Berlin and Rathenow is 80 kilometres (50 miles), and it is probable that this little town was chosen as the place to which the expelled Frenchwoman was to be taken.

The journey was extremely uncomfortable. It was not unlike the flight from Mons, although in this case it was the beginning not the end of winter, but all the way, through the chilly night, it was cold and rainy. In the open carriage it was impossible to hold up an umbrella, on account of the low branches of the trees that overhung the narrow roads, and poor Genlis, chilled to the bone and shivering with cold, became so unwell that the rough Prussian policeman, touched by her sufferings, took it upon himself to derogate from strict discipline, and, despite the royal order that he was to stop nowhere on the way, allowed a short halt to be made at a woodcutter's hut.

When at last the frontier was reached, he required of her a signed engagement that she would not again set foot in Prussia.

Mme. de Genlis showed with what courage she could face adversity by the plucky, and thoroughly French, way in which she obeyed the order. As if she were jesting in a Paris salon, instead of passing through a Prussian country town as a proscribed exile, she wrote on the paper presented to her by the official,

> "Malgré mon goût pour les voyages,
> Je promets, avec grand plaisir,
> D'éviter et même de fuir
> Ce royaume dont les usages
> N'invitent pas à revenir," [1]

and signed this witty improvisation.

Then, finding herself on the road to Hamburg, she reached, after more or less trouble on the way, the home of the Matthiessens, which she had left hardly two months ago. But to avoid being an expense to them, she took lodgings with a widow, of whom we know little beyond the fact that she excelled in running up a bill.

[1] "Notwithstanding my taste for travel, I promise, with great pleasure, to avoid and even to flee from this kingdom, the customs of which do not tempt one to return."

CHAPTER IV

THE LIFE OF AN *ÉMIGRÉE* IN GERMANY

AFTER the Berlin adventure Mme. de Genlis continued the chequered existence that she had known for nearly six years. Its changes might have suggested the illusions of romance, if she had not felt at each step the deep sadness that comes with uncertainty as to the morrow.

She naturally stayed only a very short time at Hamburg, where living was much too dear for her resources.

As soon as Mlle. Bocquet's niece, Jenny, an orphan sixteen years of age, had brought her the clothes, the harp, the music, the papers and boxes she had left at Berlin, she was busy with preparing for another journey.

Paméla and her husband had embraced her before embarking for Dublin. Fitzgerald, who had succeeded in convincing the Directory and was assured that a French fleet was fitting out at Brest and getting ready to deliver Ireland, was going, for his part in the affair, to enrol and train volunteers for his brave " Legion of Kildare."

With a view to this he had secretly provided arms and munitions of war, which were piled up in the storerooms of the Matthiessens, and thus transformed the peaceful home of the banker into a regular arsenal.

M. de Valence was also thinking of going away. He had become almost a suspicious personality in Hamburg, now a centre of agitation, torn by contradictory opinions of opposing parties, amongst whom the agents of Louis XVIII.—who were numerous, powerful, and well informed—kept a close watch on the Constitutionalists.

It was at this moment that a young German Countess,

Mme. de Wedercop, an enthusiast for Mme. de Genlis, as young folk at twenty often were, was proud to offer the celebrated French novelist a lordly hospitality in her château of Dollrott in Holstein. It was a providential interposition, and she lost no time in availing herself of it. M. de Valence escorted his mother-in-law to Dollrott. He did not remain there long, and after this we lose sight of him. But his disappearance from Hamburg must have given some support to the fable of his having gone to Ireland at the instigation of Mme. de Genlis. And the Hamburgers, and notably Herr Piter Poel, were thoroughly convinced that she and Paméla had infected Fitzgerald with their Revolutionary doctrines, and inspired the young Irish nobleman with the idea of bringing about the insurrection.

Mme. de Genlis enjoyed five weeks of rest at the château of Dollrott, in company with Jenny, whom she had taken as her secretary. She had suffered from the shock at Berlin, but in this calm retreat her mind regained the elasticity it needed for the production of fresh literary work. And the delights of this peaceful existence were so beneficial to our Countess that she wished to prolong them by settling in the country. But with her imagination inspired by the ideas of Rousseau she wanted a cottage—preferably a thatched cottage, or some little house of a sufficiently poetical aspect to deserve that charming name.

Mme. de Wedercop found it for her. It was really a lonely farmhouse, in a flat stretch of country, not too far from the château, at a place called Brevel—but the house had a thatched roof. The farmers—honest countryfolk—were "like characters in an Eclogue," with "a noble Greek air about them," and the farmer's brother realised in the eyes of Mme. de Genlis "the idea one forms of an Apollo."

But the reality was something very different from these pleasant Virgilian dreams.

The ex-Comtesse de Genlis, a poor refugee, without wealth or property, had only her pen with which to earn a living for herself and her secretary. A hundred *livres*, the price of an unfinished novel, *Les Vœux téméraires*, which had been interrupted by her expulsion from Berlin, and sold to the Matthiessens for half the cash down, was the whole of her fortune.

So the life she led at Brevel was not one of bucolic repose, but as busy as that of a Benedictine.

All the day, and for even part of the night, she was at work. In the morning she was writing a novel, *Les Petits Emigrés*, and in the evening *Les Vœux téméraires*. She was busy during her walks composing the fables for her *Herbier Moral*, which she afterwards dictated from memory to Jenny, who was also occupied in making fair copies of her manuscripts.

She took a little recreation with music and painting. And she read! She devoured the whole of the *Encyclopédie*, with the exception only of the articles on astronomy and mathematics. This formidable toil lasted eighteen months.

It was hardly interrupted by two or three flying visits to Sleswig, where the Court of Hesse resided. There were only five leagues between Brevel and Sleswig, the little Court to which Mme. de Wedercop had introduced her friend, and the Prince of Hesse had shown himself extremely gracious towards Mme. de Genlis. He invited her to his table, put his fine library freely at her disposal, lent her portfolios from his herbarium, allowed her to copy his pictures of flowers, and finally lavished on her courtesies and friendly gifts—baskets of oranges and table delicacies, that came as miraculously opportune supplies in the desert of Brevel.

These were like brief clearings in the darkened sky of this chequered life. Then once more ill fortune swooped down upon her. The poor woman was overwhelmed by bad news, added to the daily round of overwork.

First came the failure of the French fleet, defeated by a storm—dispersed without even a fight—at Bantry Bay in December 1796. Fitzgerald was denounced, hunted down, hidden no one knew where; the Royalists had got wind of the depôt of arms at the house of the Matthiessens, Thauvenay had informed the British Minister of it, and he had obtained its seizure; after which the Marquis du Crest found himself compelled to escape from Hamburg and the reprisals of the *émigrés*, and to go to Copenhagen to exploit his talents as an inventor there; and finally, the Wedercops were ruined and their property sold up.

The health of Mme. de Genlis could not stand all these blows. She became extremely agitated by nervous troubles. Her feverish imagination, always working at high pressure, began to take foolish turns and even to wander a little. As in those early days when she indulged in childish dreams at St. Aubin, and piled romance on romance, her head was filled with fancies. She took to talking out aloud when she was quite alone. She imagined she had Paméla with her, or her daughter, or Mlle. d'Orléans. She would carry on conversations with them; and in this state of nervous over-excitement she was wandering away into an imaginary existence.

Soon medical aid had to be called in. She had to go to Sleswig, to be taken care of in that city, and she had hardly arrived there when a serious attack of fever kept her for a month in danger of death.

She had none of her own relatives with her. Henriette did not come—she was busy flirting with M. de Finguerlin—and Paméla was in Dublin, where she had become "the heroine of an even more moving romance than the *Veillées du Château*,"[1] for she was watching over the safety of her husband. After hiding all day in a cellar, he would come to her disguised as a woman in the night. She was helping him once more to organise a rising, for which he had asked the help of Talleyrand, now Minister of Foreign Affairs. M. de Valence was trying to get back to France. So Mme. de Genlis, abandoned in a noisy inn at Sleswig, was fortunate in finding in her secretary, Jenny, the most devoted of nurses.

In a lucid interval between two crises of the fever she considered her case hopeless, and in her terror began to think of her conscience.

But in Holstein, an almost entirely Protestant country, few Catholic priests were to be found; and though there was a Catholic chapel at Sleswig, the priest in charge of it could not speak any language that was familiar to the sick woman.

[1] G. Lenôtre, *Paméla*.

Jenny, in her agony of anxiety, made hasty inquiries, and providentially found out that there was an aged French ecclesiastic, formerly chaplain to the Duc de Deux-Ponts, living in retirement in the neighbourhood, about four leagues from the city. She sent word to him. He came quickly, administered the last Sacraments to his compatriot, and remained a whole day with her, giving her the consolations of his ministry. Mme. de Genlis tells in her *Memoirs* how after the departure of the priest a more severe crisis than the rest seemed about to carry her off, and how poor Jenny, in desperation, suddenly threw herself on her knees, invoking Him in whose hands are all human lives, and promising to become a Catholic if the sick woman recovered her health.

God granted the miracle. "It seemed," says Mme. de Genlis, "as if she had saved me and given me life again." And indeed during all this long time of trial the conduct of Jenny was worthy of all praise.

Two months later, Henriette at last came to see her aunt, then convalescent, and took her back to Hamburg. But, as before, she declined the hospitality kindly offered by Matthiessen, and went again to lodge with the widow, while she petitioned the new King of Prussia, Frederick William III., who was more accessible than his father, to authorise her to reside again in Berlin. His Prussian Majesty gladly granted the request, and in less than a fortnight Mme. de Genlis set off at once.

In this second and final residence of the ex-Governess at Berlin, as in all the last phase of her trying career abroad, one sees a marked decline of her force of character. Depressed by such long and painful wanderings hither and thither, deprived of all influence, she had now to drag on through days of toil and misery. She had to live a life of privations and arduous work—the life of a galley-slave.

Productions of the most various kinds flowed from her pen: a book of piety, *Les Heures à l'usage des jeunes personnes*; the fables of her *Herbier Moral*; a *Manuel du Voyageur* containing dialogues for the use of French people in Germany or Germans in France, with "the expressions most used in travelling and in the various circumstances of life"; [1] then some bizarre novels—*Ida, ou le Jupon vert*; *Le Maillot*; and that impossible romance of the *Mères rivales*, full of the fictions of an extravagantly romantic mind and an uncontrolled imagination.

But with all this varied output she could not even make a living. The *Petits Emigrés*, published at Berlin as soon as she arrived there, although the book was a success, did not give her enough to pay for her board. And when she began to let the weekly bills fall into arrear (though they were so moderate that, according to her own account, Mademoiselle supplied some of the expenses herself), the hostess suddenly became ill-humoured and subjected her to endless unpleasantness. She took Jenny away from her, on the pretext that her niece's religion was in danger with Mme. de Genlis; she removed furniture from her room, told the servants not to obey her orders, and, in a word, in various ways gave her to understand that she was not in the least honoured by having to give hospitality to the French Countess merely in the name of art.

In bad health, and forced to live on a strange diet of boiled carrots, she emptied her purse to enable Jenny to go away to her sisters at Magdeburg, and then waited patiently for the day when, having received some money from her publisher, she was able to pay her bill, and remove to a modest lodging which a friend of hers, the blind Mlle. Itzig, provided for her near the Royal Gun Factory at the Silesian gate.

This Mlle. Itzig was a Jewess, with a pathetic story. She had lost her sight as the result of an unsuccessful operation for cataract, and she felt always warm sympathy and deep gratitude towards Mme. de Genlis, who with a charming ingenuity had taught her to play on the harp. In her lodging beside the Gun Factory she became closely attached to the lively Frenchwoman, who opened out such a delightful range of intellectual pleasures to her when her life seemed all sadness and darkness at only twenty-eight years of age. A real affection soon united them together. They were

---

[1] Mme. de Genlis, remembering the tragic time of her illness in the midst of difficulties in a foreign country, ended the manual with a dialogue on the way to make one's last will.

hardly ever apart, and often had with them a sister-in-law of Mlle. Bocquet, who, being more or less at variance with the latter, remained faithful to Mme. de Genlis; and together they used to take pleasant carriage drives to Potsdam, or through the neighbouring country, where, thanks to the touching patriotism of the refugees of the time of the Edict of Nantes, several of the villages bear French names.

Notwithstanding all this, Mme. de Genlis sometimes felt lonely. Mlle. Itzig could not replace her dear Jenny. A young lady companion who disappeared after a few days, leaving proof of her dishonesty, made her lose heart completely. Tied to her toilsome literary work, and absorbed for whole days in her manuscripts, she longed more strongly than ever to see her young people, whose loving attentions would recreate and console her. She had so long enjoyed the happiness of resting her eyes on the pretty faces of children, reading their innocent little souls and their young minds in all their freshness, and correcting their defects as they showed themselves.

By nature motherly and delighted to act as a teacher and protector, she could not do without children to bring up. "To be entirely without them, seemed to me," she says, "the greatest of all privations." Her old ideas on the subject of adoption came back to her—haunted her. Why not try to realise them?

When botanising in the woods, she had sometimes met a very pretty little girl whose parents were poor people.

They had a large family, and they were well pleased to yield to the caprice of the foreign lady, and send her the child every day. They even seemed to enter into her curious plans.

But at the psychological moment they refused to separate themselves from the little girl unless they were paid 60 gold Fredericks (1320 francs). Mme. de Genlis was far from possessing such a sum; and she had to give up the little girl, for whom she had been so imprudent as to buy an outfit, which she kept neatly packed in a pretty trunk. As much out of disappointment as for the sake of economy, she made one more removal, took two poor rooms in Berlin itself, and about the end of the autumn of 1799 completed in hot haste the *Mères Rivales*, sold in advance at the rate of a hundred francs the sheet to the publisher Delagarde, who had made a payment on account. But this work exhausted her to such a degree that she says she could not for a long time even think of writing. And her purse continually had an empty sound, and she was terribly badly dressed; for the small payments made to her in advance had been with remarkable imprudence disposed of in the purchase of the little outfit, and of a repeating watch.

As she was installing herself in her new lodgings there came news from Paméla, telling of the awful ending of the Irish insurrection. Lord Edward, with a price set on his head (a thousand pounds sterling), had been betrayed, discovered, wounded, condemned to death, and at last found on 4th June lying in his prison cell already stiff and cold. The unfortunate man had poisoned himself. Was it Paméla who, as rumour went, had provided him with the poison?

But in any case, contrary to certain statements, she was not that day within reach of her husband, having left Dublin ten days before for Kildare Castle, where she brought her third child into the world. It was said that Lord Edward regarded the separation as inevitable, and was not surprised at the absence of his wife.

Besides, a brother and a devoted aunt had done their best to lighten his solitude. After his death, Paméla, driven into exile, took to flight, wandered hither and thither, and at last reached Hamburg in a wretched state and asked for shelter with Henriette.

It was then that Mme. de Genlis received the news. Notwithstanding her difficult position, she offered to receive Paméla. But the hospitality of the Matthiessens and the society of Hamburg together presented advantages more desirable than the humble and precarious way of living of Mme. de Genlis at Berlin. So her offer was declined without hesitation by her adopted daughter.

Presently the mother was exerting herself to get lessons to give in houses that might welcome her talents.

It was in her search for pupils that Mme. de Genlis found

a way into the most brilliant society of Berlin, those intellectual circles where her fame was an introduction. Now those who were the acknowledged leaders, with a marked superiority, in the patronage of literature and learning were the rich Israelites. The Jewish salons, extremely elegant and wealthy, and crowded with guests, were the resort of all the cultivated minds and the celebrated men of the capital—poets, writers, artists, men of science, and Prussian and foreign diplomatists. The aristocracy, and especially the younger part of it, " brought up in the ideas of the French Encyclopædists, and philosophising like them,"[1] assiduously frequented these salons, preaching by this example the abolition of caste.

The receptions at the houses of the bankers Meyer, Ephraim, Cohen derived a special distinction from the brilliant crowds of highly educated young women. The salon of Henriette Herz and that of Rachel Levin, the future wife of Varnhagen, were extremely in request, and, on account of those who frequented them, obtained a high literary reputation.

During twenty years, from 1795 to 1815, these salons were made brilliant and glorious by the presence of such guests as Goethe and Schiller, the Prince Louis Ferdinand of Prussia and his sister the Princess Radziwill, Augustus William Schlegel and his brother Frederick, who married Dorothea Mendelssohn, the two Humboldts, Kotzebue, Jean Paul, the poet-historian Arndt, so zealous against Napoleon, Johann von Müller, Schleiermacher, Gentz, the Duchess of Courland and her daughter Mme. de Dino, and Iffland, the Talma of Prussia. The Baroness von Grotthuiss and Mme. von Rybenberg, daughters of Mme. Cohen, and the Itzigs had also their elegant circles, and the salon of the Duchess of Courland vied with those of the rich Jewesses in that union of literary and artistic grace which made one forget the distinctions of rank and social grades.

Mme. de Genlis had access to this society probably through Mlle. Itzig. It so happened that her first pupils were Mme. Cohen and Mme. Herz. She did not wish to take more

[1] K. Hillebrand, *La société de Berlin de 1789 à 1815*.

than four, so as to keep some time for writing. The two others were a Mme. Bernard and a young Privy Councillor of twenty-one, Lombard, a brother of the famous intriguing secretary who was a favourite of Frederick William II. Mme. de Genlis, for the enormous fee of a ducat (ten francs) a lesson, taught them to read French in verse and prose, to declaim poetry, and to write letters.

Touched by the poverty of their professor, her pupils before long offered to arrange a public course of lectures on literature for her.

"They were ready to lend me a very fine hall, which would have cost me nothing," say the *Memoirs*. "I would have had an infinite number of subscribers, and would have made a lot of money. But my repugnance thus to put myself forward in public was insuperable. I preferred to give lessons in my room."

The taste for lectures, which is such a feature of the intellectual education of to-day, had not come into existence at the beginning of the last century.

People were then less superficial, less in a hurry than they are now. They did not profess to be able in a few hours to extract the quintessence of a life, or of a great work, or to make a sweeping survey of them with a mere glance of the eyes. Those who were interested in men's lives and works considered that months, and sometimes years, might be given to their study.

The part of a lecturer seemed therefore hardly becoming for the ex-Governess. She refused it under influence of a strong feeling of dignity, and not from the fear of undertaking a too absorbing task, which was the reason why, about the same time, she declined to give lessons on the harp; and refused another attractive offer made by a Berlin shopkeeper, a dealer in feminine knick-knacks, who offered her four thousand francs a year if she would work for him and direct his workwomen.

People may be surprised that while Mme. de Genlis considered lecturing an anomaly, an extravagant self-exhibition, she was always happy to play a part in a comedy.

But in the eighteenth century acting was always an

amusement, while a lecture or a conference was a form of pedantry.

Now the Cohens had a theatre in their house, and a rage for producing comedies of high life. Must not this have suggested to the Countess a charming opportunity of reviving the delightful old times of the Palais Royal? Despite her fifty-four years, the taste for dramatic amusements, that she had doubtless never lost, awoke again in her. The theatre had the magic power of bringing back again for awhile the charming and sprightly Genlis of other days.

She began by composing for the Cohens some short plays turning on proverbs. Then she prepared for their little stage her *Galatée*, written as a sequel to the *Pygmalion* of Rousseau, and which in fact was played in their theatre with this piece by Jean Jacques. At her suggestion the *dénouement* of the latter was altered, and this in a very happy way.

Thus the Berlin people who were invited could compare at their ease the art of Mme. de Genlis and that of the philosopher. At the same time, they appreciated her talent as an actress, for she took a part, and her success was such that she ventured to take in the *Mariage secret* the part Mlle. Contat had played, and was received by the audience with transports of enthusiasm. Iffland lavished praise upon her, and said she was the best actress he had ever seen; and the Princes of the Royal Family, without showing any resentment for her having previously refused to be presented to them,[1] obtained invitations for themselves, and were delighted. "I had never been seen," say the *Memoirs*, "except very carelessly dressed. People did not recognise me at that distance, and wearing rouge and jewellery. Many strangers who had seen me only there thought I could not yet be thirty."

[1] Mme. de Genlis avoided the Court and distinguished strangers at Berlin out of a feeling of self-respect which did her honour. "I always thought," she says, "that when one has come down in the matter of fortune, one can only preserve one's dignity by avoiding to make oneself prominent, making advances to no one, accepting only those of friendship, and living in profound solitude."

And indeed had she not gone back some forty years! And, as if to complete the illusion, here was young Lombard, her fellow-actor and her pupil, setting himself to rehearse the scenes not included in the text of the play that once caused the exile of young Pinot.

Only he was not discreet by nature, and his passion soon rose to such a pitch that he became abominably tiresome. The suitor pestered her with love-letters full of blunders in French, and his Dulcinea regularly sent them back to him scored with corrections of his style, which made him furious . . . but next day he began again.

Mme. de Genlis shows some satisfaction in detailing to us the ravages that her belated charms made in the heart of the foolish young Councillor. She gives a sarcastic account of how, when, a little later, she spoke to him of her coming departure from Berlin, he thought it was a coquettish pretence, and seriously made a proposal of marriage to her; how after that the unhappy man, quickly disillusioned, fell into a fit of melancholy that ended in jaundice. But strange to say, Lombard, as soon as he recovered, knowing his lady was at Paris, set off on a journey thither to see her again, and no doubt to cure his passion.

It so happened that in the course of 1799 Mme. de Genlis began to hope she would see her native land once more, for Beurnonville had arrived, having been appointed Ambassador at Berlin in reward for his zeal on the 18th Brumaire. Introduced at once into Berlin society, he met his compatriot at Mme. Cohen's. Perhaps he had already made her acquaintance at the camp of Dumouriez, when the latter, at the same time as he arrested the three commissioners of the Convention, handed the General over to the Austrians at her request.

But, far from keeping up any ill-will in connection with his recollections of Mme. de Genlis, he must have reflected that this arrest had without doubt been the means of saving his life. And he generously interested himself in the fortunes of the poor woman.

Until then it had been all in vain that she had written letters, requests, and petitions, and engaged a lawyer to represent her and take the necessary steps on her behalf. She had obtained nothing.

There exist in the National Archives traces of her efforts in this direction. Already on the 13th Messidor, Year V (2nd July 1797), we find a certain Citizen Chaix, "in the name of the Citizeness Brûlart, whose power of attorney he holds," asking the Minister of Police for documents "establishing the non-emigration of the said Citizeness."[1]

Honest Chaix, meeting with a refusal even to consider his petition, and anxious loyally to earn his fees, requests an official reply from the Minister—"even if it is in the negative." It is given to him on the 29th Thermidor, by Citizen Chevrières, archivist of the former Committee of Public Safety, who, suggesting a quest from office to office, refers Citizen Chaix to "the Archives of the Central Bureau, formerly the Mairie, and the Archives of the Directory, if any exist dating from that period."[2]

Since then Mme. de Genlis had been waiting for further information.

But the intervention of Beurnonville, a man of the new time, standing well with Bonaparte, succeeded in a few days better than all possible requests and petitions, and the removal of the name of the ex-Countess from the lists of *émigrés* was soon an accomplished fact.[3]

Mme. de Genlis was at last to leave her exile, and put an end to that painful life of an *émigrée* which had been dragging on for nine years. Everywhere, except among her irreconcilable enemies, her intellectual and amiable character had attracted friends to her. At Berlin, above all, where she had met with so much sympathy, Mme. de Genlis personified French wit, grace, and manners. It seemed as if they could

---

[1] The documents Mme. de Genlis asked for, to prove she was not an *émigrée*, were: 1st, her passport for the journey to England, issued to her in October 1791; 2nd, the resolution passed by the Municipality of Paris, October 8, 1792, in virtue of which her passport for the journey to Tournay was given to her; 3rd, the warrant of arrest of the Committee of Public Safety (A.N.F.' 6521).

[2] Cf. A.N.F.' 6521.

[3] The removal of the name of Mme. de Genlis from the lists of *émigrés* is mentioned by the *Publiciste* of the 2nd Messidor (June 21, 1800). Cf. Aulard, *Paris sous le consulat*, i.

not do without her there, and that her charming sallies of wit, her comedies so full of good taste, her erudition, her critical judgments, were a refining and guiding influence in that society which was so zealous for polite letters and the cultured life. She brought to it the manners of the courtly world, the real world of Paris, which had always been its model.

Amongst the Cohens there was the deepest grief on account of the bonds of friendship that united them to their French visitor. They were at their wits' end to find some way of keeping her in Berlin. Mme. Cohen, in the hope of tempting her, one day offered her, it appears, her magnificent jewel-case, all her diamonds, if she would consent to stay.

Mme. de Genlis was assuredly touched by this proof of affection. But nothing in the world could have kept her there.

According to her custom, she started at dawn one morning in July 1800, in order to avoid the pain of leave-takings. She was accompanied by a young boy, of whom it is now time to say something.

The family name of the child was Boecker. Mme. de Genlis had christened him Casimir, but later on he produced as his names—Frederick Henry Louis Charles.

Casimir Boecker was, after Paméla,—and even more than Paméla,—the darling, the spoiled pupil, the favourite child of the ex-Governor.

Rigid disciplinarian as she had been for her own daughters and for the children of the House of Orleans, she passed over everything where he was concerned, and attempted the impossible in order to refuse him nothing.

So much weakness with regard to a very commonplace boy could not fail to excite curiosity. It was for a short time supposed that she was not the mother by adoption, but the actual mother, of Casimir. According to the Comtesse de Neuilly, he was the son of a tailor.

Later on Victor Hugo informed Louis-Philippe that the father of Casimir was the porter at the lodgings of Mme. de Genlis. But after all, it seems, we may take her word for it when she tells us that he was the son of her landlady, and, in the absence of all official documents relating to his birth, there is nothing to justify us in a contrary opinion. It was a moment when the motherly feelings of Mme. de Genlis made it painful for her to have no object on which to lavish her affection. After the unfortunate adventure of the little girl whom the parents refused to give up, her ardent and imperious longing to have children beside her made her discover a treasure in the first she could find.

The person who let her last lodgings at Berlin to her had two boys, of whom the elder was eight years of age. Mme. de Genlis endowed this child with all imaginable good qualities—to her mind he had a pretty face, a noble bearing, a superior intelligence, musical taste, an extraordinary memory—in a word, marvellous gifts.

She became infatuated with the child with all her heart and mind.

"I asked," she says, "for this child from his mother, declaring to her that I would bring him up in the Catholic religion. She consented without any hesitation, and even seemed charmed to give him to me. I took him with me, and named him Casimir, after the boy of my own that I had lost."

From that moment Mme. de Genlis never ceased to look upon Casimir with delighted eyes. He always seemed to her an angel, an incomparable jewel, an exceptional being. She lived in this illusion till her death. It was the greatest, the supreme weakness of her old heart.

On leaving Berlin, Mme. de Genlis, instead of going directly to France, went to Hamburg to see Henriette, Matthiessen, and Paméla. She found the last of these on the best of terms with the American Consul at Hamburg, Mr. Pitcairn, whom she was to marry soon after. The affair was already the talk of the city. When Mme. de Genlis arrived there at the end of July 1800, local scandal was enlarging freely on the mysterious birth of Paméla, whom all Hamburg regarded as the daughter of Mme. de Genlis. The *Hamburger Correspondant* had already revealed this as the explanation of the secret in 1792, and Herr Piter

Poel speaks of Paméla as " die reizende Tochter der Genlis " (the charming daughter of Mme. de Genlis).

There was so much of this that Mme. de Genlis arranged a scene that was solemn and dramatic enough, after which she thought no doubt should remain on this subject. Here is how her daughter, the Duchesse de Neuilly, relates it:—

" Madame de Genlis, after having gone through the formality of confessing and communicating at the Spanish chapel, assembled all her friends, relations, and acquaintances at Madame Matthiessen's. There she told them that after the religious action she had just performed, she owed it to herself to render homage to the truth by declaring that Paméla was not a daughter of hers and of the Duke of Orleans, but the daughter of a poor washerwoman, from whom she had bought her for a round sum of money. Paméla fainted on hearing this fine declaration, and her lover, the American Consul, was near doing so too. But after many tears and romantic scenes they dried each other's eyes, and Dame Genlis set off for Paris, with another adopted child, a tailor's son, to whom she had given the name of Casimir."

It would seem that after that the last word had been said on the disputed origin of Paméla. Madame thought it ought to be so regarded by all sincere Catholics.

Why, alas! are we still waiting for the definite proof, the tangible document that will finally solve the enigma of the origin of Paméla, which ever remains obscure for that great sceptic we call History ?

Mme. de Genlis considered she had given this proof, and after having made again a parting visit to her Hamburg friends, notably Klopstock, who honoured her by coming a second time to see her, she journeyed on with a light heart towards her native land.

Henriette and Paméla accompanied her on the Elbe as far as the little town of Harburg, where seven years before, during her wanderings in search of a hidden retreat, she wrote one night, in the miserable room of an inn where she did not venture to go to bed, her *Epître à l'asile que j'aurai*.

At Antwerp her son-in-law, M. de la Woestine, came to meet her. She found at Brussels her nephew, César du

Crest, who, having returned to Paris, was there during the troubles of Fructidor, and escaped, thanks to the protection of M. de Pontécoulant. Finally, Mme. de Genlis saw once more at Brussels her daughter, Mme. de Valence, from whom she had been parted for nine long years, and who went back to Paris with her.

PART V

FROM THE CONSULATE TO THE MONARCHY OF JULY

CHAPTER I

THE RETURN TO FRANCE

THE immense joy that Mme. de Genlis felt at returning to her native land, her deep emotion when she once more heard people speaking French and saw again the towers of Notre Dame, gradually gave way—alas, too soon!—to sorrowful disappointment.

In this Paris, which was all movement and excitement,—changed in many ways, but still wildly rejoicing in life and enjoyment,—she found no friends, no familiar faces—in a word, no one to bid her welcome, though *émigrés* and nobles, or at least those of them who had been spared by the great storm, were hurrying back in crowds. They were coming home to have their names struck out of the lists of proscription, and to try to recover their confiscated property; or else, impoverished and scattered as they were, they would try to build up again out of the wreck their social life.

Amongst them, how many there were who had once been the familiar friends of the Genlis!

But those aristocrats, faithful to their traditions, did not forget. In their eyes Mme. de Genlis then was, had been, and would always be, a Jacobiness. They would not give up this idea, in their hostility to the principles which she has now half renounced, and they closed their eyes to her sincere piety, a little external it might seem, but in reality ardent and evidently inspired with an intention of expiation. Even in her own family she was thought of exclusively as the Egeria of Philippe-Égalité; and the various branches of the Du Crests, living in the provinces, had long broken with her. The only one of her relatives of whom she could think during this trying new start in life was Mme. de Montesson. The two women had never cared very much for each other. In the times when the niece was in high favour and Governor of the Duke of Chartres, the aunt kept her antipathy silent

But now the positions were reversed. With more cleverness, the Marquise had compromised herself less than Mme. de Genlis, and, having providentially survived the storm, she had established herself again in splendid style in her mansion in the Chaussée d'Antin. There she displayed a princely luxury, and this was an easy matter for her, thanks to the double allowance of 160,000 francs granted to her by the First Consul as if she were a Princess of the Blood Royal. So, having ostentatiously sided with Bonaparte, she was in high favour.

We may imagine with what eagerness Mme. de Genlis, hardly arrived in Paris, and temporarily lodged in furnished rooms in the Rue Papillon, almost next door to Mme. de Montesson, hurried to visit her aunt.

She went there on the second day after her arrival. A chilling reception awaited her.

When Mme. de Genlis entered the salon of the Marquise, whom she had not seen since 1789, it was thronged with visitors. The mistress of the house, honoured with the title of "Dowager of Orleans," which the First Consul had publicly given her, made the most of her success, and did not hesitate to tell her circle all about the friendship shown her by Mme. Bonaparte, and the *déjeuners* to which that lady came as a guest at the Hôtel Montesson. Towards her niece, whom she had once flattered, but who was now poor and lonely, the aunt assumed a disdainful coldness.

Strange to say, M. de Valence, who was back in France since 1799, and was installed at the château of Sillery, which had been bought back by Mme. de Montesson, but in reality spent much of his time at the great house in the Chaussée d'Antin—M. de Valence though present on the occasion of his mother-in-law's visit, did not intervene in her favour even to the slightest extent. And yet he was the chief ruler, the prime minister of the house, controlling with an absolute sway the heart and the possessions of the Marquise.

And if it is true, as has been said, that Mme. de Genlis had helped him with her purse at Hamburg, either M. de Valence had a very short memory, or he was very ungrateful for the service rendered to him at a difficult time. It was enough to wound a woman of even less delicate feelings and less sensitive self-esteem than Mme. de Genlis; she suffered the more keenly from all these changes of sentiment towards her, and her visit was " brief and silent." " M. de Valence," she says, " went to the door with me. I told him, as I took my departure, that I was much too old to allow myself to be treated in this way, and that I would not come there again. He made a very strange kind of excuse for Mme. de Montesson. He said to me that she would be better another time; that she was in a fit of bad temper at seeing that I had not aged in any way; that it was a little outburst of feminine ill-humour that one ought to forgive her." And he ended with a word as to financial matters, to which Mme. de Genlis would soon have to give attention.

And besides this unexpected hostility—unexpected at least as regards its bitterness—there was the disconcerting aspect of Paris itself.

The delightful Paris that Mme. de Genlis had known and whose refined atmosphere she had breathed, was dead, killed by the Revolution. The houses had suffered as well as the people. The stately mansions of the past were gone. The streets had lost their names. The house fronts and walls were covered with threatening inscriptions: " Liberty and fraternity or death ! " The shops were full of objects marked with armorial bearings that showed they had once been the property of nobles since guillotined. The carriages of these same people were now transformed into vehicles on the cab ranks. Their family portraits were publicly displayed for sale. Such was the legacy of Robespierre to the survivors.

All this made a painful impression on Mme. de Genlis.

In three months she has hardly become used to recognise in the streets, under this Revolutionary caricature, the places she had once known. In her terror—her remorse, said some—it was a year before she ventured to cross the Place Louis xv. or pass in front of the Palais Royal.

"Everything seemed new to me," say the *Memoirs*; "I was like a stranger whom curiosity compels to stop at every step. I had some trouble to know where I was in the streets, of which nearly all the names were changed."

Yesterday and to-day—the everlasting contrast impressed itself upon her mind and a hundred times a day increased her sense of discomfort.

From the moral as well as from the physical point of view, Paris, at the dawn of the Consulate, differed strangely from Paris before the Revolution. One must read in her *Memoirs* the pages in which Mme. de Genlis describes for us the new manners of the city—pages so full of living interest and so well informed.

The old aristocratic life had completely disappeared. The nobles who survived just managed to live, ruined as they were, without equipages and almost without servants, and crowded together either in the Faubourg St. Germain or the Faubourg St. Honoré, which they hardly ever left for lack of a carriage. But in the Chaussée d'Antin and the Champs Elysées the parvenus triumphed in an ostentatious luxury. "Full of pride and self-sufficiency, they mistook want of politeness for dignity." The women, overdressed, vain, touchy, "kept count of visits and haggled for a courtesy. They were always anxiously on the watch, always worrying about the way in which they were treated without exactly knowing how they *ought to be treated*; with the result that they were continually irritated at imaginary want of regard for them and supposed impertinences." Stupid gossip had taken the place of the brilliant exchange of ideas of other days. There was not conversation now, only slander.

There were no more witty circles—Mme. de Genlis assures

us that she did not regret them—but the tone of talk had strangely depreciated, and was full of low forms of speech.

With what indignation does the author of *Adèle et Théodore*, the lover of the easy, polished style and the wonderfully clear language of the eighteenth century, note the expressions in current use! She considers these " new words " left by the Revolution like the filth and mud brought down by a river after a great flood. She remarks with horror that they said " *votre demoiselle* "—" your young lady "—instead of " *Mademoiselle votre fille* "; and plain " *Madame*," when speaking to a husband of his wife; a " *castor* " for a " hat "; a " *superbe denture*"—a "superb set of teeth" for "fine teeth" ("*belles dents*"); the "*Capital*" instead of Paris; and phrases like " *se donner des tons*," " *celà est farce*," etc. (" to give oneself tones," " that is a farce "). Mme. de Genlis cannot express all her contempt for these undignified forms of speech. —What would she think of the polite Paris slang of to-day, with its expressions gleaned from sport and from the cafés of Montmartre?—Finally, there is no longer any good society. People rinse their mouths at table. They treat women disrespectfully, and these take advantage of it to show themselves wanting in modesty and restraint.

And vanity, carelessness, ostentation, dull solemnity, indecent dress, outrageously theatrical toilettes, have replaced the polished grace of the *ancien régime*, somewhat hypocritical though it was, but with all its artificiality, delicate and orderly, elegant, lively, pleasing and refined.

These stupid parvenus knew very well where the shoe pinched, and vied with each other in aping nobility, trying to produce some imitation of two or three aristocrats by birth who survived among them—Talleyrand, De Valence, De Narbonne, De Vaudreuil. " It must be admitted," says Mme. de Genlis, " that they made an apt choice of their models."

But after all, unpleasant though these social changes might be, they were of less importance than the hard fact that there was not the least provision for the material needs of life.

To obtain possession again of her property was the most pressing need of the Countess, and at first sight the matter seemed simple enough, for she was not an *émigrée*. But what did this property amount to, and where was it?

According to Mme. de Genlis, her fortune would consist of a claim on the estate of Sillery, and the settlement assured to her by her contract of marriage; and further, her share in the inheritance of her maternal grand-uncle, M. des Alleurs.

In reality, according to official documents, she ought to be able to enter into possession of—

(1) Her dowry of 40,000 francs, less 15,000 assigned as common property to her husband.

(2) A personal claim of 6000 francs' worth of furniture or of cash according to her choice.

(3) Her annual allowance under the settlement of 7000 francs.

(4) Her part of the common property under the marriage contract, to be taken from the possessions of M. de Genlis. These had been confiscated and declared national property after his execution, and included lands in Picardy and the district of Agen, and the estate of Sillery, which he had inherited on the death of Marshal d'Estrées, with the furniture of the château. Now nearly all of this property had been publicly sold.

At Sillery the sale of the *immeubles* (lands, buildings, etc.) had taken place on eleven days between the 18th Vendémiaire and the 24th Messidor, Year II; the sale of furniture and effects (*meubles*) on fifteen days between the 29th Brumaire, Year II, and the 18th Fructidor, Year III. When all the accounts had been made up, a decree of the department of the Marne on the 26th Messidor, Year X, fixed the sum coming to the heirs of the "Brûlart" family at 1,147,651 *livres*, 15 *sols*, 2 *deniers*, a total reduced according to the tables of depreciation to an actual value of only 456,628 *livres*, 8 *sols*.[1]

At Genlis the property had also been sold, but had been bought back by the Marquis de Noailles, the husband of

---

[1] Cf. Péchenart, *Sillery et ses Seigneurs*, 206.

the granddaughter of Mme. de Drosmesnil, subject to the payment of Mme. de Genlis's annual allowance under the settlement.

According to the Law of Prairal (9th June 1795), confiscated property that had not yet been sold was to be restored to the *émigrés*; and the same was to be done in the case of money paid into the Treasury and representing the result of sales of " movable and immovable property " made before the decree of the 30th Ventôse. It was thus that the sum of 456,628 *livres, 8 sols* was due to the heirs of Sillery.

Now, Mme. de Genlis tells us that M. de Valence had drawn a considerable sum from the Directory. She asked him for an account of it. She resigned all family property to her children. As for the château of Sillery, it had been bought back by Mme. de Montesson for Valence.[1]

Now, the Marquis de Noailles, so far from keeping up the allowance to Mme. de Genlis, had freed himself from the obligation by giving formal notice to the Government and paying a fee of 2000 francs in assignats.

She began a lawsuit against the Marquis, and, as was to be expected, lost it.

As to the inheritance from uncle Des Alleurs, besides a sum of money of which Mme. de Genlis does not state the amount, it included an estate and château known as "Les Pannats," situated in the neighbourhood of Avallon, with the furniture and plate at the château. The estate was estimated to have the annual value of 5000 *livres* (francs).

It must be remembered that M. des Alleurs was the brother of Mme. de la Haie, and that Mme. de Montesson was the daughter of the latter. She therefore obtained possession of her uncle's inheritance and detained the part of it coming to Mme. de Genlis.

So we need not be astonished at the haughty reception given by the aunt who held the inheritance to the niece who claimed it. It was a way of giving her to understand that she had no rights to assert. The stupid compliment of

[1] It is probable that some bits of land that had not been sold were restored to Mme. de Genlis in virtue of a decree of the Year X.

M. de Valence, as he escorted his mother-in-law to the door, disgusts one, when one remembers the selfish thoughts that it concealed. And knowing as we do that Valence controlled like a master all the business affairs of Mme. de Montesson, strange reflections are suggested by his parting advice, given to Mme. de Genlis as she went downstairs, or was about to do so: "Don't trouble yourself about your business matters. I shall take charge of them. Besides, you understand nothing about such things." And if he "took charge" of the negotiations between the two women, it was decidedly not to the advantage of Mme. de Genlis.

The wealthy Marquise "did not blush at" offering her niece a single payment of 10,000 francs as the price of her renunciation of all her rights to the inheritance.

"I had nothing," says Mme. de Genlis. "It was only with the greatest difficulty that I could provide for my living. So I had to accept. . . . And then, if they had even paid me that sum down, I would have been extricated from all my difficulties, because I would have had time to write a book and sell it on advantageous terms. . . . But I received these 10,000 francs only in small instalments and at no fixed times, and I was obliged to buy all the furniture for my rooms, all that was required for a little kitchen, table and house linen, and a small supply of plate," etc.

Once more Mme. de Genlis returned to the hard school of poverty. She tried a new edition of the *Mères rivales*. By an act of unaccountable negligence on her part—for she was no novice in publishing matters—she was content with the verbal promise of the publisher, Henrichs, who bought her manuscript for 4000 francs, and according to the *Memoirs* did not pay her a farthing, although the novel was sold out in a fortnight. After all, she was rich only in enemies.

In her distress she gladly accepted the offer of Maradan, who proposed to her that she should write for the *Bibliothèque des Romans* at a fixed salary of 1200 francs a year.

But the first of her new stories did not appear until 1802. Till then she lived on reprints of her works—the *Annales de la Vertu*, a wretched compilation ; the *Heures*, which drew down on her the satire of M. J. Chénier ; the *Petit La Bruyère*, etc.

Her mind was so tired that she could not produce an original work such as would revive public taste in her favour. And she bitterly regretted the loss of a parcel of manuscripts that she had entrusted to Mme. de la Valence on her departure from Tournay in 1792, and which the latter had prudently left in the care of John Hurford Stone. Mme. de Genlis set a value of 12,000 francs on these papers, and in her vexation at not being able to recover them accused Stone of having pretended that he had lost them. But later on Miss Williams cleared up the mystery. Anxious to refute the charge against the man she loved, and to whom, it seems, she was united by a secret marriage, she tells how Stone, being in danger and forced, in the midst of the Terror, to take flight to Switzerland, handed these precious papers, about sixty *cahiers* in all, to the mother of Miss Williams, and she sewed them up in the cushions of an old arm-chair. Then in the course of the year 1794 there was a threat that her rooms would be searched, and, as one can easily understand, she feared these papers would be discovered, and—an irreparable loss !—she burned them.[1]

During eighteen months Mme. de Genlis vegetated as well as she could. However, in the spring of 1801 we find her installed in rooms she had furnished in the Rue d'Enfer, opposite the gate of the old Chartreuse. But life in Paris was horribly expensive for her, and as by a providential chance she had an offer of a holiday in the country for the summer season—perhaps with Henriette, who had just married the Baron de Finguerlin and settled on her husband's estate at the château of Carlepont, near Noyon—she accepted without hesitation.

On her return, she left the Rue d'Enfer for a little house in the Avenue de Paris at Versailles, and, once more held in the terrible grip of necessity, she wore herself out with work. Although she was unwell she wrote, wrote, in feverish haste and with admirable courage. The following verses

[1] Helen Maria Williams, *Souvenirs de la Révolution Française*, 69.

that she dashed off with her pen at this time are unfortunately only too eloquently true—

> " Je ne travaille pas, mon ami, pour mon plaisir,
> Croyez-moi, ce n'est pas la gloire qui m'enivre;
> Qui mieux que moi saurait jouir
> Des charmes d'un heureux loisir ?
> Mais je suis obligée de me tuer pour vivre." [1]

And incredible as it may seem, living under these painful circumstances, and having only her pen with which to earn her bread, she found means to gather round her and support a regular family! Besides Casimir, of whom she was so foolishly fond, she took up a child of fourteen, her goddaughter, Stéphanie d'Alyon, whose father was a chemist, formerly attached to the Orleans Princes. Moreover, three months after her return to Paris, a young German Baroness, Helmina von Hastfer, wrote from Berlin asking for her hospitality and protection. This Helmina was a strange character, badly brought up and with her head turned by romance. She had poetry in her blood,[2] according to Mme. de Genlis. She had known the Baroness in Berlin at the house of her mother, Mme. von Klencke, and was invited to the young girl's wedding with the Baron von Hastfer. It looked as if they had been united under an evil star, and neither the youth of the bride of seventeen, nor the vase of flowering myrtle sent as a wedding present by the French Countess had the gift of bringing them good fortune. Two months after her marriage the young Baroness wrote to Mme. de Genlis asking for a refuge beside her, and deserted the home of which she had hardly taken possession.

In May 1801 she arrived at the Rue d'Enfer.

She was a spoiled child, capricious, violently self-willed.

---

[1] " I do not work, my friend, for pleasure ; believe me it is not glory that excites me ; who would be able to enjoy, better than me, the charms of a happy leisure ? But I am obliged to kill myself in order to live."

[2] According to Mme. de Genlis, the grandmother of Helmina, a shepherdess named Karschin, used to indulge in dreams in the fields and compose verses, while spinning and watching her sheep. One day she composed an ode to Frederick the Great. The King heard of it, brought the shepherdess to his Court, and, charmed with her, found her a home in Berlin and got her married. Her daughter married M. von Klencke.

She united, it seems, "to the most lovable and gentle disposition and much wit and talent, an ill-balanced mind, and conduct so extravagant that, even with the greatest indulgence, it was difficult to put up with the difficulties to which it led."

Mme. de Genlis endured it for eighteen months. At the end of that time Mme. von Hastfer, thinking she could live by her own work—she copied music and was probably a poetess—went to board with the publisher Henrichs, at No. 12-81 Rue de la Loi.

After 1803 she took refuge with Madame Recamier. But the "white rose" had soon to part with the eccentric German lady, for the same reasons as Mme. de Genlis. The latter remained for a long time attached to her; she gave her warm recommendations on various occasions; she even wrote to great people, whom she did not personally know, in order to obtain help for the eccentric Baroness. We do not know what became of her.

To return to Mme. de Genlis—notwithstanding persistent hard work she could hardly make ends meet. The novelist Fiévée, who was a witness of her painful struggle against poverty, advised her to ask the Consuls to grant her a lodging, and himself wrote to the First Consul to inform him of the pitiful position of the celebrated Countess.

Mme. de Genlis believed that she had claims on the gratitude of Fiévée, and made out that she had saved his life at a time when the novelist was in prison under suspicion of complicity in the conspiracies of 1800. On the testimony of Mme. de Genlis, who, though she really only knew him through two of his novels, pledged her word for him to Bonaparte, Fiévée was liberated.

He did not accept this version of the affair; but all the same, after the 18th Brumaire he entered into correspondence with Napoleon, and Mme. de Rémusat says he was able to do so, thanks to Mme. de Genlis.

When the *Journal de Débats* became a source of trouble to Bonaparte, and the First Consul decided to appoint an editor of the paper who would be devoted to himself, he chose Fiévée for the post. Roederer had perhaps some influence in this decision. Finally, whether out of gratitude or mere sympathy, Fiévée interested Bonaparte, or the inner circle around Bonaparte, in Mme. de Genlis; and on the 29th Ventôse, Year X. (19th March 1802), Chaptal, the Minister of the Interior, wrote to the Librarian Ameilhon at the Arsenal:—

"I beg to inform you, my dear colleague, that I have granted to Madame de Genlis the use of the rooms that you have just given up. I request that you will place them at her disposal as soon as possible.—I salute you,

"CHAPTAL."

Less difficult times were beginning for the poor woman. There can be no doubt that she owed this change for the better to Bonaparte. But knowing what humble submission he required from those whom he favoured, and his Cæsar-like authority, Mme. de Genlis was malevolently accused of having basely flattered the new ruler of France and repudiated the benefits she had received from the House of Orleans. Nevertheless, we know that she went no further than to testify to the First Consul her gratitude in a very proper way, by sending him the somewhat trifling gift of the *Discours* that she had published in 1790, and the *Projet d'une École Rurale pour l'Éducation des Filles*, four pamphlets in all, which she had bound together in a little volume.

The prevailing ill will for her found another weapon against her, and even against her memory, in the fact that Napoleon, after becoming Emperor, further granted her a pension of 6000 francs, in return for which he imposed on Mme. de Genlis the duty of writing to him once a fortnight "on moral and literary questions."

"Morals and literature! Mere pretexts," it was said. "Much the Emperor cared, indeed, for such topics! He to become a pupil of Mme. de Genlis! A good joke that! Rather, it was important for him to be informed as to the usages, the views, the character of the old *noblesse*, whom he wished so much to win over—a mysterious region to the knowledge of which he was such a stranger. *Above all*, was it not important for him to know the secrets of the Bourbons ? "

From this point of view there was only a step to making out that Mme. de Genlis was a police spy, an informer. And her enemies did not hesitate to take this step. Other secret correspondents of the Emperor, such as Fiévée and M. de Montlosier, carefully concealed their employment, and in the same way Napoleon, who received these letters into his own hands under the address of Lavalette, read them himself, and burned them when he had done so. "Above all, he took care that the writings of those correspondents should not fall into the hands of his ministers."[1] So, after all, when later on it began to be publicly stated that Mme. de Genlis was keeping up a secret correspondence with Bonaparte, Lady Morgan tells us that this was " a respectable name for a higher kind of espionage."[2]

This suspicion has survived among men of our own time, thanks to certain passages in the *Memoirs* of Madame de Rémusat,[3] and a passage in which Talleyrand tells how on the evening of Austerlitz, having been told to open the imperial post-bag, he read to the victor the " report " of Mme. de Genlis, at the same time as the reports of the police.[4]

And the further fact that Napoleon never saw or gave audience to Mme. de Genlis, and that their relations were throughout confined to letter writing, seems to indicate the disdain of the master for his correspondent.

But happily the true explanation is simple enough. It

[1] Cf. Baron Fain, *Mémoires*, pp. 54–57.
[2] Lady Morgan, *La France*, t. ii., L. viii. p. 322.
[3] Madame de Rémusat, *Mémoires*, t. ii. 402.
[4] " The report, which he took more notice of, was that of Mme. de Genlis. It was long, and written throughout with her own hand. She spoke in it of the feeling in Paris, and quoted some offensive remarks which, she said, were current in the houses then spoken of as the Faubourg St. Germain ; she named five or six families who, she added, would never rally to the government of the Emperor. The rather severe expressions which Mme. de Genlis reported excited Napoleon to a violent fit of anger such as one would hardly imagine ; he swore and stormed against the Faubourg St. Germain. ' Ah ! they think themselves stronger than me,' he said. Gentlemen of the Faubourg St. Germain, we shall see ! we shall see ! " And these exclamations were uttered, when ?—a few hours after a victory won over the Russians and the Austrians." (Talleyrand, *op. cit.*, i. 199).

was nothing more than that the precarious position of this celebrated woman touched the Emperor, and he granted her a pension. And " to spare her feelings," says Méneval, he asked for a letter from her once a fortnight.

On the other hand, Barbey d'Aurevilly attributes to Napoleon the idea of having recompensed Mme. de Genlis " out of a fellow feeling for his brother princes, because she had educated the Princes of the House of Orleans." [1] For one or other of these motives the private correspondence of Mme. de Genlis with Napoleon was made an honourable pretext for her pension, something for her to do, so that it might not seem to be merely an alms. And this is corroborated not only by the partial statement of Lady Morgan,[2] but also by a very precise document lately re-discovered. It is a page of a note book, in the handwriting of Mme. de Genlis, with this heading :—

"Subjects of Notes for the Emperor."

And what subjects were they ?

" On injustice in general. The thing it is most difficult to endure.
" On Magnetism.
" On the sorceresses of Paris—Mlle. Normand.
" On dreams, etc.
" On the house of M. de Choiseul.
" On the newspapers. (*Keep this clear of politics.*)
" On the inns of Spain.
" On the occult sciences." [3]

All this is a long way from Royalist politics. But does it mean that Mme. de Genlis kept strictly to this range of subjects ?

Good heavens, no ! For we know from her own testimony that in her letters to the Emperor she confesses to him in fairly full detail what had been her relations with the Orleans family, and that these same letters contained ideas on the

[1] Barbey d'Aurevilly, *Les Œuvres et les Hommes*, t. xiv. 136.
[2] Lady Morgan, *op. cit.*
[3] Cf. Henri Lapauze, *Lettres de Madame de Genlis à Casimir Boecker.*

spirit of society and the brilliant life of the Court of old days. In this connection Mme. de Genlis must certainly have given Napoleon the benefit of her recollections, and described to him the manners of the old aristocracy. But we know also that she was continually taking advantage of these written reports to recommend to him a crowd of people. If we are to take her own word for it, a hundred individuals owed their positions to her.

There was, for instance, Mme. de Lascours, of whom she had praised the capacity as a governess. There was Cardinal Maury, "who will be a very good archbishop—he would have been a very good ambassador." There was the poet Treneuil, vouched for as " a good Frenchman, an affectionate character, and a true poet." There was M. de Bonald, suggested by Mme. de Genlis as the official writer of the Imperial Annals.[1]

She even goes so far as to claim with some pride that she protected Chateaubriand himself against severe measures on Napoleon's part. Finally, the old musician Monsigny, so thoroughly French in his inspiration, obtained a pension, thanks to her, his former pupil. Mme. de Chastenay asserts that Monsigny's pension was the only favour obtained by Mme. de Genlis, and " the solitary proof that Bonaparte read her letters."[2]

Even so this would be eulogy enough of the disinterested character of this woman against whom such an outcry was raised. Napoleon, who certainly read the requests of the Countess, thought her most unselfish and too credulous. The edifying lessons sent him by his " correspondent of the grand old times," as he playfully called her, gave him some recreation and keen pleasure. " It is not my fault," writes Mme. de Genlis, " if I did not succeed in making him devout." The Emperor had no such ideas. He smiled as he spoke of her, and said that she was the greatest enchantress in

---

[1] On this point Mme. de Genlis is certainly boasting. M. Frédéric Masson, writing in the *Echo de Paris* on the relations of Napoleon with M. de Bonald, says that it was really Fontanes who answered for the philosopher. . . . In all this long story M. Masson does not once mention Mme. de Genlis.

[2] *Mémoires de Madame de Chastenay*, i. 453.

the world, and that her letters ought to secure her for all time to come the title of inimitable.

All these indications should no doubt incline us to regard in a less suspicious light these letters of a moralising lady pedagogue, who had long ago bid farewell to political intrigue.

CHAPTER II

AT THE ARSENAL

Now that she had been extricated from poverty, and granted rooms and a pension, the barometer of public opinion was rising in favour of Mme. de Genlis.

It began with the much talked of success of her celebrated novel, *Mlle. de Clermont*—" the best thing she had done," says Ste. Beuve," whether regarded as a page of history or a page of romance,"—this revived her literary reputation.

Mme. de Montesson, always clever at seeing how the wind was blowing, suddenly remembered that her dear niece ought to come to her parties at Romainville, and her receptions at the Chaussée d'Antin; sent her word that she ought not to neglect her; and received her " with the most exaggerated show of affection."

La Harpe, lately converted, also recollected her, and wrote to her. His letter, written as some sort of reply to that which Mme. de Genlis had sent him from Holstein four years before, excused his long delay as " an oddity of the Revolutionary kind." With the zeal of a neophyte he ended thus : " Happily founded only on the love of letters and the charm of your talents, our relations never had any thing in them that could bring regret or repentance to either of us, and you yourself knew how to protect me from the seductive attraction that charms of another kind might have made dangerous for me. I am pleased to render you this just tribute."

Mme. de Genlis was quite willing to be reconciled with her aunt, but made friends with La Harpe only in a half-hearted way. As she neglected to reply to his repentant letter, he returned to the charge, and was authorised to present himself to the former Queen of Bellechasse. They talked of old times, and of the conversion of the critic, and finally he invited Mme. de Genlis to the literary gatherings, at which once a week he brought his friends together to talk.

She did not go to them. La Harpe was out of favour at Court, for he spoke too frankly of Napoleon, and his meetings of men of letters were looked upon as "mystic and political conventicles."

She considered that a woman writer whose last book had, it appeared, drawn tears from the First Consul, would only compromise herself by frequenting the society of a fellow author who had fallen under suspicion, and besides was soon to be exiled.

The publication of *Madame de la Vallière* in 1804 had, indeed, given proof of the great literary popularity of Mme. de Genlis.

When people heard that Napoleon had wept over it the general enthusiasm lauded the book to the skies, and four editions went off one after the other. But the author was none the richer for this. She had sold the book for three years for a hundred louis. But even though it brought no riches, its success was enough to enchant Mme. de Genlis. She took advantage of the flowing tide of fame to publish very soon after *Madame de la Vallière* her *Madame de Maintenon*, which under the form of a historical chronicle described with charming art the life of the Court of Louis XIV., and introduced the parvenus of the Consulate to the glories, the manners, the conversation of the "Roi-Soleil," and let them know something of the *grand seigneurs* and the great ladies of the sixteenth century, and described for them nobility and rank, the air of the Court, its brilliant and polished life, all swept away by the Revolution, and now something that the new society, wealthy, ostentatious, eager for grandeur, desired to imitate, thinking that this was all it needed to have the tone of true aristocracy. Its success was such that the engravings illustrating the work and those of *Madame de la Vallière*, exhibited in the booksellers' windows, excited a popular enthusiasm that seemed to Fouché dangerous enough for him to forbid the pictures to be publicly shown, or sold apart from the books. Then in the Emperor's circle they began to pass unfriendly criticisms on the Countess de Genlis; witness this letter of Roederer to his wife :—

"FLORENCE, 28th *April* 1806.

"I have read *Madame de Maintenon*. It is a book written to prove of how little importance a mother may be and how great may be the importance of a governess. And then the wit of Madame de Genlis does not seem to me to add much charm to that of Madame de Maintenon. Finally, there are things repeated a hundred times, which ought not to have been said at all. The style is nearly always commonplace and sometimes trivial. I do not dwell upon the pretentiousness and affectation of repeating unceasingly a word which neither in the times of Madame de Maintenon, nor in our own, has been in use in diplomatic language, namely, the word *sovereign*. They used to say then 'the prince,' 'the king,' 'the monarch.'

"All the book can do is to confuse people's ideas of the reign of Louis XIV., while it throws some light on the views of this intriguer, whose pen has never been used except for her personal ends. I must ask you to pardon my speaking thus of your friend."[1]

Madame de Lage is not more kindly.

But on the other hand Mme. de Genlis obtained the friendly support of Fontanes. She had sent him a copy of her book, and received an extremely flattering reply from this eminent man of letters—

"It has been said," he wrote, "that Fénelon was the foremost writer in the art of making virtue seem something lovable. It seems to me that you share this glory with him. Fénelon had enemies; well, you must have yours also. The injustice, of which you appear to complain in your writings, is a thing that belongs to all times. I doubt if even in an age more worthy of you, Madame de Sévigné and Madame de la

[1] Roederer, *Œuvres*, ii. 67.

Fayette would have pardoned your surpassing them. It is true that La Rochefoucault, La Fontaine, and La Bruyère would have been at your feet; but where are such men nowadays!"

M. de Fontanes was, as every one knows, the personification of courtesy.

The literary reputation of Mme. de Genlis shone, then, brilliantly in Paris, and flung its rays over the whole of France. She was further exalted by her sister novelists, and there were more than a hundred of them already in Paris. They were just then frightened at the romance of *Delphine*, and feared to see Mme. de Stael take up their branch of literature,—she who till now had kept strictly to the region of philosophy and literary criticism. They dreaded above all that she would reopen her salon; she had just lost her father and was then travelling in Italy. So they vigorously opposed to her the celebrated lady of the Arsenal.[1]

In a word, all the polite world was proud to pay its compliments at the Arsenal. Only the nobles who had not yet rallied to the Empire stood apart, but there were the diplomatists, the poets, foreign visitors of distinction, leaders of fashion, Imperialists of to-day, Royalists of to-morrow.

When it chanced that circumstances made it difficult to come openly, some romantic stratagem would be brought into use.

Thus young Mme. de Chevreuse, the daughter-in-law of the Duchess de Luynes, several times disguised herself as a flower girl in order to gain access to Mme. de Genlis, and the latter gave her the pleasure of allowing this charming amusement to go on for some time.

In the autumn of 1804 Mme. de Chevreuse had "quite declared herself," and was in correspondence with the author

---

[1] Mme. de Maltzan wrote on 12th October 1808 to the Countess of Albany,—" We no longer talk of Madame de Staël: no doubt she is preparing to wake us up. ... Madame de Genlis has now more successes than she has, but I think it is by giving us as recent work things she wrote in middle life." (Cf. Pélissier, *Le Portefeuille de la Comtesse d'Albany*.)

of *Madame de la Vallière*. Anatole de Montesquiou, though a relation of Mme. de Genlis, would have at all risks presented himself in the guise of a black-bloused printer's messenger, bringing her her proof sheets, if Maradan would have allowed it. Tired of arguing the point, he had to have recourse to a regular introduction. And being now so much sought after, the Comtesse de Genlis again fixed a day for visitors, the Saturday. It was the last salon that she arranged.

To tell the truth, it was in many ways very different from the elegant " blue salon " of the Palais Royal, or even the political gatherings at Bellechasse. If the mistress of the house kept up the ways of society before the Revolution in her talk, her attitude, her cultured ease that was at once noble and full of animation, there was nothing else to recall the air of the Court.

The salon at the Arsenal was not a fashionable assembly of people who made and unmade reputations; nor was it a circle of wits, whose sprightly sayings circulated all over Paris; it was rather the study, the workroom, of a laborious student of the Muses, that was thrown open in the interval between the writing of two pages of history or romance, to admit a number of educated people who were sociable as well as learned, who had a liking for intellectual matters, and were more refined that the new made society of the day. They went seldom or never to the imperial receptions, but they had for their hobby art, poetry, literature of all kinds—French and foreign—and finally they were philosophers enough to be willing to come together without much comfort or luxury.

For it must be said that to go to Mme. de Genlis's " At Homes " meant overcoming all kinds of discouraging circumstances.

The Arsenal was out of the way and difficult of access. With its labyrinth of vaulted archways and gates, courtyards and stairs, it was like a fortress.

Miss Edgeworth, who was passionately desirous of making the acquaintance of the author of the *Rosière de Salency*, which she had seen acted at Mme. Campan's, was very nearly lost, with her father and their carriage, in this tangle of vaulted passages, and in the courtyards where nobody knew anything about Mme. de Genlis. The merest chance made their coachman stop before a winding staircase in bad repair, and lighted only with a candle-end in a wretched tin lantern hanging in the angle of the wall. "There was just enough light," she says, "to show us the bareness as well as the extreme dirt of the stairs. Only for this lamp, which could hardly be the only one alight in the building, there was nothing to indicate that it was inhabited."

At the second storey, where the "authoress" resided, there was the same air of abandonment. On the landing, which was barely lighted by a miserable taper, they saw "two large double doors, very dirty, one to the right, the other to the left, each one with a bell of the size of what one would find in the bar parlour of an English inn." But it was no good ringing and knocking, for no answer came. At last, as the result of questioning an ill-humoured porter, it was found that there was a third bell—and this the right one—lost in obscurity and therefore invisible.

When it jingled, Stéphanie Alyon, who attended to the door, "badly dressed but with her hair beautifully arranged," led the visitors, "with the grace of a young girl who has learned to dance," through two badly-furnished anterooms into the little salon where Mme. de Genlis was sitting.

This room still exists. It had been the boudoir of the Duchesse de Maine before it was assigned to Mme. de Genlis, and it is now the private office of the librarian of the Bibliothèque de l'Arsenal. It is a room of moderate size, lighted by a large window, and its arrangement remains the same as in these old times.

The pearly grey woodwork, in the rococo style of Louis Quinze, frames, with its carved mouldings over the three doors and the double-panelled glass of the mantelpiece, medallions in monochrome, representing mythological subjects in the pure style of the eighteenth century. Facing the window and flush with the wall, is a cupboard with double-folding doors fitted with silk screens. The fireplace, of noble proportions, sent out, in Mme. de Genlis's time, if there chanced to be a fire in it, a puff of smoke to meet the visitors as they opened the door. It appears that still from time to time it attests its antiquity by the same token.

By the feeble light of a single lamp one made one's way to the arm-chair, which the mistress of the house occupied, usually near the fire. And while exchanging the first polite greetings, one was surprised at seeing all round a strange confusion, suggestive of a bric-a-brac shop. "There was no taste in the furnishing of the room," says Fiévée, "no care for it, not even that effort at cleanliness which is to the end, and almost necessarily, a matter about which old ladies are particular. She had lived in palaces but she had not the least idea of how to keep in order, I won't say a mansion, but even the simplest household. One never saw anything like it."[1]

In fact, one ran up against a thousand things of the most varied kind, work-baskets, writing-desks, Chinese vases, bird cages. Chairs were missing or hidden under heaps of books and music, "all the apparatus of art and all the tools with which she busied herself."

A green silk fire-screen, displaying a long stain of oil, and her beautiful harp, all bright with gilding, stood in front of her writing table, represented by an old deal table, worm-eaten, worn out, and blotted with ink. This table of itself might suggest a poem. One day Frédéric Barrière saw upon it, all at the same time, tooth brushes, a coil of hair, two open pots of jam, some eggshells, combs, a breakfast roll, a bottle of hair wash, the remains of some *café-au-lait* in a cracked cup, irons for goffering paper flowers, a candle end, an unfinished water-colour drawing of a garland, a little Brie cheese, two stout volumes, and two sheets of paper with verses scribbled on them. Finally, an ugly leaden ink-pot took the place of the magnificent inkstand the Queen of Spain had sent as a present to her, and which, like all the presents she received, the Countess had given away.

To complete the description, the mirror over the mantelpiece was "a gathering place for dust and cobwebs that defied the broom; for the broom, stretched on a slip of

[1] Fiévée, *Madame de Genlis*.

carpet, was so crippled, so battered out of joint, that it seemed past all work, like the bellows, another invalid, hanging in the chimney corner by a string that was worn and near the breaking point." [1]

In the midst of this disorder, and herself in careless guise, Mme. de Genlis received her guests, as if she were still at the Palais Royal. She displayed as much grace and tact, and exerted herself without stint. Thanks to her practical knowledge of the world and her natural sociability, she saved the situation despite its unpleasant features. As soon as one sat down beside her, one forgot the painful impression of her lodging, and could only listen to her, reply to her, admire her, allow oneself to be carried away with wonder at the charm that made one its own. "One must, like me, have passed long years in her society fully to understand all the attraction she exercised," writes Brifaut, "all the magic resources of her mind, this Proteus of a thousand forms; all the gifts of pleasing she derived from a well-stored and ready memory, an unwearying imagination, and a talent for observation that gave her at once the measure of the strong and the weak points of every one, the chief secret of her power." [2] He tells us further that Mme. de Genlis " possessed the special art of making one believe that she took an interest in one even when no such thing existed, of whispering into one's ear words of praise that she had carefully weighed beforehand, but which seemed to come involuntarily from the heart, of charming one's self-esteem, arousing one's attention, and disposing one to feel a gratitude based on what ? On a friendly look, a polite smile, a formal grasp of the hand, slight and fragile proofs of an affection which one liked to think one had secured. As soon as she wished it, one was caught." [3]

In fact, Mme. de Genlis was still something of a coquette. And she had also kept the capricious humour of coquetry. All the cares and courtesy " lavished on her so freely that you felt sure that your credit was established with her for ever," was a dead letter as soon as you had repassed her

---

[1] Cf. Brifaut, Œuvres, t. i., p. 281, etc.
[2] Brifaut, op. cit., i. p. 280.   [3] Ibid., p. 279.

MME. DE GENLIS IN LATER LIFE.

threshold. "You went away enchanted with yourself, and when you came back what did you find ? A woman who was cold, dull, bored; the empire of her heart was for others."[1]

Thirty years earlier these capricious changes of mood would have been regarded only as the whims of a pretty woman, and might have been praised by poets as such. But now, alas ! Madame de Genlis had no longer the roses of spring on her fresh cheeks, or the bright glances of youth.

The terrible marks of misfortune and suffering had marred her countenance and brought some bitterness to her smile. Her cheeks were pale and hollow ; her lips, now almost thin lines, told of a mouth that once was pretty ; the skin was discoloured and dried up. But in her eyes, under the lessened shadow of her eyebrows, there still lingered a spark of gaiety, and her nose, of the beautiful Roxalana type, had not yet lost its shape. But her chin was becoming pointed, and two or three locks of hair that was turning grey escaped from under the lace cap on her high but now wrinkled forehead.

Miss Edgeworth notes that Mme. de Genlis, so anxious to please the masculine element, shows herself less amiable to her own sex. Her Irish visitor could discern behind her petulant vivacity, a background of bitterness, the nervous melancholy of a woman tormented by literary jealousy, and made irritable by ill fortune. But she was the fashion, and that was enough, so a very numerous circle frequented her salon at the Arsenal. There was the Comte de Choiseul-Gouffier and his wife the witty Princess de Beauffremont ; Victorine de Chastenay and her mother Mme. Kennens ; Mme. de Brady, the Baroness Dubrosseron ; Mme. de Vannoz, who was compared to, and often set up against, Delille ; Mme. de Bon, the translator of Sir Walter Scott's *Lady of the Lake* and any number of English novels ; Mme. Tallien ; Mme. Hainguerlot ; Mme. de Bellegarde ; Mme. Roger, the future Countess de Montholon ; Mme. Daubenton ; and Mme. Delarue, the niece of Beaumarchais. So much for the feminine side. We must add the names of the Countess of Albany and the Countess d'Harville, the only one of her

[1] Brifaut, *op. cit.*, i. p. 281.

former lady friends who revisited Mme. de Genlis after the Revolution.

The men also belonged to that literary class which was trying to find once more the delights of intellectual life among the ruins of an overturned world. Naturally they were favourable to the new régime which had made a calm prevail after the cyclone of the Revolution. The poets especially came in numbers; Brifaut, a future Academician, and a mediocre rhymster, but a man of the world, lavish in his offerings of incense to women, and by choice an opportunist; Désaugiers; Millevoye, suffering from poor health, but crowned with laurels at twenty-five; Charbonnières, who believed and declared he was the nephew of the Abbé Delille, a little stupid, but always welcome to the mistress of the house on account of his incessant epigrams against Mme. de Staël; and M. de Tréneuil, another poet and the successor of Saugrain at the Arsenal—all were regular visitors. There, too, were Count Joseph d'Estourmel, then a young Auditor of the Cour des Comptes, an insatiable reader, and a habitué of the library of the Arsenal, where one could hear, in the storey overhead, Casimir's wonderful harp; M. Laborie; the vaudeville writer, Radet; Cousen de St. Malo, Count de Courchamps, soon to be the author of the *Souvenirs de la Marquise de Créqui*; the septuagenarian Descherny, still an admirable singer, " an enthusiastic disciple of Rousseau, and an extreme *philosophe*; M. Pieyre, formerly assistant tutor to the Orleans Princes; the violent Royalist, Coriolis d'Espinouze; the learned Count de Laborde, whom his hobbies had made famous, a consummate musician and an enthusiast for Casimir; old Prince Kurakin, the Russian ambassador at Paris, whose ugliness was proverbial, and whose coat of cloth of gold covered with the insignia of all manner of orders, set in diamonds, made him a man of mark everywhere. Then there were D'Offremont, M. de la Tremblaye, Dussault, the editor of the *Journal des Débats*, M. de Sabran, the Count de Rochefort, young Anatole de Montesquiou, the Abbé Sabatier de Cabre, an old acquaintance of the Genlis, who was always intriguing, the Baron de Lascours and his wife. They formed a distinguished enough company which was reinforced from time to time by some foreign visitors.

As was fitting, conversation was the main business at these gatherings, interrupted from time to time by the poets, who brought their works with them to give readings, or who recited verses in honour of the mistress of the house. Millevoye, Radet, Charbonnières and some others even composed in her honour a garland of flowers of poetry in imitation of that which once helped to make Julie d'Angennes famous.

And it will be asked, was the drama forgotten at the Arsenal? No it was not; but the form of it was changed. The time was long past when the sprightly Genlis could make her appearance and win a triumph on a stage improvised out of two folding screens. She was no longer of the age for playing youthful heroines, or even noble mothers, and the theatricals that once were such an effective means of showing off her face, figure and bearing, her graceful manners and her voice, could now do no more than interest her as a spectator. So they became a mere pleasure for the eyes, an ingeniously contrived spectacle consisting of one or more *tableaux vivants*, which the fertile imagination of Casimir set off with poetry and appropriate music.

One of these spectacles is mentioned in the *Memoirs*. It was *David and Saul*. David, or rather Casimir, appeared in the guise of a little shepherd, charming with his harp the madness of Saul, " whose fine face and gestures spoke even more powerfully than all the sounds of the harp."[1] But Saul was represented by Talma himself.

This " living picture " was produced on 25th January 1810, for the celebration of Mme. de Genlis' birthday. Mme. Dubrosseron organised a series of similar tableaux on subjects selected from the novels of her friend.

So this was what made up nearly all the social life of Mme.

---

[1] Cf. D'Estourmel, *Derniers Souvenirs*, 341. Madame de Genlis gives another version of this scene. According to her account, Saul was represented by the actor Michelot. But no doubt it was given on more than one occasion—once with Talma, the other times with Michelot.

de Genlis. At this time, except at her receptions, she seldom saw anyone. She never went to the Imperial Court, but only to a few houses where good company was welcome—to that of the Marquise de Grollier among others, and to the salon of the Duchess of Courland, where the famous Dr. Gall gave a course of phrenology.

Was it there or was it at the Arsenal, where he was received one day "when there was grand company," including Talleyrand, the Vicomtesse de Laval, Mme. de Choiseul-Gouffier, and the Duchess of Courland, that the doctor discovered that Mme. de Genlis had "the bump of religion and elevation of soul, and that of perseverance developed to a really extraordinary size"? On which Talleyrand, always ready for a witty sally, said, "You see, Mesdames, that she is not a hypocrite." Finally, Brifaut introduced her to M. Sage, and the latter invited her to a supper with Talma, whom she annoyed to the extent of putting him quite out of countenance by her lavish eulogies of Lekain.

But she preferred to cultivate the friendship of a little intimate group, a privileged circle of intellectuals whom she called "the Inseparables." Their hour was nine o'clock each Saturday evening, and it was for them only, such were her orders. At the appointed hour the Inseparables arrived. There were Fiévée and the Abbé de Cabre, the Count de Choiseul-Gouffier and the Baron de Lascours, the tribune Carrion-Nisas, the poet Marigné, M. de Sennovert, the collector Baron Vivant-Denon, and perhaps Cardinal Maury; with Brifaut, Tréneuil and D'Estourmel, all conversationalists, educated men, with a stock of piquant anecdotes. "Then began," says Fiévée, "a wild talk. There was no ordered discussion, no settled plan, no prudence. One said everything that came into one's head, and in this freedom one realised how much self-respecting restraint there is in pleasant amusement united to intellect." Midnight arrived too soon, bringing the end of these fine literary gatherings. "At last," says Fiévée, "it was time to end and go away; but then among the Inseparables there began another conversation of running commentary on the conversation from which they had just torn themselves away."[1] To close this account of society at the Arsenal, we must not forget those notable persons who, having exceptional claims upon her, visited and did honour to the Muse in her refuge. They were given private audience. There was, for instance, Fontanes, for whom *Madame de Maintenon* served as an introduction, and whom Mme. de Genlis met later at Mme. de Montesson's. He came three or four times. So did Désirée Clary, who had now become the Maréchale Bernadotte.

Then there was Cardinal Maury, always on a friendly footing with the Countess. This friendship dated from long ago. And since the time when Maury, then only an Abbé, had come to Bellechasse to read confidentially to her his address on his reception into the French Academy—a speech which but for Mme. de Genlis would have been spoiled by an enormous error of taste[2]—these two veterans of the Court of Louis XV., who had fought with honour in the combats of 1789, had never ceased to esteem one another. There was a literary comradeship between them; and each freely communicated to the other projects and plans for books, criticisms, problems of style or of erudition, and finally political opinions.

After 1809, Maury, having been made Archbishop of Paris, could not continue to visit his old friend so frequently. He did not entirely give it up, but he seldom came. One of the last occasions when His Eminence was at a party at the Arsenal seems to have been 25th October 1810. "As he will not be able to make further visits," wrote Mme. de Genlis to Casimir, "he has asked me to choose a day in the week for coming to lunch alone with him. I shall go on the Sundays. . . . His sentiments are admirable and his conduct perfect."

King Jerome of Westphalia honoured the Arsenal with

---

[1] Fiévée, *Madame de Genlis*.

[2] The Abbé Maury had intended to make in one passage of his address a direct appeal, in interrogative form, to his audience, and to reply to them if he was contradicted. Madame de Genlis happily prevented him from carrying out this project of getting up a political discussion.

two or three visits. Finally, Chateaubriand, who in 1802 offered his *Génie du Christianisme* to Mme. de Genlis, made her acquaintance a little later, and seems to have come once to see her.

And there was yet another visitor, admired, flattered since long ago by the lady who had vowed an indestructible friendship for him.

As in former days, " the better to enjoy the charm of his conversation," she received him quite alone. He nevertheless was dry, cold, indifferent, essentially an egotist. But what a value " this apparent indolence " gave to his friendship. . . ." A sign of approbation, a smile, an air of being interested, were in him really something enthralling," she exclaims in her *Memoirs*. And as for his mind, " that mind so versatile, which without an effort and without pedantry could display its brilliance on the greatest occasions, and yet in everyday intercourse could also brighten conversation with epigrams, or with inimitable grace lend itself to the most frivolous badinage "—nothing could be compared to it.

Do we not recognise in this portrait that old friend of so many women, who still remained the friend of Mme. de Genlis ? Do we not recognise Talleyrand ? And truly it was with him, and perhaps with him only—for in this respect Brifaut never got beyond pleasantly agreeable conversation —that she remembered the old time, and opened the gates of memory. With him it seemed as if she was once more a lady of the Court, laying aside for awhile the governess, the authoress; and the corner of her old heart that she kept for him seemed still to perserve a last glow of the feelings of other days. Was not Talleyrand, indeed, the only one who had ever sought to dominate her ?—However, in this he had only wasted his time. But she, who even in love kept her intellectual strength, may she not have been more deeply moved by this man of such wide-reaching allurements, who had, alas ! all women devoted to him and deceived them all. She, who was so caustic to most people, could not refrain from praising in a tone of affection that is almost surprising, Talleyrand's kindness of heart, and " his good actions performed with such simplicity." He was, as we very well know, the very opposite of simplicity, but if we are to take Mme. de Dino's word for it, he liked it in others. Who knows but that he was inclined to appreciate that rare virtue in Mme. de Genlis, with her outspokenness, her sudden and charming changes of mood, and that vivacity, still full of playfulness, that so readily put her at her ease with another in conversation. She must have made him feel tired of Mme. de Laval and his other lady friends, his " old seraglio," as they were irreverently called. But he was now a greater personage than ever, and he was too much of a cynic to abandon himself in the case of Madame de Genlis in her declining years to an autumn friendship that might still have some tenderness in it.

And besides, Talleyrand was not the most familiar of the visitors at the Arsenal. There was another of whom she said, " He knows my heart perfectly." [1] Him to whom she wrote, " My friend, I am externally the coldest person living." I have seen so much affected sentiment. I have heard so many false protestations. The expressions and the language of the heart have been so profaned to me, that it is no longer possible for me to make use of them. But listen to my silence; it is worth more than my words." [2] And again :—

" My excellent friend, I am in every way happy at thought that a person so perfectly amiable as you, is at the same time so worthy of affection."

And this privileged, this chosen one, an ecclesiastic like Talleyrand, and almost as much compromised as he, this confidant was the Abbé de Cabre. He was very devoted to Mme. de Genlis, and obtained a pension for her from the Queen of Naples. He seems indeed, among the many who were indifferent or scoffers, to have had a really kind feeling for her. In return she confided in him, she let him see sometimes a little of her heart, which was so embittered, so disenchanted, so lonely, in order to calm its restlessness, and

---

[1] The Comtesse de Genlis to the Countess d'Albany, October 12, 1806 (Pélissier, *op. cit.*).

[2] Lettres inédites de Madame de Genlis, published by Pélissier, *Intermédiare*, February 22, 1908.

break away from the isolation that surrounded her as she remembered Bellechasse and its little world of children. And in her devotion to teaching, and also out of her fear of solitude, she had again added to her household a poor little boy, picked up we know not where: it was Alfred Le Maire.

Foreseeing that Casimir and Stéphanie d'Alyon would marry, she adopted him. Perhaps he would be there to close her eyes at the last. Meanwhile she was giving him an education,—spelling, arithmetic, poetry,—but above all she tried to put a useful occupation in his hands, and direct him to a musical career, that of a harpist, for which it seems he had some gifts. In a word, she was as interested in him as if he had been one of her own children, and she brought him up as an admirer of Casimir. When the latter went away in 1810 for a series of concerts in Germany—leaving by the way the son of a precocious love affair with Mlle. Duchesnois, Henri Achille Rafin, born on 10th January in that year—Mme. de Genlis brought in a certain Mme. Roussel to take care of Alfred. But the boy, if possible, made a poorer return for her interest in him than even Casimir.[1] So one wonders why she "uprooted" him from his old surroundings.

It is quite certain that Alfred would have preferred to lead a vagabond life with urchins of his own age, rather than bend himself to the fine manners for which he was not fitted by his nature. But the instinct of the pedagogue in Mme. de Genlis was not repelled by so small a matter as this.

That instinct found further scope for its exercise when, in 1812, Napoleon appointed his correspondent lady inspectress of the schools of her district of Paris. It was

---

[1] "He is not a child after my heart," she writes in the autumn of 1810. "Nothing strikes his imagination: he has not a bad heart, but he has no delicacy of feeling; it will be difficult to give him noble manners. He is not stupid, but he is so backward for his age that he takes no interest in anything. It is impossible to speak seriously with him even for half of a quarter of an hour. He is dirty and negligent to excess. But with all this one has to treat him gently and with kindness. Naturally he is not very communicative. . . . Since your departure I make him be very respectful to me, but I have to treat him with extreme patience, for there are days when he is quite broken down" (*op. cit.*, 81).

an honorary position without any salary, but it might console her for not having some higher post. Mme. de Genlis had, in fact, expected for a short time in 1806 to become once more the governess of princes,—in this case of the children of Joseph, then King of Naples. The idea perhaps came from the Abbé Sabatier de Cabre, who acted as an intermediary between Mme. de Genlis and the Queen of Naples, and thought he could obtain for her the education of the Emperor's nieces.

"Mme. de Genlis, who believed she was born with the vocation for training and instructing others and imparting to them her principles and opinions,"[1] took advantage, according to Méneval, of her correspondence with the Emperor to ask for his approbation of this idea. On the other hand, we find her writing to Mme. d'Albany: "I do not yet know if I shall go to Italy. It is a favour that I have neither asked for nor desired, and which I can hardly even look for. To rest, to be forgotten, to have a little garden, these are my constant wishes. But when one has been stripped of everything, one does not rest, and one has not enough freedom to go and bury oneself in solitude. However, it is still possible that a single word may oblige me to start for Naples, and in that case it is quite certain that I shall fulfil my duties there with as much zeal and affection as if I had myself chosen my lot."[2] But already the suspicion that dogged her least steps had put aside these plans and disappointed the hopes of the poor woman. The Marquise de Lage de Volude writes from the hostile standpoint to M. de Sabran :—

"It is said that this Genlis is aspiring to be the governess of the *Corsicans*. I think that Bonaparte knows the people about him too well to allow his nephews and nieces to be entrusted to this shrew. If Josephine were to die, you would see that she would want to marry the Emperor, as the other governess married the King. This idea occurred to me when reading her *Madame de Maintenon*. Just you

[1] Cf. Méneval, *Napoléon et Marie Louise*, iii. 285.
[2] Mme. de Genlis to the Countess d'Albany, *op. cit.*

read it attentively and you will find you have something to tell me. I had not the time to write in the margins the thoughts that struck me, but her character is continually coming out in it. As she speaks of her heroine, she takes every opportunity of making one think of herself."[1]

Mme. de Lage had no reason to be so excited. When he received the letter of his correspondent Napoleon had knitted his brows. He did not want to bring Mme. de Genlis into the imperial household, and he made his wishes on this point at once known to Mme. Julie, who, at the suggestion of the Abbé de Cabre, softened the disappointment of her refusal and of the Emperor's disapproval of Mme. de Genlis by a pension of a thousand crowns. The latter showed her gratitude by a gift of several of her manuscripts. But she makes out in her *Memoirs* that the post was offered to her, and that she refused it out of attachment for the House of Orleans.

Strange to say, having failed to obtain this advantage for herself, she thought of getting it given to Victorine de Chastenay, and made some efforts with this object. It is well known how the witty Canoness de Chastenay, wishing to have a place in the Court of the Empress, and not in that of Naples, refused the post, which went to Mme. Dannery.[2]

Whatever she may have said on the subject, Mme. de Genlis, so far as her own feeling went, would probably have preferred the post of governess to the Emperor's nieces rather than her actual position. But her failure on this point took nothing away from her privileges as the correspondent of Napoleon, and the good offices of the Queen of Naples did not indicate any loss of favour. Those around her soon had proof of this, especially the librarian of the Arsenal Ameilhon, against whom she always scored a success in her disputes with him. Now they were always in perpetual rivalry, living under the same roof, and not able to endure each other. The story of their disputes

[1] Comtesse de Reinach-Foussemagne, *La Marquise de Lage de Volude*, 242.
[2] Mme. de Chastenay, *Mémoires*, ii. 58.

has a touch of the serio-comic novel, and one feels a regret that some writer like Alexandre Dumas *père* has not told it to us in his lively style.

The arrival of Mme. de Genlis had been hailed with anything but pleasure by Ameilhon, who regarded it as nothing short of an intrusion. To have for his neighbour a literary lady, who had no claim to occupy a place in a domain which he considered as his own, hurt his self-esteem, and, besides this, deprived him of a suite of rooms into which he had long been wishing to move.

And if it had even been possible for him to ignore the presence of this neighbour!

But, not content with living next door to him, she disturbed the peace of the librarian even in the very heart of his kingdom, having obtained from high quarters an authorisation to borrow books from the library without any restriction. As for the number and duration of these borrowings, everything depended on her wants, the work she had in hand, and, if it came to that, on her good pleasure. Then, divining the ill-disguised hostility of Ameilhon, she took a delight in playing the autocrat with him, using him as a humble subordinate, and making him give way to her wishes. There was not one of the regulations that could hold good against her, and the librarian had each day, hat in hand, to bow to the orders of Mme. the Comtesse de Genlis.

Did he seem to be touchy or recalcitrant?

Did he venture to raise his voice, and claim in a threatening way some volume that Mme. de Genlis had kept too long?

She seized her pen, complained to the Minister, and he gallantly took her part, and she gained the day.

In 1812 she formed the plan of publishing an Abridgment of the *Mémoires* of Dangeau. It was a colossal work, for the original manuscript consisted of more than forty folio volumes. She accordingly had brought to her the magnificent manuscript copy in fifty-eight quarto volumes—one of the finest things in the Arsenal library, which had been purchased by the Marquis de Paulmy at Mme. de Pompadour's sale, and she kept it for nine months running. But she did not foresee that Napoleon would become alarmed as to certain comparisons suggested by the criticisms of Dangeau on Louis XIV., and that on the eve of publication, notwithstanding the good offices of Talleyrand, the "Abridgment" would be kept waiting in vain for his *imprimatur*.

Mme. de Genlis had marked with lines in the margins of the original manuscript the passages to be extracted for her work, passages which were then copied out chiefly by Stéphanie d'Alyon. She now protested that the public, or the first comer of them, might go to the Arsenal library, read Dangeau in the fifty-eight quarto volumes that had belonged to Mme. de Pompadour, note the passages marked by the marginal lines, collect them, and, thus appropriating her abridgment, publish it quite legally in Belgium or elsewhere.

Quickly she took her pen and poured out letters, protests, petitions. On which Napoleon sent for the beautiful manuscript, locked it up in his private library, and kept it. When he heard who had been the cause of this blow poor Ameilhon nearly died of rage. He moved heaven and earth, sent out letters full of recriminations and protests, went direct to the Minister, and, as she assures us, forgot himself in unheard-of scenes with Mme. de Genlis, urging her to demand the return of Dangeau. It was all no use. The beautiful manuscript did not come back to the Arsenal.

Mme. de Genlis did not stop there in the way of success. When Saugrain[1] died she asked for the suite of rooms that the conservator had occupied. Needless to say she obtained it, with the further favour of a grant of 1500 francs for the expenses of moving into it (25th Brumaire, Year XIV). "But what must seem odious to us," says the learned historian of the Arsenal library, "the widow of Saugrain—of the man who had saved the library during the Revolution—was turned out to clear the rooms for Madame de Genlis."[2] And then, if the Countess would only move quickly and quietly!

---

[1] "Till then the position of those who directed the library had not been clearly defined. Ameilhon was the librarian; Saugrain had the title of conservator-librarian; and the Minister corresponded now with one, now with the other" (Henry Martin, *Histoire de la Bibliothèque de l'Arsenal*, 405).

[2] *Ibid.*, 422.

But she delayed, and, as if on purpose, took an endless time over it, while her tardiness blew into angry flame the irritation in the hasty mind of Ameilhon, who was waiting for Mme. de Genlis's lodging, and anxious to move into it, or at any rate place his books there. At last one fine day, all his patience being at an end, he conceived the plan of removing the doors. The enemy had gone out that day. But on her return the gaping entrance revealed her rooms to her with all privacy gone from them. What an outrage! what an impertinence! The librarian must answer for it. Going straight to the reading-room, where he was sitting, she imperiously lectured him, and before all the readers gave him the sharpest scolding he had ever heard. It seems that, quite ashamed of having failed to such an extent in the respect due to a woman, Ameilhon made excuses and had the doors replaced.

But she was implacable, and revenged herself in a clever but very cruel way. A printer's boy had brought her by mistake some proof-sheets of Ameilhon's *Histoire du Bas-Empire*. She joyfully set to work scratching out, striking lines through, and correcting "not mere printer's errors but faults in style," and on the Saturday evening passed round the proof-sheets, riddled with her corrections, for the amusement of the Inseparables, who laughed heartily at the expense of the librarian. "M. Ameilhon thundered about it," she says. Poor man!

He had already tried to have his dear neighbour sent away, when in 1811 the opening up of the Rue de Sully led to the demolition of several buildings in which there were heaps of books. He had claimed her apartments as being required for housing of the books thus displaced. It was his ill-luck to fail once more. But time, which is cleverer than men in bringing things to pass, was soon to give him the satisfaction of witnessing, before he died, the departure of Mme. de Genlis.

For a long time the old Arsenal had been very damp. Walls and wainscots were becoming saturated, until at last the panelling of one of his enemy's windows fell to pieces. She asked for repairs, but Ameilhon, on being consulted, drew up with a ready pen an estimate the total amount of which frightened the Minister; and just then his department was very short of money.

Nevertheless, the Government had granted Mme. de Genlis a lodging for life, and there was no other vacant. Obliged to give up the rooms at the Arsenal, that were now becoming uninhabitable, she took advantage of this state of things to make a demand for compensation.

A fresh petition explained to the Minister that, wishing to retire to the country and there continue her literary labours, the Countess was willing to renounce her right to lodge at the Arsenal, and asked for a sum of 8000 francs " to prepare the place of my retirement." An imperial decree, dated 12th April 1811, granted her what she asked for " out of the vote included in the budget of the Ministry of the Interior for unforeseen expenses." All the same, she was in no great hurry, and on 30th April, with a view to hasten her departure, Ameilhon wrote to the Ministry: " I hear from various sources that Mme. de Genlis is preparing to leave the Arsenal, and that she will at last restore to the library the rooms she has occupied so long to the prejudice of one of the chief officials of that institution."[1]

In the course of the month of May, Mme. de Genlis vacated the place. Ameilhon was not long to enjoy the gain he had fought so hard for; he was ill, and he died soon after, but not without Mme. de Genlis having in his last days shown him some kindness, some friendliness. As for herself, she could not shut her eyes to the fact that in leaving the Arsenal she was leaving also the brightness of her life.

No doubt we shall see her shed some remnant of light on the days of the Restoration. But these will be the last gleams of a reputation that was to go on declining during some fifteen years.

[1] Cf. Henry Martin, *op. cit.*, 429.

CHAPTER III

1812—THE RESTORATION

MME. DE GENLIS pitched her tent for awhile in the Rue des Lions St. Paul, with many regrets for the Arsenal, where she had the illusion of living in a kind of palace.

The suite of rooms, damp, "Gothic in style and ridiculously planned," could barely suffice for her diminished household. Casimir was just then giving his concerts in Germany; Mme. Roussel was establishing herself in Italy; as for Paméla, she would not rejoin her adopted mother. Casimir had met her three years before in an inn at Dover, where she had taken refuge after her separation from Pitcairn. She was in a miserable state, and was living under the name of Mme. Dufour. He brought her back disguised and hidden away below decks in a vessel placed at his disposal by Prince Esterhazy, and Paméla landed at Calais on 15th February 1808, not without exciting the suspicions of Fouché.

After Mme. de Genlis had made an appeal in her favour, Napoleon, thinking that he might obtain interesting information from her, gave orders that she was to be allowed to come to Paris, and permitted her to reside there. But Paméla, considering that the kind of life her mother by adoption offered her was of too mediocre a kind, refused her hospitality, and, dreaming of triumphs to come, set up housekeeping in a luxurious style at a considerable distance from the Arsenal. But what really came her way was debt. By 1811 she owed 8000 francs, and already, in 1810, her creditors had sold up her furniture. However, they could not seize a pension supplied by the Fitzgerald family, and another from

Pitcairn, these amounting together to 6800 francs, besides some minor sums of money. On this income she lived in a cottage, to which some rooms had been added, about five leagues from Paris—that Paris which she could visit only on Sundays and holidays, when legal processes could not be executed.

So there remained with Mme. de Genlis only Stéphanie d'Alyon and Alfred Le Maire.

As we have said, she was at the Rue des Lions St. Paul only for awhile, for she was not lying when she told the Minister that she wished to retire into the country. Her idea was, in fact, to buy a farm for about 20,000 francs, end her days there, and then leave it to Casimir. " You will choose the place," she wrote to him on 11th February 1811, " either near Lyons, or near Brussels, or near Strasburg; for as to the neighbourhood of Paris, it must not be thought of. You would do nothing there, and you must not contract any more debts." She inclined towards Strasburg, " and those little courts, where one could get on very pleasantly."

The farm was never bought, because Mme. de Genlis was short of money. " When my affairs are arranged," she said; but they never were arranged.

Want was always holding her poor fireside in its grasp. Any other but she could have lived at her ease on the pension from the Emperor, that of the Queen of Naples, and the profits of her works. There is no denying that Mme. de Genlis scored great success with the publishers. Almost all her works appeared in new editions. About 1812 her *Souvenirs de Félicie* were in the third edition; the *Veillées du Château*, the *Vœux téméraires*, and the *Petits Emigrés* in the fifth; the *Petit La Bruyère* and the *Chevaliers du Cygne* in the fourth; the *Mères rivales* in the sixth; the *Duchesse de la Vallière* was getting on to the eighth or ninth; and *Madame de La Fayette* was an immense success—the first edition, on sale at the booksellers' at eight o'clock in the morning, was sold out to the last copy by ten in the evening. Finally, she had completed her *Siège de la Rochelle*, which was translated into every language in Europe, and the *Bergères de Madian*, which went into a second edition in the same year in which it was pubished.[1]

Once more, anyone else but Mme. de Genlis would have made ends meet. But she was terribly wanting in system, and above all the caprices of Casimir were everlastingly exhausting her resources. This great big boy—mediocre, lazy, sensual, phlegmatic, a drinker, a spendthrift, and a hypocrite —enchained her old heart by some kind of spell, for he never seems to have had any touch of feeling, and his only merit was his agility with his fingers. In her inexplicable blindness, Mme. de Genlis thought he was a genius destined to immortal fame, and refused him nothing.[2] So all, or nearly all, her letters tell of a remittance of money to this acrobat of the harp, who excelled in tricky displays, arpeggios and lightning variations—at best a poor kind of talent. But for this Casimir she empties her purse, kills herself with work, and deprives herself even of necessaries.

Casimir Boecker might spend 1800 francs in a single month at Strasburg, and ask in letter after letter for twenty or thirty louis ; she did impossibilities in order to send them to him, with a heap of good advice : " You must eat this, and not drink that—I order you to have some light summer vests made for yourself, and *this at once*." There is advice as to drinks and pills—she forbids him to smoke—she exhorts him to penitence, and tells him to go to a confessor. She had indeed a great anxiety about Casimir's salvation, and all her letters without exception end with the three letters " G.D.E." or with the three words —strange to say in *English* —" God, Death, Eternity " ; or with the maxim, " Honour always and in all places divine religion." Certainly these were admirable sentiments, rare enough with the mothers of the eighteenth century; but we are somewhat disappointed at seeing that Mme. de Genlis continually mixes them up

---

[1] The manuscript of this work is now in the library of St. Petersburg, to which it was presented by Casimir on 5th April 1837.

[2] " I have never received such dull letters as yours," she writes to him in 1804. " What a correspondence ! But I pass it all over, and you have none the less in me the best of mothers and of friends. . . . I have always a delightful presentiment which tells me that a great change will take place in your mind, and suddenly you will become what you might be " (Lapause, 3).

with another kind of litany, the versicles of which reveal a singular utilitarianism. There are such phrases as "Get married; make a good marriage," emphasised with, "If I were in your place, I would have made a grand marriage this very month," or, better still, "*Try to turn your thoughts towards a rich widow*, and above all keep right with God." It is the everlasting contradiction of human nature making piety the ally of ambitious views; the everlasting mingling of sacred and profane, of which Mme. de Genlis from her childhood was an instance, accustomed as she had been to such things as part of a system or method.

And let us not accuse her of hypocrisy. In her actual state of mind, preoccupied solely or almost exclusively with Casimir, the settling in life of this adopted son, the securing of his future by a rich marriage, became for her a fixed idea. She only thinks of that. If she were to die, Casimir would have no means of livelihood. Casimir would be lost. Casimir would be incapable of directing himself. What he needs is a peaceful life in easy circumstances. (Many still limit their ambitions to such desires.) So she looked round her for the fiancée of whom she dreamed, she made inquiries, she worked out schemes. At one moment there was an idea of Caroline Collard, the daughter of Hermine whom we saw at the Palais Royal, and who had since been married to Jacques Collard, at that time deputy for the Aisne. But the plan came to nothing.

All the time Mme. de Genlis could not help recognising the fact that the obscure origin of Casimir necessarily limited his prospect of a brilliant marriage, and she tried to find a remedy for this drawback. She heard from someone that in Austria, according to a custom still in use in some of the French provinces, young Catholics, presenting themselves to receive the sacrament of Confirmation, were accompanied by a godfather. And it appeared that at Vienna the person confirmed adopted the name of his sponsor.

By the direction of his adopted mother, Casimir accordingly was confirmed at Vienna, and Mme. de Genlis claimed that he should call himself M. de Morald, after one of the names of the Prince de Ligne, who had been his sponsor at confirmation. Unfortunately Lamorald was not a surname but only a Christian name, and in fact Casimir used it as such after this.

In the beginning of 1812 Mme. de Genlis, by dint of ferreting everywhere and exhausting herself in the matrimonial quest, found herself on the eve of success. Witness the letter she wrote to Casimir on 29th January 1812, from which we take the following passage :—

"For my part, I have been employed only in looking for a wife for you, and besides Lucy I have five to propose to you. Amongst these there is a charming girl of seventeen, of whom I have as yet said nothing to you, because I had such slight hopes. She was at your last concert, and the thought of you is fixed firmly in her charming head. She is delightfully pretty, without being beautiful; but she has a face, a look, a smile that are matchless, and a very pretty figure. She is the only daughter of a man who adores her, and besides an honourable position has a settled income of 25,000 *livres*. I so thoroughly interested him by my account of your perfections and of all I mean to do for you, that he asked to be allowed to introduce his daughter to me. We talked much about you. I read for him, as if by chance, M. Jeckel's first letter. Those details about your studies delighted him. He repeated, 'That young man will go far.' He is a M. Carré (*sic*). . . . He has been for thirty years the chief doctor and administrator of the hospitals of Lyons."

Mme. de Genlis had in fact a year before discovered the lady who was to be the *fiancée* of Casimir—Mlle. Adèle Carret, whose father had become one of the leading councillors of the Cours des Comptes, and was a member of the Legion of Honour. The marriage took place on 19th November 1813.

Previously to it, in order to form a property for Casimir, who possessed nothing, she had sold to him by a deed drawn up and witnessed by Maître Morand, a Paris notary, on 2nd July 1812, "the full and entire personal property in all the literary works whatsoever produced and published either under her own name or under that of Sillery." She further tried to secure for him a source of profit by taking out a patent for a game of cards painted with flowers which she had invented.[1] Besides this, at the close of 1812 she asked for a sinecure for him, the post of Inspector of Publishing. Finally, being desirous of making some kind of a show, she moved into a fine suite of rooms in the Rue Ste. Anne, then known as the Rue Helvétius.[2] It was there that, living in better style, thanks to the sale of a herbarium with sketches in water-colours which the King of Westphalia, Jérome Bonaparte, had bought for 6000 francs, she began a new series of weekly receptions. On these days, if we are to believe her, her salon was never empty " from five in the afternoon till one o'clock in the morning ; without counting the days when there was music or they played proverbs." We may be sure that proverbs and romances were intended solely to bring Casimir to the front. But, on the other hand, the Inseparables continued to rally round their old friend. D'Estourmel tells us that he was then one of her favourites, with Anatole de Montesquiou and Brifaut. She called them laughingly her lovers, and she wrote : " At sixty I find I am able, like Mademoiselle de l'Espinasse, to love three lovers at once." It was a mere jest, with which no one would dream of reproaching her.

The marriage of Casimir marked the close of the musical and theatrical parties. With her mind for the present at rest as to the future of the young man, who had set up house at Ecouen, and at once gave up all work and settled down to a quiet life, Mme. de Genlis, it seemed, need only repose upon her laurels. Perhaps she would have done wisely if she had

[1] This curious card game consists of fifty-two cards grouped according to the flowers of the four seasons. The king, queen, and knave of each suit are represented by mythological personages. All the other cards each represent a plant or some flowers, the number of which corresponds to the value of the card. The pack, entirely original in design and workmanship, painted in water-colours by Mme. de Genlis, is a real curiosity of art. Mme. de Genlis subsequently gave it to a friend, the Marquise de Bourdeille, who had a literary and artistic salon about 1830. Thanks to the kindness of the Marquis de Bourdeille, we are able to give a specimen of it here.

[2] It was to Mme. de Genlis that the Rue Ste. Anne owed the resumption of its Christian name. She was proud and happy to obtain this by the intervention of M. de Charbonnières, the friend of the prefect.

shut up her desk. But could her active mind ever be at rest? At this time she was editing a little paper, the *Journal Imaginaire*, in which under the guise of imaginary works under the names of various authors, she sharply criticised the literary productions of the day.[1] And her great quarrel with the biographer Michaud was in full swing.

At all times Mme. de Genlis had a liking for controversy. She rightly considered that there was nothing more apt to keep alive public interest in connection with her name, and she liked it all the better when it gave her the opportunity of using her pen, like the sword of an apostle, against the *philosophes* and their disciples. Consumed with an ardent zeal for religion, animated with a bellicose devotion that was sometimes a little bitter, she acted at times as a Christian woman roused to anger and indignation by the Voltairianism of her times, and as an uncompromising champion of morality.

If she refused, then, to increase or even to sanction the influence of the *philosophes*, it was only her duty as a good Catholic, and it fell in with her inclinations.

When she was asked to contribute to Michaud's *Biographical Dictionary* her first care had been to ask who were the other contributors.

She saw on the list her enemies Auger and Suard, and thought she might tolerate them. But at the name of Ginguené, the agent of Voltaire and Diderot, she broke off the negotiation on the pretext of being too busy.

Nothing was more natural than that Mme. de Genlis, on being subsequently assured by the organisers of the work that Ginguené had been excluded from it, should reconsider her decision and accept a payment in advance. But when she found out that she had been misled by a mere pretence, and this was all it was, she withdrew her promise and sent back the money she had received. Nothing could be fairer.

" M. de la Borie wrote to me," she says, " that they had not been able to get rid of Ginguené, and that they hoped I would reconcile myself to this. I did nothing of the kind. . . .

[1] The *Journal Imaginaire* was begun at the Rue des Lions-St. Paul in 1812, and ceased to appear in 1813.

I sent back the money and got a receipt for it in regular form, and by this adventure all I gained was thirty fresh enemies, who still remain such for me."

But there also remained for her as a balance on the transaction a lot of articles on celebrated women, which she had prepared for the *Biographical Dictionary*.

These collected in a volume, with the addition of somewhat rambling commentaries, in which she ventured upon a hundred criticisms of Voltaire, Diderot, and false philosophy in language that was at once sharp and polished, formed her book on the influence of women on French literature (1811), a kind of handy dictionary of celebrated Frenchwomen, that began with Queen Radegonde, and came down to Mme. Cotin, passing in review all the queens of France on the way. But even more than the historical part, and the preface which was a plea for women authors, certain passages where personal feeling came out, excited an amused interest, as for example the pin-pricks aimed at the French Academy, which before this had preferred to honour Mme. d'Epinay as a teacher rather than Mme. de Genlis. "If there were an Academy of women in existence," she exclaims, "one ventures to say that it would find no difficulty in conducting itself better and coming to sounder judgements,"—an opinion of which we may well leave her all the responsibility.

It was a fine chance for the editors of Michaud's *Universal Biography* to reply to the disdainful treatment Mme. de Genlis had given them, and they took good care not to neglect it. They had their revenge, in well-written and severe reviews, by Auger (*Journal de l'Empire*) and Népomucène Lemercier (*Gazette de France*), amongst others.

To which Mme. de Genlis replied by a first pamphlet against the *Biographie Universelle*, soon followed by another.[1]

---

[1] See Genlis, *Examen critique de l'ouvrage intitulé Biographie universelle* and *Suite de l'examen critique* (Paris, Maradan, 1811). Mme. de Souza wrote to Mme. d'Albany on 22nd July 1811: "Madame de Genlis has had published to-day a little pamphlet in which she tries to show that she was right in her attacks on Fénelon, Madame Cotin, and Madame Necker. But she does not quite prove that it was her business to attack them" (cf. Pélissier, *op. cit.*, 107).

Auger, in the name of all its editors, and especially of Suard and Ginguené, replied with some cruel truths in a little work against Mme. de Genlis,[1] and she tried to have the last word in a third pamphlet.

She carried on the whole controversy cleverly and energetically. She made plenty of judicious criticisms. The *Biographie* fared badly. It had not many celebrated names in its list of contributors. Mme. de Genlis proclaimed its weakness in this respect in the plainest language, touching the tender spot.

She compared with the Voltairian group recruited by Michaud a number of names of those who, to her mind, could "if they liked" carry through a rival work in victorious competition against Michaud's enterprise. And her insight was absolutely remarkable.

Among the names she selected were: Delille, Bonald, Chateaubriand, Millevoye, Legouvé, Baour-Lormain, Mercier, Arnault, etc., who since that time have all most certainly won for themselves fame or at least celebrity.

The public—that is to say the literary public—followed with attentive interest the various phases of the quarrel. Begun in the month of August 1811, it went on through 1812, and made so much stir that the Minister Pomereuil, "an ardent *philosophe*," ordered the censorship to suppress forty pages of Mme. de Genlis's pamphlets. She did not hesitate to intervene with this powerful personage, and was received discourteously. "Why the devil, Madame," he exclaimed, "are not you tired of screeching against philosophy for thirty-five years? You have given yourself a lot of useless trouble in coming to see me!" Happily, she had some good friends to support her in the camp of religion—the Abbé Frayssinous, the future Bishop of Rodez, whose influence extended to a number of Catholics of good position since his famous conferences had first been forbidden and then authorised afresh; and Cardinal Maury, who still came to talk with her, though on rare occasions.[2] Besides

---

[1] L. S. Auger, *Ma brochure en réponse aux deux brochures de Madame de Genlis*.

[2] A letter of Mme. de Genlis to Cardinal Maury speaks of an evening they

this spiritual support she received many encouraging letters, among them one from M. Pieyre, whose admiration consoled her for her rude reception by the Minister. Finally, she obtained an imperial authorisation to produce an expurgated and corrected edition of the works of the Encyclopædists, and this was an official encouragement to continue the war against their detestable influence.

Meanwhile the political horizon was darkening with storm-clouds. There came news of the disastrous campaign in Russia. Then 1813 passed by, and France was invaded—the Allies attacked Paris—Marmont and Mortier signed the capitulation. The imperial Colossus was tottering, and at the same time, following the general movement that was detaching nearly all his old adherents from Napoleon, the enthusiasm of Mme. de Genlis took for its guide and model the man of the day, the contriver of the Restoration, and the chief actor on the stage at the moment—Talleyrand. Convinced, like so many others, that the Prince of Benevento would bring back the Bourbons and at the same time be their master, she addressed to him, on 6th April 1814, this long letter, in which she recommended Casimir for favours to come:—

"*The Comtesse de Genlis to Prince Talleyrand*

"At last we are seeing the *dénouement* of this long tragedy, of this pompous and sanguinary drama, of which the plot was so defective, so badly developed, and of which the incidents had so little probability. If anyone ever makes out of it a *historical romance* it will be very gloomy, and full of catastrophes and theatrical surprises, but there will be no common sense in it.

"After having thought a great deal about my actual position, I have called to mind that I lived fairly well for nine years in foreign countries with a little work. It is likely I have not now so long to live, and as I have enough for my needs I am giving up the idea of working for a newspaper, and certainly I shall not ask for a pension, even

had lately passed together, and leads one to believe that it was at the Countess's (cf. Mgr. Ricard, *Correspondance et Mémoires du Cardinal Maury*, t. ii.).

if they are giving such to several writers. I can very well
do without it. But I have just one favour to ask of you.
It will secure repose and happiness for the remainder of a
life which has been full of vicissitudes and hard work, a
life of bitter suffering caused by much ingratitude, a life of
persecutions and unjust treatment—in fact, my own. This
favour would be the granting of a place as Inspector-General
of the Post Office to Casimir. I am convinced that people
have prejudiced you against this young man. They cannot
have said that he is wanting in brains or talent, or that
he is a gambler or a libertine. But those who envy or
hate anyone attack his character when they cannot attack
his conduct. They will have told you that he is giddy,
imperious, violent, and that he is foppish. Ask Mme.
d'Harville, who has known him since his childhood, and
who has the tenderest affection for him, what he really is,
and she will tell you, like me and all those who know him,
that it is impossible for anyone to have more gentleness,
goodness, more of sound reason and most perfect feeling.
Because he made a few excursions on the roofs of the
Arsenal, and twice or thrice rode eighty leagues at headlong
speed, they said he would make me very unhappy; it is
generally by escapades like these that he makes one anxious.
I am far from approving of his conduct lately, when, while
fighting was in progress, he passed five hours on the battlefield collecting and carrying off the wounded, for he is
married, and even for my sake he ought not to have acted
thus. But I protest that he has never caused me any
trouble except in this way. They blame him for never
having reaped any advantage from his admirable talent;
but he loves the *art* and abhors the *trade*. He has too
much intellect, and that intellect is too cultivated,—he
has too much loftiness of soul, for a profession in which a
fortune is made by thinking only of money, and by devoting
oneself to a kind of society quite different from that which
he can really like. Besides, he wanted to pursue other
studies, to learn Latin, get through a great deal of reading,
and learn to write well. If he wished, he could be a very
distinguished man of letters. It is impossible to have more

wit, a better judgment, and more imagination. Finally, among a thousand good qualities he has two that are very rare —great frankness and perfect discretion. If you knew all that he is, you would judge him to be well fitted for more than one kind of public position. He knows German perfectly—it is his native language. He has neglected English, which he used to speak wonderfully well, but he would need only a couple of months to pick it all up again. And these serious studies have not led him to neglect his artistic talents. He composes like an angel; he is unequalled on the harp; he paints landscapes; he has a crowd of other agreeable talents. And he can acquire many more, for he is only twenty-four years of age. Such is the young man for whom I ask this position. He is married to one of the most charming creatures living. You will secure happiness for this young and interesting household and for me. I hope this will tempt you. My gratitude will be equal to my joy, and you can rest assured that after such a favour I shall never be so indiscreet as to make the least demand upon you. I have been inviolably attached to you from the depth of my soul since first I had the happiness of knowing you, and it would be most pleasing to me to owe to you the tranquillity of my life. Deign to send me a word in reply on this matter, so that I may be certain that you have received this letter. Remember that you have given me a right to count upon your kindness and friendship, and you will excuse this action of mine, and allow me to say to you that if you destroy the hopes that this gives me, you will make me very miserable. If you make this hope a reality, I cannot express to you how deeply I shall be touched, how happy and grateful I shall be. . . ."[1]

Is Mme. de Genlis to be accused of versatility?

Yesterday at the feet of Napoleon, she runs to the Bourbons as soon as the news of their restoration seems to be certain. Quite happy at returning to Royalist ideas, " which I have always held," she says ingenuously, " as all

[1] Unpublished letter, British Museum, Add. MSS.

my works prove "—she was among the first of those who acclaimed on the Boulevards the return of the Comte d'Artois on 12th April 1814.

She might boast that she had never frequented the Imperial Court—for lack of an invitation, but she did not say that—and she went to pay her homage at the Tuileries as soon as Louis XVIII. announced that he would receive all the ladies. In this our Countess followed the example, not only of the people of Paris, but also of the marshals, of the Emperor's oldest comrades in arms, of Talleyrand, and of M. de Valence. The latter, after being made a senator and general of division in 1805, had signed the resolution for the Emperor's deposition, and at the first Restoration was given a seat in the Chamber of Peers. All these had not, to an equal extent with Mme. de Genlis, the excuse—always the same, alas!—of their means of livelihood being in danger, for now that Napoleon had fallen and left France, a time of anxious uncertainty had again begun for her.

The same motive—with some mingling, however, of affection and attachment—made her go to the Duke of Orleans and Mme. Adélaide almost as soon as they returned to the Palais Royal, now half dismantled. Aided by the pleasant memories of Bellechasse, she hoped to renew the relations that had been broken off during the time of the emigration, but also, as respectfully as possible, to put forward her claim to her retiring allowance as governess.

Ripened by sorrow and exile the Princes had somewhat forgotten the tutorship of Mme. de Genlis. They had left that world in which she had kept them young, they had found themselves, and they saw life with other eyes than those of the past. And their welcome showed signs of all this. Only that Marie Amélie was so kind and gracious, and in her delight at knowing her husband's old teacher, embraced her and addressed friendly words to her, the first interview would have been rather cold and stiff. Matters improved later. In 1816 we find Mme. de Lage, then at Figuières with the Duchess of Orleans, noting that between the mother and the daughter " a shadow continually interposes—that of La Genlis. The pupil is still under the evil influence of her teacher."[1] Mme. de Genlis had therefore been able, without much difficulty, to re-establish the current of sympathy between herself and her pupils by means of long letters to Mademoiselle and to the Duke of Orleans.

At the end of June the Prince sent word that he was going to make a visit to his former "Governor." Then, being obliged to defer it, he wrote Pieyre a two-page letter full of affectionate sentiments and of his desire to contribute to the happiness of Mme. de Genlis, etc.

On 3rd July 1814, Mademoiselle sent her word that she would come on the following Monday.

Nay, even the Dowager Duchess, generously forgetting her grievances of the past, in her great goodness renewed her friendly relations with her former enemy. So Mme. de Genlis writes to Casimir—

"DEAR CHILD,—All goes well. You have no idea of the success of my novel, the *Marais Pontins*[2] in every way. The Duchess of Orleans was very much touched by it. I had not sent it to her, but she bought it. She sent M. de Folmont to me this morning. It is the greatest proof of good feeling for me that she could have given. He spent an hour *tête-à-tête* with me, and he was most politely obliging and friendly. He told me that the Duchess would see me with the greatest pleasure, meeting me by myself as I had asked, as soon as she was free from the people to whom she was giving receptions morning and evening. This would be within eight days. She would then be able to close her doors in the mornings. . . ."[3]

But these undeniable proofs of politeness would not supply the means of livelihood at a moment when she was absolutely without funds, and when the troubled state of public affairs caused general mistrust, and hermetically sealed up money boxes and purses.

How could she think of being able to sell new manuscripts

---

[1] Comtesse de Reinach-Foussemagne, *op. cit.*, 242.
[2] *Les Hermites des Marais Pontins* (1814).
[3] Lapauze, *op. cit.*, p. 230.

at a time when the allied troops were encamped in France, and when the Government's want of financial credit made every one timid? The times were hard for those who, like Mme. de Genlis, were living almost from hand to mouth, and were unable, or did not know how, to cut down expenses.

The greatest expense was that of her rooms. So, at the end of April 1814, she had left the Rue Ste. Anne, and then made several moves one after another. In July we find she has taken refuge at Ecouen, with Casimir, who himself was living on his wife's resources—the allowance made by her father, Councillor Carret, to the young couple.

In this temporary shelter, expecting every day some proof of Talleyrand's interest and of that of the Princes her pupils, she worked industriously at new books. But nothing came from the Rue St. Florentin, where certainly there were other affairs than those of Mme. de Genlis to be thought of; and nothing either from the Palais Royal. It was at Ecouen, no doubt, that, weary and full of anxiety, she became more imploringly urgent in her petitions, and on 10th July 1814, wrote the Prince of Benevento this letter full of infinite distress—

"My position has been frightful since the Duke of Orleans went away. I have had neither pension, nor income, nor resources of any kind; I have lived only by borrowing and pawning things. . . . If the King grants pensions to literary people, it seems to me that I can put forward better claims than most. However modest it was it would be enough for me, even if it were only 1200 francs. Your decision in this matter will do everything. Think of my position; and that I am sixty-nine years old; deign to remember that you have permitted me to be your friend and to count upon your kindness. I am without any resources. . . . etc."[1]

This same letter announced another great work that she had in preparation, her *Histoire de Henri* IV., begun in eager haste with a view to winning the good graces of Louis XVIII., "for it is full of allusions that are flattering to the Bourbons and very damaging to Bonaparte."

[1] Cf. Charavay, *Amateur d'Autographes*, No. 125, 1st March 1867.

Unfortunately, events wrecked all her forecasts. The *Histoire de Henri le Grand* was ready just too late. It was issued by the publisher on 20th March 1815, the very day that Napoleon, returning from the island of Elba, made his triumphant entry into the capital.

Thunderstruck, Mme. de Genlis tried to parry this fresh blow of fate by a letter to the Emperor, for which fifteen years later she offered her excuses to posterity. "It was," says the *Memoirs*, "the only letter in all my life in which I made use of flattery." And what better way than that of praise was there for reminding Napoleon of the interrupted correspondence, and the pension attached to it?

We need not be surprised that the Emperor had not time to think of such a trifling person as Mme. de Genlis.

He was never again to give any sign of life to the correspondent of his great days, who now fell back into the most painful poverty.

Casimir gave her some trifling support, but he had no great means. He was now living at Mantes, in the Rue aux Pois, and trying to get pupils for the harp.[1] Overstrained, weakened by work and anxiety, Mme. de Genlis fell ill at Mantes—hence an increase of expenses (for the illness lasted six weeks), and hence loans "at usurious rates." To complete her ill fortune, Louis XVIII. refused to continue the pension the Emperor had granted her. It was a period of dark adversity, in the midst of which many would have lost all courage. But she, with her marvellous energy, her old habit of holding out, soon pulled herself together again.

Who would help her? The Abbé de Cabre? He was too much in the disfavour of Talleyrand. As soon as her strength would allow, she began a new campaign of petitions. Her post as Governess of a Prince of the Blood Royal gave her a right to an annual retiring allowance of 12,000 francs. The Duke of Orleans at last granted her one of 8000, and, besides, got into the way of sending her a present of 2000 on New Year's Day.

Talleyrand gave proof once more that he was capable of pity by buying a box of manuscripts from her for 20,000

[1] Note from M. Grave of Mantes.

francs—rough drafts of novels and romances, "useless and very useless papers," which he gave the same day to the Princess Helène de Bauffremont, who had an ardent desire to possess them.

Refurnished with money, Mme. de Genlis ceased to be an expense to Casimir, and at the end of 1816 she returned to Paris. But instead of setting up again in a fashionable quarter, she chose a place of retirement, far from noise and agitation, in the house of the Carmelites of Vaugirard.

But what was this convent ? Who were these Carmelites? Up to the time of the Revolution we find no trace of them at Vaugirard, and it was not until the reign of Louis Philippe that the order was temporarily installed at No. 86 rue de Vaugirard. Contemporary publications throw no light on the question; and the *Memoirs* of Mme. de Genlis give only the topographical clue of placing the convent in the neighbourhood of the Abbaye-aux-Bois. But an English lady who visited the author of *Adèle et Théodore* in 1817 is more explicit, and speaks of the chapel, "a mournful monument of the massacre of bishops and priests in 1792," as being separated only by a low wall from the garden of the Carmelites.[1]

The reference is plainly to the old house of the "Carmes."

Now, at the time of the massacres, the Carmes stood between two houses of nuns, the Benedictines of the Blessed Sacrament and Notre Dame de Consolation; but there was no Carmelite convent there. But the clue to the mystery lies in the identification of the existing Catholic Institute of Paris with the former monastery of the Carmes.

In fact, the monastery and its garden—after having been abandoned by the monks after September 1792, confiscated as national property, then let by the Convention to a gardener who erected a drinking-bar and dancing-room under the aged trees; transformed into a state prison, then into a barrack, then into the official printing office of the Directory, then once more, at least as far as the garden was concerned, converted into a dancing place, a *bal des Zephyrs*, then bought by a joiner—were at last bought back on 15th August 1797 by the brave Mlle. de Soyecourt, a Carmelite

[1] Lady Morgan, *La France*, ii. 319.

nun. Her father and mother had been imprisoned under Robespierre and were both dead, the former guillotined on the 5th Thermidor, the latter dying of the hardships of imprisonment at Ste. Pélagie. Sister Camille de Soyecourt repaired the buildings as best she could, and, being joined by some other former Carmelite nuns, little by little restored the Order.

Further purchases enabled her to regain possession of the gardens and out-buildings of the Carmes, then the houses abutting on the Rue de Vaugirard, in which she installed " some pious ladies who devoted themselves to the education of young girls." [1]

In 1817 the chapel of the martyrs, which had been opened for two years to the veneration of the faithful, had become a place of pilgrimage. It was separated from the convent by a low wall and a garden known as " the great garden." On the other side of this wall, in the enclosure of the convent, and attached to the main building where the nuns lived, there was a little building, a kind of wing, in which rooms were let to lay women who wished to live there in silence and peace. It looked out upon a narrow strip of grassy lawn. It was to this little building, which was not subject to the rule of enclosure of the convent, that Mme. de Genlis retired. When she was at Bellechasse she had known Mlle. de Soyecourt, who was then a boarder in a convent, the garden of which was next to that in which the Orleans children took their recreation, and a slight bond of friendship had united them. This was renewed in 1817. Mme. de Genlis went gladly to this retirement, pleased to be once more in a place that memory made dear to her, for the convent of the Daughters of the Precious Blood, where she was living at the time of her marriage, had stood only a few steps away at the corner of the rue Casette.

And those who were good at gossip, including old Mme. de la Reynière, still in vigorous health and always hostile to Mme de Genlis, said that she had gone there to end her days in monastic observances " disappointed with the vanities of the world and the false hope of celebrity."

[1] Abbé Pisani, *La Maison des Carmes*, 1610–1875.

But if we are to credit Lady Morgan,[1] Mme. de Genlis's room still blossomed strangely with the perfumes of the world. "Her apartment might pass for the oratory of a saint or for the boudoir of a coquette." The English woman thought she was in some region of romance. She mistook, it seems, for a "beautiful bedstead in the Greek style" the commonest of bedsteads in mahogany veneer, and for "draperies of blue silk," an old bed quilt. But, after all, the beautiful gilded harp, always kept in tune, the alabaster vases, the fresh flowers everywhere, the piano heaped with new music, seemed elegant trifles beside the great crucifix of ivory, that Pius VII. had asked to see during his forced stay in Paris, and the chaplets and rosaries hanging on the walls, one of which was regarded as a priceless relic because a few days before his death Fénelon had held it in his hands as he prayed. And then the many books, scattered on shelves and tables, were a testimony to the serious side of the mind of the woman who lived in this cell, and their titles paid homage to her indestructible faith, that had been made more ardent by the recollection of the errors of her youth.

In the midst of these studious surroundings Mme. de Genlis, still keeping her good looks, erect, and with her bright eyes lighting up the worn features of her face, seemed to set time at defiance. And, nevertheless, violent nerve pains, the result of the intellectual overstrain to which as a diligent worker she condemned herself, were almost entirely depriving her of sleep. Bent all day long over her writing-table,[2] seldom receiving visitors, and still more rarely going out, she might be supposed to have retired from the world. If one wished to see her and enjoy the charm of her conversation, one had to write to her more than once, renew one's request, and finally come and ask for her at her room. It was thus Lady Morgan, anxious to meet the celebrated French

---

[1] Lady Morgan, *op. cit.*, 324.

[2] She published during the fifteen months of her stay at the Carmelites her famous abridgment of Dangeau, for by persevering efforts she had at last obtained the use of the manuscript; and, besides, she published her romance *Les Battuecas*, three stories, etc.

woman, penetrated to her presence, and that Mme. de Krudener made her acquaintance and succeeded in making her very interested in her. But for a long time Mme. de Genlis had shown herself disinclined to satisfy the curiosity of strangers. Even at the Arsenal she had written to the Abbé de Cabre, "Allow me to tell you, dear friend, that I would be greatly embarrassed if Madame d'Albany brought to me ladies who are unknown to me. I am continually declining such visits. If they want to come and hear some music, well and good, but if it is only *to see me*, I am not worth the trouble, and it is no pleasure to me to receive people who have only this trivial curiosity, and besides have no wish to make friends with me."[1]

She might have made friends with her neighbour Mme. de Vilette, the famous " beautiful and good lady " of Voltaire, who seems to have shown her desire to be neighbourly by kindly letters and even by an invitation to dinner. But Mme. de Genlis took her stand in obstinate coolness, and out of her horror for Voltaire kept Mme. de Vilette at a distance.

Besides, she limited her goings out to some flying visits to the Abbaye-aux-Bois, where Madame Récamier held her Court, and where Paméla had gone into respectable retirement, the Orleans family paying for her board and lodging—four thousand francs—which in this way were beyond the reach of seizure by her creditors.

The adopted daughter had made advances to the ex-governess. But there was an ill-concealed coldness between them. On the side of Paméla it took the form of an air of mistrust, a kind of rancour and disregard. It seems that she held Mme. de Genlis responsible for her actual position.

On the part of the latter, it was inspired by prudence. For the widow of Fitzgerald was a source of anxiety to the royal police. She was the subject of unfavourable official reports. In 1815 she was said to be "receiving in her rooms in the rue St. Lazare many persons known for their bad political opinions, General Grouchy, M. de Pontecoulant," etc. A report of 16th November 1816 makes out that "she has an

[1] L. G. Pélissier, *Lettres inédites de Madame de Genlis*.

understanding with the Orleanist party and receives considerable sums from them."

This report is based on some small sums that Mme. Adélaïde had lent to her to stop the proceedings of a creditor, besides the pension for board and lodging at the Abbaye-aux-Bois, which was paid directly by M. Pieyre. The loans were the result of her still finding the means of contracting debts that entailed legal proceedings.

Worried by creditors, and suffering from a rheumatic pain in the head that mostly forced her to keep to her room, Paméla was nevertheless always dreaming of love.

Soon she will have herself carried off by the Duc de la Force, and taken to the elegant Villa Chambord at Montauban. There she will be seen as late as 1880, in the satin costume of a Watteau shepherdess, watching sheep decked out with ribbons and roses, like a heroine of the Golden Age.[1]

But at the Abbaye, as long as she stayed there, Mme. de Genlis visited her regularly, and this enabled her to become more intimate with Mme. Récamier, who, moreover, sometimes visited her at the Carmelites.

[1] Cf. Vicomte de Reiset, *Anne de Caumont la Force*, p. 386.

CHAPTER IV

THE LAST PHASE OF MME. DE GENLIS

THE last period of the life of Mme. de Genlis was entirely taken up with literature and religion.

All her anxiety in these last years turned upon her writings and the question of putting her own conscience, and the consciences of those who were near to her, in order. Her fame as an author placed her in communication with literary people of all kinds, and, as we shall see, she knew at this time all the literary celebrities of the first part of the nineteenth century. The ardour of her devotion placed her in the front of the anti-Voltairean movement, which Chateaubriand had inaugurated, and her heart was set on marking her position in it by writings and literary enterprises directed against the Encylcopædia and the Encyclopædists.

It was a noble occupation, befitting a closing life, and a woman who was now free from all family life. Her granddaughters had long since married, Félicie de Valence to the Count de Vischer de Celles, a Belgian nobleman, then one of Napoleon's prefects. "It was autumn and springtime," said Brifaut. Rosamonde de Valence had married Marshal Gérard. Anatole de la Woestine had retired to his father's house in Belgium. He had joined the Royalists in 1814, making an exaggerated display of decorations and crosses, and his new friends had persuaded Louis XVIII. to dispense with his services. The Marquis du Crest was living at Meung-sur-Loire, on a pension for which the House of Orleans had kept him waiting three years, until by threatening them with a law-suit and revelations he secured with great trouble 4000 francs, which might have been more but for his making a disadvantageous compromise. The ex-Chancellor of the Palais Royal consoled himself by dreaming of his beloved inventions and of the marriage which (to her misfortune) his daughter Georgette had contracted with the musician Bochsa. As long as Mme. de Montesson lived, Georgette du Crest, protected by her and introduced to the Empress Josephine, passed a fairly happy time. After the death of the Marchioness, who did not leave her even the smallest legacy, she bravely prepared herself for an artistic career, in order to make a living and educate her daughter Coraly, in whom Mme. Adélaide no longer took any interest.

Mme. de Montesson died, on 3rd February 1817, after a long illness, at her splendid country house at Romainville,—she had let her mansion in the Chaussée d'Antin to Ouvrard. She was cared for by Mme. de Valence, who was then living with her, and by Mme. de Genlis, who was so devoted as to spend four or five hours a day at her aunt's bedside. She showed very poor gratitude for the care of her nurses, and even at the point of death gave further proof of the antipathy with which her mother had long ago inspired her for the Mezières and their descendants.

Under the influence of this feeling, and especially of her affectionate preference for M. de Valence, the last will of Mme. de Montesson was a monument of injustice.

Mme. de Genlis and the Marquis du Crest were disinherited for the benefit of Valence, who was made almost sole legatee. As if out of pity, she left each of them a mere 20,000 francs. Anatole de la Woestine received " the legacy one might have left to a lackey,"—4000 francs. Moreover, M. de Valence, who, according to Georgette du Crest, had the bad taste to draw up the will, far from doing anything to mitigate its results, asserted against Du Crest a charge of old date upon his 20,000 francs, and went so far as to refuse to let him have even a picture, the work of the Marquise de Montesson. After the death of the lady, Mme. de Valence spent most of her time with one of her daughters. Then the pupils of Mme. de Genlis had left her one after the other. Casimir, married as we have said, and now father of a family, was living at Ecouen. Stéphanie d'Alyon was also married. Alfred Le Maire had been sent by his benefactress to Belgium. She had now no one near her except M. de Valence, for whom she still kept some secret affection. And in 1819 she went to stay at his mansion, No. 9 Rue Pigalle. Before that, tired of the Carmelites, she had returned to Casimir's home at Ecouen, where her mind was haunted by the plan she had so often formed of owning a house of her own, shaded with trees, which she could later on leave to her beloved Casimir. This went so far that she conceived the idea of asking Louis XVIII. for it in these terms:—

"Sire,—I am over seventy-one, and with my health enfeebled by prolonged work and great troubles. For myself I only long for solitude and a little rest. But in whatever part of Paris I might stay I would not find the tranquillity that I need.

"There are at Versailles, besides the rooms of the palace, a large number of vacant apartments, which are at your Majesty's disposal, amongst others the whole of the Hôtel d'Angeviliers. It is there that I would like to end my days. But I would never have taken the liberty of troubling your Majesty with a request merely for a lodging for myself, which perhaps would be only for a few days. I could not have been induced to take this step only for something that I have greatly at heart.

"Seventeen years ago I brought back from Germany a boy from Berlin who was then eight years of age. To me he owes his religion, his education, the most brilliant talents, the cultivation of a mind that nature had made capable of acquiring and assimilating everything. To me he owes the cultivation of a soul that is in a high degree exalted and beautiful, and has the noblest feelings; to me he owes a marriage that makes him happy, and I owe to him all the consolations and pleasures of my home life for the last twelve years. But the arrangements I have made as to my works will not suffice for me to purchase a little country house, and nevertheless all my happiness depends on ending my life with him, and thinking that I shall leave him after I am gone the enjoyment of the quiet refuge where we will have together cultivated literature and art, and where he will have received my last lessons and my last breath. So the favour I venture to ask of your Majesty is a place of residence at Versailles given to me under his name,—granted to Casimir Boecker. It is only under this condition that I would enjoy it or have any desire for it. This favour would produce no public effect. I would confine myself to saying that I had obtained a lodging at Versailles, and this is all that people would know or say. If your Majesty—with a condescension that one can hope for from you alone—deigns to grant me this favour, there will be nothing wanting to my happiness and nothing equal to my gratitude. How greatly I shall then enjoy a tranquillity that I have long desired in vain, and which will be so honourable for me, because it will be a favour from your Majesty.—I am, etc. . . ."[1]

It was a prettily worded petition. Roederer, who had received such things at Naples, including one from the Comtesse, and who read the document while playing cards with the King, said that "there was not a writer of begging letters in all Italy who better knew her business." Nevertheless Louis XVIII. was deaf to her request, and Mme. de Genlis, taken once more with her liking for changes, moved again, returned to Paris, and put up in the Faubourg St. Honoré. Without being aware of it, she was coming back to the unsettled humour of her early youth. Her last years were like a continual moving. One might say that she has hardly taken up her abode in a neighbourhood before she began to dislike it. Restless, haunted by the fear of death, she believed, says a gossiping historian, that she might escape the grim visitor by changing her address.

In fact, in the twelve years from 1818 to her death, she was jumping about Paris from district to district, so that she lived in more than fifteen different places, without counting her visits to the country—to Marshal Gérard's home at the Château of Villers, to Mme. de Custine's at Fervacques, to Mme. de Grollier's at Epinay, and elsewhere.

[1] B.N. MSS., *Nouvelles acquisitions françaises*, 1304.

At the end of 1818 we find her living in the Rue Neuve des Petits Champs, and in the summer of 1819 she went for a country holiday to Villers. This visit gave her the opportunity of consulting General Gérard, whose opinion she greatly valued, on a family affair that was troubling her.

The fact was that Anatole de la Woestine was making a claim for the payment of his mother's dowry, 100,000 francs, of which the half not actually paid over was a charge on the inheritance of M. de Genlis, which, it will be remembered, was administered by M. de Valence. Now, the young man declared that he had been deprived of his rights, and talked of nothing less than beginning a law-suit against M. de Valence.

Mme. de Genlis recognised that Anatole had very serious claims to put forward, and General Gérard agreed with her. She tried to act as a mediator, and wrote from Villers to her grandson. But Valence would not listen to reason, and became obstinate, and the matter could not be arranged. Seeing this, the grandmother went to pass the autumn with Henriette at Carlepont. But on her return to Paris, having no place of her own, she asked M. de Valence for hospitality, and he granted it to her " with all possible grace."

In going to stay at the Rue Pigalle, Mme. de Genlis was influenced by two important motives. She hoped to bring Valence to an agreement with young La Woestine, and in the second place to attempt his conversion, to help him to die well.

She expected to settle the former affair in three weeks, but at the end of that time nothing had been done. M. de Valence fell seriously ill, and then she only occupied herself with the second point. A man who, to use the conventional phrase, enjoyed " life," a lover of good cheer and pleasure, a reckless gambler, he had during all the years he had lived been a proof of that saying of La Bruyère that the rich delight in excess. Worn out and wearied, with his constitution like that of an old man, and tried by the campaigns of Spain and Russia, he broke down rapidly under the final strain that his attempts to enjoy the heritage of Mme. de Montesson entailed upon him. He was dying of having

" lived " too much. A Peer of France, reestablished in the good graces of royalty after temporary disgrace following on the Hundred Days, he had been living in grand style. But in the midst of all his opulence and dignity he would have been left uncared for if Mme. de Genlis had not come to his help. And he kept on saying that he would die if she left him.

Mme. de Genlis stayed with him. " Besides," she says, " M. de Valence had taken that strong liking to me that all people when seriously ill have had for me." [1]

She had lodged at first in the top floor of the mansion in a large room which commanded a magnificent view and had splendid air. But to be nearer the invalid she came down to the lowest storey. The treatment was easy for her to superintend, for it consisted only in a severely plain diet. But as Valence did not come to table, Mme. de Genlis, out of a thoughtful wish to spare trouble, took her meals with her lady companion at the *table d'hôte* of a pension, kept by ladies who once ranked as aristocrats, but had been ruined by the Revolution.

It was during this stay with her son-in-law that, at his request, and to please him, she had her portrait painted by Mme. Chéradame.

However, Mme. de Genlis had not obtained any practical result as yet with regard to her two great objects. She saw at the end of three months of regular treatment that M. de Valence seemed to be regaining strength, and he soon began to take supper again at the Café Robert, to stay up late, and to play for high stakes. But as she was being suffocated in her apartment in the entresol storey, badly ventilated as it was, with a low ceiling, " a regular barrack room," where the working of a pump close by woke her up at daybreak, he offered to give up to his mother-in-law his own room," the only good one in the house," and to remove to the fifth floor. She would not consent to this, and preferred to get a change of air by taking rooms at the Bains de Tivoli.

This did not last long. After a short time Valence

[1] Genlis, *Mémoires*, iv. 218.

sent word to her that if she refused his request it was quite certain that he would fall ill again and die. So she came back to the little room in the entresol. Her way of life then depended on that of the general. She visited his friends, presided in his salon, received his guests with him, went out with him, and accompanied him to the *cabaret*. She appeared at the magnificent dinners given by M. de Valence to his colleagues of the Chamber of Peers—dukes, generals and other political friends, all Liberals, wildly eager for thorny discussions in which old Mme. de Genlis was not allowed a word. She gives us an amusing account of one of these dinners, at which the guests, amongst whom were four peers, four marshals and three generals, talked nothing but politics from one end of the table to the other without taking any notice of her. When they went to the salon they seated themselves in a circle in armchairs, without any further care for Mme. de Genlis, and began to discuss affairs of state. "They shouted loudly enough to deafen one," she says; "they interrupted each other, quarrelled and made themselves hoarse. . . . It was a perfect image of the Chamber of Deputies."

It must be said that they did not consider her as one of themselves, as they were Liberals and she an extremist on the other side. But by a curious chance the extremists called her a "phrase-monger," no doubt out of dislike for the speeches addressed to the Chamber of Peers that she composed for Valence. Notwithstanding these differences of opinion, and thanks in some degree to her position at Mme. de Valence's, Mme. de Genlis was nevertheless very much in fashion in the year 1820.

Whatever opinion one might have as to the value of her works, her name, surrounded as it was with the respectful consideration that comes of celebrity, counted for much. It recalled the perfume of a period of politeness and good taste of which she was one of the few survivors. It counted to her credit that she had depicted in her historical romances the manners and tone of the Court, of which after the license of the Directory one could only form an idea in imagination.

Besides, in spite of current talk, Mme. de Genlis was a

moralist. The errors of her youth had not prevented her from always defending the principles of an irreproachable code of morals founded on the Gospel. Since her return to France she had always taken up this position more strongly, and she might well be pardoned if in her struggle against the Encyclopædists she had sometimes been too declamatory in her argument. It now seemed that her only object in writing was this defence of good morals. Everyone in the literary circles of Paris knew of her project of recasting the *Encyclopédie*, purifying it and remodelling it. Meanwhile, in expectation of the time when she would be in a position to carry out her plan, she published an expurgated edition of *Émile*, with appropriate notes dealing with the dangerous passages or ridiculing them. And she repeated this kind of criticism, but with reference to her contemporaries, in a little monthly magazine which she founded under the title of *L'Intrépide*.

Slight as may be the influence that is now assigned to the *Intrépide*, it was not at the time disdained by men of letters, or even by writers of genius. Chateaubriand and Lamartine—to name only these—attached a good deal of value to its support. Chateaubriand was so pleased at Mme. de Genlis having praised his little work on the death of the Duc de Berri, that he wrote to her on 27th May 1820, " Your indulgence, Madame la Comtesse, is the result of your talents. You are willing to give me a share of your own fame. I accept the present because it comes from you "; and Lamartine showed much disappointment at her having criticised his first *Méditations*. It did not matter that she recommended him to Madame Adélaïde.—If she speaks truly, it was this recommendation that disposed those in high places to name Lamartine an attaché to the Embassy at Florence. But a poet does not readily pardon anyone who has written of him that he does not belong to a good school, that his expressions are ill chosen and obscure, his verses ambitious, and his phrases formed at haphazard.[1]

[1] Genlis, *Mémoires*, vi. 178-180. She says also of Lamartine (vii. 79): " I had praised exceedingly his talents and his poetry, and I had criticised with much politeness some really ridiculous verses. . . . It was infinitely

On the other hand, Astolphe de Custine was made famous by Mme. de Genlis, and did not thank her for it. This singular young man, of a capricious disposition and an unhealthy and presumptuous spirit, inspired her from the first with an ardent interest. She had made his acquaintance in May 1819 at the house of old Mme. de St. Julien, a last survivor of Ferney and still a brilliant conversationalist at the age of ninety-two. Perhaps it was because Astolphe reminded her of the tastes of old times, and recalled the memory of that poor friend of her youth, the Vicomtesse de Custine, and of the Comte, her brother-in-law, who had been in love with Mme. de Genlis before the days of the Palais Royal.

She at once regarded the young man as belonging to her; she had an idea of protecting him, of lecturing him, of becoming his literary guide, of all which he made fun later on. But in the first stage of their acquaintance young Custine was delighted at the interest Mme. de Genlis took in him. She began a literary correspondence with him, and wrote to him: ". . . I shall not say a word to you about *friendship*. Every line of this letter speaks to you of that with which you have inspired me, for all this good advice would be very ridiculous if it were not dictated by the most affectionate feeling. I love at once or never. I have predicted that you will be an extraordinary man. You will make pass me for a sorceress. I am quite prepared for it; I have already the age of a Sibyl, and, thanks to you, it will be admitted that I have also the prescience of one. . . ."[1] Young Astolphe, won by her charm, confided in her, sent her verses and asked for her advice.

"It was not the fault of Madame de Genlis," writes the biographer of Mme. de Custine-Sabran, "that she did not inspire the grandson of her friend with a long-out-of-date

trying to me to show such impartiality towards an author who, when *himself* sending me his work, had with his own hand written on the first page: 'M. de Lamartine begs Madame la Comtesse de Genlis to accept this very slight homage of his respect for her and his admiration for her genius.' "

[1] Unpublished letter, B.N. MSS. Français, *Nouvelles acquisitions*, 1304.

affection," [1] and she never suspected the cynical ingratitude of which he gave proof later on. Perhaps he felt ill-will for her on account of the failure of her project of uniting him in marriage with the daughter of the General's widow, Mme. Moreau, a splendid match, very favourably regarded in Royalist circles and much desired by Astolphe. At the request of Mme. de Custine the Countess had in fact undertaken the negotiations, but, happily for Mlle. Moreau, an obstacle—the reluctance of the General's widow to part with her daughter—broke them off at the decisive moment. The disappointment of young Custine was very great, but the curious thing was that his friends in Germany, especially Rachel Levin (now Mme. de Varnhagen), who had known Mme. de Genlis at Berlin, were active in turning him against her. Rachel indeed wrote to Custine at this moment: " Your mother, that dear lady, cannot be happier than I am at this rupture. Believe me, that intriguing woman (Mme. de Genlis) will not be easily tired out. You will have only too many experiences of the same kind." [2]

For the moment Astolphe was offering incense to the old Countess, and this too in verse. In this matter he was in competition with his uncle, M. de Sabran; going to the Princesse de Vaudémont to read her the letter of Mme. de Genlis to Mlle. d'Orléans on her old watch, and replying with a pleasant madrigal with old-fashioned and witty grace in it. M. de Sabran, as his contribution, rhymed the two stanzas, which she reproduces in her *Memoirs*. At the same time, Anatole de Montesquiou, another cavalier-in-waiting, dedicated to her a rondeau in the same affected style. All this was a far-off echo of the eighteenth century. One might have imagined oneself to be still in the times of the Boufflers, the Latteignants, the St. Lamberts.

And it was indeed this vanished time that Mme. de Genlis reminded one of. They came to her to breathe its perfume, like that of a faded sachet whose scent recalls old memories. And writers especially, and not the least of them, felt themselves attracted to her. Besides her old friends of the

---
[1] A. Bardoux, *Madame de Custine*, 367.
[2] Quoted by Bardoux, p. 368.

Arsenal, many another asked for the favour of being received at the Rue Pigalle.

There was M. de Bonald, whom the Chevalier d'Harmensen had to introduce to her. Many years were to go by, it is true, before the austere philosopher knocked at her door. There was Lacépède, at whose table she dined with M. de Valence. There was M. de Lingré, a youthful moralist, the author of a very good book of maxims. There was Delille; and the Duc de Bassano; and Pougens. Fiévée, whom some difference kept for a while apart from her, sought a reconciliation, and Mme. de Genlis, who liked very much to hear him talk politics, gladly agreed to it. M. de Norvins read her his verses. They all greatly appreciated her judgment, her good sense, her conversation, and came to talk with her; and besides these there were learned men like M. de Sommariva, the Baron Vivant-Denon, Count Arthur de Bouillé, M. de Courchamps, Baron Trouvé, the Abbé Desmazures; men of rank like Lord Bristol, Sir Sidney Smith, the Duke of Mecklenburg, and better still, the Grand Duke Paul of Wurtemberg; and the pleiad of young poets who submitted their verses or dedicated them to her. So when, in 1821, the *Genlisiana* appeared, it added nothing to the fame of her whom it sought to depict; the traits of character and the actions of which it reminded its readers had long been public property. They had not the attraction of novelty, and they could not harm a celebrated woman nearly eighty years of age, who had an established reputation as a writer on moral questions. Besides, as if to guarantee her position, the Orleans Princes kept on excellent terms with their former Governess, and the Duchesse de Bourbon had up to the day of her death lavished marks of friendship upon her. Among all who knew her one voice only was raised in support of malignant attacks upon her, and to the general surprise that was the voice of Paméla. That dislike to be near her mother by adoption which we saw in her in 1808, had ten years later become a kind of underhand ill-will against her, which grew stronger, and, cherished in secret, at last broke out without a trace of restraint. On what subject and in what connection? Paméla had got the idea of asserting to Mme.

Adélaide some supposed rights of her own to the favours of the Orleans family. It certainly had something to do with the secret of her birth. And this in itself was enough to result in her being ignominiously driven away from the Palais Royal by the indignant Princess, who sent word to her that she wished never again to see the intriguer or to hear a word about her.

M. Pieyre had written " four furious pages " to Mme. de Genlis on the subject. He expressed for Paméla, " for her infamous lies and her inconceivable hypocrisy, the uttermost degree of contempt."

" Good heavens ! " exclaimed Mme. de Genlis in a letter to Casimir, " is it of this person whom I once loved so much that I now write thus, not only without mortal sorrow, but with a kind of pleasure ! "

In fact, any friendly feeling between the two women had, after long weakening, at last broken its last link. It had become very strained, very frail, and all correspondence between them now ceased

Mme. de Genlis—more lonely than ever, for the Abbé de Cabre had died in the course of 1821—now turned her attention again to M. de Valence. It was a case of helping this man, who had seen too much of " life," to die a decent death. And his state of health was deplorable, and made worse by continual excesses and imprudences in his way of living. It could not fail to inspire anxiety about him.

Gangrene had shown itself and was making rapid progress in his limbs, so that everything indicated that the end must come soon.

It will be remembered that at an earlier date Mme. de Genlis had attempted the conversion of Valence; and her zeal against the Encyclopædists had had some influence on the mind of the old pleasure-seeker. She persuaded him to adopt certain good practices—the abstinence on Fridays and Saturdays, the Mass on Sundays, and some reading; but there was a long way from this to a sincere conversion, and his temporary recovery had banished far off all thoughts of religion. When she found that he was again in danger,

Mme. de Genlis, who herself was so seriously ill that she received the last sacraments, dictated to Casimir a long letter for Valence. Casimir had already taken it upon himself to bring to the bedside of the dying man the former confessor of Mme. de Montesson, but had gained nothing by his efforts.

But the pressing letter of Mme. de Genlis, arriving when all hope had been given up, persuaded M. de Valence to make his peace with God. When he was at the last extremity he sent for Mme. de Genlis's confessor, a curate of Notre Dame de Lorette, the Abbé Gavoile, and, according to the precept of the apostle, worked out his salvation in fear and trembling. He confessed and received absolution, and expired during the extreme unction. It seems that Mme. de Valence and her daughters were present at his last moments. However this may be, their grief was overwhelming. A ghastly circumstance made it more painful for them. The corpse of the deceased was of such great bulk that it required a very large and heavy coffin, and it seemed as if it would never be got down the rather narrow stairway of the house. It took a full hour to manage this. Mme. de Genlis, still ill, and unable to rise from her bed, heard as she lay there " the collisions against the wall as this mournful and heavy burden almost slipped from the hands of its bearers, who all the time were uttering terrible cries." " I never suffered more," she says. But she had the consolation of thinking that her efforts had been crowned with success, and had resulted in this wretched Valence being led to make a good end.

Some time before, the dispute between him and young La Woestine had been settled in a friendly way. General Gérard, the husband of Mlle. de Valence, bought from his father-in-law the Sillery estate, for 800,000 francs, under condition that if he resold it at a higher price he would share the profit with Valence, and that out of it they would pay to La Woestine what was due to him. Mme. de Genlis says that General Gérard sold it for 600,000 francs, and that they gave 100,000 to M. de la Woestine, " in settlement of the lawsuit begun by him." In reality, the estate and château of Sillery were bought by M. Hédin on 6th June 1821 for 400,000 francs.

After the death of M. de Valence and the sale of Sillery, the Comtesse de Genlis remained for six weeks at the mansion in the rue Pigalle and then returned to the Bains de Tivoli. It was there that she completed her convalescence and also the most violent of all her works against the *Encyclopédie*, and above all against Voltaire—the famous *Dîners du Baron d'Holbach*. In this book she fought the *philosophes* with their own weapons—that is to say, with quotations taken from their writings, chiefly from their correspondence. She made it an imaginary record of the talk of Holbach's guests at his dinner-table—Diderot, the Abbé Morellet, Dalembert, Duclos, Helvétius, the Abbé Galiani, Raynal, the Chevalier de Chastellux, etc. The subject, the inexhaustible subject, of conversation was the letter from Voltaire that Dalembert received on every post-day. Mme. de Genlis made use, for this purpose, of the correspondence of the " patriarch "—at least of as much of it as was then known—and of the *Memoirs* of Morellet, which had lately been published. But the interest of the book did not centre upon these dialogues, written with a purpose, between the members of the same coterie. It depended on the vigorously written introduction, containing two terrible indictments against Voltaire, in which she explained her purpose. And after having been so long in the fight, Mme. de Genlis had had ample leisure to polish up her weapons. She now brought them all out. It must be allowed that often she chose them well. Without dwelling on the somewhat combative tone of her essay, one ought perhaps to say of her philippic, it must be admitted that Mme. de Genlis saw quite clearly the failings of Voltaire —the extent of his inferiority to Racine and Corneille ; the coldness of his poetry ; his lies, his immorality, his intolerance ; finally, that literary jealousy which led him systematically to calumniate everyone who was suspected of being a genius. She says with much justice that the immense extent of his influence " is no credit to the false philosophy," and " proves that the corruption of human nature is easier to mislead than to enlighten." She judges his age and the man who dominated it from the Christian not from the mere literary point of view. And in this sense, and for the matter of that in the philosophic sense, she is right again and again. She maintains that the century of education, of literary masterpieces, of philosophy, and of good morals was rather the seventeenth than the eighteenth, and once more she is right. It will be objected against her that she saw only the bad side of Voltaire. But writing as a moralist, and a Christian moralist, she might indeed remain silent as to his talents; and she took this course, though there is no doubt she could appreciate Voltaire as a writer.

The *Dîners du Baron d'Holbach* made a noise. One can easily imagine who were its admirers and who its unfriendly critics.[1]

The work appeared in 1822. As soon as it was published, there was such a " prodigious demand " for it that it could not be supplied quickly enough.[2] Even two years later a preacher in the pulpit of St. Roch spoke highly in its praise.

Encouraged by this success, and happy, as she liked to repeat, in working for religion, Mme. de Genlis set actively to work on her new edition of the *Encyclopédie*. It amounted to nothing less than an entire transformation. Our Countess had read the immense compilation twice through. She undertook to expurgate Diderot's articles, to revise all those on mythology, etc.

And she undertook with joyous ardour at the close of her career this titanic work, that might have alarmed a writer in the full vigour of life. She had already confided

[1] Mme. de Genlis asserts that the publication of the *Dîners du Baron d'Holbach* was followed by the coming of anonymous letters and threats of revenge, so that she did not dare to go out unaccompanied to Mass. Mme. de Choiseul escorted her and kept her in sight; nevertheless, an insolent young man assailed her, it appears, in the church,—with words only, presumably,—and the romantic imagination of Mme. de Genlis made her believe that soon after she saw an unknown person who had got into her room, and was advancing upon her with fury in his eyes, when at that moment the Count de Rochefort arrived, and " the unknown made his escape without delay" (*Mémoires*, vii. 252, 253).

[2] Cf. L. G. Pélissier, *Portefeuille de la Comtesse d'Albany*, 2nd December 1822.

her plans to an illustrious visitor at the Rue Pigalle, M. de Chateaubriand, to whom the idea seemed so admirable, that he interested himself in it, came back to talk about it a second time, and on 23rd March 1828, put 2000 francs at the disposal of Mme. de Genlis, with that condescending grace that was characteristic of him.

"It is a mere trifle," he said, "for so useful a work, but perhaps I shall have more funds at my disposal in the last quarter of the year, and I could not make a better use of them than in giving you the means of instructing and charming a public that has become accustomed to admire you."[1]

Finally, this colossal project had the good fortune to please Louis XVIII. He gave proof of this by granting Mme. de Genlis a pension of 1500 francs, payable from the budget of the theatres, and dating from 16th September 1828.

"I have a very shabby pension of 1500 francs," she writes to Casimir, "with a fine letter about my talents, my writings, their utility, etc. Anyhow it will do to pay the rent and the servants."

Mme. de Genlis was then living in the Place Royale (now the Place des Vosges), and her finances had great need of being livened up. Apparently the royal pension did not suffice for this, for our poor Countess was thinking of lodging at less expense in a convent, and to diminish the outlay she hoped to share her rooms with Mme. de Valence. However, the latter was happier with her daughters; she lived sometimes in Belgium with the Comtesse de Celles, sometimes at Villers with Rosamonde, Comtesse Gérard; and Mme de Genlis set to work to search for two rooms with a lodging for a servant, but they must be healthy, with good air and a lofty ceiling, which is "the thing most difficult to find in all the world."

From this point of view a first floor suite then vacant at the Abbaye aux Bois did not suit her, and a convent answered better her desire for retirement and austerity. She has said herself that in old age the sight of the pleasures

[1] Chédieu de Robethon, *Chateaubriand et Madame de Custine*, p. 226.

and vain amusements of the world is painful and seems foolish. Feeling that she was on the threshold of eternity, and although she was remarkably free from illness, and at nearly eighty-four read and wrote without glasses, she was dominated by the fear of death, and wished to prepare for it by penitence. For several years she had been in the habit of periodically making good resolutions, generally the same, for they were quickly forgotten. This one, however, she kept: "Not to wear silk any more or jewellery, except her wedding ring." "Considering how she dressed, whether in silk or woollen," says Fiévée, "I think that God did not see much difference. But her carelessness about dress could not prevent her having a most distinguished air."

Mme. de Genlis tried therefore to find a place of retirement with the Dames du Saint Sacrement. The attempt proved impossible for her, on account of several drawbacks, among which the impossibility of having a confessor every week was the principal. At the end of four months she moved to the Rue Taranne. But increasing complications in her affairs, and the debts of which she did not take time to check the accounts, for she was all day bent over her writing-table, very soon forced her to leave the place. Sad, lonely, deserted, and in no state to extricate herself from her difficulties, the poor woman was glad to receive help from Casimir. He rented a suite of rooms for his mother by adoption in the Rue Neuve St. Roch, furnished it, organised the housekeeping, found a servant and a cook, and leaving for awhile his wife and children—by 1824 there were three of them—at Mantes at his place in the Rue des Pois, came to stay with Mme. de Genlis.

This state of things lasted six months, after which Mme. de Genlis, having become ill through trying to keep the Lent strictly, Casimir proposed to her to come to his home at Mantes in the spring. He had to be beside the domestic hearth just then, for his wife brought into the world, on 3rd April 1824, a son—Marie-Joseph-Gabriel-Édouard Boecker.[1] But Mme. de Genlis kept the rooms in the Rue Neuve St.

[1] État-civil de Mantes (communicated by M. Grave).

Roch, leaving them to the care of her two servants. She came back to them for the New Year's Day of 1825, wishing to see all her friends again and receive their good wishes; and it was a real joy to her to gather round her her daughters and nieces, and M. de la Woestine and his daughter Léocadie, the offspring of his second marriage and a Bavarian canoness, and Paméla and the rest. There was, alas! one missing from this family party; it was the Marquis du Crest, who had died on 9th April 1824; but his widow and Georgette, in deep mourning, reminded the old Countess of the absent one.

She stayed only two months in Paris; just long enough to see through the press the first two volumes of her *Memoirs* which were about to appear, and draw up the prospectus that was to launch them. It was at Mantes, therefore, that there came to her the echoes of the work, the protests, the outcries of people named in these two volumes, drawn from the life and described in them. Even descendants of those she mentioned did not fail to cry out as if they had been flayed, and talk of calumny and scandal. Sainte-Beuve has remarked that "no doubt in her desire to conceal and to attenuate many things she has revealed a good many others." And her revelations, those of a person who has seen and heard what she talks about, and who describes it with a lively pen, skilled in drawing with a single line the whims and oddities of others, especially of women, and in making herself come out well in all circumstances—these revelations fell into the midst of royalist society like a stone into a pond of frogs. There was an outcry. The late Mme. de Montesson, who had lived only to court public opinion, found posthumous defenders against this "devilish niece" of hers. Others, descendants of the contemporaries of the youthful Genlis, filled the newspapers with their corrections,—notably the son of the Chevalier de Bonnard, who defended his father in the *Journal des Débats*.[1] Others wrote to her and overwhelmed her with protests, to which she paid hardly any attention. Again and again Mme. de Genlis, after this descent into the literary arena, found herself exposed to a succession of

[1] *Journal des Débats*, May 1825

attacks. We have remarked elsewhere how carelessly she relied upon her untrustworthy memory, which was assisted and often misled by her imagination, and with what incomparable art she forgets dates and circumstances that she had no reason to be proud of. We need not return to the subject.[1] Did she remember at eighty-four the failings of the past? She was, on the contrary, all delight at being once more the subject of every one's talk, and enchanted with the stir this publication had made. She was in a hurry to follow it up with the next two volumes, and for this purpose came back to Paris to make arrangements with Ladvocat. It was the end of May 1825. But she did not again appear at the Rue Neuve St. Roch.

Ladvocat had looked for and found another place for her. It was in the outskirts of Paris, so far out then that one thought one was almost in the country. It was in the *maison de santé* of Dr. Canuet at 10 Grande Rue de Chaillot. There, far from the noise of the city, she could find quiet and the care she needed for her health. This journey came just at the time of the celebrations on the occasion of the coronation of Charles X., which she saw from the carriage of Mme. de Choiseul. But she had no longer the elasticity of youth. Having failed to resist the temptation to eat freely of an enormous box of Rheims gingerbread, a present from her pupil the Duke of Orleans, Mme. de Genlis suffered violent colics, became nervous, and sent in all haste for Baron Alibert, the physician of Louis XVIII. We quote this pressing note, which, considering how unimportant was her indisposition, gives a somewhat amusing picture of the old lady's fears:—

"I have been some days in Paris, my dear doctor. I arrived in perfect health, but to-day I feel myself very sick. I have very sharp pains in the stomach, a thing I have never before had. I suspect it is a kind of tympanic colic, for there is much local swelling and tension. What should I do? Send me word this very day, or come at once to my help. I have confidence only in you.

[1] See on this subject the opinion of Stendhal, *Correspondance*, i. 290.

"Good-day, dear doctor. It is four o'clock in the afternoon. My address is No. 10 Grande Rue de Chaillot.
"D. COMTESSE DE GENLIS."
"*Thursday, 9th June* 1825."[1]

Of course this mere indigestion had no serious result. But the house of Dr. Canuet was not to be the last refuge of Mme. de Genlis. Haunted by the idea of ending her days in the shadow of the cloister, she removed on 12th October in the same year to the convent of the Dames de Saint Michel. Her lodging there was " a very bad and very lofty " room, where, as the winter came on, she found that " one would need all the skins of a flock of sheep to stop all the cracks and all the holes in it," and that this icy habitation would be fatal to her. So there was a fresh removal. Her new apartments were in the Rue Neuve de Berry, in a school for young girls. It was there that, still hard at work, she published the *La Bruyère des Domestiques* and the *Soupers de la Maréchale de Luxembourg*, works of the last declining period of her life, but not entirely without passages full of intelligence and sound sense.

Finally, in 1827, at the age of more than eighty-four, she made her last move, and retired to a family boarding-house kept by a certain Mme. Afforty at No. 24 Rue du Faubourg du Roule. She hoped to make from there a final pilgrimage to St. Aubin, but she could only do it by letter, and this was her last place of residence. There it was she heard the firing of July 1830, for there was fighting nearly opposite the house, at the royal stables in the Rue d'Artois, the site of the present Rue de Berry. Her niece, Georgette du Crest, came from Clichy, where she lived, to tell her the news —how the insurrection had broken out, how the troops under General Gérard were masters of the Revolution, how the Duke of Orleans had been named Lieutenant-General of the kingdom, and it was thought would soon be King of France. "God guard him from accepting it," exclaimed Mme. de Genlis. "I wrote thus to him years ago, and my

[1] Unpublished letter, Library of Nancy. The signature and date only are in the hand-writing of Madame de Genlis.

opinion of him is the same as then. He has all the virtues of a good father of a family, but none of the qualities required for the chief of a party—no ambition and no firmness of character. . . ."[1]

The governess strangely deceived herself. And if Heaven had granted her greater length of days, Louis-Philippe, a King, and a King that really governed, would have proved to his old teacher that, having learned from her to rule himself with integrity, he could therefore all the more surely and bravely guide the car of the state. But she clung so obstinately to her opinion that, even after the republication of her "Letter from Silk" in 1828 by the enemies of the Duke of Orleans, and even after 9th August when Louis-Philippe had accepted the crown, the object of his desires, she persisted in saying, "He will repent of it. Happily I shall not be a witness of his regrets. I shall be dead."[2]

She was, in fact, then hardly recovered from one of those illnesses of old people of which age is the most serious cause.

In her case the malady had attacked the head. Her ideas became confused, her speech failed, and a continual drowsiness dulled her whole body. At the very outset, with keen foresight, she recognised what her state meant, and wanted to write to her august pupil to recommend Casimir to him. But she could not manage to hold the pen, or even to dictate the shortest letter. A torpor she could not overcome made all her ideas vague the moment she tried, with a hopeless effort, to keep the thread of them. Mme. de Valence, Casimir, a devoted friend the Comtesse Anquetil, and Georgette cared for her day and night. This last relates an amusing incident relating to this illness of Mme. de Genlis. One day one of her doctors, finding her lying in an uncomfortable way, gently raised her up while the nurses rearranged the bed a little. She suddenly roused up from her torpor and exclaimed: "Whatever are you doing, Monsieur? Are you trying to run away with me? Such a thing never occurred to me in my life, and I don't think it ought to happen at eighty-four. Please lay me down at once."

[1] Georgette du Crest, *op. cit.*, ch. xiii.   [2] *Ibid.*

LOUIS-PHILIPPE, KING OF FRANCE.

To a question of Georgette as to how she felt she replied, "Be silent. You are distracting me!" It was afterwards known why she did not wish to be distracted. "It was," she said, "because I believed I was dying. I thought I recognised what one must feel when the soul is departing, and I was afraid it would go while you were talking to me."

A remarkable thing happened. The last Sacraments brought her back to life. On the morrow of the day when she received them she was better. Two days after her health became excellent. They saw her once more reading and writing without using glasses, hearing admirably, surprising every one by her wonderful memory, and resuming the almost vegetarian régime that she had adopted for thirty-five years. Her meals consisted almost entirely of vegetables boiled in water without salt, and fruit of all kinds, grapes from Fontainebleau, oranges, and enormous quantities of strawberries. Chicken broth and a drink of honied barley-water completed her fare, from which she had excluded, for good and all, wines, coffee, and liqueurs. It then seemed to those around her that her health had been solidly restored, and that if she received no sudden shock she might go on till she was a hundred. As for Mme. de Genlis herself, she went on quietly with her literary work and her romantic projects. Was she once more dreaming of making a fortune when, on 2nd June 1829, she formed a partnership with two young people, a doctor and a bachelor of law, with a view to putting on the market a balm to cure rheumatism, a patent medicine of her own invention?

Her idea, no doubt, was that the profits of this discovery, if there were any, should go to Casimir—everything was for him—he was the object of her last and her only affection. It cost her something to leave the world without having first secured a comfortable future for this careless young fellow, who had now set up as a teacher of the harp at Mantes. She would have liked to make him rich—very rich. There is a letter of hers dated 20th October 1829, dictated by Mme. de Genlis to a friendly amanuensis, in which, after extolling the good qualities of Casimir, she recommends him to a person in high position who was absolutely unknown to her.

Death came suddenly on Friday, the last day of 1830.

That morning her maid, Mlle. Sorel, came as usual into her room at eight o'clock. Her mistress asked her for a glass of *eau sucrée*, and told her to let her rest until ten.

"At nine o'clock," her niece tells us, "her doctor arrived to wish her a Happy New Year. The maid hesitated about allowing him to go in before the hour fixed for awaking her mistress. But the doctor insisted, saying that he could not come to see her next day, as he would be obliged, as an officer of the National Guard, to make several visits in connection with the corps, and that he must really give her his good wishes now.

"He therefore went in, and was surprised at seeing that she remained asleep, notwithstanding the noise made in opening the shutters, and that she looked very yellow. He went close to her, and spoke to her without receiving any reply. He took her hand; it was icy cold. Alarmed at this he tried her pulse and felt the region of the heart. It was not beating. Mme. de Genlis was dead! ... Her features had not changed; she was holding a handkerchief to her mouth like some one wiping the lips after drinking. The glass standing near her was empty.

"The doctor tried to do something for her. He put some alkali in the mouth. But it was all of no use."[1] Mme. de Genlis was no more!

As soon as this was known a magistrate was sent for, and went through the sad formality of sealing up her belongings. But no will was found, for the inventory makes no mention of one being among the papers of the deceased.

It was, however, well known, for she had often mentioned it, that she wished to rest in the cemetery of the Calvary on Mont Valérien, and arrangements were made accordingly.

Mont Valérien had been from time immemorial a holy and venerated place. Since, in the year 1180, the village

[1] Georgette du Crest, *op. cit.*

of Suresnes, ravaged by the plague, had seen its sick cured at the fountain on the Mount, the water of this miraculous spring had drawn crowds of pilgrims from twenty leagues around. Some hermits took up their abode there, and in 1640 Louis XIII. authorised the erection of the Calvary. The protection of Louis XIV. made it more widely known. As the feasts of the Cross came round, and especially in Holy Week, the faithful came in crowds, venerated a relic of the true Cross, the gift of the Elector Palatine, and formed processions in long array. In the eighteenth century Bernardin de St. Pierre and Jean-Jacques Rousseau came there together, and dreamed of the happiness and peace of soul of those who believed. The Revolution broke everything up, and left the Calvary in the possession of Merlin de Thionville, who sold it to M. de Gay, the incumbent of the Abbaye-aux-Bois. Rebuilt, and much visited by the Royalists, it excited the jealous suspicion of Napoleon, who, after various projects, decided to build a barrack there. 1815 interrupted the work, and Louis XVIII. restored the Calvary to its original destination.

Then Monsignor de Forbin-Janson established the Pères de la Foi there, and they reopened the ancient cemetery for those who out of devotion might wish to rest under the sacred shadow of the Cross.

All the aristocracy were eager to obtain allotments of ground for graves, and before long the enclosure sheltered the last repose of privileged nobles, cardinals, bishops, generals, admirals, Chevaliers of St. Louis and of the Legion of Honour, and some ladies of distinguished families.[1] Then, during the Revolution of July, the monastery was sacked and the Calvary damaged, and one of the first acts of Louis-Philippe was to forbid any more burials in the aristocratic cemetery. The decree was dated 25th December—that is, five days before the death of Mme. de Genlis, and it had not yet been put in force.

Nevertheless, a special permission from the King was required before the new law could be suspended in favour of his old teacher. Louis-Philippe granted it " in view of

[1] Cf. Robert Hénard, *Le Mont Valérien*.

the fact that she had chosen her place of burial under the shelter of the Calvary and under the care of the Priests of the Mission." But the *Constitutionnel* did not fail to protest and to ask "why under so thoroughly constitutional a Government decrees could exist that were not applied without exception."[1] But notwithstanding the *Constitutionnel*, Mme. de Genlis was buried at Mont Valérien.

If they could have seen her will, they would have found there this provision as to her funeral—for she had thought of everything, even of the persons to whom invitations should be sent—"I wish to be buried without any display." But nothing was known of this; for her executor under her will, M. Anière, formerly a magistrate at St. Denis, a friend of Mme. de Genlis, who had known him at Mantes, was then in Switzerland, where he heard of her death only through the newspapers, so that the will, which he had in his keeping, arrived too late.

There had been only brief announcements of the death of the Countess in the newspapers of 2nd January 1831,— the *Gazette de France*, the *Débats*, the *Quotidienne*, and the *Constitutionnel*. The *Constitutionnel* and the *Gazette* in very short notices mentioned only, to the honour of the deceased, that she had been the King's governess. But the *Temps* devoted to her a long biographical article, in which it was easy to recognise the bitter and rancorous pen of one of Michaud's contributors.[2]

The *Gazette* announced the funeral service for Monday, 3rd January. In reality it took place on Tuesday the 4th, at St. Philippe du Roule, the parish church of Mme. de Genlis.

By the order and at the expense of Louis-Philippe, who nobly offered this last public testimony of esteem for his old teacher, the ceremony was splendid. The obsequies of "Madame la Marquise de Sillery, Comtesse de Genlis, formerly

[1] *Constitutionnel*, January 8, 1831.

[2] *Le Temps*, January 3, 1831. The article ended thus: "Outside of this conventional world Madame de Genlis could neither describe nor understand anything. She seems never to have examined human passion except in the embroidered vests of the Court of Louis xv., and never contemplated Nature except through the Venetian blinds of the summer-house at Bellechasse."

lady-of-honour to Her Highness the Dowager Duchess of Orleans, and Governor of His Majesty the King," were celebrated with a magnificence that " was in complete contrast with the modest and simple ways of the deceased."

The church with its portals draped, and its nave entirely hung with black, with the great catafalque covered with black hangings embroidered in silver, and the sanctuary bright with hundreds of tapers in silver candlesticks, presented the imposing spectacle of a great Catholic funeral service, always the same through the centuries.

The chief mourners were the Marquis Anatole de la Woestine, Colonel of the 6th Regiment of Hussars and grandson of Mme. de Genlis, and Marshal Comte Gérard, the husband of her granddaughter, Rosamonde de Valence. Then came the officers of the Palais Royal representing the King and the Princess Adélaide; Casimir and his eldest son; Louis Boecker, aged ten, a godson of Mme. de Genlis; and finally, a group of friends, small in number, alas! for death had terribly thinned their ranks and the departed was very old.

It was the funeral of a grandmother, all of whose contemporaries belonged to two generations ago, and where the only representative of these old days was the Comte de Sabran, for Talleyrand was at the Embassy in London, Anatole de Montesquiou was absent, and except Fiévée there were few among her colleagues of the literary world who remembered her. The carriages of the Court with the Orleans liveries closed the procession, which wended its way to Mont Valérien.

There a discourse brought the ceremony to an end.

But who was it that had the honour of pronouncing the funeral oration of Mme. de Genlis? Georgette du Crest says it was the Latin scholar Lemaire. But she must be mistaken, and other narrators attribute it to a provincial man of letters, a scholar and member of several learned societies, who died Inspector of the Academy at Bourges, but is quite unknown to the present day—a certain Pierquin de Gembloux. We have, in fact, found in the list of his works the mention of a discourse delivered at the grave of Mme. de Genlis, with these words in parenthesis: " It was the only one that was delivered."[1] One might well have wished that some less obscure voice had praised the memory of a woman whose career was celebrated, and who numbered nearly fifty years of literary reputation. Besides, M. Pierquin de Gembloux was for her something less than an ally, and little more than a stranger, for he had married a cousin of Mme. de Montesson. By this open grave he made up in some small degree for the neglect and injustice with which the late Marquise de Montesson had disdainfully overwhelmed her dear niece; but the laurels that he bestowed on the dead woman were not of the kind that are rich enough and vigorous enough to endure. They withered as soon as they were bestowed. The discourse has, unfortunately, not reached us. We only know that Anatole de Montesquiou read it and eulogised it. And all this passed without causing any stir and in the midst of indifference. Mme. de Genlis had lived too long. Her name, as a contemporary publication remarked, " seemed already a recollection of the past, of antediluvian or at least of ante-Revolution date, and people murmured a *Requiescat in pace*, as a sufficient tribute to her memory."[2]

Now that Mme. de Genlis was gone, there was the winding up of her affairs. Her direct heirs, Mme. de Valence and Anatole de la Woestine, had the legal inventory of her effects drawn up. The first meeting for this purpose took place on 18th January 1831, the second on Wednesday, 23rd February. They revealed no hidden treasures. Mme. de Genlis had died poor.

They found several agreements relating to works sold outright to publishers, and having now no value, as full payment for them had been made long since; two assignments of literary property in payment of bills signed by her; another, a settlement with the publisher Roret, " for the assignment to him of two works, one the *Manuel épistolaire*, the other the *Manuel encyclopédique*, at the price of 800 francs for each, reduced to 400 francs in all, paid to Mme. de Genlis, seeing that the work delivered under the title of *Manuel encyclo-*

---

[1] *Travaux scientifiques de Pierquin de Gembloux*, p. 3.
[2] *Ephémérides universelles*, December 30, 1830, t. xii.

pédique was only a copy of an older work."[1] They found also the curious little agreement concerning the anti-rheumatic balm. As she was boarding at Mme. Afforty's, the Countess had very little furniture of her own. The few objects belonging to her were valued at a little under 800 francs. The beautiful ivory crucifix blessed by the Pope, which Mme. Afforty was taking care of, is valued at only 80 francs.

Then bills came in, mostly from shopkeepers, representing the expenditure of the current year: a shoemaker, a dyer, a pastry-cook, a provision dealer, a jeweller—for hardly 900 francs in all. Who can say whether the jeweller's account did not refer to a "ring of brilliants" which Mme. de Genlis wished very much to have attached to her beautiful crucifix? Then there had to be added two months' board and lodging, and 2000 francs due to Maître Morand, notary, for costs—making the total of her debts 3710 francs, 70 centimes. Meanwhile, her will had become known.

At the moment of the death of Mme. de Genlis M. Anière was at Carouge, near Geneva, whence he sent it by post to the President of the Tribunal of the Seine on 9th January. It arrived on the 18th.

This long recital of the last wishes of the Countess was dated 6th August 1827. It left to Mme. de Valence and to the Marquis de la Woestine all her rights as an author with reference to her various works, with the exception of one single work already reserved to M. de Bouillé,[2] and it distributed to her grandchildren, great-grandchildren, nephews, and friends little legacies, knick-knacks, and books—everything she possessed: her wedding-ring to Mlle. Pulchérie de Celles; her beautiful crucifix to M. de Morlaincourt; her ivory palette to Henriette; her guitar to Mme. de Choiseul; her snuff-box to M. Pieyre, etc. Various copies of her works went to Paméla, to M. de Courchamps, to M. de Sabran, to the Comtesse de Brady, to Georgette du Crest, to the Comte de Rochefort, etc.

Mme. Récamier was to have the manuscript of an un-

[1] *Inventaire*, Étude Mouchet. Cf. on this point Quérard, *Supercheries littéraires*.

[2] *Les mémoires de la marquise de Bonchamps*.

published novel, the *Château de Coppet*. But the most important clause concerned Casimir. Mme. de Genlis, relying upon the gratitude of her august pupils King Louis-Philippe and the Princess Adélaide, begged them to give to Boecker the reversion of half of her pension, or 5000 francs.

Finally, another clause bequeathed to the children of Boecker and to Alfred Le Maire the sum of 2000 francs, which was to be increased to 4000 francs if the payment was delayed for six months. The loose cash that might be found in her drawers was to be given to the poor of the parish.[1]

Louis-Philippe respected the last wishes of his old governess: Casimir had henceforth an assured livelihood. Georgette du Crest, moreover, attributes to the royal generosity the payment of the two thousand francs left to young Le Maire, and not only this one payment, but, if she speaks truly, an annual allowance of 2000 francs. However, her statement is unfounded.

As to the other bequests of money, who undertook the payment of them? In making them, doubtless Mme. de Genlis did not assume that she could give away what she had not got.

Now an entry in the archives of the registry, dated 21st June 1831, notes with regard to the Genlis inheritance: "Heirs unknown."[2] It would appear, then, that Mme. de Valence and M. de la Woestine renounced all claims under the will; the Treasury even lost some trifling fees, for lack of a balance to draw upon.

And here, it seems, the story of Stéphanie Félicité du Crest, Comtesse de Genlis, comes to its close.

We must, however, to be quite complete, add to it some posthumous details, for her tomb has a history of its own. Where precisely was this tomb among those that lay under the shadow of the Calvary?

It is a difficult and much-disputed question, on which it is impossible to give a certain decision on account of the lack of precise documents.

Recently the author of an article on Mont Valérien

---

[1] *Testament*, Étude Mouchet.
[2] *Archives de l'enregistrement*, registre des décès, 1831.

that appeared in the *Revue hebdomadaire* claimed to have seen it, and the *Journal des Débats* repeated the statement—speaking of the " aristocratic cemetery, where all the families of the Faubourg St. Germain are represented, and where there sleep bishops, marshals of France, a descendant of the Kings of Scotland, and Étienne Félicité, Comtesse de Genlis." [1]

These lines were printed in 1902. Now at that date the remains of Mme. de Genlis no longer reposed at Mont Valérien. They had left the pious enclosure sixty-eight years earlier. But, after all, some trace of the tomb might yet remain; and, in support of this supposition, the same author speaks of having with difficulty deciphered on a cross the name of the celebrated Countess. He was more fortunate than we have been. For, notwithstanding long and patient researches, it has not been granted to us to rediscover in the cemetery of Mont Valérien the tomb of Mme. de Genlis, or even the traces of it or its former site. And nevertheless, if the cross existed in 1902, it is not rash to suppose that, a few years after, time would not have entirely destroyed it. But among the rows of tombs that remain, now sheltered under the fresh foliage of a delightful little wood, there is not the smallest stone bearing the name of Genlis. And neither the collection of epitaphs from the cemetery drawn up with scrupulous care by M. de Hennezel [2] nor the work of M. Robert Hénard [3] make any mention of it. More than this, a learned friend of ours who lived at Mont Valérien before the date of the article referred to has made the cemetery the subject of special studies, illustrated with photographs,[4] and he has never seen any trace of a tomb with the name of Mme. de Genlis.

As to official documents, they are absolutely non-existent. The old register of burials at the Calvary kept by the Pères de la Miséricorde and begun in 1825 still exists, it is true, but

[1] L. Feuquières, A l'Intérieur du Mont Valérien. *Revue hebdomadaire* of the 22nd and 29th November 1902.

[2] Vicomte de Hennezel d'Ormois, *Les épitaphes de l'ancien cimetière du Mont Valérien*, Paris, 1905.

[3] Robert Hénard, *Le Mont Valérien*, Paris, 1904.

[4] They have been carefully reproduced by Feuquières and Hénard.

unfortunately it stops at the month of June 1880.[1] The official record of the exhumation would no doubt have given us some useful information, but it was burned with the civil registers of Paris in 1871.

It seems, then, more than unlikely that in 1902 the former tomb of Mme. de Genlis in the cemetery of Mont Valérien was still to be seen. Perhaps the remains of a cross, a fragment that had by chance survived, and was lying among scattered stones, might have been found. But the real position of the grave is unknown. The most that can be said is that an examination of the tombs still remaining in the fourth row leads by induction to the conjecture that Mme. de Genlis was perhaps buried in that place. One of them is, in fact, that of Valérie Boecker, who died in 1828. She was a daughter of Casimir and godchild of Mme. de Genlis. The next grave is that of Hales de Morlaincourt, who died in 1829, aged four, a great-grandnephew of Mme. de Genlis through his mother, Félicité Pulchérie de Sercey. Near him were buried another Morlaincourt, his sister, in 1830, his brother in 1832, and his father in 1837.

Various photographs of this corner of the cemetery dating from ten years ago show that the neighbouring graves in the same row had been dug up for disinterments, and that the monuments belonging to them had disappeared. One of them was probably that of Mme. de Genlis, who would have been laid here among her kindred. Besides, the tombs that come before and after the Boecker and Morlaincourt graves all belong to the period of 1827–1830.[2] This is all that can be positively stated as to the first place of burial of the body of the celebrated Countess. As to her last resting-place, one can indicate the spot without any possible doubt, for it still exists.

The remains of Mme. de Genlis, transferred to Père Lachaise on 21st December 1842, now repose in the eighth line of the twenty-fourth division, under a stone sarcophagus

---

[1] *Archives de la Seine.* Register of interments in the cemetery of Mont Valérien (communicated by M. Lazard).

[2] *Archives de la Seine.* Registre des sépultures: de Hennezel, Hénard *op. cit.*, and communications by Dr. Gillard.

THE LAST PHASE OF MME. DE GENLIS

surmounted by a funeral urn, and decorated with a medallion by Sornet, representing the side face of the Countess.

The sarcophagus, adorned with marble panels, stands on a tomb, on the front of which is the inscription :—

STEPHANIE-FELICITE-DUCREST DE SAINT-AUBIN

COMTESSE DE GENLIS

Née en sa terre de Champ-Céri près Autun (Saône-et-Loire)
Le 25 janvier, 1746

Morte à Paris, le 1ᵉʳ janvier 1831.[1]

This monument is classed as one of the historical tombs, and is now kept in order at the cost of the city of Paris. Formerly the Valence family fulfilled this pious duty.

During the three quarters of a century since the soul of Mme. de Genlis departed to the realm of the shades, time has accumulated its fine dust upon her memory. Oh, how the old governess of Louis-Philippe is forgotten in this land of the living, where once all worldly success was vouchsafed to her. However, there is something to survive her—namely, her voluminous—perhaps too voluminous—series of works, over which it is worth while to cast one's eyes. For in more than one place they are worth attention and full of interest.

[1] See *Inventaire des recherches d'Art de la France*, iii. 203.

PART VI

THE PUBLISHED WORKS OF MME. DE GENLIS

The works of Mme. de Genlis constitute a veritable library in themselves, comprising as they do novels, plays, memoirs, historical volumes, educational volumes, poetry (an item of not much account), theology and pious manuals, diaries also, even a dictionary, as well as politics, catalogues of art and botany.

At least a hundred and thirty volumes in all, without counting re-issues and revised editions, and volumes of extracts from her correspondence, which has never been published in full.

"One would have to be very daring," said Sainte-Beuve, "to pretend one had read them all"; upon which M. Faguet remarks that Sainte-Beuve would seem to have read only three of them, and it certainly looks as though he limited himself to the *Memoirs*, the *Leçons d'une Gouvernante*, *Adèle et Théodore* and some of her stories, among them *Mlle. de Clermont*.

Sainte-Beuve probably reinforced this very limited series of Mme. de Genlis's work by examining the tables of contents included in some editions, and, with these before him and his incomparable acumen, enabled him to detect its essential features, and its literary and moral value so accurately, that even with a wider knowledge of the books it may seem daring—to use his own word again—to venture to speak of them after him.

However deep one may go into Mme. de Genlis's work,

indeed, one will not arrive at any conclusions different from those of the great critic, except in regard to a few points of detail.

Sainte-Beuve divides it into four chronological sections: Before 1789, the Revolution, Napoleon, the Restoration. This is not a hard and fast division; he gives it merely as an aid to synthetical treatment, and it is not to be taken quite literally.

For instance, Sainte-Beuve noted quite correctly that Mme. de Genlis' first works, published under Louis XVI., have all a direct bearing upon education;[1] but he overlooked her dramatic efforts, whether her *Théâtre d'Education*, properly so-called, or her *Théâtre de Société*, in which the theatrical and worldly elements were infinitely in excess of the educative.

She wrote very little for the theatre, though an actress all her life. Her few volumes of comedies—mere drops in the ocean of her productions—all belong to this first period of her life, when she was devoting her mind to education; the single exception was her *Galatée*, which was written in Berlin. If Sainte-Beuve had read these plays he would not have failed to talk about them.

It is necessary also to amplify a little Sainte-Beuve's treatment of her work during the Revolution. He alludes to it very summarily, leaving it to his readers to fill in the details.

Mme. de Genlis did, of course, exercise her pen in regard to the new ideas, writing whenever she herself had any new thought to formulate or whenever she wanted to support the policy of the Orleans Party, or to explain and defend her own conduct. Occasionally her *Discours* or her *Leçons d'une Gouvernante* serve her as catapults from which she may sling stones at her enemies, who retaliate—and with interest. But this revolutionary period does not extend beyond 1797— that is to say, not beyond her *Précis de ma Conduite*, the last book in which she plays the part of a political Egeria. In regard to principles, moreover, it marks a step back from the *Discours* and the *Leçons*; while it appears to palliate and

[1] *Adèle et Théodore, Les Annales de la vertu, La Réligion Considérée*, etc.

excuse—almost even disavow—the violent blows administered in these earlier writings.

Her pen ceases to be revolutionary from the date of the appearance of the *Précis*. Before coming to the Napoleonic period note ought to be made of this change, and all the more that, while in exile, she published a series of romantic stories which had an immense success—*Vœux Téméraires*, while she was at Altona, *Mères Rivales* in Berlin, etc.; besides continuing to work her vein as pedagogue and as moralist in such publications as the *Manuel du Voyageur*, a sort of *vade mecum* in four languages, the *Petit La Bruyère* and the *Herbier moral*.

The revolutionary period should be regarded as ended, if not in 1797, in the year 1798, which saw published the *Reflexions d'un ami des talens et des arts*, destined to incline the Directorate towards clemency in regard to La Harpe and Suard. The Napoleonic period, " her best moment," according to Sainte-Beuve, includes the *Bibliothèque des Romans* and the historical romances.

Sainte-Beuve has not troubled to deal with the fourth and last period, beyond pointing to its abundant insipidity; that at least is the most conspicuous feature of Mme. de Genlis' last works of fiction. The most insignificant, most uninteresting theme, the most commonplace plot, serve to string together a succession of moral platitudes. But if her faculty for weaving romances and for writing with elegance has failed her, her religious zeal and her anti-Encylopædist energy are more notable than ever before.

These qualities come out most vigorously in her *Dîners du Baron d'Holbach* (1822). We may say what we like about this book, we may smile at its bellicose sentences, its bullying tone and its fanaticism, but we cannot deny its force and weight; as Sainte-Beuve showed himself disposed to do when, in referring to it, he said that Mme. de Genlis was becoming more and more the " Mother of the Church " and the mortal enemy of Voltaire.

In the brief study of Mme. de Genlis's work which I am about to undertake it seems to me preferable to deal with her books in the three different categories into which they naturally subdivide, rather than in accordance with Sainte-Beuve's chronological table. I shall deal with Mme. de Genlis first as Moralist, then as Dramatist, finally as Educationalist. The task will not take me so long as might be expected, for there was not much depth in her. Her merit lies in her alertness and social tact, her good sense and intelligence, the ease of her style and often the originality of her ideas, qualities invaluable to a psychologist, knowing how to develop them and turn them to account; but Mme. de Genlis does not work things out, she does not go deep enough. Her fluency carries her away. Her books seem to flow from her like meandering rivulets, now flashing brightly, now reflecting the flowers beside the banks. The page once written, she never rereads it; she confides to the paper her impressions of the moment, and her writing reflects all her many moods.

She is at her best in dealing with education, for in this field her practical experience gives solidity to her work. In her dramatic efforts also her stage experience is of service to her, and her construction in consequence is better here than in her novels. In all her other work, indeed, she is content not to take much pains. Knowledge had come to her easily and speedily, while her feeling for morality and religion was inbred. She herself believed that the moral and religious principles inculcated by means of maxims and anecdotes were sufficient in themselves to establish the value of even the feeblest of her books.

Despite her prolixity, there is something that pleases in her writings, even to the end: she is fair-minded; she has a consummate knowledge of the world, and she has always some indefinable charm. She undoubtedly wrote too much; but those of her works which depict for us the life of her own time—the *Petits Émigrés*, the *Vœux Téméraires*, the *Dictionnaire des Etiquettes*, and finally her *Memoirs*—deserve to survive.

Her juvenile books, the *Veillées du Château*, for instance, a good half of *Adèle et Théodore*, and above all her *Théâtre d'Education*, are still worth putting into the hands of children and even young people. Her educational works, as we shall see, are extremely interesting and ingenious.

The rest of her published work—apart from those which provide biographical information in regard to herself—does not count for much. Suggestive ideas may be found in them here and there, and observations with wit and fancy in them, but much patience would be required to take one through all the multitude of meaningless pages in search of them.

CHAPTER I

MME. DE GENLIS AS MORALIST

In considering Mme. de Genlis' work we have to recognise that it is all definitely moral.

From the very beginning, even before she puts her pen to paper, she is intentionally a moraliser, a character much resembling that of the pedagogue, for by moralising we mean pointing out faults and showing people how to do rightly,—in a word, instructing them.

This intention of moralising is always there, whatever her subject may be, education, history, theology, botany, the theatre or literary criticism, whether she is constructing mere romances or only stories with some amount of probability in them. Even when she is writing apparently only for the sake of writing, or because she has seized some slight pretext for it, she recognises no other reason for her literary activity except this moral intention, and if by any chance the reader should forget it she takes care to remind him of it.

Every one of her works has a moral aim announced, with a copious preface. "I firmly believe that my romances are really moral treatises," she says in her preface to the *Mères Rivales*, "therefore I trust I shall be forgiven if they are not quite so frivolous as so many other romances." In the preface to *Madame de Maintenon* she declares that "A historical romance is the most favourable form for the development of really moral conceptions." We might give any number of such examples, but we must not forget the preface to the *Veillées du Château*, in which we find an "outline sketch" which shows the spirit in which she entered upon all her work. The moral to be taught was always present in her mind. Unlike those who deduce a moral from some given subject, Mme. de Genlis composed and invented anecdotes, stories, romances, or comic episodes to suit the moral which she wished to enforce. She says: "Instead of attempting to find a moral in each story after it was written, I composed and arranged each story to illustrate some moral truth."

Her work therefore does not at all resemble those constructions made of small stones carefully shaped and polished, each one containing some spark of truth so brilliant as to illustrate with its tiny light some hidden vice, some depth of the human heart, as in the writings of La Bruyère or of La Rochefoucauld. Is her architecture a mere logical monument which, aiming at being useful or even super-useful, if I may be permitted to use such a term, is solid but not very pleasing? To admit this would be to accuse her of having written heavy and tiresome books. What a mistake we should make if we laid too much stress on her confessed intention of writing only for the sake of enforcing some moral! if we failed to recognise in her the clever tactfulness of a woman of the world!

Before her time no one except Rousseau had so thoroughly realised the inefficacy of moral treatises, and no one had practically acted upon that principle, so often expressed by Jean-Jacques and becoming at last a fixed idea with him, that moral teaching ought to be made attractive. "There is no detail of morality," says Mme. de Genlis, "which cannot be treated attractively, and no book about morality can be useful if it is tiresome. This truth is not sufficiently recognised. That is why the moralists have produced so many treatises, so many 'thoughts,' so many 'reflections,' dissertations, discourses, essays, etc. . . . why should they exclude sentiment and imagination from their writings about morality?"

Therefore Mme. de Genlis will moralise, but without repelling or irritating her readers; she will show morality in action, in the form of romances, comedies, tales, letters, etc. As she has sufficient imagination to invent the most extraordinary stories, she is able to intermingle in the cleverest manner her morality and her tales of intrigue or of romantic and astonishing adventures; she not only moralises, but she also keeps her readers interested and amused.

Does she wish to prove that love is an illusion, that it holds out a promise of felicity but can only disturb and destroy it? She weaves a story, the *Palais de la Vérité*, a tissue of legends and allegories the heroes of which are genii and fairies, with wonderful details, both pathetic and droll,—like that of the fairy Zolphire condemned by a maleficent foe to spend her life on a see-saw,—and dramatic complicated adventures which she unravels to the great delight of the reader. Does she desire to prove the strength of maternal love capable of withstanding the worst trials? She writes *Alphonsine*, the most incoherent romance that has ever been written. We will not relate how Diana de Mendoce, wedded to a horrible Spanish bandit, the Comte de Moncalde, is after an ambuscade shut up in a cavern and there gives birth to her daughter Alphonsine, whom she brings up in subterranean darkness for five or six long years; this tale, crammed full of adventures, ought to be read by the bored and morose people of to-day.

When her task is to show the ways of the modern world, corrupted by too much civilisation, and to paint the charms of simple, virtuous life in the country, she writes the *Battuecas*. In that book she gives an imaginary picture of a small Spanish tribe, which, having sought refuge in an inaccessible valley hemmed in by mountains, dwells there without any contact with the world. "It is," says George Sand, "a small rural republic governed by artlessly ideal laws. Its inhabitants cannot help being virtuous. It is the golden age with all its happiness and all its poetry." When a young Battuecas wandering by chance along the disused road which leads to the outside world, enters into civilised life and discovers that it offers not only grandeur and beauty, fame and pleasure, but also hypocrisy and misery and many other evils, he returns gladly to his narrow valley.

It is unfortunate that Mme. de Genlis did not keep entirely

to the highly original plan which she had conceived. But she was most illogical. After having denounced the wearisome writers of reflections, essays, thoughts, and moral discourses, she falls into the same error by writing heavy treatises on morality. What else can we call her book *Réligion considerée comme l'unique base du Bonheur*, the *Annales de la Vertu*, the *Petit La Bruyère*, the *Etude du cœur humain*, the *La Bruyère des Domestiques*, and many others of the same sort? It is quite remarkable how utterly she fails in such attempts. As soon as she abandons the imaginary world and the romantic fictions which serve as a framework for her morality and hide the feebleness of her arguments all her good qualities disappear.

She has neither the depth nor the power nor the knowledge required for elaborating a character or a philosophical essay; as soon as she ventures on this higher ground she becomes embarrassed, she is unable to frame striking maxims, but she stumbles on, using a mass of verbiage devoid of real ideas. Then she compiles, borrows, copies, loses herself in details, and only occasionally escapes from this tangled wilderness by giving a well-aimed stroke or making an interesting observation. This is clearly seen by glancing through the pages of the *Petit La Bruyère*, the best of the bad lot I have just mentioned. In this book, as in La Bruyère's immortal *Characters*, we find portraits, maxims, and character sketches. But what a pale imitation of that great writer! Certainly it was intended for children, though it is not at all suitable for such young people. A child of twelve is not able to understand maxims and portraits, also it is very dangerous to incite little boys and girls to notice the whims and the oddities of those around them. Yet in order to entertain them she gives descriptions of the faults of various children who might well be their companions. They read about Hortense, who is capricious, vain, badly educated, impatient, idle; Chloe, who is a coquette; Rosalina, who is too talkative. Among the boys we have Ernest the fop; Stephen the miser; Irenæus the coward; Otho, who mocks at everybody. As a curious specimen read this sketch of Adrian, a youthful pedant: "Adrian is twelve and a half years old, he is very clever, he has a well-trained memory and a great taste for literature, he is already an author in a small way, he has a feeling for the rhythm of versification and knows its rules fairly well, he has already written several little pieces of poetry. Well, if Adrian would only believe that time, study, and good advice are necessary for success, he might some day show real talent in this line. But Adrian thinks that he is already a poet and a very good one; by that mistake he makes himself very ridiculous." This beginning is not so bad in itself, but it goes on for three whole pages. Mme. de Genlis is entirely blind to the absurdities which characterise her own book, but at the end she atones for them by a few happy thoughts, such as: " Piety should neither be advertised nor concealed "; " Youth is seldom able to avoid a fault except by flying to the opposite extreme." And then in the very same book she writes long pages on the necessity of rendering morality lively and agreeable!

However inconsistent Mme. de Genlis may be, we must confess that we may learn a good deal from her moralisings. Except in her actual treatises, we shall find all her work full of sensible observations which throw a wonderful light on the minor habits and the small weaknesses of the society of her time. Of course she has not sufficient ability to construct a museum like that of La Bruyère, but her natural curiosity and her instinctive moral sense have, during the whole course of her long life, prompted her to write an infinite number of most interesting observations and criticisms. There is not much to be gained by dwelling on the moral characteristics of her work—there are too many, they permeate it, they overcrowd it. But two essential ones may be mentioned: first, that although living in a licentious age her morality is very pure; secondly, that it is incomplete because intended almost exclusively for the upper classes.

Although dealing with such a variety of subjects and interspersing them with so many varied precepts, Mme. de Genlis continually recurs to two or three important themes, family affection, maternal and filial love in all its forms. In all her writings the home has the highest place of honour, it is thus exalted because, being founded on religion and on the precepts of the Gospel, it is a school of all the virtues. When she treats of maternal love the work of this singular woman has a real tinge of passion due to that fondness for exaggerated sentiment characteristic of the age in which she lived and by which she was in this respect so strongly influenced. In her inmost heart she loved other people's children better than her own, yet we find her depicting maternal tenderness with an incredible depth of feeling and perception which could hardly be expected in a nature so cold and, in certain ways, so arid.

The favourite *leit-motivs* of Mme. de Genlis, after family affection, are the simple life, rural life, the love of Nature (a direct inspiration from Rousseau) as opposed to the corruptions of the town and of the Court; learning, as opposed to vanity, luxury, and frivolity; and finally charity, as atoning for all other faults. She avoids speaking about love and seems to hold herself aloof from it. When she has to depict it she does it hastily by exclamations, interjections, broken sentences; she can only imagine it as a passion. Then, of course, she is up in arms against it, she is on guard, she withdraws. On all points of difficulty she invariably refers to the Gospel, that eternal rule of all morality, but it is not so much for the morality of the Gospel as for its religion. This is a characteristic of her work which deserves some attention.

It is well known that as early as 1785 Mme. de Genlis entered on a campaign against the philosophers, and especially against Voltaire, in her book *Religion considered as*, etc., and she maintained the war until her very last breath. Taking up a purely moral and religious ground, fighting against the philosophic spirit and identifying it with atheism and immorality, she never lost an opportunity of stirring up public opinion against it.

We are surprised sometimes to see her suddenly start a diatribe against Dalembert, Condorcet, or Voltaire; she does so because she cannot bear to write a book without inserting some public accusation against the false philosophy. That is the polemical side of her work and the least solid.

We may neglect it and dwell more on the intention which she has so perseveringly manifested throughout her long career. It grew stronger in each new work up to the famous *Dîners du Baron d'Holbach*, a veritable fortress firing shots from every opening. This book, although written in 1822, shortly before her death, is wonderfully vigorous. The whole set and especially its chief, Voltaire, were very badly handled by this feminine pen, so skilful in stigmatising their defects.

Mme. de Genlis clearly saw that Voltaire was preparing the way for a new departure by upsetting the sane traditions of the seventeenth century. We have already shown how plainly she pointed out his negative cynicism, his literary intolerance, his deplorable facility in telling lies, his audacity in ruining all morality and in scoffing at all good men, his hypocritical wheedling of those in power; yet at the same time he was entirely opposed to the democratic spirit.

Strangely enough, she was one of the first to accuse Voltaire of being unpatriotic and to point out his numerous plagiarisms; *Zuline* a transposition of *Bajazet*, *Mérope* borrowed from *Maffei*, *Semiramis* and *Rome sauvée* stolen from Crébillon. Now we know quite well how little originality there was in the dramatic conceptions of the patriarch of Ferney, almost all his tragedies have English ancestors, but Mme. de Genlis said it long before the specialists of the present day. Doubtless she did not exhaust the question, but we ought to notice that she knew about it and studied it.

In examining the doctrines of the *Encyclopédists* she gives proof of similar intelligence; she goes back to their predecessors, Bayle and Fontenelle; she knows—we cannot say how or from whom she ascertained it—but she does know that the *Encyclopédie* was not original in its negations but merely took and popularised a number of opinions professed by Hobbes or by Spinoza and also ancient heresies condemned long ago by the Church. As to the philosophers themselves, she stamps each one with his characteristic mark. D'Holbach is the heavy materialistic atheist whom we know so well, Dalembert dry and sarcastic, Diderot a skilful destroyer endowed with artistic feeling; Morellet,

Galiani, discourse brilliantly and utter epigrams, etc., all of them irreligious, sceptical, licentious, menacing God, priests, kings, and all morals.

Mme. de Genlis had taken up a noble cause. The apostle of morality and of truth, she had a splendid mission in defending the rights of human dignity in the name of the Gospel; she was a defender of the Church and of the Faith. How is it then that she was not able to write more vigorously? Why was the *Dîners du Baron d'Holbach*, in which she used every weapon she could lay hands on, written in the declining period of her life and of her success? Why did it not come before the *Génie du Christianisme* and before the "Martyrs" which obtained all the glory like major stars outshining in the literary heavens all the smaller ones.

The reason seems to be that Mme. de Genlis was a moralist in an age that was not moral. In the eyes of posterity that will be her title to honour. Neither her education nor her environment nor her century gave any inducements towards morality. All around her, in the Palais Royal, at the theatre, in the salons, and in literature, haughty carelessness, insolent corruption, and elegant vices were in fashion, there was nothing to predispose her to act as a "Mother of the Church." Yet, whatever style of life or of literary work she adopted, she always preserved her moral sense. As soon as she sat down to her work-table and began to write, no pernicious or even doubtful thoughts come into her mind, she is conscious of having a responsibility, or exercising a sort of ministry.

When we think of the prose and verse produced in her time amid general sensuality and religious indifference, we cannot help being grateful to Mme. de Genlis—in spite of what the Marquise de Créquy said about her—for preaching virtue, faith, and piety.

Her morality was especially adapted, as we said before, to the men and women of her own world. She flattered herself, but without any reason, that she was the first author who had tried to instruct and improve the common people; she has occasionally described artisans, dressmakers, seamstresses, and servants, but neither her subjects nor her style responded to the needs of the people. They were suitable for literary or worldly members of society, they appealed to the aristocracy and the middle class, they had not that solid simplicity, that rather brutal directness, which alone are intelligible to common people.

She did indeed at times remember the Revolution, and we get stray whiffs of the ideas of 1789, especially of equality. Therefore, George Sand called the *Battuecas* a socialistic novel, although the author certainly had no such notions in her head when she wrote it in 1816. The idea of equality was, however, consonant with her scheme of preaching universal morality, and that scheme included not only educated people but also the masses who, being regarded as children, had the same title to her consideration. We must admit that, as regards the masses, her work had no result, but with children she was particularly successful. This leads us to the consideration of her efforts as a dramatic author.

CHAPTER II

MME. DE GENLIS AS A DRAMATIST

AT the present time we can hardly imagine morality as a leading feature of a play. It does not now occupy the stage; it seems to have deserted it as an uninhabitable place. Light comedy helped to banish it, and now the only " moral " plays are those wearisome productions written to suit schools for boys and girls. A lively and interesting comedy, well written and yet moral, would be put down as the result of a wager. It is perhaps surprising, but into this sterile field Mme. de Genlis dared to venture, and she achieved success.

Her dramas and her comedies, whether intended for young people or for fashionable drawing-rooms, her *Théâtre d'Éducation* or her *Théâtre de Société*, are irreproachably moral and yet wonderfully amusing and interesting. All those who have studied her works give the palm to her *Théâtre d'Éducation* as being the best of all. It was certainly an original idea to write little comedies without the aid of amorous intrigues, and fit to be played by little girls ten years old.

She did not always restrict herself to this limited sphere, but whenever her educational ingenuity set itself to instruct and amuse children by plays suited to their comprehension, they were perfectly successful. There was no lack of subjects. Any observer of life, especially of the life of high society, will notice every day a score of situations, tragic or comic, worthy of being dramatised. But a piece which does not touch on the only subject which is the chief support of the stage seems destined to be childish, wearisome, and insignificant. To treat morality as a living subject is not so easy as some people imagine.

This art furnished Mme. de Genlis for the first time with a means of experimentally testing the process which afterwards she employed so frequently, composing her works for the sake of demonstrating some moral truth or some wrong which she wished to set right. In that way she created some charming moral fables. As an antidote to the vanity of little girls, she constructs a small play called the *Flaçons*, in which two coquettish little girls, becoming suddenly convinced by a fairy's artifice of their ugliness and deformity, try to cure themselves of frivolity and to acquire more solid qualities. Then when the fairy offers them two magic phials—one which will restore their former prettiness, while the other will improve their hearts and minds—a charming scene is enacted before the looking-glass. The children, finding themselves so very ugly, are about to choose the phial of beauty; but then, in order not to distress their mother and the fairy, they make the necessary sacrifice. In the end the fairy arranges everything satisfactorily.

It would be impossible to describe the charm of this little play, simple and natural in its tone and perfectly intelligible to young children. Some of the passages referring to the perils of the world are quite pathetic, and even now do not seem old-fashioned.

Another delightful piece of work is *Colombe*: its cooing dialogues were designed to cure little girls of jealousy. Others, like *L'Enfant Gâté* and *Dangers du Monde*, are ingenious though apparently simple comedies which appeal for a verdict against the customs of her day, against the weaknesses of that society which Mme. de Genlis knew so well. Then there are some which extol the virtue of purity (*La Rosière de Salency*), maternal love (*La Bonne Mère, la Curieuse*), charity (*l'Aveugle de Spa*).

It would be a mistake to think that the *Théâtre d'Education* is devoted only to rather dull subjects. Sometimes it deals with sentimental affairs, happening as it were behind the scenes, and it makes a psychological study of the characters. Here we have a series of plays designed not only for children and young people, but also for their parents. In these the lights and shades of stronger feelings are depicted; there are social criticisms which forecast 1789 The high society in which Mme. de Genlis shone at the very time when her plays were being acted had not always been merciful to her; in her rôle of moraliser she had to castigate its vices. She did not fail to do so; a schoolmistress by nature, she scolded well. Thus the *L'Intrigante* shows the influential woman who procures favours for her friends, and in succession promises to three different people the same post at Court, the same admission to the Academy of Painting, the same governorship. In the *Portrait*, a good three-act play full of well-planned scenic effects, she feelingly depicts a passion which, beginning badly, grows purer amid dramatic scenes that are sketched with consummate art.

We need not say much about *Cécile*, in which Mme. de Genlis indulged in a scathing and almost revolutionary satire on the Convents; in it there is a certain Mère Opportune, a Rabelaisian personage—a part certainly not fit to be acted by children or in their presence. It is difficult to understand how this bitter, violent piece came to be acted at Bellechasse before the Duchess of Orleans. The *Vrai Sage* is a comedy rather too outspoken for young girls,—certain things are mentioned which they ought not to think about, —but in it Mme. de Genlis strikes a deep, strong note which shows that she possessed extraordinary dramatic talent. Here is a scene which would do credit to Dumas *fils*.

The Chevalier, a sort of Don Juan, has his eye on Colette, a young and pretty peasant girl. This is the way in which he reveals his intentions to his friend Verceil:—

The Chevalier: "Well, in that case, Colette will come to Paris merely for my sake, and I will undertake to console her for your change of plan."

Verceil: "You may be sure that her father will not consent to her going away."

The Chevalier: "Then I shall do without it."

Verceil: "What! you intend to abduct Colette?"

The Chevalier: "Abduct! What an absurd word! You

cannot apply it to a girl of that class. You can abduct a young lady, but a peasant girl you merely carry off."

Verceil: "Then, according to you, violence has a different name when it is practised on the weak! This is just a case in which it seems to me that the abuse of strength and the hope of impunity give a tinge of meanness which makes it doubly atrocious."

The Chevalier: "You take a too tragic view. Colette is not the sort of girl to live in a cottage. I want to bring her out and make her fortune. Would that be a great crime? Besides, I shall take steps to prevent her father having any more rights over her. I shall have her inscribed at the Opera as a dancer."

Verceil: "Colette a dancer! That's nonsense. What a reception she would have! She does not know how to dance."

The Chevalier: "That does not matter. It is an ingenious system which is often used as an excuse for removing a pretty girl from the absurd authority of low-class parents. A substantial shopkeeper might perhaps find some way of maintaining his rights, but what possibilities are there for a poor rustic, coarse and ignorant and unable to stir far from his hut?"

Another passage, where Verceil launches forth in the style of Beaumarchais, would have pleased the philosophers: "I always remember it, and I never blush for it. I am the son of a tradesman, who by honesty, ability, and hard work was able to acquire a considerable fortune. His moderation and beneficence have gained public esteem for him and have even killed that mean, secret envy with which a proud and poor nobility often regards the good fortune of a parvenu. Therefore, when resentment or anger reproach me for my birth, I do not feel humiliated by such insults. The blood in my veins is not illustrious, but it is pure; it has transmitted into my heart a love of virtue and a horror of vice and bad principles." Is it not strangely reformist for a work written in 1782? On the stage these passages produced a great effect. Stage effect was Mme. de Genlis's strong point; in producing it she showed most wonderful skill. To conduct an intrigue, to entangle it, to prolong it so as to postpone the pathetic moment, to insert a tirade, to excite emotion, to stimulate it to its utmost point, all these artifices of the dramatic author were but child's play for this woman whom M. Faguet said, "She was a born actress, a born manageress, an aristocratic Montansier, with wonderful gifts for theatrical work."[1] He was the first in our time to recognise her genius.

Since he has revealed them we now acknowledge the merits of "Tendresse Maternelle," that pearl in the *Théâtre de Société*, that act full of intense emotion, transplanted by Mme. de Giradin into *La joie fait peur*, and from which Musset has borrowed the character of the abbé in his *Il ne faut jurer de rien*. But we do not recollect that La Harpe considered the *Mère rivale* good enough for the Théâtre Français; and that the love scenes at the telephone, so often introduced by modern authors, have a prototype in the *Cloison* of Mme. de Genlis; she had foreseen the situation, *minus* the telephone.

She had a real vocation for the stage, and she obtained her experience when still quite young. Into the amateur theatricals which were the rage in the high society to which she belonged she introduced phrases and sentiments far superior to their narrow setting. She had high moral and social aims, she handled romantic adventures, marvellously imagined, with consummate art, using combinations and contrasts with all the skill of a professional dramatist—a dramatist of the period, of course.

Ingenuity, remarkable skill, a determination to moralise, technical experience, these are Mme. de Genlis's theatrical characteristics, charming when they were employed in dialogues for young actors and young audiences, though they are apt to lose their interest when expended on plays like those in the *Théâtre de Société*. The latter have also a fundamental fault, being mostly three- or five-act pieces. Five acts of the eighteenth century phraseology—that is too much for any modern audience to endure.

[1] E. Faguet, *Propos de Théâtre*, 2e série.

CHAPTER III

MADAME DE GENLIS AS AN EDUCATIONALIST

As I have remarked already, Mme. de Genlis is no longer read. All that is remembered of her now is that she was an admirable educationalist. *Adèle et Théodore* and the *Leçons d'une Gouvernante,* so familiar to our parents in their childhood, are unknown to-day.

They are held of no account, like so many other pedagogic treatises.

They are of use, however, in enabling us to reconstruct with precision Mme. de Genlis's whole system of education—the most complete system imaginable—inasmuch as it begins with the child while still in his cradle and leads him on to manhood without leaving him for a moment !

From infancy to the age of twelve—such is the cycle embraced in *Adèle et Théodore*; from the age of the use of reason up to manhood, such is the period covered by the *Leçons d'une Gouvernante*. And if we remember that it was in the field of education, as Sainte-Beuve says, that Mme. de Genlis realised her gifts to the full, we shall be ready to devote some special attention to these two books.

Naturally, all was not original in her methods—we shall see presently in what respects she was an innovator. Like all her contemporaries, she derived much of her inspiration from Rousseau, and this is particularly noticeable in *Adèle et Théodore*, in which we find principles from *Émile* put into practice, side by side with Mme. de Genlis's own theories. But another very profound influence, permeating all her thought, is that of Mme. de Maintenon.

The directing of education towards realities and persistence in the effort to overcome *ennui* and the passions—these principal elements in the Saint-Cyr method have the first place also in that of Mme. de Genlis. She bases herself indeed upon a groundwork of ideas originating in the seventeenth century—largely in Mme. de Maintenon and in Fénelon; but, influenced by Rousseau, she adapts these ideas in accordance with his reforming notions. On one point she breaks away entirely from them: namely, the scope of instruction.

According to Mme. de Genlis, a child cannot have too much education.

The *acquiring of knowledge* is at the very root of her system, as is evident from *Adèle et Théodore*, which is essentially an educational work, and from which the anecdotes, included with a view to enlivening it, might with advantage have been omitted.

The general ideas of this book belong for the most part to Rousseau: the adapting of education to the age of the children; keeping the lessons and exercises and moral instruction well within their powers of comprehension; teaching them all kinds of ordinary things; always being frank and candid with them; paying particular attention to their physical well-being—food, clothes, hygiene; above all, never leaving them out of sight, watching over them always, in their games and on their walks no less than in their studies—such were the main principles. It is from Rousseau also that she derives this view of Latin: "I consider a knowledge of Latin very useful, but not indispensable, as it was held a hundred and fifty years ago. It was then impossible to acquire any idea of the beautiful otherwise than by learning the Greek and Latin languages, but nowadays anyone perfectly acquainted with French, English, and Italian may read a number of works superior to, or at least equal to, anything antiquity can offer."

A wrong idea, put into practice in our modern educational programmes with the disadvantages of which we are all aware.

But the other influence, that of Mme. de Maintenon, makes itself felt simultaneously.

Following the example of the founder of Saint-Cyr, Mme. de Genlis accustoms the child to do useful things. The idea of utility runs through the system, modifying that of the acquiring of knowledge of every description.

That is to say, that instead of giving her pupils the superficial, conventional education then in vogue, Mme. de Genlis aimed above all at what would be practical and of real value.

It was the custom for young people to study Greek and Latin, chronological tables, and historical summaries, a little geography, a little heraldry, a little prosody, music, dancing, and riding. Orthography and literature were greatly neglected, the sciences were left on one side altogether with a few exceptions. Their turn came generally when, towards his fifteenth year, the young aristocrat began to take up the career of arms; but the veneration professed in the eighteenth century for antiquity maintained the classical mythology universally, and the exploits of Hercules and Theseus were as familiar as the catechism or the sacred history.

Mme. de Genlis did not propose to change all this. She retained the speculative studies in her programme, though she gave precedence to the practical. Her first concern was to teach the child what he could learn.

Rousseau had said: "It is important that he should not do anything unwillingly"; Mme. de Genlis, however, took the line that the boy should be accustomed to overcome his unwillingness in regard to the learning of useful things, and that it was quite practicable to bring this about without fatiguing him.

Making a good use of one's time was an all-important feature of this system of utility. The best way of getting through a good day's work, she always held, was by utilising what are generally spoken of as spare moments. With this in mind, she parcelled out the day minute by minute, so to speak. No hours, except sleeping hours, were without their task, or outside her supervision. Even the hours of recreation were turned to account by means of instructive games. After supper, there were a variety of manual exercises—the making of boxes and hampers and horse-hair rings, the cutting out of paper figures, etc., etc.

Details of the order of the day as arranged in the case of her godchild, Alfred Le Maire, have come down to us. That which was adopted in the case of the children of the Duke of Orleans is not to be found recorded in full. Louis-Philippe declared, looking back upon it when he was King, that Mme. de Genlis educated him and his sister " with ferocity." His day, we may take it, began at 6 a.m., winter and summer, and ended at 10 p.m. He does not seem to have been allowed time to digest his supper, for his Italian lesson began a quarter of an hour after it, involving the study and translation of Metastasio—a heavy and tiring piece of work. And at no period of the year could he ever hope for any relaxation in the régime.

Mme. de Genlis would not listen to any nonsense about holidays. It was her contention that studies should never be interrupted. "Holidays," she wrote, "have done more harm to education than all the incompetence of teachers."

During their journeys, of course, which broke in somewhat upon studies, practical things took the place of books; but Mme. de Genlis devoted her attention to her pupils unceasingly.

Rousseau had said in *Émile*: " I would have teacher and pupil regard each other as so inseparable that they should plan out in common the order of all their days."

In this way Mme. de Genlis sought complete control over those in her charge. She sought to educate their minds and govern their hearts. The daily records of the studies at Bellechasse were evidences of this.

These studies, save for philosophy, comprised every form of knowledge. The living languages come first, then history, literature and natural history, chemistry, botany and mineralogy, architecture and mechanics, Greek and Latin, and the study of the law; something of medicine, chemistry and anatomy; drawing and music, and finally a very strengthening system of physical development upon new and very complete lines, including gymnastics, fencing, swimming and riding.

Everything in this programme that a woman could teach Mme. de Genlis attended to herself. She called in only such assistants as were indispensable, and these she supervised and directed even in regard to minute details, leaving them no initiative whatever: M. Lebrun for geometry, mathematics, chemistry and common law,—after 1789, Biauzat was charged with the task of explaining to the young Princes the difference between the laws of the Ancien Régime and those of the Assembly; the Abbé Guyot for Latin, Greek and religious instruction; M. Alyon, for chemistry and botany; the Abbé Mariottini for Italian, M. Pieyre acting as a sub-tutor. The Abbé Guyot's functions Mme. de Genlis reduced to a minimum, and it will be remembered that he resigned his post when she took it upon herself to prepare Louis-Philippe for his first Communion. The Abbé Mariottini also left owing to certain domestic quarrels, and Mme. de Genlis, knowing enough Italian herself by this time, did not get anyone else in his place.

The subjects which remained entirely for Mme. de Genlis then were grammar, history, and literature, geography, mythology, the fine arts, anatomy, gymnastics, German, English and Spanish. She set aside two and a half hours every day for history and literature, and if, contrarily to the wishes of Rousseau, she made use of chronological tables and summaries, she contrived to vivify them in various ways. The students' rooms at Bellechasse were hung with reproductions in tints of the heads of Roman emperors and empresses, and of pictures representing the most important scenes in ancient hisotry; there were ingeniously devised sets of written tables. "I would read out a heading from one of these tables," Mme. de Genlis tells us, "and they would narrate to me from memory the story connected with it. For instance, I would say: 'Ægeus; the sail';" and the pupil would repeat the details of the return of Theseus, the vanquisher of the Minotaur, with the account of the death of Ægeus caused by the white sail, which ought to have been raised on his ship being forgotten.

Literary extracts were selected from history, mythology and books on geography to enable the children to commit certain points to memory; and the painter Myris executed several series of small pictures illustrating sacred and ancient history, as well as episodes in the history of China and Japan. These were done expressly for use in a magic lantern—the "Historical Magic Lantern" was the name given to them.

Mme. de Genlis thus describes her method of teaching literature. " I began by reading to them the works of the poets of the second or third rank. I endeavoured in the course of these readings to impart to them an excellent spirit of criticism. We had plenty of material for criticism, for as it is much easier to recognise the faults of mediocre work than to appreciate the beauties of what is really fine, my pupils soon became very good judges of the poems of Mlle. Barbier, Campistron, Autreau and others of that class ; and certainly at that age they would have been very bad judges of Corneille, Racine, Voltaire, Crébillon (*sic!*), La Fontaine, Molière, etc. Educational authorities may smile at this progressive method of tasting literary beauties. At least we must admit that it was ingenious.

But it was in regard to the teaching of modern languages that Mme. de Genlis was most in advance of her time. Far from following Jean-Jacques, who ranked this study among the useless forms of education, she was the first to understand their importance. She was the first to realize that it was not enough to read Dante and Shakespeare with a dictionary, and that it was not much good to stock one's memory with extracts from odes and plays if one could not hold a conversation of five minutes with an Englishman or an Italian; that it was not much good to be conversant with the dead if one could not hold converse with the living.

Convinced of this, she divided the day up into four quarters—each devoted to one language exclusively.

On the morning walk a German gardener (who also supervised the young Princes' gardens at Saint-Leu) went out with them, and nothing but German was spoken. German was the language also during the midday meal. During the afternoon walk an English man-servant took the place of the German gardener, and nothing but English was spoken until after dinner. Italian was spoken during supper, which was followed by a lesson in that language and in Italian literature. At a subsequent period Mme. de Genlis contrived to find time for a Spanish hour as well.

At the age of eight the young Princes and the Princesse Adélaïde, as well as César du Crest and Henriette de Sercey, were able to speak and construe the three languages, German, English and Italian. At twelve Louis-Philippe was, in addition, fairly well grounded in Greek and Latin.

In regard to the Fine Arts, Mme. de Genlis was also very well equipped. It would have been difficult to find anyone better versed in music. Herself an admirable harpist, and familiar with all the traditions of the great musicians, her qualifications in this field were indisputable.

Carmontelle, an amateur artist, was entrusted at first with the teaching of the elements of drawing. Later Mme. de Genlis, breaking away from the ordinary routine, set her pupils drawings from models made to show the muscles. A Polish painter named Myris, a good draughtsman, was afterwards installed at Bellechasse, and David came from time to time to supervise the instruction and judge of the work done.

Side by side with all these studies, properly so-called, Mme. de Genlis's pupils were kept busy with gardening and all kinds of gymnastic exercises: working pullies, carrying baskets upon their heads, and pitchers of increasing weight in their hands, walking in slippers weighted with lead, etc. They were taken also to visit manufactories of pins and of furniture, and mustard and vinegar factories, as well as to workshops of carpenters, basket-makers—to say nothing of the theatre. The development of their bodies proceeded simultaneously with the development of their minds; there was no coddling, no spoiling, however tired the young Princes might be, and very little was made of their occasional cuts and bruises.

Sainte-Beuve has commented on the fact that Mme. de Genlis was much given to the introduction of the dramatic element in her educational methods. She used to get the children to enact scenes and tableaux from history on a portable stage which was set up in the large dining-hall; and in the park of Saint-Leu, where the trees and workhouses and the little river served as accessories, they would perform the principal scenes from the travels of the Abbé Prévost, and give many other historical and mythological representations. David took great pleasure in these theatrical efforts, and supervised the artistic side of them. He was enthusiastic in particular over a little production entitled *Psyché persecutée par l'Amour*.

But it was not merely in these circumstances that Mme. de Genlis's pupils came under the influence of the drama. The theatrical element was constantly to the fore in their life. It was to be found in their declamation of verses, in honour of the Duchess of Orleans; it was present on the occasion of the decorating of the Thanksgiving Altar at Spa; and there were traces of it in the diaries of the young Princes and in the demonstrative affection of the pupils for their governess. Her contemporaries were not blind to all this. They charged her with loving the limelight, and with injuring her pupils by all these scenic displays. It may, however, be contended that Mme. de Genlis's system was only theatrical in respect to outward forms, not in its essentials, as indeed its positive results bear witness, for neither Louis-Philippe nor Mme. Adélaïde can be accused of theatricality.

The question deserves looking into more closely. Nothing could really be more practical, more materialistic, than this system of education, exercising as it did the memory more than the understanding, the eyes more than the brain, reducing the imagination to the simplest expression, turning the intellectual faculties into a machine. Sainte-Beuve points out the disadvantages of their very modern and one-sided method, with its entire lack of all feeling for antiquity. He notes also to what an extent Mme. de Genlis's programme repressed all originality and exuberance and vigour in those subjected to it. Louis-Philippe might believe himself to be versed in all the different branches of knowledge, and might be able to discuss everything under the sun; he was a conscientious pupil, diligent, attentive, but not original, and with nothing of the artist in him. He had been discouraged from dreaming, and had learnt only to be far-seeing, practical, sometimes a little mean.

On the other hand, it must be remembered that the

severely hygienic régime to which he had been subjected—the way in which he had been taught to bear heat and cold, wind and rain, to sleep upon bare boards, to endure fatigue and even hunger, and to fend for himself in all possible circumstances, fitted him wonderfully for meeting with the courage and dignity we all know of the hard vicissitudes which were his lot during the years of the Emigration.

The schooling which he had from Mme. de Genlis had been a democratic schooling, anticipating strangely that which is given to the young Princes of to-day. It made of him a man of the new age—even in the matter of indifference to religion.

For in this one respect he had not been a good pupil. Presumably, Mme. de Genlis, with all her qualifications, was not as good an instructor as a simple priest like the Abbé Guyot might have proved. So that in its results in this case the system was essentially modern in doing more for the body than for the soul. In any case, the throne of France gained a man of action, a man of worth and intellect who knew how to govern—in short, a good king. This we owe to Mme. de Genlis. It involves no small praise for her methods.

The same system of education—"substantial and free from all frivolity"[1]—that was given to the young Princes was given also, as we know, to those other young "collegians" of Bellechasse, Mlle. Adélaïde, Paméla, and Henriette.

Mme. de Genlis has expounded her ideas on the subject of the education of girls in two small works which are quite unknown to-day and which are curiously interesting: the *Discours sur la suppression des Couvents de Réligieuses et l'éducation publique des Femmes* (1791) and the *Projet d'une École rurale pour l'Éducation des Filles* (1801).

The *Discours*, written and published during the Revolution, takes an unfavourable review of the education given in religious establishments, as might be expected in the case of an expert like Mme. de Genlis. She declares roundly that the girls are taught little, because the schools have no purpose

[1] E. Faguet, *Sainte-Beuve et le Feminisme.*

except to free indifferent and neglectful parents from the toublesome duty of looking after their own children.

The convent is a safe refuge in which instruction is indeed given, but in which it counts for less than anything else. There are convents without classes and convents with classes.

In the former " the girls are kept in separate rooms with governesses to teach them, ... the nuns take no part whatever in their education." The governesses were lady's-maids retired from service, as in the time of Mme. de Maintenon: "peasants or at best townsfolk of no social standing who knew only how to hold up their heads, how to lace a corset, and how to curtsy ";[1] and they were paid only about 500 or 600 francs a year.

Masters came to give the additional instruction in other subjects chosen by the parents—the number of the masters varying in accordance with the rank of the pupil. Whence it followed that these convents were extremely expensive, and were supported mainly by the nobility and wealthy financiers.

The education given in the convents with clerics, notably those of the Ursulines and the Filles de Marie, was generally speaking not as good as it might have been, but it was superior, Mme. de Genlis held, to education by parents to whom the bringing up of their own children was not a sacred duty coming before everything else. In both kinds of convents the great thing, the great security, was the cloister; and Mme. de Genlis, in her anxiety to retain this, devised a plan for the establishment of cloistered schools in which the girls should be indoor boarders, but not the mistresses—as in the case of our Lycées for girls to-day; and in which the masters should give their lessons in parlours with a grating in the door, and in which men should never enter the cloister. We must remember that at the moment of the publication of this *Discours* the National Assembly had abolished the abbeys and convents, and that, more intent upon destroying than on building up, it had made no provision for filling the enormous breach caused by the departure of the religious orders which had been occupied in the education of girls as well as boys.

[1] Mme. de Maintenon, *Entretiens sur l'Éducation* (1703).

It was this breach that Mme. de Genlis thought to fill by the creation of her cloistered schools.

What was to be taught in them?

The curious thing is that in 1791, on the eve of the Terror, Mme. de Genlis takes as the ground plan of her proposed method the Saint-Cyr system, with its governing idea that education should be adapted to the sex and social standing of the pupils, and that, as women were not destined to take part in public affairs, sweetness, modesty, prudence and regard for a spotless reputation were the qualities to be developed in them. Her programme, then, was to be the Saint-Cyr programme: very thorough religious and moral instruction; the elements—not more—of history, mythology, geography and common law, a little medicine and chemistry, and some accomplishments—the drawing of flowers, vocal music, simple embroidery. Above everything else came knowledge of the management of the house, and the girls were to sew all their own clothes. That was to form a woman's education.

What had become then of Mme. de Genlis's innovations? They consisted in an extreme regard for hygiene and diet. Gymnastics were an important feature.

The study of the laws governing the country was also in the nature of an innovation, and constituted an open door for feminism. Not that Mme. de Genlis would have wished to see women become lawyers, professors of economy, or members of the Chamber of Deputies; but she did foresee such things. "When a woman becomes a widow," we find her saying, "she quits the modest rank in which nature and the laws have placed her, and takes up her position among men, she replaces a citizen, and so doing becomes a citizen herself." Decidedly, we are on the eve of Feminism. Our Feminists of to-day may be interested to learn how Mme. de Genlis proposed to bring home the laws to her sex. "It would be desirable," she writes, "that in these educational establishments some kind of altars or small columns should be placed, after the fashion of the Ancients, either in the class rooms or the recreation rooms, with the fundamental laws and principal articles of our constitution engraved upon them. This, of course, is derived direct from Rousseau—it is the "education made attractive" of his dreams.

Ten years later Mme. de Genlis amends this educational scheme, rendering it more useful and practical in the second work which has been mentioned, the *Projet d'une École rurale pour le Éducation des Filles.*

The groundwork of it is still the Saint-Cyr system, informed with its horror of idleness and worldly dissipation—those schools of the passions. But whereas Mme. de Maintenon was content to evoke and stimulate the love of work, Mme. de Genlis adds the work itself with a view to embellishing the mind; and whereas Mme. de Maintenon fortified the inner life by means of intellectual austerity and privations—the abstention from useless reading, for instance, and especially of books calculated to nourish vanity of mind—and by a mode of moral therapeutics based upon fasting and abstinence which resulted in the subjection of the woman, and in restricting her to a life of domesticity and dependence, Mme. de Genlis held that woman should have an individual worth apart from mere moral worth, and sought to endow her in addition with mental accomplishments.

Leaving such a school, a woman was prepared for her walk in life, whatever it might be. All positions were provided for, save only that of the frivolous and useless, idle woman of the world—the type of woman that Feminism has always fought from the days of Fénelon and Mme. de Maintenon down to our own time.

To the actual school, situated in the country, a farm was to be attached, with a mill in addition to the poultry-yard, kitchen-garden, orchard, vineyard, wine-press and fish-pond.

Here is the complete curriculum as Mme. de Genlis sets it forth:—

Religious and moral instruction.

Writing, arithmetic, English, German and Italian. In the study of these languages, all that is to be attempted is to make the pupils to speak them well, to read prose fluently and to write a letter correctly. They are not to be made to read poetry.

Some elementary notions of history and geography. The drawing and painting of flowers.

Everything that concerns the interior economy of a house:—

1. Supervising the laundry work.
2. Washing and ironing clothes themselves once a fortnight.
3. Taking care of poultry.
4. Managing a dairy.
5. Managing a fruit-garden.
6. Supervising a kitchen and cooking for themselves, so that they may never be taken in regarding the price and quantity of the ingredients to be used.
7. Everything concerned with distilling.
8. Supervising the bakery, and getting to understand the different ways of making bread for the household.
9. An infinity of household recipes.
10. A knowledge of botany, at least as far as plants in general use are concerned, and a knowledge of the principal drugs.
11. A knowledge how and when to sow, together with actual practice in gathering in the crops and in vintage.
12. Practice in sewing, knitting, net-making, embroidery, carpet-weaving, lace-making, artificial-flower making. In addition, a man of business to be in the house to teach them all they need to know with regard to managing a property, and in reference to the laws bearing upon wills, inheritances, dowries, guardianships, etc.

. . . .

Mme. de Genlis was not entirely without justification when she complained of the way in which she was plagiarised. It is certain that she was much plagiarised during the generation of Louis-Philippe. It was some considerable time before she was forgotten—she was still read forty years ago. To-day she is too much neglected. Perhaps these pages will help some future readers to pick out the best of her works. They will find many original passages and much that is interesting and full of good sense.

The list of her books which follows will aid them still

further in their researches. I shall be glad for my part if my efforts shall have helped to freshen the faded laurel wreath which indicates the right of Stéphanie Félicité du Crest, Comtesse de Genlis, to take her place beside Mme. de Maintenon in the history of the literature of France.

APPENDIX

LIST OF THE WORKS OF MADAME DE GENLIS

Théâtre à l'usage des jeunes personnes. Paris, 1779-80. 4 vols. 8vo. (Reprinted, 1785, in 5 vols. 12mo.)
Théâtre de la Société. Paris, 1781. 2 vols. 8vo.
Annales de la Vertu. Paris, 1782. 2 vols. 8vo.
Adèle et Théodore. Paris, 1782. 3 vols. 8vo.
Les Veillées du Château. Paris, 1784. 4 vols. 12mo.
La Religion considérée comme l'unique base du bonheur et de la véritable philosophie. Paris, 1787. 8vo.
Discours sur l'éducation de M. le Dauphin et sur l'adoption. Paris, 1790. 8vo.
Discours sur la suppression des couvents de réligieuses et l'éducation publique des femmes. Paris, 1791. 8vo.
Discours sur l'éducation publique du peuple. Paris, 1791. 8vo.
Leçons d'une Gouvernante à ses Élèves. Paris, 1791. 2 vols. 12mo.
Discours sur le luxe et l'hospitalité.[1] Paris, 1791. 8vo.
Les Chevaliers du Cygne. Hamburg, 1795. 3 vols. 8vo.
Épître à l'asile que j'aurai, suivi d'une Épître à Henriette de Sercey. 1796.
Précis de ma conduite depuis la Révolution, suivi d'une lettre à M. de Chartres et de réflexions sur la Critique. Hamburg, 1796. 12mo.
Les Petits Émigrés. Paris, 1798. 2 vols. bound in one, 12mo.
Réflexions d'un ami des talens et des arts. Paris, An. VII. (1798). 8vo.
Manuel du Voyageur. Berlin, 1798. 2 vols. 8vo.
Herbier moral. 1799. 12mo.
Les Vœux téméraires. Altona, 1799. 3 vols. 12mo.
Les Mères rivales. Berlin, 1800. 3 vols. 8vo.
Nouvelles Heures à l'usage des enfants. Paris, 1801. 18mo.
Le Petit La Bruyère. Paris, 1801. 8vo.
Nouvelle méthode d'Enseignement pour la première enfance. Paris, 1801. 8vo.
Projet d'une École rurale pour l'éducation des filles. Paris, 1801. 8vo.

[1] In 1797 all the "Discours" were republished in a single volume under the title of *Discours moraux et politiques.*

Mademoiselle de Clermont. Paris, 1802. 16mo.
Nouveaux Contes moraux et Nouvelles historiques. Paris, 1802. 3 vols. 12mo.
L'épouse impertinente. Paris, 1804. 12mo.
Souvenirs de Félicie L——. Paris, 1804. 12mo.
La Duchesse de La Vallière. Paris, 1804. 2 vols. 12mo.
Les Monuments religieux. Paris, 1805. 8vo.
Étude du Cœur humain. Paris, 1805. 12mo.
Le Comte de Corke. Paris, 1805. 2 vols. 12mo.
Madame de Maintenon. Paris, 1806. 2 vols. 12mo.
Alphonsine. Paris, 1806. 3 vols. 12mo.
Esprit de Madame de Genlis, ou Portraits, caractères, maximes, pensées, extraits par Demonceaux. Paris, 1807. 12mo.
Suite des Souvenirs de Félicie. Paris, 1807. 12mo.
Le Siège de La Rochelle. Paris, 1808. 2 vols. 12mo.
Bélisaire. Paris, 1808. 2 vols. 12mo.
Sainclair. Paris, 1808. 16mo.
Alphonse. Paris, 1809. 8vo.
Arabesques mythologiques. Paris, 1810. 2 vols. 12mo.
La Maison rustique. Paris, 1810. 3 vols. 8vo.
La Botanique historique et littéraire. Paris, 1810. 8vo.
De l'influence des femmes sur la littérature française. Paris, 1811. 8vo.
Observations critiques . . . ou réponse de Mme. de Genlis à Messieurs T. et M. et sur les critiques de son dernier ouvrage de l'Influence des femmes. Paris, 1811. 8vo.
Examen critique de l'ouvrage intitulé " Biographie universelle." Paris, 1811. 8vo.
Suite de l'examen critique de l'ouvrage, etc. . . . Paris, 1812. 8vo.
Les Bergères de Madian. Paris, 1812. 12mo.
La Feuille des gens du Monde ou le Journal imaginaire. Paris, 1813. 8vo.
Mademoiselle de La Fayette. Paris, 1813. 2 vols. 12mo.
Les Hermites des Marais Pontins. Paris, 1814. 8vo.
Histoire de Henri le Grand. Paris, 1815. 2 vols. 8vo.
Jeanne de France. Nouvelle historique. Paris, 1816. 2 vols. 12mo.
Le Journal de la Jeunesse. Paris, 1816. 12mo.
Les Battuecas. Paris, 1816. 2 vols. 12mo.
Abrégé des Mémoires du Marquis de Dangeau. Paris, 1817. 4 vols. 8vo.
Les Tableaux du Comte de Forbin. Paris, 1817. 8vo.
Zuma, ou la découverte du Quinquina. Paris, 1817. 12mo.
Dictionnaire critique et raisonné des étiquettes de la Cour, usages du monde, etc. Paris, 1818. 2 vols. 8vo.
Les Voyages poétiques d'Eugène et d'Antonine. Paris, 1818. 12mo.
Almanach de la Jeunesse. Paris, 1819. 18mo.
Émile (édition Genlis) avec des retranchements, une note et une préface. Paris, 1820. 3 vols. 18mo.

APPENDIX

Catéchisme critique et moral de l'Abbé Feller, avec préface et notes. Paris, 1820. 2 vols. 12mo.
Contes, nouvelles et historiettes par Mme. la Comtesse de Genlis, Mme. la Comtesse de Beaufort de Hautpoul, Mme. Dufresnoy, M. le chevalier Lablée. Paris, 1820. 2 vols. 12mo.
L'Intrépide. 1820.
Le Siècle de Louis XIV. Paris, 1820. 3 vols. 12mo.
Palmyre et Flaminie. Paris, 1821. 2 vols. 8vo.
Prières, ou Manuel de Piété. Paris, 1821.
Six nouvelles morales et religieuses. Paris, s.d. (1821). 12mo.
Les Jeux champêtres des Enfans. Contes de fées. Paris, s.d. (1821). 12mo.
Les Dîners du Baron d'Holbach. Paris, 1822. 8vo.
Les Veillées de la Chaumière. Paris, 1823. 8vo.
Les Parvenus. Paris, 1824. 3 vols. 12mo.
Les Prisonniers (contenant six nouvelles et une notice historique sur l'amélioration des prisons). Paris, 1824. 8vo.
De l'Emploi du temps. Paris, 1824. 8vo.
Les Athées conséquens, ou Mémoires du Commandeur de Linanges. Paris, 1824. 8vo.
Pétrarque et Laure. Paris, 1825. 2 vols. 12mo.
Thérésina. Paris, 1826. 12mo.
Inès de Castro. Paris, 1826. 2 vols. 12mo.
Le La Bruyère des domestiques. Paris, 1828. 2 vols. 12mo.
Les soupers de la Maréchale de Luxembourg. Paris, 1828. 8vo.
Mémoires inédits sur le XVIIIe siècle et la Révolution française. Paris, 1825–28. 10 vols. 8vo.
Le dernier voyage de Nelgis. Paris, 1828. 2 vols. 8vo.
Étrennes politiques pour 1828. Lettre au Duc d'Orléans. Paris, 1828. 8vo. (This is a reprint of the "Letter from Silk," issued by enemies of Louis-Philippe and Mme. de Genlis. There was another reprint of the same kind in 1831.)
Manuel de la jeune femme. Guide complet de la maîtresse de maison. Paris, 1829. 18mo.
Athénaïs. Paris, 1832. 18mo. (A posthumous work, left in MS. to Mme. Récamier, and published for her by Didot in 1832.)

Besides these works, Mme. de Genlis edited the *Mémoires de la Marquise de Bonchamps*, and wrote a series of articles under the title of *Lettres de Marie-Anne* (1790). Two unpublished MS. works of hers are in the library of the city of Nancy: (1) *Catalogue sommaire du cabinet de tableaux de M. le Comte de Sommariva*, written on vellum, with illuminated titles and tailpieces. (2) *Essai sur les Arts*, with water-colour sketches as illustrations.

Printed by
MORRISON & GIBB LIMITED
Edinburgh

CPSIA information can be obtained at www.ICGtesting.com
Printed in the USA
LVOW09s2005011213

363412LV00020B/859/P